TEACHING METHODOLOGY AND CHILD DEVELOPMENT

TEACHING METHODOLOGY AND CHILD DEVELOPMENT

V.K. NANDA

ANMOL PUBLICATIONS PVT. LTD.
NEW DELHI - 110 002 (INDIA)

ANMOL PUBLICATIONS PVT. LTD.
4374/4B, Ansari Road, Daryaganj
New Delhi - 110 002
Ph.: 23261597, 23278000
Visit us at: www.anmolpublications.com

Teaching Methodology and Child Development

ISBN 81-7488-833-0

PRINTED IN INDIA

Published by J.L. Kumar for Anmol Publications Pvt. Ltd., New Delhi - 110 002 and Printed at Mehra Offset Press, Delhi.

Contents

Preface

"Child is the father of man," thus future of a nation depends on the development of children. 'Child development' in its diverse aspects is elaborately discussed in the present encyclopaedia.

Organised in five volumes, the first volume of the encyclopaedia contains information on 'Principles of Child Development.' 'Child Development Counselling' is the theme on which learned articles are compiled and collated in the volume second. Volume three consists of useful and authoritative material on Nutrition and Health for Child Development. Teaching Methodology and Child Development is the major theme of volume four. Volume five of the encyclopaedia is devoted to Development of Interactive Abilities in Children.

All the articles are judiciously selected from authoritative sources. We are grateful to all the learned authors and academicians whose writings are cited or substantially made use of in these volumes. Students, teachers, researchers, administrators, policy planners and professionals from different streams of disciplines will find this encyclopaedia informative and useful.

V. K. Nanda

1
Planning for Teaching

There is no area of the modern school curriculum which needs more realistically to be based upon the facts of man's existence than does the programme of health instruction. There is little danger of being overdramatic on that point. Quite literally what the adolescent girl learns about cancer in her health class may save her life later. What the young man may learn about his responsibilities in marriage can well protect his marriage from the incompatibilities which are fatal to so many.

If we are to achieve such useful results, the effort in health instruction must be carefully planned and skilfully executed. It is not reasonable to remain aloof from the facts of living and prepare teachable material with merely the hope that it will do someone some good. On the contrary, teaching in this area must begin with an analysis of need and proceed from there to an organisation and presentation of material geared to all that is currently known about the learning process. The haphazard throwing of facts at students, an unrealistic organisation of course content, the teaching of material too simple or too complex for the group—these are ruinous of the chances for good results. The teacher who plans to function effectively in health instruction must be aware of basic principles applicable to the selection and organisation of material to be taught.

FUNDAMENTAL CONSIDERATIONS

Planning of the specific course in health, or of the entire curriculum as it relates to health, must be done with certain fundamental considerations in mind. These are:

1. Personal Action

To effect favourably the personal life of an individual is the ultimate goal not only of health teaching but of all public health work. Surely all health teaching must be focused directly at the impact it makes upon a *given person*. The favourable changes which may be made in a person's life are the changes that count. Whenever one sees a table showing, for example, that a thousand mothers die for every hundred thousand births one must recognise that each of these thousand was *an individual*. Nothing could be effective in saving their lives expect as it touched each one of them. If instruction could have done it in some cases, then it had to be instruction which was *acceptable and used by that woman*. Sanitary engineers have improved the public health by cleaning up a water supply and thus protecting *individuals* against typhoid fever. No health lecturer ever spoke for an hour to five hundred people and did any good whatever expect in so far as the people themselves individually lived by the advice given. "The public health" is but the sum of the individual "healths" of the people who make up the "public". Thus, all health teaching must be directed at persons—no impersonal general approach will be as effective.

2. Needs and Interests

Such teaching, therefore, must be based upon, must be related to, must in fact be identical with the needs and interests of consuming learners. There need be no confusion about this point. There are some who erroneously believe that acceptance of this principle will commit the teacher to the willy-nilly pursuit of every whim and fancy raised in class and will prevent the attainment of any solid block of learning by the class as a whole. It does not imply this at all. It does imply, however, that any course and any curriculum must be based on the personal problems of the members of the group individually and in society. These personal needs will not be ignored in favour of "general background", alleged problems, or the "things the teacher thinks they should know".

People of all ages have needs. They have interests. Sometimes they are articulate about them, sometimes not. Sometimes students readily reveal their interests. Sometimes they hide them. The teacher of health instruction must have the ability to dig them out wherever they are, to organise them for class purposes, and to use them as the material with which the class deals. (We will discuss later how these interests may be discovered.)

We can hope for a greater acceptance of health information if it relates to the problems of students than if it is arbitrarily selected and unrelated to these real problems.

On what grounds can we justify the satisfaction of personal needs in health teaching? Three general statements may be made to support this view.

(a) *People will not think vitally about a subject unless the subject is vital to them.* The material which is selected to go into a course in hygiene ought, according to this statement, to be material which is an intrinsic part of the life of the learners. W.H. Kilpatrick once said that learners must see and feel the utility and pertinence of what is being learned as a matter of present concern to them. Only thus will they intelligently join in the movement or apply the knowledge to an actual situation. The closer the conscious relationship, the better the learning.

In view of these statements, then, the best way to get students to think vitally about their health problems would be to seek out those problems of living which are vital to them. Their interests and felt needs play just such a role. What would be the vital needs and interests of students in, for example, the subject of fatigue? They would probably want to know how best to go through the day without "that tired feeling", or perhaps the reason why a person feels "all run down". The problems close to their lives are those of common occurrence, rather than concern over the construction of lymph vessels or the formation of carbon dioxide and lactic acid.

To seek out the individual and class interests and use them for subject matter is to recognise the principle that the best learning takes place when the learner reacts vitally to the subject material. The immediate problem is most fruitful of results because of the identity of the subject-to-be-learned and the learner himself.

(b) *Learning, for the most part, is highly specific.* Students do not, as a general rule, first learn generalities and then later make their applications. Learning about a particular thing takes place by specific experiences with each particular subject. A great deal is known, for instance, about the physiology of muscular exercise, the kinds and types of muscles, and the importance of muscular exercise in life. Enough is understood so that certain broad conclusions can be made regarding the benefits of exercise. But in teaching the known facts about exercise and its place in life, the best point of departure is the interest of the student in active recreation, and not the conclusions or generalities reached after prolonged study of muscle action. Illustrating this point of view, syllabi can be found in which the order for discussion on the subject is: (1) structure of muscles, (2) how muscles act, (3) kinds of muscles, (4) involuntary muscles, (5) keeping muscles in good condition, (6) the value of exercise, (7) desirable forms of exercise. The generalisation which physiologists have made regarding the structure of muscles (1) and the ways in which they act (2) was reached after a study of the more immediate and specific problems of muscular exercise (6) and (7). That is, the world learned about the structure of muscle after it learned about the action of muscles in exercise and about the specific effects of exercise upon the muscles.

A more hopeful way of approaching this unit on active recreation would be through the specific experience of the student in such problems as: Is swimming a good form of recreation? When should one learn to play golf? Should one in middle age indulge in strenuous sports? What sports are best for high-school girls? Or, how best can one keep in good physical condition? Some such recognizable problems as these would be a more acceptable point of departure and elaboration than "the structure of muscle" because they are specific rather than general experiences.

There are very good reasons to question the desirability of teaching generalisations or abstractions first. To know that digestion is principally an acid reaction or that there is phosphorus in bone may be interesting factual material to the physiologist or the anatomist but to the ordinary consumer, the student who merely wants help in solving his problems of living, these are not relevant facts until they can be shown in relationship to the known problem. They remain unrelated generalisations until their bearing upon some specific matter calls them up.

Clearly, then, the wealth of material now known about exercise should not be presented in its general divisions. It should, instead, be offered in terms of specific problems of the individual, such as the type of game which will develop muscles, the nature of muscle stiffness, the reasons for fatigue after exercise, and other specific interests of the learner.

What the adult world has learned about the prevention of disease in the individual has by now been classified into certain generalities concerning protective substances, blood function, and the action of micro-organisms. In learning about these things, however, one first approaches them in terms of the specific elements involved in the general statements. The learner's interests are in such health matters as catching cold, blood poisoning, and vaccination, rather than in phagocytosis, the side-chain theory, or the general notion of immunity.

The idea that a person has of an abstract matter is dependent upon the sort of situations in which that matter has been previously experienced. Symonds makes this perfectly apparent when he says: "A misconception that is found throughout all education is that learning proceeds from the general to the particular. . . . Conduct begins by the formation of separate skills and habits. . . . It is a curious anomaly that we take the end result in our own learning and try to make it the beginning in the learning of children". In other words, the generalisations which we make about health, such as "the mouth is an avenue of entrance of disease", or "exercise is beneficial to health", are conclusions which are not readily apparent at first except by persons with trained minds or by those with an exceptionally high degree of intelligence. The generalisations or logical arrangements of experiences are continuous with, but represent the later stages of the learning process, and should not be used as points of departure.

Students have traditionally been taught to understand the

best health practices only after they have studied the anatomy and physiology involved. Thus, to understand the importance of the balanced diet, they have had first to know of enzymes, amino acids, calorimeters, and nitrogen equilibrium. Or, in order to understand how to develop a wholesome adjustment to life, they have approached the problem through the fissures of Rolando, the centres in the medulla, or the cortical areas.

The wealth of material in human anatomy, physiology, bacteriology, and the other great sciences which have revealed the workings of human life is teachable *in explanation of a human problem. The material is largely wasted when given as new material and merely to teach the student the structure and function of his body.* It may even be said that there is no use at all in teaching the structure and function of the body unless the learner can use the material taught to further his development and solve his problems. If that is true his problems and his development offer the point of approach for the science. Otherwise the science may become wasted because, being unrelated to anything on in the life of the learner, it is dry and dull.

(c) *Interests manifested by questions or outspoken curiosity represent the individual's attempts to maintain a favourable relationship with his environment.* We may call these articulate interests. They are revealed to the teacher by the spoken word in the form of questions arising out of some situation in which learning is taking place and in which the need for a new adjustment to environment has appeared.

Raup has described this as a constant effort on the part of the human being to maintain a state of favourable adjustment with his world. Raup's contentions are based upon the universality of the characteristic of living things to be continually seeking a balance, or a "complacency", between themselves and their environment. How do interests or outspoken curiosities relate to the human desire to maintain this state of complacency? Suppose a student has been taught that smoking is injurious to health. This idea has, in the past, seemed perfectly reasonable, and the student has reached a state of quiet conviction on that point. One day he reads an advertisement in which it is stated that a prominent athlete smokes and that smoking has a steadying influence upon the nerves. He is immediately disturbed, for he feels that his former learnings are being contradicted. His complacency in the matter of smoking is upset. Then follows an effort to discover the truth. After all, is smoking really harmful? What evidence have these people when they say that smoking steadies the nerves? Doesn't smoking dull the brain, thereby upsetting the nerves? Dozens of questions immediately crowd into his mind, and he seeks some person, some source, which will give him satisfaction in the matter and help him solve his problem.

The questions or curiosities this disturbed student may have represent his efforts to return to a state of complacency or stability with his world. He wishes most earnestly, sometimes desperately, to re-establish his mastery, his complacency in the situation and thus any teaching which helps the problem is avidly seized upon by drives from within and is accepted as helpful in the situation.

The implications of this conception of complacency to the teaching of health are numerous. We may assume that students are almost constantly faced with stimuli of varying sorts which necessitate some action if they are to maintain their complacency. Daily experiences bring changes from former ways in which living was best accomplished. The individual is in a more or less constant struggle to maintain his complacency. To seek out his problems, explain and answer his difficulties, lead him into better ways of making his adjustments to life—these are opportunities for a teacher of health.

Assume that students come to a hygiene class some morning in a state of complacency regarding food. They have had a good breakfast; they are generally well fed; their interest in food and nutrition is, for the moment, dormant. The subject of the day is announced but evokes no general response in their minds. If, however, this subject is stated in the form of a question, the complacency of the members of the class is disturbed to a certain extent. Their conception of some matter has been challenged, and they react by answering the question either to themselves or aloud. Thus, by thought-provoking questions they may be stimulated out of their complacency regarding nutrition. Then, with the discussion well established, each student may take from it what information he needs to restore himself to his former state of balance. If the complacency regarding the first question is not restored completely in the make-up of any one student, he may ask another question. Given the answer by his own reasoning or with the help of the teacher, his balance is then restored. By this continuous raising of questions, and the discussion of them, the subject of nutrition can be covered, time permitting, to the satisfaction of most of the students.

Supposing, however, that no question is forthcoming at the very beginning of the class hour. Does this mean that no teaching on the subject of nutrition ought to be carried on that morning? No brief is held for the stand that the teacher should wait until some need, desire, or whim appears in the mind of some student. To refuse to teach because no one in the class has any immediate interest in the subject at hand is not reasonable in the light of the purposes of modern education. Dewey puts the responsibility directly upon the teacher in this situation: "If the teacher is really a teacher and not just a master or 'authority', he should know enough about his pupils, their needs, experiences, degrees of skill and knowledge, to be able to share in a discussion (not to dictate aims and plans) regarding what is to be done and be as free to make suggestions as anyone else". Further, his "problem [the teacher's] is that of inducing a vital and personal experiencing".

The question arises here, however, as to the ability of any one person to learn much if he is utterly dependent upon the questions of others to bring out the discussion. Will there not, in the question method, be a waste of time for any particular individual? At times there probably will be. But it may be noted that the greater part of our learning takes place in social situations in which we listen to others discuss the problems of life. In the long run, the pooled interests of a group will probably make for progress in the learning of any one individual in the group, rather than for regression.

The health knowledge of a student by the time he reaches college is an echo of the particular kinds of information which have been taught him at home and in school. The home still carries on the greater share of health teaching, and yet it is likely to be one of the major sources of superstition and misconception regarding health. Health education, at best, is not a very exact science; and it will be many years before definite statements can be made about all matters of health. This situation makes for perplexity in the student's mind. He may have learned one "fact" at home, a conflicting "fact" at school, and a third elsewhere. These apparent inconsistencies, when discovered, will usually be grouped around larger problems which then can become the principle segments or areas for discussion of the health or hygiene course.

In summary of the foregoing three statements in support of the use of student needs and interests it must be clear that the successful teachers will constantly relate the material to be taught with some experience of the student. School and college students are in the developing, expanding, questioning, thinking period of their lives. Life to them is a series of new adventures, challenges, perplexities, and they keep seeking new ways of doing things. They must continually make decisions and they normally seek the right to make their own. Health instruction, therefore, should be constantly related to this process of decision making; should constantly aim to give the material with which these decisions can be made; and should constantly reveal consequences, open new ways of behaving, and lead the student into a life which can be guided by the wealth of scientific information available.

The converse of this point of view uses the learner as a means to an end. It uses him to serve some purpose other than his own. It has him learn things for values not apparent to him. He is asked to "make a showing" or to "pass a test" or to learn "because I believe you should". Such values are psychologically not conducive to permanent and applied achievement. The many produce temporary results, but lasting values from the process are rare. Much of schooling is forgotten because it was meaningless. In health education when teachers do not make the material meaningful it is more than a missed opportunity. It is frequently tragic in its effect upon health. Kant's dictum is particularly pertinent here; he cautions us to "so act as to treat humanity whether in thine own person or in that of any other in every case as an end withal, never as a means merely". That is a command to make health teaching useful—not a mere collection of facts but a living experience in the study of life and how it is lived.

3. Intrinsic vs. Extrinsic Material

Daily problems of living present the most favourable media for effective learning about health. It is within these experiences that one seeks the answers rather than having the answers to problems thrust upon him. A learning experience has the elements within it of the ongoing activity, the hindrance, the search for promising ways to overcome the hindrance, the application of the trial of the ways, the resumption of the activity or the solution of the problem. We learn by this pattern and its variations. It has meaning to the teaching of health. For example, we find our work interfered with by acute indigestion; we seek relief; we try water, soda, pills, and tablets. We try medical attention and possibly surgery. We apply the solutions. One works, and in the whole process we have learned much about medicine and quackery, about pills and tablets, about food and food idiosyncrasies, and about causes of indigestion. The learning was intrinsic to the problems; it was meaningful and cogent. But it might also have been inaccurate. The teacher's role is to guide the student into a solution of his problem at the same time building within him convictions and techniques which will be useful in other and similar problems.

Our problems are so numerous that they are not, of course, all of the same simplicity. Some are very complex and to solve them requires learning in many areas of living. One learns of marriage, for example, not by studying some of the rudimentary phenomena of sex life but by delving far into the factors which make for successful marriage. The economic, the psychological and the social factors are all important. When they are taught they become better learned when their relationship to the personal problems of marriage is apparent. *Thus material is intrinsic when it deals with or helps solve a problem and its relationship to the problem is seen.* It is extrinsic when it is learned merely for its own sake and without reference to any ongoing activity or problem in the life of the learner. The material intrinsic to the solution of a problem has the better chance of being effectively learned.

4. Motivation Through the Group

Most organised teaching about health matters takes place in a class. The individual finds himself a member of a group. The teacher discovers that he is trying to get individual action without intimate association with the personal problems which need solution. If personal action, rather than knowledge or favourable attitude, is the *ultimate* goal in health teaching, then the teacher, not being in such an authoritative position as to *command* action, must give some thought to all the factors which will favourably motivate.

The young teacher will often be dismayed at the apparent "wastage" in teaching. People do not always do what they are taught! They sometimes seem to pay little heed to the health advice given to them in the classroom. There are many who have spent years in school and college and yet the experience has meant very little to them in terms of behaviour changed for the better. And so the modern teacher is constantly trying to study the ways to reduce this wastage and thus make the teaching more effective. It is a problem of discovering the magic formula for presentation-motivation-acceptance—and use . If the teacher can arrange for the presentation of the materials to be learned in such a way as to motivate the students to accept them, the chance of usage is greater than otherwise. But how?

The answer to the question is not altogether available as yet. Not enough is known about the factors and conditions which will produce action. Or about the relative influence of some factors with some people. Some youngsters are easily swayed by the group they run with, others not. Some come to class with home notions fixed firmly, and no amount of didactic instruction will shake the ideas loose. Let the group take a different view of the problem, through, and the stubborn one may come around with surprising ease.

It may all have something to do with our overall social background. Our children are brought up in an atmosphere of debate and discussion. They hear forums, read of Congress, are aware of labour-management discussions, enter into disputations among themselves—are, in effect, brought up in an atmosphere more democratic than authoritarian. Hence, when they bring to class preconceived ideas on health, on smoking, diets, sex practices, alcohol, they are frequently less likely to accept scientific explanations as authoritative than they are a group acceptance as persuasive.

The teacher may well attempt two things as he aims to utilise group opinion and group action in teaching. He should make every effort to find out what the values are which cause a student to have the ideas he does. For example, a student may refuse medical care not because he is ignorant of what the physician has to offer or because he is ignorant of his own condition. He refuses because "where he comes from" going to a doctor is sissy. Or the high-school girl will consistently dissipate not because she knows no better but because by so doing she finds the prestige she seeks which is denied her at home. Teachers who seek out these deeper motivations frequently attain valuable insights into how to change the behaviour into a sort more favourable to the welfare of the student.

The second suggestion which is important in this connection pertains to the group itself. There is an increasing body of evidence from modern social psychology to show how effective group discussions can be in producing personal action. It is a far cry, of course, from the didactic lecture of a professor to two or three hundred students (not one of whom he knows, nor do they know each other) to the small group discussion with the teacher participating in the search for a decision or solution.

Suppose a high-school group is about to tackle the question of smoking. The chances are great that every member of the class has an attitude about the subject—some of the attitudes are more or less violent or emotionally based. Several alternatives are open to the teacher: (a) he can lecture on the subject giving one side of the controversy only; (b) he can give both sides; (c) he can authoritatively "tell" the students what and what not to do; (d) he can set himself up as a question answerer and allow students to raise their questions with him; or (e) he can make the problem a truly group one with the main issue clear, the secondary questions discovered, small class groups or committees at work on the sub-issues, debate and discussion held freely and without rancor, and some group decision arrived at.

He has those and other choices. The last one described has great promise. It allows the individual to bring his own values to the group to test them in group discussion which must be kept free and not oppressive, and eventually to ally himself with the group as he seeks support for his changed ideas or changed behaviour. The essential thing in method in conducting classes on this discussion-decision basis is to allow complete freedom for all to present their ideas, to work out their confusions and disagreements, and to formulate a conclusion based upon their experience.

The teacher's role is of great significance. He does not, as some erroneously believe, step out of the picture and allow students to come to a decision on the basis of their pooled ignorance. The teacher takes part, adds facts, opinions, helps formulate judgments, opens new resources, aids in finding evidence, arranges for resource people to be used. The teacher keeps the discussion free, encourages the timid, sublimates the overly aggressive and domineering, moves the group along to a decision or conclusion, but never usurps or dominates.

By such group action many individuals find the all-important personal action more readily taken.

5. Motivation and Emotion

Psychiatrists and other students of human behaviour are aware of the part emotions play in forming attitudes and guiding behaviour. If the teacher can associate pride with keeping fit, fear with the absence of protective vaccination, joy with active recreation, results in terms of continuous behaviour are more likely to occur. As J.C. Whitehorn has expressed it:

> . . . It would be helpful, I think, to keep ourselves consistently reminded of a basic motivational principle; namely, whether we are considering human attitudes on social or interpersonal issues

or human prejudice regarding food, the development of attitudes is brought about through emotional experiences, and it is through emotional experiences that any modification of attitudes is accomplished. I venture to express a very broad generalisation: mere information never of itself changed an attitude. This is not a trade secret among psychiatrists. Other know it, too. But I doubt if the members of any other professional group are so thoroughly aware as are the psychiatrists of the ineffectiveness of mere information. In order that information may have some influence on attitudes and behaviour, it must be related to one's sense of values, and value judgments are essentially tied to emotional processes.

Far too many times health classes are said to be boring, dull, static. Probably the reason for such a sorry condition is that the teacher teaches dead rote fact, without application, without meaning without imagination, controversy, or appeal. To have students feel as well as think, take sides on an issue, show enthusiasm for what they are doing, is surely not to be condemned, but encouraged. There is ample opportunity for this kind of total response in health instruction.

6. Health as Motivation

"Health" itself is not a good motivating factor. We have become accustomed to appealing to young and old alike to do or not to do this and that "for the sake of your health". The admonition that such and such is "good for your health" is used indiscriminately to get children to go to bed, to eat their cereal, or to wear their overcoats. Many appeals are made in the name of health. Advertising channels use it liberally for sprays and soap, for mattresses and automobiles. The health of the nation is well solicited. One is urged on every hand to protect his health against the many dangers which beset him.

And yet, using health as a motive is a dubious practice, and the reasons are three: In the first place the concept of health is essentially a generalisation and thus not well understood. Few people will do things for reasons they do not understand or understand poorly. Ask a child what "health" means and he will generally respond that health means "being big" or "eating my cereal". An adolescent will think of it as being "physically well". He will think of it in terms of recognisable and immediate experiences. It is more meaningful to a child to be encouraged to eat his fruit or drink his milk because he will be stronger if he does than to tell him blandly that such things are good for his health. Likewise, there is a better chance of getting overcoats worn in cold weather if one makes it clear that the "flu" will interfere with school activities which are fun. A specific appeal to a specific ongoing and important interest is much more likely to be successful than the appeal to a generalisation which is not well understood.

In the second place health should be presented in its true light as a means to an end rather than as an end. Health is a tool to be used. Only to the sick and the hypochondriacal does it become an objective. To the well it is something to use, to spend, to rely on through life. It is expendable in the sense that it is there to be used in the attainment of life's purposes. As Williams has expressed it many times, health is not mass, but function. It is not something to husband but something to spend. Not that it is to be wasted. Good health is a condition of the organism which is to be used in attaining one's goals. It should be used freely. Whenever the teacher sets health as an end in competition with other ends, then health will frequently come out second best. Many are willing to attain the other objective and let a little health go for the moment. Let the teacher show, however, that the performance of "health" activities will contribute to the success of the ends in view (i.e., sleep tonight will assure a better game tomorrow) and here is a better chance for getting the sleep.

Health as a motivator is likewise of doubtful value because of the hazard of making hypochondriacs out of people. There are millions seeking alibis for failures, millions who yearn to be the centre of the stage for even a fleeting moment, millions who crave sympathy and affection. To these their health is a sure thing. Teach them to guard it, do things or avoid things because of it, make them "health conscious", drum "health" into them from infancy, and they develop the morbid interest in it characteristic of the hypochondriac, the quack, the faker, the bore. Health becomes a crutch, an excuse, an all-absorbing fetish. These people excuse failure because of poor health. They have no claim to glory but know that the recitation of symptoms will get an audience any time. They claim their share of sympathy with a vengeance.

These are too frequently the results of urging people to do things "because they are good for your health". It is much better to find the reason for doing the thing in the direct result of its doing. Health as a word and as a motive should be used sparingly if at all in teaching about it. There are excellent reasons for getting sleep, being vaccinated, and eating well. They need not be obscured by using a single general term "health".

To teach people to be "health conscious" is a doubtful practice for the reason that the great physiological processes go on best without interference from the psyche. The loss of self-consciousness is desirable for the sake of one's effective functioning. This means that the teacher of health must see that the interest in learning about health matters is transferred from the self to the idea or activity which would be the beneficiary of the knowledge learned. For example, one would transfer the interest in vitamins from their importance to growth to their relationship to playing hockey or basketball. One would, likewise, transfer the interest in active recreation away from doing it "for one's health" to playing golf or tennis for the fun of it or for the sake of being with friends. The West Pointer maintains a rigid posture not by concentrating on the position of his visceral organs but by attempting a bodily reflection of an ideal of the Service. One seldom plays golf for health's sake, and to play tennis for "exercise" is suitable only for those who (a) must actively seek such therapy in convalescence or (b) must find an excuse for their love of golf and tennis.

There are times, however, when it is desirable to think consciously and act overtly in terms of health. We would want the camper to boil or chlorinate his water on purpose to prevent disease. We would want children deliberately to give up the old swimming hole because its water is filled with *B. coli* and we would want any persons with early symptoms of an ailment to be introspective enough and to know enough to call a physician for aid. Sometimes we have to act consciously about our health and it thus becomes the responsibility of the teacher to give enough information describing the consequences of our acts to allow the learner to make intelligent choices. Health conduct is, after all, largely a matter of choices. We choose to smoke or not to smoke, to go to sleep or to stay up another two hours, to seek an early diagnosis or to wait a couple of months to see what develops, to eat this or that, to cross in the middle of the block or to go up to the corner. The selection is the student's. It is his life, his welfare, his happiness at stake. The business of the teacher is *to provide him with the data which will help him make these choices.*

Thus to get everyone to "take a conscious interest in his health" can be badly overdone from several points of view. It can lead to a morbid interest in health. It can interfere with physiological function, and it can serve as a spurious reason for doing an otherwise reputable thing. At the same time students must be taught to handle reasons, facts, points of view, data in such a way as to be prepared to make an obvious and important choice when serious matters are at stake.

With such basic principles of instruction in mind one can reasonably expect results from a programme of health instruction. Individuals lives should be improved. Thus the aim of school health instruction must be clarified.

THE AIM OF SCHOOL HEALTH INSTRUCTION

The principal aim of school health instruction is to secure favourable behaviour or conduct in all situations involving an individual's health. Broadly put, the aim of health instruction is to teach people to live well, to live scientifically, efficiently, economically, and happily. Behaviour is what counts. In the last analysis it is what we do that is of greatest significance. As Durant says, "We become what we do." There are other aims of instruction. Two, at least, are traditional, almost classical. They are: to acquire knowledge about health and to establish proper attitudes about it. Health knowledge is, of course, the framework upon which are built the attitudes and behaviour. It is the grist out of which the judgments, the decisions are made. Knowledge is basic, primary, and important. "Had I *known* that, I would have done so long ago". Knowledge forms the base for action, and if the principal aim of health instruction is healthful behaviour then knowledge must be acquired and given freely and plentifully as part of the experiential base from which a course of action is chosen.

To impart knowledge is the simplest thing to be done in the classroom. Students can be taught, tested for retention, and taught some more. Whether the learning becomes effective in the pattern of living depends in part upon the way the knowledge was acquired and also upon a great variety of other competing variables over which the teacher has little control. The teacher knows it is not enough to teach *about* vaccination. To be vaccinated against smallpox is the only thing that counts. All the knowledge about it in the world will not protect against smallpox. Action is the thing. But knowledge appropriately given is the first step in getting vaccination accomplished. Knowledge is sought even though behaviour is the most important, the only important, outcome.

Health attitudes are widely described as desirable too. They are, to the extent that they facilitate the achievement of specific behaviours. An attitude as described by Webster is "an habitual way of regarding anything". How do you feel about healing cults? Are you against them in general? In favour of them? Do you believe that all drugstore cures are fakes? Do you put any stock in superstition? Habitual ways of answering these questions would be, presumably, attitudes; and yet they cannot be determined to exist really until the behaviour or conduct of a person reacting in situations involving the subject is noted. One's attitude toward chiropractic, for example, would not be proved until one went or did not go to a chiropractor for treatment. One might be quite opposed to immunisation and yet when going overseas submit willingly to typhoid and smallpox "shots". An attitude in students toward tobacco or toward continence can be built up through the acquisition of knowledge and experience *but it is tested for its existence through observation of behaviour*. Verbal or written statements of "how I feel about" things are fairly unreliable, often coloured by "how do you *want* me to say I feel?" Hence as a working objective of school health instruction health attitudes are neither as important as knowledge and behaviour nor as readily evaluated.

More specifically the objectives of school health instruction may be offered as follows:

1. To secure behaviour (action, conduct, habits) favourable to a high quality of living, and to point the way to those acts which, if performed, will assure this high quality.
2. To assist in the development of a well-integrated personality, enjoying life with no reliance upon false superiorities or inferiorities but with a stability rooted in a capacity for accurate self-appraisal.
3. To clarify thinking about personal and public health matters, to remove the superstitions, the false beliefs, the ignorance; and to substitute the accuracy of science, where available, for the darkness of falsehood and misbelief.
4. To facilitate the development of a security against the threats and destructive forces of the world through the acquisition of scientific knowledge, the formation of scientific attitudes, and the practice of the scientific behaviour.
5. To enrich the life of the community and commonwealth through the collective action of individuals well taught in the advantages of health measures to be taken for the common good.
6. To establish the ability in students to see cause and effect, to recognise consequences, and thus to preserve life and the fullness of it.

THE THREE PATTERNS OF INSTRUCTION

To bring this sort of education about, to make a constructive contribution to the life of any individual, the school must exercise great care in the selection of the material to be taught and must teach in such a way as to get the greatest acceptance. There is more material available about life and its functions and processes than can ever be taught to students in the usual school setting. The educator realises also that much of what he teaches may be either rejected, ignored, or forgotten. In giving instruction about health the material taught, therefore, must be intrinsic to the life of the student; if it is, it will have a better chance of being accepted by him and built into his life.

To fulfil this opportunity three patterns of teaching have evolved in school health education. Some schools use only one of them, some use two and in some places all three patterns are in operation. *They* the same situation. In the three chapters to follow they will be amplified as being:

1. The Programme of Direct Teaching

Direct teaching represents to many the best, most concrete and practical way to offer instruction in health. It involves the organisation and presentation of material from personal and public hygiene to students who are enrolled in a class specifically to receive that kind of instruction. There are no divergent or competing interests and "health" is the "subject" to be taught.

2. The Programme of Correlation

The programme of correlation involves the use of other areas within the curriculum as vehicles by which health material is taught. There is much of personal and public hygiene which *may* be taught in the biological sciences, the social sciences, home economics, and other curricular areas. Whether it is or not depends upon the receptiveness of other areas to health material and the skill with which the correlation is brought about.

3. The Programme of Integration

Integration differs from correlation in that it infers by definition an organisation of learning experiences around a central objective. It has three applications in contemporary education: integration applied to the curriculum, integration applied to the total school programme, and integration applied to the developing child or to the student. A completely integrated school health programme is a rarity, not because it would not be desirable, but because its attainment is difficult in many current settings. It is, however, when carefully and fully developed, the richest of the three patterns in terms of learning about health and living a healthy life.

2

Teaching Methods and Child Development

Group Discussions

Most teachers prefer to conduct their classes on the discussion plan rather than the lecture plan. They feel the discussion is better because it gets more students actively participating in what is going on and with participation learning is more likely to take place and to affect behaviour. The problem in health instruction is the problem of learning in other areas as well: how to get action from a learning situation. Teachers must remember that students bring to class varied backgrounds of experience, prejudice, knowledge, willingness to learn, and intelligence, and to find a teaching method which can cope with all of these and succeed in producing the results in terms of action is the great question in all of education.

To date, there is no clear evidence that one teaching method is *always* better than all others. There is reason to believe, however, that individual action is more readily attained if the individual can find endorsement for that action within his group. Apparently, merely to give information in class and to test for knowledge is not enough to assure action. Information received is only part of the story. The teacher must pay some attention to other motivations, and surely group sanction or endorsement and group agreement to act are of great importance in affecting individual behaviour.

Hence, the teacher can seldom, if ever, afford to be arbitrary or dictatorial. Nor can he afford to be complacent over the inculcation of knowledge. His classes must be so conducted as to allow for free discussion, presentation and weighing of evidence, personal analysis and testimony, and summarisations and conclusions.

It takes several years of experience to lead class discussions successfully. Beginning teachers should not expect to handle the discussion method expertly. It is easier to lecture than to conduct a discussion because there are no interruptions, no questions to be answered, no calls to meet issues except on one's own terms. One must realise, however, that the health lecture, like many other lectures, is a less effective instrument in getting the purposes of health instruction accomplished. Because so many teachers prefer to use the class discussion, the following suggestions are offered:

1. The teacher should know well the general objectives of the unit and keep the flow of discussion moving toward their accomplishment.
2. The teacher should keep the main points under discussion, the issues, if any, clearly before the group.
3. Students should be taught to back up their views with evidence, and in lively discussions the teacher should encourage students to demand evidence in place of personal opinion or hearsay.
4. In the original planning of the problem or unit the teacher should make sure that there is enough preliminary discussion to bring out the issues or directions which the later investigations and discussions might take. As many students as wish to should express themselves while the teacher is taking note, on the board or elsewhere, of these principal sub-problems. When the subject has been amply explored in this preliminary way, the teacher should boil the issues down, if necessary, to the place where they can be handled well and then present them clearly to the class for selection and development. In so far as is reasonable, students should be given their choice in the pursuit of investigations, but the teacher must always prevent misbalance by assigning some good students to bolster the cause of poorer ones.

5. In class debates or presentations by students the teacher should keep the presentations reasonably on the track, should try to get all students to participate, and should draw out the shy and diffident ones with friendly encouragement. The brighter, more aggressive students should not be allowed to monopolise the conversations.

6. The language of the classroom should be largely non-technical. The teacher should remember that he is not preparing medical students, and only the mastery of technical words for "unit" use is needed. When a point cannot be made safely or well without the technical word it should be used, but explained and spelled until all understand it.

7. The details of anatomy and physiology, of structure and function, are useful only *in explanation* of personal or group problems. Let the problem be raised first, then seek the answer from anatomy or physiology if that's where it is to be found. For example, one may wish to deal with matters of nutrition. Don't begin the unit with the five classifications of food, or with the mouth, the esophagus, and the stomach. Begin it with a discussion of what lunch to pack if you're working or the problem of how to live on seventy-five cents a day and like it.

8. Learning about health, or anything else for that matter, proceeds from the specific to the general. We learn about disease control, for example, by talking about one disease first, like tuberculosis, and eventually drawing general conclusions about water-borne, air-borne, and contact diseases. It is much more difficult to develop effective learning about food if you begin with proteins, carbohydrates, and fats, which are generalised classifications, than if you begin with Tuesday's breakfast or with lunch for the working student.

9. "Health" itself is not much of a motive. Very few people—mainly the sick—do things for the sake of their health. Good food is eaten, rest is taken, eyes are examined for the sake of more immediate purposes. Few golfers ever hit a 200-yard shot and reflect how wonderful that is for their

livers. Games aren't played generally for exercise, or for health. Good food is eaten for the clearer purpose of being efficient the next day, or making the team, or just to feel good. Health, as a motive, is not very effective compared to the appeal of more understandable purposes.

10. Instruction in the classroom is certainly not the only source of health information. Students learn from dozens of other sources. The teacher is in competition with the movies, press, commercials, parents, friends, books, and other teachers. He should make it his business, then, to be accurate, fair, and scientific, and to realise that the least he can do is to present the facts—the individual himself will make the choice of behaviour.

11. The teacher should be prepared to answer many questions but should not be afraid to admit it when he does not know the answer. In such instances he should have a pretty good idea where the answer can be found.

12. The teacher should always begin each hour with a transitional word or two, tying today with yesterday, and use frequent summaries of the discussion thus far, always summarising and tying together each unit or major subpart of each unit.

13. The teacher should frequently use timely illustrations, particularly when discussing abstract or general problems.

14. The discussion should not begin with the issue upon which prejudice is strongest but on a problem which will "warm up" the class.

15. The teacher should never answer a question with a question, nor should the entire period be taken up with questions from the students and answers from the teacher. The latter should turn many of the questions back on the class (never on the asker) for reply, gaining information on the problem that way and then putting the capstone on the matter himself before going on to the next question.

16. As the discussion on the problem nears the end the teacher should be prepared to stimulate and help phrase summary

statements. These should be in the nature of significant high points or directions.

17. Following the development of an appropriate summary for the problem the teacher should then draw out of the class suggestions for action—things to do or not to do—directions to take. These will not always be clear cut; they may be developed in the form of alternatives. At all events, the group should be given a chance to express itself in terms of recommended action or point of view.

Supplementary Methods

Good teachers will use more than one or two classroom methods. They will rely neither on the lecture nor on the question-answer-debate type of discussion wholly. They will vary their teaching practices in accordance with the nature of their group and the nature of the problem under discussion, and sometimes they will vary their techniques for variety's sake alone. There are many other ways to conduct a class or a discussion on a subject. For example, the teacher might use (1) individual or committee reports in which the persons reporting have had a chance to do some research on their problem, present their findings, and thus open the problem for class consideration and action; (2) experiments, class activities, or field experiences—some problems are more readily solved by experimentation or doing something than by talk, and field experiences, which will be discussed in a later paragraph, are almost always useful; (3) socio-dramas and the so-called role-playing, in which a health problem is presented to the class in dramatic form with a prepared script or some members present contrasting views as advocates for purposes of enlightening discovery of issues and facts; (4) written questions from the class submitted either to the teacher or to an "expert" or a panel of persons prepared to answer; (5) panel discussions representing an effort to get at the facts and issues and to resolve conflicts or come to conclusions; (6) invited outside speakers.

There are other promising ways. Some teachers occasionally use written work in which a student describes his relation to a problem, his perplexities, and his findings and opinions. These then serve anonymously as the base for class discussion. Areas of hygiene where there is some controversy or some popular misconception, such as considerations of socialised medical practice, drugs and narcotics, nutritional fads, healing cults, marriage problems, and others, are particularly good material for these supplementary teaching techniques.

Field Experiences

Field trips are also becoming increasingly popular in health education. It is realised that to learn about healthful living *only* from books is a somewhat limited experience. To find out how people actually live, the way they meet or fail to meet their problems, the way the community safeguards the health of its citizens, or to gain an on-the-ground insight into the larger social problems related to health provides a richer, more meaningful approach to an understanding of personal and public health. There are, of course, many trips available to students in a school which approves of such extramural activity. An enterprising teacher might arrange for the class to:

1. Visit hospitals, clinics, or public health agencies, to observe and study their programme.
2. Observe and study the work of commercial laboratories for the production of serums, drugs, and medicines.
3. Survey the recreational programme of the community in relation to needs.
4. Study slum areas in relation to disease, housing needs, and the connection between crowded conditions and crime.
5. Study through personal experience the work of quacks, charlatans, religious healers, and others who purport to heal the sick.
6. Observe the work of government in the inspection and control of food and water supply, restaurant and hotel sanitation.
7. Study building and zoning ordinances for their relation to safety, health, and welfare.
8. Survey local traffic control problems in relation to improvement.

9. Seek out local fire hazards with suggestions for improvement.
10. Sample public opinion on a variety of contemporary problems such as medical care, superstitions and fallacious beliefs, dietary practices, attitudes toward insanity, causes of disease.

There are but ten of a long list of possibilities. The field trip can become an important adjunct to any course of study in health education or it can be a waste of time. To assure the former and prevent the latter the following conditions should be observed:

1. The trip or study should have a definite bearing on the matters at hand. It should be *a part of* that which is being studied at the moment and should not intrude upon a sequence of thought being developed at the time.
2. The trip should be thoroughly talked over *before* it occurs, with purposes and prospective outcomes thoroughly understood by the committee or class making the trip.
3. On the trip discussion of what is going on, or being seen, should be directed to the purposes for which the trip is made.
4. When the group has returned to the classroom the trip should be summarised, the gains itemised, the lessons drawn so all will understand.
5. The trip should not be taken merely as an amusement, or to satisfy morbid curiosities, or as a chance to get out of school for a half-day. A trip to a penitentiary or to a court must be related to a health problem under discussion and cannot be justified if made merely to satisfy curious people as to how criminals are treated or what "The Big House" looks like. Likewise, trips to waterworks or dairy barns are futile unless they bear upon problems of food sanitation.
6. All safety precautions for the care of students making the trip should be taken. These should be planned in advance. Bus transportation, chaperons, directions, even police

escorts should be arranged to prevent any remote possibility of accident or other untoward event.

7. Arrangements with the hosts for the trip should be made far enough in advance to allow them to prepare to receive the students and to make their visit worthwhile.

If these conditions can be observed the exploration and study of community activity give the study of health an important realistic touch.

The Use of Community Agencies

As in the development of worthwhile field trips, there is every reason to associate the school course of study in health education with community agencies working in the health field. Too long has there been a lack of understanding on the part of each—the school and the agency—as to purposes and programmes. Students gain in understanding of health problems when reciprocal relationships are established and the health agency is invited to participate in the programme of school health education.

Means of perfecting this relationship are numerous. As Miss Tucker has well expressed it, "There are three effective ways for making the school health programme more community centered. One is to bring the community resource people into the school-room. Another is to take the students into the community where they will actually participate in health projects. A third is for the school activity to take part in joint planning for health through a community health council." Illustrations from actual situations of this three-way relationship may be cited as follows:

1. In one city the public health engineers and the fire inspectors made their annual report after visits to the schools and consultation with not only school officials but students as well. The report became a joint report.

2. A local dental society offered to assist the school in the construction of an adequate dental education and care programme. Students participated in the planning.

3. School-community health councils (with student representation, of course) may be formed for discussion and action on common problems where such health organisations do not exist. Representative teachers and students participate on the health council of a community.
4. Summer pre-school roundups of parent-teacher associations are sometimes held.
5. The state highway patrol and the traffic bureau of the local police department have worked with school children to the successful furtherance of the ends of the department and the protection of the children.
6. Parent-teacher groups, women's clubs, service clubs, and other interested groups have frequently sponsored, financed, and conducted the local school-lunch programme.
7. State and local departments of health, as well as numerous volunteer agencies like the tuberculosis associations and Red Cross chapters loan films and slides of interest, provide literature and speakers of value to school health classes.
8. With students participating, a disease control programme for the schools was planned by the school-community council, approved by the board, and executed by the school personnel.
9. Students in hygiene classes have frequently attended meetings of metropolitan health councils and made the activities of the councils a study for the benefit of all, including the health council.
10. Students in classes have also attended public forums, meetings of medical, labour, educational, or other groups where current issues of medical care are being discussed.
11. The school and local branch of any voluntary health agency can be of great mutual aid. The students can assist in the sale of seals, participate in programmes, extend information; the association can furnish services, literature, and other informational services on the subject, and in part interpret the problem to the community through the school.

12. Students asked for and got a field trip with the commissioner of public health to visit swimming pools and bathing beaches for joint discussion and action concerning the sanitation and safety of the facilities.

13. Students have, on numerous occasions, assisted local dairy councils with their programmes of public education.

14. There are many other instances of reciprocal services—all to the ultimate benefit of the health of people: police protection at meetings and games; fire department inspections and instruction in fire safety; Boy Scout cleanup days. These and the activities of organisations for crippled children, fraternal organisations, chapters of the National Foundation for Infantile Paralysis, the American Legion, and dozens of other local, state, and national organisations all provide opportunity for enriching the health education programme in the school if effective correlation can be established.

Other Resources

The teacher of health education has almost unlimited resources at his command. His principal problem will be to use them effectively and not wastefully. *There is no particular point to using a motion picture, or a set of slides, or a field trip unless it bears on the point at hand and makes a real contribution to its understanding*. Some teachers have a naive faith in the efficacy of visual aids. These have merit—but only to the extent that they are cogent to the problem under discussion and are themselves well constructed and interesting. There is certainly nothing sacred about a motion picture on a health subject. The picture must be held to the same standards of educational effectiveness as a book is.

Certainly no teacher needs to be limited in health education only to a single textbook and his own lectures and discussions. The subject can be made immeasurably more vital and functional in the lives of students if other resources are used.

Text and reference books still remain the principal resource, other than his own knowledge and skill, which a teacher has or should have at his disposal. There are good textbooks written on personal hygiene and there are some very poor ones. In adopting a text one should be extremely careful to assure its worth as a teaching instrument.

If one does not use a single text, then a set of six or a dozen or an unlimited number of good reference books in the library will be needed. As a matter of fact, even with a text reference, books and magazines are needed because no school text ever written has covered or will be able to cover the entire range of student problems and interests. Students must have access to additional readings as the occasion demands, and for that reason the teacher should make the effort to provide such references at the rate of one to every eight or ten students.

Students should be taught to use these reference books in their search for the solutions to problems. Many teachers list selected readings from them for each unit of work.

Misinformation and Unscientific Material

There is a danger that misinformation and unscientific material will creep into courses of study and syllabuses. Personal hygiene is not, in every respect, an exact science ready to be applied to human life with predictable results. Much of hygiene is conjecture, assumption, or reasoning based on related scientific evidence. Some hygiene is based only on personal experience. Someone finds that morning calisthenics make him feel fit to eat a hearty breakfast so he forthwith teaches or, worse, writes that such frivolities are good for everyone. Someone reasons that, because water is an essential for life and we rid ourselves of so many pints each day, to drink eight or ten glasses a day is one of nature's requirements for anyone. In one school syllabus they speak of "surplus nervous energy". There is no such thing. In another, flat-chestedness is alleged to be predisposing to tuberculosis. There is no such relationship. It is widely thought that breathing exercises are important to bring "fresh air" to one's lungs or to "build up resistance to disease". No such relationship can be established scientifically.

Hygiene teachers are constantly tempted to give the final

and definitive word on the causes of colds, the hours of sleep required, the best treatment for constipation, or the ways to prevent mental aberrations. So many people know so many wrong answers to life's problems that the conscientious teacher has a difficult time resisting the temptation to speak with authority. One who is widely read and who keeps up with scientific developments learns to distinguish a folk tale from fact, fraud from an honest report, and quackery from science. Nothing but constant study and wide reading will develop this talent for discrimination. Such preparation is a requisite for hygiene teaching.

Furthermore, the teacher must recognise fully that he is in no position to diagnose or recommend treatment for mental or physical ills. Students will frequently ask: "What can I do for this cold?" or "If I feel thus and so do you suppose it could be cancer?" The teacher should *not* attempt any solution to such problems either for an individual or before a group. A quite general discussion summarising what is known about the treatment of colds will be adequate in the first instance, and no more than a description of principal symptoms of cancer would be appropriate classroom material in the second.

The Omission of Large and Important Problems

Sometimes syllabuses are designed to omit certain problems or areas which are important to students. There may be a section on the nervous system, for example, with no treatment at all of adjustment to school or to friends, emotional control, or the prevention of worry. Frequently sections or chapters on sex hygiene are conducted with no mention of continence, premarriage problems, or instinct *versus* intelligence in "falling in love". Not infrequently syllabuses are developed with no provision at all for a discussion of nostrums, quackery, medical care, or healing systems.

These omissions are unfortunate. They occur for a variety of reasons. Sometimes the instructor is unprepared in one area so it is deliberately left out. Sometimes time is limited and other areas of less importance are chosen because they are easier. Sometimes the instructor fears controversy and avoids it. On other occasions he simply does not know the problem exists.

Whatever the reason, good course-of-study construction does not allow these omissions. No course of study can be complete without a careful covering of all the major health problems confronting the American people.

Rewards and Prizes

Teachers are frequently moved to use rewards or prizes or other motivating forces in health education. Membership buttons in a health club, ribbons for performance, group prizes for the room making the "best showing", medals, cups, insignia, even cash prizes are sometimes used to stimulate good health practice or the acquisition of knowledge. The world seems constituted to accept such as legitimate teaching devices.

There are many rewards which may be associated with an activity either as an incentive or as recognition of good work well done. Furthermore, some are tangible or have tangible value while some are intangible. A student may become vaccinated, for example, because everyone else is and his room wants to win the blue star for 100 per cent vaccination; or perhaps a certificate is given each child who performs fine hygienic practices daily for a month. Or possibly five dollars is awarded the student who writes the best essay on "Why I Should Drink Milk". Possibly only self-satisfaction is the reward for abstaining from tobacco and alcohol until one is "of age". Grades, money, public commendation, trips, cups, self-satisfaction, approval of the group, publicity, group membership, "being captain"—these are all available for use as the teacher strives for health knowledge and health behaviour on the part of students.

Are they all of equal value? Are they all equally justifiable in terms of their educational soundness? Obviously, they are not. They all may be placed somewhere on both of two scales, the one ranging from useless to result-producing and the other from intrinsic and valuable to extrinsic and distorting of values. Such a rating of rewards will depend upon the interpretation and use of criteria. If a teacher cares not for the effect of the reward itself upon the child but only for the results gained, he will use one kind of reward. If he believes the reward should be only a recognition of good work, he will use the same reward but in an entirely different manner. It is the difference between "If you will go to bed every night for a week before 9 o'clock, I'll give you a dollar," and "Because you've been good and not stayed up late this week, here's a dollar". Grades in health classes are particularly susceptible to this difference. "If you'll pass this knowledge test you'll get an A," or "Because you did well on that test you have earned an A". Rewards used in some ways may produce dishonest reactions, distorted egos, antagonisms, and completely distorted values. Used in other ways they may be productive of continued good work and clear understandings of where values are.

What criteria, then, may be applied *before* a reward is fixed upon or *before* a system of rewards is set up? These are suggested:

1. The reward should be inherent in the activity—not separate or unrelated to it.
2. The reward should lead the winner on to further activity in the same line of endeavour.
3. The reward should have values no different from those of the activity itself.
4. The reward should produce no consequences in the individual winner which are unacceptable socially.
5. Above all, the reward or anticipation thereof should not serve as an incentive; the incentive must come from the satisfactions within the activity.

In short, when rewards in health education are used to help the student face the realities of life, achieve something, organise and integrate values, *then* they are moral instruments. When they warp values, teach false values, distort ego, and dissipate energy, then they must be thought of as immoral.

SPECIAL PROBLEMS

In the arrangement of any course of study, the construction of any syllabus, or the teaching of any unit or course, certain problems appear to be of special importance.

The Area of Sex Hygiene or Social Living

The study and discussion of sex hygiene offer great possibilities for affecting favourably the behaviour and attitudes of young people. The evidence is overwhelming that instruction is needed to guide children through adolescence and into maturity and marriage. Great good can be done if courses of study can include consideration of these problems and if teachers in charge of health instruction are well prepared to meet the issues.

Many school principals and teachers are reluctant to deal with the subject because they fear an adverse public reaction. Many others have such a distorted notion of what sex education is that they think of it narrowly as only education about venereal disease or about how to beget children. Others with equally distorted views and vulgar predilections conceive of it only as teaching youngsters things they should not know about the anatomy of the genitalia and the mechanics of intercourse. To such benighted views any well-informed person takes well-founded exception. Instruction in social relationships including even the phases directly related to sex life can be handled cleanly, scientifically, objectively, and broadly by skilled and informed teachers. There need be nothing obscene about the discussion of boy-girl relationships. There is nothing vulgar or hurtful about the many well-taught courses on marriage problems which are found in universities today.

Three well-known approaches to classroom instruction exist in this area: (a) through animal and plant life (the "birds, bees, and butterflies" approach); (b) through the anatomy and physiology involved; and (c) through human life situations. Of the three, the last is far and away the best, most productive of good results, and most helpful to young people as they wend their way through the complexities of premarital and marital life. Admittedly it is helpful to have students come to the unit with some understanding of terminology and processes gleaned from the animals—from ponies and pollen. Nevertheless, to learn of human sex life by an original study of animals and plants is to pitch the early understanding of sex matters at a low level from which some individuals are never able to rise. Actually, there is little similarity (only in gross anatomy and basic function) between the sex life of animals and that of man. The presence of the intellect, of the ability to plan, think, react emotionally, worry, and be sensitive, and the existence of the complexity of marriage customs, conventions, laws, and similar impediments cast man's sex life in an entirely different setting from that of sheep. To help people we must plunge directly into a consideration of people's problems. "The only proper study of man is man himself."

To begin with anatomy and physiology is equally unfortunate. Youngsters are early curious about anatomy. But even as beneficiaries of graphic portrayals of the detail of genitalia and the reproductive apparatus, the students may miss entirely the great social and emotional controls needed in intelligent sex behaviour. Such anatomical information is only incidental to the solution of problems.

The best approach is through human life situations as they arise and as they become important and meaningful to students at any age. How a seven-year-old boy should act when going to a girl playmate's birthday party is a human life situation and thus part of sex education. Whether to "go steady" in high school, how to conduct oneself at a dance, what legal requirements should be met before marriage, and how much money a fellow should have to get married on—these and thousands of other similar human problems give the best approach to classroom discussions. They should be utilised to the fullest—*and they may be discovered from the students themselves.*

Here, for example, is one listing of forty-five different but related questions which came from students, and which may serve as a basis for student-teacher discussions in senior high school. Units of work constructed from these and other human problems represent the best kind of sex hygiene instruction:

Family Health

The problems of high-school students in social and family living.

(a) Current problems:

1. What behaviours, manners, courtesies, and customs are desirable among boys and girls in order to establish harmonious social relationships within the school? (a) Conduct on dates, (b) Conduct around the school, (c) Language and ""horseplay", (d) Dress, (e) Drinking.
2. What is the basis for attraction and friendship between boys and girls? (a) The nature of "sex appeal", (b) Similarities in interests, (c) The need for attention, (d) The relative importance of social status, (e) Loyalties.
3. How can one go about meeting the boy or girl one would like to meet? (a) Introductions, (b) "Pickups", (c) Organisations.
4. Is it desirable to establish a "steady date" in high school? (a) Variety in friendships.
5. What responsibilities do a boy and girl have to each other and to the parents of their companions? (a) Arriving home from dates, (b) Differences in family standards, (c) Safety on dates.
6. What knowledge of the reproductive structures and functions is necessary to the establishment of an intellectual understanding of one's own life and life in relation to others? (a) The essentials of structure and function.
7. How can a boy or girl control the reproductive urge? (a) The use of the intelligence in relation to emotion, (b) Interests, (c) Moral standards, (d) Recognition of consequences.
8. How should girls care for themselves during menstruation? (a) Rest, (b) Bathing, (c) Exercise, (d) Medical care.
9. What is menstruation and what are its normal characteristics? (a) Purpose, (b) Regularity.
10. Are intimate complete relationships before marriage

justifiable? (a) Moral standards, (b) Probable consequences, (c) Effect on later marriage, (d) The futility of "the conquest".

11. What are the best sources of information on matters of love and marriage which are available to high-school students? (a) People, (b) Books, (c) Movies, (d) Miscellaneous literature.

12. What are the best ways to gain this information?

(b) Premarriage problems:

13. What consideration should be taken into account in the selection of a marriage partner? (a) Maturity, (b) Health, (c) Background, (d) Interests, (e) Age, (f) Looks, (g) Education, (h) Job.

14. How can one tell when one is ready to assume the responsibilities of marriage? (a) Age, (b) Income, (c) Maturity, (d) Willingness.

15. What should each partner know about the health and background of the other before agreeing to marry? (a) Health, (b) Heredity, (c) Disease.

16. How much money should a couple have to get married on? (a) Tastes, (b) Locality, (c) Standard of living, (d) Child planning.

17. Should opposites marry?

18. Should engaged couples be allowed greater intimacies than others? (a) Local customs, (b) Effect on marriage, (c) Effects of restraint.

19. How long should engagements last?

20. What attitudes should be cultivated regarding the influences of "in-laws" on the forthcoming marriage? (a) Parental decisions and advice, (b) Gifts and support, (c) Living with parents, (d) Visits and vacations.

21. What legal requirements must be met before marriage? (a) Health certificate, (b) Licence, (c) Banns, (d) The minister.

(c) Family Planning:

22. How soon and how can a sexual compatibility be established in marriage? (a) Individual difference in response and desires, (b) Attitudes, (c) Trial and error.

23. How soon should couples plan for and have their first child? (a) Financial arrangements, (b) Religious beliefs, (c) Health, (d) Readiness for children.

24. How soon should a physician be consulted?

25. What sort of examination should be made of the prospective mother before pregnancy?

26. What should be known by the couple about how life begins? (a) Function of reproductive organs, (b) Genetic mechanisms.

27. Under what conditions would further childbearing be detrimental to a mother's health? (a) Medical judgment, (b) Strain.

28. What changes in diet as well as rest and other personal habits should be made during pregnancy? (a) Medical judgment, (b) Rest, (c) Exercise, (d) Diet, (e) Household work.

29. What are the early signs of pregnancy? (a) Tests for pregnancy.

30. What sort of care should a mother have following the birth of the child? (a) Medical advice, (b) Sympathetic family.

31. How long after the birth of a child is a physician's care needed?

32. What sort of adjustment is required of the husband during pregnancy? (a) Patience, (b) Sharing of duties, (c) Restraint, (d) The development of affection.

33. What should be known about hospital costs, insurance plans, and needed home equipment in anticipation of a child?

34. What assistance do the federal and state governments give to wives and families of servicemen? (a) The funds for maternal health, (b) Sources of information.

35. What plan should be made by the family regarding recreational interests, friends, and distribution of time within the home? (a) Planning as a group, (b) Selfish interests, (c) Income and expenditures.

36. How can differences of opinion within the home be reconciled? (a) Frankness, (b) Willingness to settle differences, (c) Authority, (d) Customs and traditions.

(d) The care of children:

37. How much attention should a child have from the parents? (a) The rights of infants, (b) Fondling, (c) Spoiling the child, (d) Decision making.

38. To what extent should the presence of a child affect the relationship between the husband and wife? (a) Continuation of joint interests, (b) Sharing affection, (c) Building the family.

39. What medical care (e.g., diet, immunisation, control of infections, habit regulation, correction of defects) should be provided for the child?

40. How can one tell if the baby is developing normally? (a) Weight, (b) Motor controls, (c) Length, (d) Vision, (e) Hearing.

41. How many toys and other playthings should be provided for the child? (a) Overstimulation, (b) Purposes, (c) Values.

42. Should the parents plan in advance for the emotional responses and psychological growth of the child? (a) Response to people, (b) Crying, (c) Development of character traits, (e) Imitation.

43. How should the child be prepared for school? (a) Attitudes, (b) Skills, (c) Clothing, (d) Immunisations, (e) Sociability, (f) Personal habits.

44. What attitudes should be developed in the child in preparation for the visits to the physician and dentist?
45. At what age should parents plan for the social development of the child in his relationship with playmates and adults?

From those forty-five human problems and the many others which are similar a teacher with the class or a committee can construct several small units of work. The arrangement, i.e., "current problems, premarriage problems, family planning" need not be used for unit titles; in fact, they probably should not be so used in that they are too general and perhaps too academically logical.

As an example of the kind of instructional units which might be prepared from such a collection of student questions the following three units out of an outline containing eight recommended for senior high schools are suggestive of what may be done:

Suggestions for the Use of These Units

1. The order in which the units are here presented may, and no doubt should, be changed to meet the particular classroom situation in which they are used.
2. The questions in each unit are merely typical or "priming" questions. Others would be useful in guiding the discussion.
3. Teachers will make selections of the reading in terms of the availability of the books and of time.
4. Additional or fewer experiences may be conducted, depending upon the zeal of the class and opportunities available.
5. Effort should be made to teach these units not on a lecture basis but using as fully as possible student discussion, committee work, panels, and individual reports.

Unit 1: The Economics of Home-making

1. What minimum income will allow for reasonably comfortable family life?

2. Are living costs and family expenditures the concern of the whole family?
3. How are family budgets made? Are they useful?
4. What share of the family income should be allotted to medical and dental care, maternity expenses, child care?
5. How can a family remain happy even though financially insecure?

Reading Selections:

1. Foster, Robert G., *Marriage and Family Relationships*, Chapter 11.
2. Groves, Skinner, Swenson, *The Family and Its Relationships*, pp. 177-217.
3. Johnson, Randolph, Pixley, *Looking Toward Marriage*, pp. 63-66.
4. Moore, Leahy, *You and Your Family*, Chapters 12 and 15.
5. Wood, Mildred W., *Living Together in the Family*, Chapter 10.
6. Pierce, Wellington G., *Youth Comes of Age*, Chapter 13.
7. Bowman, H. A., *Marriage and Moderns*, pp. 357-373.

Suggested Experiences:

1. Small committees can prepare sample budgets for varying incomes in relation to current living costs.
2. Studies can be made of expenditures in the city or nation for medical, dental, maternity care.
3. Heads of families may be brought to the class for participation in the discussions.
4. Intra-class discussions may be arranged on any controversial problem within the unit.

Unit 3: The Social Life of Married Couples

1. How much entertaining is expected of young married couples?

2. Should young married couples ever double-date?
3. How much fun can be had on limited incomes?
4. How much should others be told of the problems of home?
5. Should wives ever "gossip" about their husbands, and vice versa?

Reading Selections:

1. Foster, Robert G., *Marriage and Family Relationships,* pp. 178-181.
2. Groves, Skinner, Swenson, *The Family and Its Relationships,* pp. 375-409.
3. Wood, Mildred W., *Living Together in the Family,* Chapter 11.

Suggested Experiences:

1. Two or three married persons might visit the class to tell of their social life; what it involves, what it costs, where they go, and what they do.
2. Small committees might make special investigations of segments of the problem and report back to the class.

Unit 8: Where Can One Learn?

1. Where can one find good books to read on this subject?
2. How can one discriminate between good and unsound literature on marriage and home life?
3. How reliable are popular magazine articles?
4. What persons can be trusted for having scientific information about these problems?
5. How can one check what one learns from casual conversation, over against scientific fact?

Reading Selections:

1. Ohio Department of Education, *Some Suggested Sources and Materials for Health Education,* pp. 3-4 and 21-23.

Suggested Experiences:

1. Arrange with the local library to send over a dozen scientific books on marriage and friendship.
2. Arrange for a small committee to present the class with a list of reliable sources of information.
3. Arrange for a group to evaluate the popular sources of information such as movies, radio, conversation, and to present criteria for judging.

General References for Students:

1. Foster, Robert G., *Marriage and Family Relationships,* The Macmillan Company, New York, 1944.
2. Groves, Skinner, Swenson, *The Family and Its Relationships,* J. B. Lippincott Co., Philadelphia, 1948.
3. Johnson, Randolph, Pixley, *Looking Toward Marriage,* Allyn and Bacon, New York, 1943.
4. Moore, Leahy, *You and Your Family,* D. C. Heath & Co., Boston, 1948.
5. Pierce, Wellington G., *Youth Comes of Age,* McGraw-Hill Book Co., New York, 1948.
6. Wood, Mildred W., *Living Together in the Family,* American Home Economics Association, 620 Mills Bldg., Washington, D.C., 1946.

Or a coordinated unit on social living as part of a year's work in hygiene for high-school people may be illustrated by the following excerpts from such a unit now being conducted. This unit fits into a one-semester course required in the senior year. The class meets five days a week for eighteen weeks and boys and girls are taught separately although joint meetings are sometimes held. Six weeks of the eighteen are devoted to this unit on social living.

The entire unit deals with six problems areas: dating, adolescence, how to choose a mate, getting ready for marriage, heredity, and building a family. The teachers proceed to the first areas—on dating—something as follows:

Example of specific questions discussed—dating.

1. What is expected of a date?
   (a) Behaviour.
   (b) Manners.
   (c) Courtesies.
   (d) Customs.
2. What changes occur when dating begins?
   (a) Stimulation for personal grooming.
   (b) Desire for release from parental direction.
   (c) Social status.
   (d) Group loyalties.
3. How can an individual meet a potential date?
   (a) Introductions.
   (b) Pickups.
   (c) Organisations.
   (d) "Blind dates".
4. When should the individual start dating?
   (a) For parties.
   (b) For double dates.
   (c) For single dates.
5. What can be done on a date?
6. Is it necessary to drink or smoke to be popular?
7. What hours should high-school students observe?
8. Should girls ask boys for dates?
9. Can girls have a week when they assume the dating responsibilities of boys? "Twirp Season."
10. Is Dutch-treating permissible or desirable?

11. What makes a boy or girl popular?
12. Is a girl expected to invite her escort in after a date?
13. How can one refuse a date and encourage the boy to call again?
14. Is there such a thing as dating too much or too little?
15. Are necking and petting necessary for popularity?
16. What are the advantages and disadvantages of having a variety of friendships?
17. What are the advantages and disadvantages of going steady?
18. Is kissing expected on a first date?
19. Should one use dates as a means of meeting people? (even if he does not like the date)
20. Should the boy ask the girl's parents what time she is expected home?

Projects:

(a) Organise a panel to discuss questions of primary concern.

(b) Make a questionnaire and submit to various groups.

(1) Check the average answer of the boys as compared with the average answer of the girls.

(2) Check the average answer of the senior as compared with that of a junior.

(3) Check the average answer of the student as compared with that of the parent.

(c) Write a skit or play in which the various questions are answered with situations.

(d) List personality traits that make for popularity.

3. General activities:

(a) Panel discussions based on needs of students.

(b) Joint class meetings considered necessary by students to develop better relationships and further understanding.

(c) Speakers for combined groups—topics.

(1) Senior Prom—the male viewpoint; the female viewpoint.

(2) Further discussions in separate classrooms.

(d) Movies; filmstrips (example).

(1) "Junior Prom."

(2) "Manners Made Easy."

(e) Student-planned assembly programmes for entire student body.

(f) Student speakers from other countries discuss their methods of handling similar problems.

4. Additional methods of achieving curriculum objectives.

(a) Cooperation with the home and community-home. Visitation programme adopted as a school policy establishes an understanding of home life, background, and social training.

(b) Cooperation with the senior class in regard to social functions.

(c) Cooperation with school organisations in correlation of problems.

(1) Intramurals—mixed volleyball teams; badminton; dancing; ping pong.

(2) Game room—leisure-time activities.

(3) Council of student representatives—school policies; assembly programmes.

(d) Group participation in class planning.

(e) Supervised study enables instructor to give individual attention.

(f) Required reading lists provide additional information for specific sections of the unit.

(g) Reference library in classroom—emphasis on the value of student research.

(h) Use of a manikin purchased by the Health and Science departments for classroom discussion.

Any one of these units is susceptible to interesting treatment involving student participation. The teacher should *not* do all the talking. A sex lecture is generally ineffective. The student should be expected to participate by raising questions, discussing, contributing information, working on committees, and making investigations. To study the matter of child adoption by sending a committee to visit an adoption agency or nursery and report their findings to the class would be effective. Likewise, a visit to a maternity ward, an investigation at the district attorney's office of abortion rackets, an exhibit in the classroom of a complete layette borrowed from a department store, and a class-developed code of behaviour are examples of opportunities for students to participate. The emphasis on *doing* as well as mere talking can take much of the tension off discussions in this area and both teachers and students can feel more comfortable.

How broad is the field of sex instruction? Are there sub-areas which, for the good of the total situation, the teacher had best *not* handle? The field is tremendously broad and great discretion and good taste must always be used by the teacher in admitting to or barring from the syllabus or discussion certain areas of doubtful propriety or actual taboo. No one has ever suggested that the schoolroom was the place to "cover the water front", as it were. There are some areas best left untouched, some which might be appropriately admitted depending on the local situation, and others which could be admitted with safety almost anywhere. A rough screening of the material available for teaching would, on the foregoing basis, appear something as follows:

I. Areas of possibility—acceptable for school discussion virtually everywhere:

(a) Primary Years:

1. Functions of elimination as they relate to the genitalia including protection and care.

2. The phenomenon of birth—the coming of the baby—reproduction in plants and animals.
3. Early social friendships—manners and courtesies between sexes.
4. Early conceptions of sex differences.

(b) Intermediate Years:

1. Mental and physiological changes attendant upon growth—continuation of sex differences.
2. Continuation of social and ethical relationships between the sexes—social friendships.
3. Early lessons in hereditary influence.
4. Basic sources of information on sex problems.

(c) Puberty and adolescence:

1. Secondary sex characteristics and phenonomena.
2. Full discussion of friendly relationships between the sexes—social and ethical problems—social standards—origins of social relationships.
3. Discussion of preliminary emotional experiences.
4. Continuance of information on the phenomena of reproduction—further discussion where necessary of genitalia and reproductive process.
5. Mate choosing—the nature of affection and love.
6. Continence—ethical, biological, and psychological factors.
7. Venereal disease—prevention and care.
8. Factors important in the establishment of a home.
9. Scientific sources of information.

(d) Adulthood:

1. The case for and against birth control—social, ethical, and biological.

2. Parental responsibilities.
3. Home and family life problems—homemaking.
4. Care and development of children.

II. Areas of caution—may be unsuitable for school discussion because of lack of satisfactory scientific information or because of local objections.

1. The basis for sex and emotional control in human life.
2. The relation of intelligence to love.
3. The biological foundation of morals.
4. The process of birth—conception—delivery—normal and abnormal phenomena.
5. Sterilisation.
6. The testicular and ovarian hormones.
7. Rejuvenation.
8. Artificial impregnation.
9. Sexual practices during pregnancy.
10. Sex perversions.

III. Areas of taboo—no place in the classroom.

1. Abnormal sexology—sexual aberrations.
2. The *modus operandi* of sexual intercourse.
3. Techniques of birth control.

Obviously teachers of health education must be well prepared to handle safely and efficiently the materal in this area. Certainly the answers to many student problems will not be found in the details of anatomy and physiology of the reproductive systems. Much more is needed. Teachers expecting to be helpful to students throughout these units on social living should have a fairly well-rounded background in the organic, psychological, and social factors which influence behaviour in these situations. *Adequate preparation is essential.* It would be recommended that much of this material be left untouched unless the teacher is prepared to do a competent job on it. It is difficult to delineate what knowledge is necessary; impossible, in fact, to place here specific suggestions. The teacher should read the outstanding basic books on the subject and, after reading them, should proceed with a continuous plan of improving his understanding of the area.

Knowledge of the social problems of the adolescent, their nature, cause, and solutions, is basic. The knowledge of the anatomy and physiology of the reproductive system is but preliminary in preparation to the true dealing with the problems. The students deserve highly competent handling of this entire field.

Teachers experienced in dealing with the subject frequently come to these conclusions about it:

1. "Instruction concerning sex should be a normal part of courses designed to have a much broader educational purpose. Life science, biology, or hygiene form excellent mediums."
2. "The unit on sex hygiene should not be placed prominently near the beginning of the course, nor should it be last. Teachers and students should have ample time to become acquainted."
3. No prominence at all should be given the approaching unit—no special announcements, no segregation or division of the class *just for this unit,* no special visitors, nothing which is out of the usual routine of the course. The unit should be "taken in stride".
4. "While a clear-cut and thorough factual knowledge is a necessary preliminary to ethical interpretations, the social implications of sex should be presented with sincerity and conviction."
5. The teacher should retain throughout the unit a nice sense of humour—not letting the discussions get too "heavy" and being alert to turn potentially embarrassing moments into moments of laughter. The discussion must be kept on an objective, understandable, and human plane, being allowed

neither to become grim, tense, and heavy nor to degenerate into a "smut" session.

6. The teacher should feel no hesitation about using the slang of the day in discussing a point at issue. Vulgarisms and obscenities are, of course, barred but the harmless slang expressions for dates, love-making, or marriage are acceptable and help to ease a situation which otherwise might be tense.

7. "Fear is not nearly as effective a deterrent as positive idealism; therefore, loyalties, family ideals, self-respect, self-restraint, and moderation should be taught rather than the danger or horrors of venereal disease."

8. "Children tend to absorb only that information which serves immediate needs or answers immediate questions. Some provision for continuously meeting the child's sex problems is manifestly ideal. If this is not feasible, as many problems as possible should be met *prior to* adolescence. . . . When, too, instruction is delayed until adolescent development is under way . . . the teacher's job becomes more difficult."

9. Teachers should be very wary indeed of talking from their own personal experience. Because of the wide range of individual variations and differences in sex reactions there can be no safe "typical" experience. People vary tremendously in sex behaviours and, hence, personal experience is highly unreliable.

10. "While single lectures in high school by some outsider may be preferable to ignoring the subject completely, they are typically objectionable because they allow little opportunity for discussion and clarification, are frequently 'taken the wrong way' or made fun of, and are often saccharine and general."

11. "Parents in schools where units on sex, reproduction, heredity, marriage, or social relationships are taught should be informed in advance of the course, given easy opportunity to learn of its content, and told something of the methods and procedures to be used. Suggestions for

improvement of the course should be solicited from parents and other interested adults."

12. Special instructors for this aspect of a health or biology course should not replace the regular teacher unless those specialists, as in an integrated project, are contributing specialised knowledge along with others.

13. "The instructor should at all times be strictly honest in all statements, ready to encourage and to answer frankly all questions and careful to distinguish fact from belief or interpretation." Likewise, the instructor should readily admit that he does not know the answer if such is the case and proceed then to help the students and himself find it. There is certainly no disgrace in not knowing the answers to human problems. A teacher concerned about "losing face" by admitting he does not know should safeguard his pride by telling the class at the outset that the answers to many of their questions remain in the realm of the unknown and that they can only hunt for clues together.

14. Teachers should not be chosen for this kind of instruction only on the basis of their scientific preparation. Because the discussions are so close to students, so intimate and affective of a student's life, the soundness of character of the teacher is of even greater importance.

15. Segregation by sexes is not a requisite for effective instruction. Few items of importance must be omitted to save embarrassment in mixed classes. Certainly if the class starts out mixed it should stay that way through the unit on sex hygiene. Likewise, there is no reason to believe a skilled man could not teach successfully a group of girls or a woman a class of boys. It depends entirely upon the skill, preparation, and seriousness of purpose which the teacher brings to the group.

16. When should the work be given? There is no "ripe" time in particular for the unit on sex hygiene. Every year, every day is the strategic time for instruction. There are needs for this kind of instruction from infancy to senility. No one unit given in some magical semester will clear away all previous

questions and solve all problems which will arise in the future. Need for instruction, or at least advice and counsel, is continuous. Units of work in any school year from first grade through college will be fruitful. Certainly any year of the senior high school would reap a full harvest of questions and problems.

The Area of Mental Hygiene

The study of mental hygiene is increasing in popularity and prominence as time goes on. Treatment of it in hygiene classes has become a necessity. Formerly a hygiene teacher needed to pay little attention to problems of psychological health; the organic or scientific aspects of health were considered adequate coverage. At present, however, the situation is radically different. Partly because of a growing understanding of the interaction between "mind" and "body"—psychosomatic relationships—and partly because of a growing student demand for consideration of psychological problems, the area is now a major one of any health course of study.

It requires no special treatment. The same techniques of problem discovery, grade placement, and student participation apply here as elsewhere. Students are in need of discussion of their problems, not their anatomy. The description of the brain and spinal cord, gray and white matter, the nature of instincts and reflexes, the location in the brain of the centres for sight, hearing, and memory—all such detail is no doubt very interesting to some but to many it is dull.

In this area there are student problems to be prevented or solved and student questions to be answered. It is futile to think that instructional classroom services are all that are needed to deal with the psychological and behaviour problems in school. Guidance programmes, psychological counselling, and an analysis and reform of the psychological aspects of the teaching-learning process are needed effectively to influence student adjustment and behaviour. Classroom instruction is only a facet of the needed programme.

Such instruction, by constructing units of work as in other areas of health, can bring helpful classroom discussion on questions like the following:

1. What are the characteristics of a normal mind—and a normal adjustment to one's environment?
2. Does one have to learn to adjust or does it come naturally?
3. What does intelligence or mental processes have to do with health?
4. Does good health include the way a person thinks?
5. What does heredity have to do with making a normal mind?
6. Is self-analysis a good thing?
7. Is it harder to get along with people now than it used to be?
8. Can one's mental health be built up like physical health?
9. Does a person's physical health affect him psychologically?
10. How can one prevent nervousness?
11. What is temperament? What are moods?
12. Is there such a thing as nervous or emotional energy?
13. Can worry be prevented? Fear? Insanity? Epilepsy? Alcoholism?
14. Is there any intelligent basis for superstition?
15. Is it human nature to worry and fret?

And here are examples of the kinds of problems which are susceptible to some form of class treatment:

1. Homesickness.
2. Fear of competitive games.
3. Wanting to play and be alone.
4. Dislike for the opposite sex.
5. Stealing, cheating, and lying.
6. Temper flare-ups.

7. Poor sportsmanship.
8. Cruelty to others and to animals.
9. Inability to accept criticism.
10. Insistence on own way.
11. Inability to make decisions.
12. Dependence upon others for praise and attention.
13. Daydreaming and absent-mindedness.
14. Fears.
15. Feelings of inferiority and inhibition.

As an example of an attempt made by one group to deal with problems in this area, the following unit has been worked out:

Unit I: Adjusting to College Life and Mental Health

1. What are some common problems that men encounter at the University?
2. What counselling agencies are available to young men to help them with certain of these problems?
   (a) Adjustment problems in general and vocational guidance.
   (b) Financial problems needing scholarship assistance, loans, or employment.
   (c) Problems related to inability to study properly or effectively.
   (d) Problems related to difficulty in mathematics or reading.
   (e) Problems of speech or hearing.
   (f) Problems of marital or premarital character.
   (g) Problems related to health.
   (h) Learning how to dance.

(i) Legal aids.

3. What is personality? Mental health? How does personality take shape?

Good mental health comes then when you (the personality) satisfy your drives, feelings and emotions and still meet in a satisfactory manner the demands of your social and physical environment.

How does personality take shape?

The Way We Learn

(a) Introjection

(b) Identification

(c) Sublimation

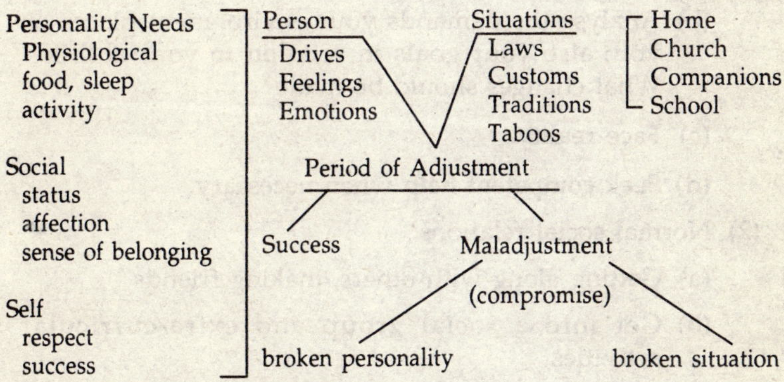

4. What mental mechanisms do we sometimes use to resolve our conflicts? Are these harmful?

Competition Between Personality and Environment

Escape Reaction	*Fight Reaction*	*Constructive Compromise*
Dodge responsibilities.	Refuse to cooperate.	Make decision that will bring the most enjoyment and satisfaction in the long run — a test of growing up.
Become sick: malingerer; "gold bricker".	Bitterness.	
	Troublemaker.	

Make-believe "attitude" is unhealthy way to escape environment.	Griper.

5. What are some of the personality traits that make for successful adjustment on the job and in society?

appearance	expression
agreeableness	intelligence
manners	self-confidence
interests	dependability
temperament	loyalty

6. What practices can one follow which aid him to develop a pleasing personality, mental health, and efficiency?

(1) Scientific attitude.

(a) Analyse yourself.

(b) Analyse the demands your environment places on you; also your goals in relation to your abilities. What changes should be made?

(c) Face reality.

(d) Seek competent help when necessary.

(2) Normal social relations.

(a) Getting along with others, making friends.

(b) Get into a social group and extra-curricular activities.

(c) Recreational life; hobbies, physical activity, etc.

(3) React, but react favourably.

Control means the utilisation of nervous energy in developing a new and healthful activity that may take the place of an unwholesome activity.

(4) Mental work, itself.

(a) Learn to do your own work; mental efficiency follows the same law of function as does physical—i.e., only become a good runner by running, only become efficient in speaking by speaking, writing by writing. The man that copies another man's theme learns only to be a good copier. The man that leans on someone else only learns to become dependent on others.

(b) Budget your time; balance of work, play, and rest.

Required reading for students:

1. Diehl, H.S., *Elements of Healthful Living,* New York: McGraw-Hill Book Co., 1950, chapter on "Mental Health".

References for students:

1. McKinney, Fred, *The Psychology of Personal Adjustment.* New York: John Wiley & Sons, Inc., 1949.
2. Overstreet, H. A. *The Mature Mind,* New York: W. W. Norton & Co., 1949.
3. Dunbar, Flanders, *Mind and Body,* New York: Random House, 1947.
4. *Hygeia,* "Normal Abnormalities", September, 1938.

Films available through teaching aids:

Emotional Health, A McGraw-Hill Text-Film.

Controversial Areas

There are several areas of potential controversy in health education. One can get into an argument over almost anything from the unimportant problem of drinking a certain amount of water each day up to the always perplexing one of whether some of the "doubtful" areas of sex hygiene should be taught. Principally, however, the elements of objection are to be found in the areas of sex education, healing, the administration of medical care, alcohol and tobacco, and preparation for teaching. The first four of these are teachable areas, the fifth is a professional one. The teacher will have to face them all with conviction based upon evidence and experience.

The sources of controversy vary. Sometimes citizens in the community object to certain teaching, e.g., about Christian

Science. Sometimes the school principal dislikes to have the teacher deal with pre-marriage problems. Sometimes the medical society may object to the lack of training of a teacher for instruction, or to certain views expressed concerning socialised medicine. It is simply impossible, in the course of a year's good teaching, to avoid controversial areas. One should, therefore, have a technique for meeting objections, embodying, perhaps, some of the following:

1. Teachers should keep rather full notes of what they and students *say* or *do* in these areas of controversy. This is for "the sake of the record". It is always helpful, when someone demands to know "What is it you are teaching these young people?" to be able to *show* them.

2. Teachers should keep as full a record as possible of the *student problems or questions* asked about the areas. It frequently helps to show that the teacher did not "put such things in the heads of students" but that such things were already there and were being given an airing for purposes of getting information scientifically rather than from unauthorised sources.

3. When critics bring the issue to the principal (they will rarely bring it to the teacher himself), the teacher, if called to discuss the matter, should meet the issue fairly, courageously, aggressively, and with the best interests of the students in mind. There is no cause to be intimidated by critics of any sort. Teachers should, when the provocation arises, be prepared to take the case to any "judge", present the need and its answer, and be content to rest the case with the authorities for settlement.

4. Sometimes, in face of rumours of objection or of stated criticism, teachers find it helpful to go directly to the critics, lay the cards on the table, and seek a settlement. Frequently such personal conferences will result in a "settlement out of court" which is to the advantage of students.

5. Teachers should remember that, even though they are public servants, they are *professional* and need not quiver to the whip of every local politician or run away and hide

when the local dowager and arbiter of society begins to wag the tongue. With surprising frequency the community applauds the teacher who stands up for his rights and defends the opportunity of children to learn.

6. Any such attitude of aggressive defence must be based solidly on a scientific position. If a teacher has been dealing with religious healing, for example, in any other terms than in full view of all that is known about psychosomatic medicine, then he has a much weaker defence. If, in dealing with boy-girl relationships, the teacher has allowed vulgarisms to creep in, or has made the discussion too personal, or has simply taught the unit unprepared to do so, then he is vulnerable. One can meet controversy successfully if one is sure of his position. There is nothing quite as contributory to such confidence as a thorough and constant preparation in the science of hygiene *and* in the science of education.
7. Much potential objection from dealing with sex hygiene, venereal disease, insanity, and other extraordinary areas can be avoided if one tries *not* to be spectacular or shocking, uses simple terms, *avoids the abnormal and the morbid,* and keeps a sense of humour throughout.

3

Direct Teaching

The most popular and best understood teaching practice in our schools is to offer a "course" in something. If a college student wants to learn about geology he "takes a course" in it. Or several courses. If a high-school boy wants to learn about science or mechanics he enrolls for a course in physics or industrial arts or some other convenient and aptly named area of information. Over the years the educator has been able to cut our vast accumulation of knowledge into related pieces, offer them as courses or units, and out of them construct a curriculum.

And so it is not unreasonable that we should do the same with "health". A person ought to be able to "take a course" in it. And so he can. This is one of the three curriculum patterns in modern health instruction. It is the oldest of the three patterns and it has gained and lost and gained again in its popularity. Right now it is popular. Great effort is being made to include the study of health or hygiene at least once and preferably two or three times at the secondary level and to arrange the elementary curriculum so that a child will have a more or less continuous experience in the study of healthful living. And in many colleges students may elect from a variety of courses in personal hygiene, general hygiene, nutrition, disease prevention, mental hygiene, marriage and family problems, and others.

This sort of arrangement is known as the direct or specific approach to the teaching of health. It involves a time, a room, a syllabus, a teacher, probably a textbook—all the appurtenances of any other "course". The class is required or elective, usually for credit, and meets regularly for discussions or field experiences or lectures or whatever devices the instructor chooses to use to teach the material.

CHARACTERISTICS OF A GOOD COURSE

A good hygiene course at any level will have certain characteristics. It will be a course in which students actively participate in fact finding, discussion, field experiences, and in the forming of conclusions. It will not consist merely of a series of lectures on health topics. The series of health lectures, even the occasional health lecture by an "outside authority", is of doubtful merit. The lecture allows for virtually no active participation by the students, and although it may be productive of some knowledge the learnings from a series of lectures are less likely to be useful, functional, and secured learnings. The discussion method is much more acceptable to students in that it allows for participation and creates a feeling of being a part of the process, which is conducive to greater and more effective learning than is passively receiving advice from the rostrum.

A good hygiene course will keep its students busy. It will have assignments growing out of or in preparation for the problem at hand. It will allow for extra-class experiences, will take the students afield in search of solutions to problems, will involve reading in more than a textbook, and will use aids to teaching, such as motion pictures, whenever they contribute really to the learning going on. The course will not be a dull lecture-recitation affair with quizzes covering the numerically assigned chapters in the required text.

A good hygiene course will deal with live problems of everyday living. It will seize upon a contemporary drive for funds for cancer research and make the subject of malignancy a study for several days or weeks. It will deal with local traffic problems and current disease rates. It will seek to explore issues involved in contemporary health legislation and will debate the issues currently noted on the subject of medical care. It will fearlessly and yet with dignity explore contemporary problems of friendship, marriage, and heredity, and it will not hide its head in the sand while the great problems of delinquency, venereal disease, or divorce sweep over the school population.

A good hygiene course will allow the students to share in its planning. The teacher can never be sure of his omnipotence. He may not know "what they should be taught". "They" may have ideas and their ideas should be discovered and used. This is true not only for day-to-day teaching but in the selection of the larger problems which go to make up the whole course. A great turning point in the popularity of hygiene courses was reached when teachers ceased being altogether all-wise and all-dominating in the selection of material to be taught and recognised the equity of students in the determination of health problems to be discussed. Hygiene in both school and college has been unpopular in many places. It has been dull, boring, unproductive, and a waste of time for its students, largely because the teacher presumed to choose the health material to be taught and thus the students found little of interest in it.

Given these four characteristics a hygiene course is well started on the road toward popularity and effective function in the lives of students.

THE SOURCES OF STUDENT PROBLEMS

It must be clear that the teacher who organises and conducts a course in health instruction is in a very important and strategic position. A number of decisions which he will make will determine the success or failure of the course for the students. Decisions relating to textbooks, references, field trips, and the like are significant, but the most important set of decisions to make will determine the content, the material, the areas to be studied. These are all critical and upon the wisdom shown in making them depends the acceptance or rejection of the material by the students. The teacher has immense responsibility and must face it with full realisation of the potential consequences of his decisions.

There is no reason for a health course unless the teacher hopes the material taught and the experiences undergone will affect favourably the lives of the students.

As has been said before, knowledge is secondary in importance to the acceptance and use of the material in *living*, in *conduct*, in *behaviour*. Such acceptance requires that the material presented be interesting, meaningful, and identical with the problems and needs of the students who are doing the learning.

How, then, does one find student problems? By asking the students. Or by inquiring into their lives to discover the problems of which they may not be aware or about which they will not tell. Neither the teacher, the adult, the textbook writer, nor the parent can safely say he *knows* student problems unless and until he has explored their sources seeking objective evidence of their existence, seeking the problems themselves. No guesswork will do. No view from Olympus is safe. No parents, even, can be safely counted on to reveal problems of their children just because they are parents. The problems and interests have to be dug for, sometimes ferreted out, and when revealed *these problems then become the stuff out of which the modern functional hygiene course is built.*

The search for needs of students, for their true interests, will take the investigator to several different sources not all of which are equal in productivity. A teacher can explore many of them, and should, as a source of material for the course. Others, interested in research, can take more time than the teacher usually has at his disposal and make more thorough explorations.

So far some twelve sources of student needs and interests have been tapped by those who seek to discover student needs:

1. Student Questions

Given a fair and honest chance to ask questions, students will ask them in abundance. The questions, for the most part, are reliable indications of need. They are, in fact, needs themselves. More times than not the student asking the question wants the answer for his own purposes, because it is important to him, or he would not have asked it. Curiosity emerging in the form of questions may be taken as evidence of need, and discussion can be arranged in answer to the problem.

There are several ways by which such questions can be gathered and, whenever they are gathered, they should be recorded and catalogued so as to be easily associated with a unit or area of work.

(a) Students may be asked to submit, in writing, three (or any number) questions on a subject of the day, each day the class meets (or once a week, or once every change of unit).

(b) Questions which students ask in class may be recorded by the teacher or an assistant at the time they are asked.

(c) Teachers, counsellors, nurses, and other personnel throughout the school may be asked to record (usually on 3" x 5" cards) each question having a health flavour which is asked of them. Such cards could be collected once a week and would provide an interesting supplement to questions asked in class.

(d) A word list containing, say, fifty of the key or common words in health can be presented to an entire class with the request that they take the hour writing (again one question to a card) their personal questions stimulated by the words. It is surprising the number of questions which will be forthcoming when a priming suggestion has been given. The writer has collected something over forty thousand such questions from high-school and college students by this method.

(e) By using a health problem inventory such as the one published by Dr. Oliver Byrd, the teacher can get a good indication of the range of interests held by students. On such inventories students are asked to check or circle the health topic or item they would like to have discussed. By tabulating the results the teacher can readily determine where the emphases of interest are in the class.

2. Parental Testimony

Parents can, if they will, throw considerable light on important problems suitable for class discussion. They see the fatigue from too much school excitement, the developing bewilderment in face of adolescent sex problems, the hit-or-miss sort of dietary practice, and the worries and emotional strains attendant upon "keeping the pace". The teacher may not be as sensitive to these and similar problems as the parent. Some means should be devised to take advantage of these insights from the parents, and the following have been used:

(a) Personal visitation: As often as possible, teachers should visit with parents and in general conversation attempt to get them to reveal the health problems which are important in the lives of their children.

(b) Monthly or semester reports. The anecdotal report card or similar device can be used to stimulate parents to reply telling of health problems as they see them.

(c) Questionnaires of various kinds. These have been sent to parents with the request that they answer such questions as: "Does your boy (girl) show signs of nervousness before tests or examinations?" "Does your boy average nine hours' sleep each night?" "Does your girl show evidence of fatigue as a result of her school activities?"

Or, to change the form, an invitation is extended to the parents to allow the school to assist them in the solution of problems, and to accomplish this the parents must indicate what the problems are. Forms are sent to parents worded, perhaps, as follows:

The school wishes to cooperate fully with you in regard to the health of your child. Perhaps we could, in our classes, reinforce or add to your discussion of certain health problems. If you would indicate below what these problems are we would take them up for discussion:

Principal health problems of my son, as I see them, are:

1.

2.

Etc.

Or, in still another form, a check list of topics might be sent out with the request that parents check once for problems of interest as they have observed their children and twice for crucial or very important problems; thus:

. . . . x . . . .   1. Smoking

. . . . x . . . .   2. Late hours

. . . . x x . . . . 3. Self-medication

. . . . x x . . . . 4. Nervousness

. . . . 5. Eating irregularly

. . . . 6. Sleeplessness

. . . . 7. Drinking

. . . . x . . . . 8. Lack of concentration

. . . . 9. Etc.

(d) Scheduled meetings with parents. Often a teacher will find parents so willing to contribute what they know of health problems that they will agree to meet with the teacher two or three evenings a month for a month or two to discuss them. The teacher will find this a very revealing and helpful device. Parents will frequently talk freely and the teacher can record the principal problems as they are revealed.

3. Opinions of Experts

Similar in value to parental testimony would be the opinions and observations of experts in child life or in health education. There are those who are spending their lifetime studying the nature of children's problems or who, because of their professional work, have excellent opportunities to gain insight into the problems of childhood and adolescence. Physicians, school counsellors, favoured and sympathetic teachers, psychiatrists, public health and social workers—these and others could be used very much as parents are used to reveal the problems of students as they, from their professional vantage points, have seen them.

Frequently the observations of reports will reveal a set of problems quite different from those uncovered by parents and there is often a nice supplementation of the one by the other.

4. Morbidity Statistics

What is the nature of the illnesses of the age group being taught? From what diseases do they suffer? What are the principal causes of their illnesses? If one could get such information locally and for the age groups being taught, one could make the morbidities the subject of discussion on the theory that if some of them are preventable by education then we had better find out what they are and bring them into class discussion. If, for example, tuberculosis is a serious problem among adolescent girls in a city or state, and if there is anything about tuberculosis which, when taught, might help save some girl from contracting the disease, there is justification for bringing the subject into the course. Or, likewise, if it can be shown that there is an increase in the venereal disease rates in later adolescence, then to do a job in preventive education would require the introduction of the subject early in the high-school curriculum. A study of morbidity tables will throw light on the urgency of many such problems of any age.

5. Mortality

Similarly a study of death rates for any age will reveal opportunities for education concerning the causes. If there is something teachable about the five or ten principal causes of death among college students, for example, then most certainly the college should make the effort to instruct about them with the intent of preventing death, if possible, through alteration of conduct. Mortality figures, like morbidity, are revealing in that they show where important emphases in hygiene courses might be put.

6. Analyses of School Life

School life itself produces health problems. There is no reason to believe that "going to school" is altogether a healthy experience. Many a child, as a direct result of having to go to school, now has impaired vision, or is nervous and emotionally unbalanced, or has tuberculosis, or caught scarlet fever and now has impaired hearing. The school experience leaves its mark. It is only hoped that the mark is usually a good one and not a scar.

To find these sources of problems, to discuss adjustment to demands of housework, to examinations, to the social life of the school, to the complexities of friendship, and to analyse the school environment for sources of infection, for dirty locker rooms and showers, for unsafe traffic arrangements, for dangerous shop and laboratory facilities, comprise an opportunity which should not be missed by any teacher hoping to make the instruction truly *functional*.

7. Analyses of Home Life

What problems are created by the home? What sort of health conditions are found there? How do school children live? It has long been axiomatic that all the fancy teaching in the world about vitamins and balanced diets will not help much if, at home, there is scarcity or monotony in the meals. With delicacy and discretion the teacher must discover the health problems created by the home, the instabilities due to paternal neglect, the skin diseases from crowded bedrooms, the fatigue from noise and late hours, and bring the problems to the classroom for appropriate discussion and action. The teacher must visit the homes to see at first hand the sources or nature of these problems, must talk with public health and social workers who have seen the homes, must read contemporary studies on home life and in every way attempt to collect data on health conditions within the homes of the children. Here is further intrinsic material for classroom use.

8. Analyses of Community Life

If there are great sources of infection in the community environment, if there are no playgrounds useful in combating idleness, if the water or food supply is unsafe because of lack of sanitary measures, or if the dust and dirt in the city air is such as to be a hazard, then these problems and others like them become proper material for attention in classes. They represent intrinsic material because they are problems confronting the students as they live. The teacher must be observant of community problems, must gather accurate data about them, and must read the many analyses of community life with sufficient insight to see the health problems involved.

9. Analyses of Literature

What do students read? Do Superman and his ilk create health problems or are "the funnies" innocuous in this regard? What books do students read? What ideas of romance, sex behaviour, emotionality may they get? What do authors write about? What do newspapers and current magazines contribute to broadening the understanding and improving the conduct regarding health? These are all cogent questions for the teacher to have answered. They represent an area of investigation for the one who has plenty of time for such research. The effect of all kinds of reading material upon the health of people needs to be explored and evaluated. It could be done by various means—by making word frequency analyses of different types of literature, by testing for current events relating to health, by tracing sources of delinquency, infection, or other deviations to determine whether they have a relationship to what people read.

10. Analyses of Modern Communications

It is reasonable to believe that the influence of motion pictures, radio, and television on health and behaviour is very real and may be for good or for evil. Such pictures as *The Magic Bullet* and *Burma Surgeon* enhance the understanding of people concerning medicine in particular and health and science in general. Radio and television programmes like "Dr. Christian" and the many shorts put out by medical organisations, universities, and similar sources give opportunity for the observation of human behaviour, leave an important impression, and have a direct bearing on the health and behaviour of students. The teacher would do well to keep posted on studies of the effect of modern communications on the health of people; further, it would be profitable to make the health implications of current movies and television and radio programmes the subject of class discussion.

11. Analyses of Physical Examinations

To make the findings from physical examinations the subject of classroom instruction is not always a plausible and profitable thing to do. To interpret such findings individually to the person who was examined is more effective in producing results in terms of correction or prevention. Nevertheless, some use can be made of the whole medical examination experience in class instruction by discussing such matters as the purpose and frequency of examinations, their scope, and the meaning of the findings, and emphasis can be placed on the importance of follow-up action as the test of the utility of the examination.

Group findings are sometimes useful but usually only in terms of the relation of an individual to them. To discuss the number of carious teeth or infected tonsils found may be somewhat interesting and valuable but only to the extent that such findings can be made meaningful to an individual who *has* carious teeth or infected tonsils or who may have them in the future.

To find these data the teacher needs access to the records at least in statistical form. The study of summaries of conditions found reveals the relative importance and extent of the problems.

12. Analyses of Social Records

To the extent that personal problems show up eventually in social data the study of the latter is useful in gaining clues to the former. For example, the divorce rate in most communities is alarmingly high. What are the causes of these failures in marriage? Juvenile crime rates are high. What causes relating to health may be cited and studied? Church membership among young people is proportionately not what it should be. Does this contribute to the psychological welfare of adolescents or not? These and others forms of data on social problems are fruitful for class discussion. They should be studied and used.

The foregoing twelve sources of data on student health problems are constantly undergoing exploration. Teachers and research workers frequently publish additional data on their discoveries. Furthermore, additional sources appear from time to time. There may be more than twelve places to look and surely there are more techniques available for exploring the twelve than have been mentioned. Very real contributions can be made in this area of exploring human needs. Without such discoveries health instruction remains a remote and blindly operating thing. Once human problems have been revealed, there remain the problems of testing them for importance and cruciality and of organising them into a course of study.

Testing for Cruciality

If every question asked by students and every problem revealed by exploring the eleven other sources of health problems were to be used as teachable material, the hygiene course would easily occupy one hour daily for all sixteen years of the school and college span! The curiosities and problems of students concerning their health are endless. Some selection, therefore, must be made of those most suitable or most important for use in the time available in school. The revealed problems are not all of equal importance or of equal suitability, and some measures must be taken to weigh the cruciality of the problems in order to bring to the classroom those which are of greatest significance and a discussion of which would be of greatest profit to the students involved. Several tests of cruciality may be used:

1. The Frequency with which a Question or Problem Appears

One might think that the more often a question is asked the more important it is. At least its frequency shows widespread interest and thus its reception as intrinsic material is assured. The reverse, however, would not be true necessarily. Important questions such as "Is cancer hereditary?" or "Of what importance is sexual incompatibility to divorce?" might not be asked frequently and yet the evidence from other sources indicates the problems to be important, even crucial, to many people. A question such as "Is eating between meals bad for health?" will be asked over and over in spite of its relative unimportance to life, yet other questions more closely related to the attainment of a healthy life will seldom be voiced. The teacher must not, therefore, take frequency as the only criterion of cruciality. High-frequency questions may be important but there are a lot of others of less frequency which also should find a place in the deliberations of the course.

2. The Judgment of Students

On the theory that the consumer should be consulted, the student should be asked every now and then to react to the importance of certain questions or certain segments of the course. This can be effected in many ways. For example, the teacher or research operator, given time, patience, and some money, could make a list of a hundred or more questions or problems judged important for the age group for whom the planning of a course is being done. Mimeographed copies of the list could be reviewed by several hundred students each marking the questions on a three-point scale "of great importance", "of importance", "of no importance", to "me"; or the same list could be given to the same or another group of students with the request that they judge them in terms of whether they think the subject would be of importance to or should be taught to others of their age. Then, by scoring perhaps on a 2-1-0 basis, the questions could be rearranged in terms of their importance and a selection be made accordingly.

Students have judged whole areas of health problems in such fashion and thus have guided the selection of categories of problems for inclusion in the course.

There are other ways of getting students to judge cruciality. They will do so verbally, or they may be given outlined areas to select from and from debate and discussion among themselves come forward with statements as to relative importance. The important thing is to get student reaction. The adult is unsure of his ground unless he does.

3. The Judgment of Adults

Some adults, principally experienced public health and social workers and physicians, have reliable judgments on the importance and cruciality of problems. Teachers and parents also have good judgment on cruciality, provided their experience is broad and long and not merely local or personal. Some problem may be of utmost importance to one parent because his one child is affected, but in the long or broad range it may not be crucial to others. It is probably better to sample all opinions, dividing the adults according to their status and comparing results. The techniques may be similar to those used on students. A list of questions or problems may be provided and the adult asked "Do you think a full discussion of this should be given to high-school (or any other age) students?" or "How important would you consider this problem to be to high-school students?" or "Would you recommend that this problem be given a place in a twelfth-grade course in hygiene?" "Check: Urgently recommend it——. Recommend it ——. Do not recommend it ——". There are several ways of getting adult judgment of cruciality, and the view of the adult is desirable in selecting a few areas from many for class use.

4. Current Popularity

In times of local or national epidemics of poliomyelitis it is important and worthwhile to be working on the problem in the classroom. The interest is that much keener and motivation better. Local problems of accident prevention, delinquency, leisure use, or any of several others which are susceptible to local variations and peaks of interest or concern may be studied effectively at the time of their public popularity. One must always be reminded, however, that the whims of public interest are unreliable and that there may be terrific public furor about one mad dog giving one child rabies when ten children may have diphtheria for want of a control programme. Or the leisure-time problem of the youth of the community may be much more serious and have nothing done about it while the community turns itself inside out to discuss the pros and cons of whether the school should teach hygiene in mixed or segregated classes. The intensity of public zeal for a problem is not always an accurate measure of its cruciality in the lives of students.

A judicious balance of all four of these means of determining cruciality should be used. They have been presented somewhat in order of the weight which should be given them.

UNITS OF WORK

A good hygiene course usually consists of a series of units for investigation, study, and discussion. These units may be large or small but are most successful when they take not less than a week and not more than a month of fairly consecutive class meetings to handle. They usually deal with some contemporary problem or group of problems. The units of work chosen need not, in any one semester, cover the entire range of personal hygiene. Characteristically teachers feel they must "get clear through the book" or touch at least lightly on every subject in the short period of time allotted to them. This is a mistake. If the time is limited, say, to a one-hour-a-week course for one semester, it would better to plan a few units and do them well than to touch on everything usually found in textbooks. It would not be wise to give one or two hours each to appearance, nutrition, exercise, sex hygiene, care of the eyes and ears, disease prevention, mental hygiene, medical care, nostrums and quackery, and care of the teeth. In fact such an organisation of work, familiar though it is, is one of the reasons why hygiene remains poorly received and ineffective in the lives of the students. It would be better to choose three or four of these large areas, develop functional units of work within them, spend adequate time on each unit, and hope for greater time allotment another year.

If such a discriminating selection of principal areas to be covered can be made in relation to the class days available, the problem of constructing the units of work within the areas can be faced and solved. At this point the teacher must bring into play all he knows about the principles of learning and of the philosophy of interest.

If an analysis is made of many hundreds of such units from many such courses it will be found that various organisational arrangements are used. The psychological plan will be discussed first because it is based on all of the foregoing material relative to teaching of hygiene and thus offers promise of being the most effective style.

PSYCHOLOGICAL ARRANGEMENTS

The psychologically constructed unit of work is based on demonstrated or revealed student needs and interests. Its material is alive and meaningful. Its point of view is predominantly contemporary and it aims more at the solution of problems now than at the laying up of a store of information for possible use later. It teaches the science of human life in relation to the need for it and not as background generalisations which the student might use later on when he grows up. Whatever use it makes of the detail of anatomy and physiology, of chemistry and bacteriology, it uses in *explanation of a problem,* as material helpful in the understanding of the matter at hand. It would never teach the anatomy and physiology of the human body *per se* and for no other purpose than to teach anatomy and physiology. It would never begin a unit or chapter with the background of science. *It would always use science where the science is necessary to explain a point.*

There are, of course, several versions or kinds of psychologically arranged units, some long, some short, some using texts, some not. Here follow several examples of psychologically approached units taken from working course outlines now in operation. They deserve to be studied for their essential use of student interests and for the vitality of their approach.

Examples of Units

A. A unit on medical care suitable for late senior high school.

1. What is a chiropractor, osteopath, naturopath?
2. What is Christian Science? What is a faith healer?
3. What is medicine, and what is a physician?
4. What legal and professional differences and similarities exist between healers?
   (a) Assignments of readings in the text.
   (b) Investigation of local and state laws pertaining to licensing and the practice of healing arts.
   (c) Assignment of reading of descriptive material from advertising copy.
   (d) Planned visits, if feasible, to offices of various practitioners.
5. Are some illnesses "mental"?
6. Can physical states cause mental distress?
7. Can religion cure diseases?
   (a) Assignment of reading on psychosomatic relationships.
   (b) Investigations of results of faith healing.

8. How should one choose a physician or a dentist?
9. How can one tell the difference between a good doctor and a poor one?
10. What rights does a patient have when he chooses and uses a physician?
    (a) Committee assignment to the local medical society.
    (b) Class discussion with a physician.
11. What community resources are there for medical care?
    (a) Field trips to clinics, hospitals.
    (b) Consultations with local council of social agencies and charitable organisations.
12. When should one use a physician or dentist?
13. How safe is self-diagnosis and self-treatment?
14. Of what value are drugstore or advertised remedies?
15. What protection does the public have against false and misleading claims?
    (a) Assignment of readings on self-medication.
    (b) Assignment of readings on analyses of drugs and patent medicines, and on protective legislation.
16. Summary and conclusions.
    (a) The nature of the scientific method.
    (b) The right of the individual in a free society to selection and his companion responsibility for intelligent use of this right.
    (c) The clarification of psychosomatic states.

This unit makes ample provision for student participation through reading, discussion, and investigation. The teacher finds a ready response and must exercise skill in helping the discussion on the subject at hand. At the end the teacher assists the class to formulate a series of statements, representing their summary of the unit and the conclusions they have drawn from the discussions.

B. The following unit, on the control and prevention of tuberculosis, makes use of the familiar questions which junior-high-school students have regarding that disease. The unit is taught in six class periods or less and requires library resources and motion pictures.

A Unit on Tuberculosis Control

1. Is tuberculosis inherited? Does it run in families?
2. Is tuberculosis transmitted? How?
3. What parts of the body does tuberculosis affect?
4. How long does it last?
   (a) Assignment of readings in text and references and view of *This is T.B.* or other good introductory motion picture.
5. How can I find out if I have tuberculosis?
   (a) Assignment: Investigation of nature of laboratory tests, sputum test, X-ray, field trip to clinic and testing laboratory.
6. Is tuberculosis curable?
   (a) The sanatorium or hospital.
      (1) Surgical aids in advanced cases.
         (a) Pneumothorax and thoracoplasty.
      (2) Educational benefits.
   (b) Rest.
   (c) Home treatment of tuberculosis.
   (d) Rehabilitation.
7. How can I prevent tuberculosis?
   (a) General health.
      (1) Presence of tubercle bacilli.
   (b) Early detection.

(1) Tuberculin testing.

(2) X-ray at regular intervals.

(c) Elimination of bovine sources.

(1) Testing of cattle.

(2) Pasteurisation of milk.

(3) Education of the public and discovery of the carriers.

(a) Various associations which carry on this work.

(d) Assignments: Committee reports on the pasteurisation and other health measures of the local dairy, sanatorium care and cost, availability of X-ray service. Readings in text and selected references.

8. What is the local and national tuberculosis problem?

(a) Mortality and morbidity figures.

(b) Age groups affected.

(c) Financial repercussions.

9. What are *my* responsibilities in control?

(a) As a high-school student.

(1) Keep in good health.

(2) Have periodic X-rays.

(3) Become informed on the health problem and its implications.

(4) Educate those around me to the problems involved and the latest medical developments.

(b) As a citizen in the community.

(1) Become informed upon the particular problems of the community.

(2) Aid in preventive and control measures of the community.

10. Additional projects should be used as time and interest warrant. The following are recommended:

    (a) Distribute pamphlets containing tuberculosis information from departments and local tuberculosis association.

    (b) Investigate the immediate community problem.

    (c) Provide speaker and discussion of tuberculosis before parent groups.

    (d) Provide an X-ray or tuberculin test for everyone in the school.

    (e) Have a "Tuberculosis Prevention Week" in school.

        (1) Arrange for X-rays this week, invite parents in.

        (2) Pass out materials concerning tuberculosis, put up posters.

        (3) Strive toward 100 per cent X-ray programme.

        (4) Follow up cases found.

    (f) Organise field trips to a dairy, local health department, local tuberculosis association, and other places of interest.

C. A unit for middle-high-school students on "How to Get Along with Others". This unit, more elaborate perhaps than some others in its use of student self-analysis, student discussion, and outside resources, was, nevertheless, well received and profitable. It had as its objectives the development of satisfactory patterns of living, interest in the welfare of others, fair play and self-control, a wholesome attitude toward the opposite sex, and an understanding of courtesy and the value of good appearance.

It utilised the findings on each student of the California Test of Personality and the check list "Problems of Life and Health".

I. Procedure

The procedures used were suggested, planned, and carried out by teacher-pupil planning.

1. Each pupil selected a problem for study in which there was personal interest and need.
2. The class was organised into discussion groups as follows:
   (a) Pupils whose problems were similar were organised into small groups to study their problems.
   (b) The groups were organised in such a way as to give each person some responsibility, such as group leader, recorder, or resource person.
   (c) Each pupil served as discussion leader for at least on group meeting. Each group made a report to the class describing methods used to solve their problems.
   (d) Each group planned some activity in which all members of the class participated.
3. The class, the school, the homes, and the community were the principal laboratories used to help pupils solve their problems. Resource people and organisations outside the community were also utilised to help with the solution of a few special problems.
4. Problems:
   (a) What are the characteristics individuals like to see in their associates?
   (b) What makes an individual popular?
   (c) How do you get people to like you?
   (d) How should you act toward people older than you?
   (e) How does one's personal appearance affect others?
   (f) In what ways can one show friendship for others?
   (g) How can one develop self-control?
   (h) How can one become an intelligent conversationalist?
   (i) How does a person overcome shyness?
   (j) Why should one participate in some form of recreation?
   (k) What are some good hobbies for teen-agers?

(l) What are the signs of a healthy personality?

5. Individual Activities:

   (a) Each pupil selected a personality problem based on interest and need and tried to find a solution to it.

   (b) Pupils held personal conferences with a psychologist to discuss findings of his "California Test of Personality".

   (c) Pupils interviewed leaders in the community to secure information related to their problems.

   (d) Pupils read books and current literature to get facts concerning their problems.

6. Group Activities:

   (a) All groups held planning meetings and discussions to help their members solve their problems.

   (b) The groups planned excursions to agencies and organisations to secure information which would be helpful to them in solving their problems.

   (c) The group planned and gave to the class a report summarising their findings.

7. Class Activities:

   (a) The group on etiquette planned, prepared, and served a tea for the class, their parents, and the faculty.

   (b) The group studying various phases of personality used the class in the following ways:

      (1) The entire class developed a rating sheet which they wanted all other members of the class to rate them on. Mimeographed copies of the rating sheet were made and distributed to the class. Each pupil rated all other members of his class.

      (2) Each pupil left the classroom while the class evaluated his personality traits. A written summary was given to him upon his return to the room.

(3) The pupils developed a rating sheet of ten items. These were sent home for the parents to use in rating their children's personality traits.

(4) Each pupil made a written summary of all helpful suggestions obtained from the ratings and outlined methods for using them.

(5) The class made a survey of the community to discover recreation facilities available for them.

(6) On several occasions, the class planned discussions on various problems the class requested be discussed in order that the entire class could help each group and individual in solving their problems and in planning their activities.

(7) The members of the class were used for the following demonstration of good grooming: hair shampoo, manicuring nails, applying make-up.

(8) Several people were invited to speak to the entire class on special problems.

(9) Several films on appropriate subjects were shown. See list under "Teaching Aids".

(10) Several trips such as a class visitation to Ohio Hospital for Mental Illness were planned and taken.

II. Guidance

The group work in health classes is closely related to counselling or guidance. This is a relationship that works two ways. The group situation shows up individuals who need guidance or counselling. The guiding or counselling situation reveals the need for certain kinds of group experiences. To understand the individual members of the health class and their relationships, there are certain records and techniques that can be used by the teacher so that he can help the students plan and provide suitable worth-while class projects. A few of these are listed below:

1. Teacher-pupil personal conferences.
2. Student's cumulative record.
3. The results of tests, graphs, and charts used in class.
4. Sociometry techniques.
5. Teacher-parent personal conferences.
6. Teacher ratings of the students.

The unit as prepared had additional material on evaluation and teaching aids describing the usual subjective judgments sought from students and others on the value of the unit, and a listing of appropriate books, pamphlets, and films.

D. A unit on the effects of alcohol, tobacoo, and narcotics. This unit was designed for the eleventh grade and for a daily period of three weeks. For purposes of reproduction here it has been greatly reduced. Its wise use of contemporary and familiar problems as approaches to the area is clear, however.

Part I: Advertisements Dealing with Alcohol, Narcotics, and Tobacco.

1. Is all advertising bad?
2. How do we critically analyse advertisements?
3. How much of an advertisement is backed up by scientific fact?
4. Do baseball players and other great athletes really use the products they advertise?
5. Can advertising help us make a wise choice?
6. What are some of the pressure groups which attempt to promote the use of alcohol, tobacco, and narcotics?

Readings:

1. Cody, Lee D., "What's Behind That Label?" *Hygeia,* Vol. III, September, 1935.
2. Harays, Henry, *The Education of the Consumer.*
3. Harding, T. Swan, *The Popular Practice of Fraud.*

Suggested Experiences:

1. Study billboards as to psychological appeal and authenticity of statements made concerning alcohol, drugs, and tobacco.
2. Study testimonials and determine how they are secured and the amounts paid for them.
3. Detect false and misleading statements made.
4. Small committee to interview a local business manager for information on advertising rates.

Part-II: Terms Heard at Home and in the Community.

1. What is a drunk?
2. What is an addict?
3. Etc.

Readings:

1. Gregg, F.M., and Rowell, Hugh Grant, *Health Studies*, pp. 78, 181-203, 283.

Selected Experiences:

1. Bring in a list of words which might have some relation to alcohol, drugs, and tobacco.
2. Read the newspaper for a week and bring in words and terms that are used in affairs connected with alcohol, tobacco, and drugs.

Part-III: Effects of Drugs, Alcohol, and Tobacco on Society.

1. Do drugs and alcohol cause problems in juvenile delinquency?
2. How many accidents and deaths are caused by the use of alcohol or dope?
3. Why is there an international control on narcotics?
4. Etc.

Readings:

1. Clemensen, Jessie W., and Laporte, William R. *Your Health and Safety*.
2. Rice, Thurman B. *Living*.

Selected Experiences:

1. Visit local police departments and study the records of juvenile delinquency to find how many offenders are in trouble because of alcohol or narcotics, also what the local and state laws are concerning use of these.

2. Report on international efforts to control sale of narcotics. (Committee)

3. Etc.

Part-IV: Economical Aspect

1. Is it true that some parents use all their wages for drinking, smoking, and use of drugs, instead of buying vital supplies for the home?

2. How much money is spent on alcohol and tobacco per year?

3. Etc.

Readings:

1. Cockefair, E.A., and Cockefair, A.M. *Health and Achievement,* pp. 375-381, 450, 483.

Suggested Experiences:

1. Have a small committee secure data on the yearly alcohol and tobacco bill. Discuss valuable uses toward which this money might be directed.

2. Etc.

Part-V: Harm of Drugs, Alcohol, Tobacco, to the Individual.

1. What poisons are found in tobacco?

2. Why shouldn't boys and girls of high-school age smoke or drink?

3. What is harmed by smoking?

4. Etc.

Readings:

1. Biddle, Harry C., and Bush, George L. *Dynamic Chemistry*, pp. 673-679.
2. Rathbone, Josephine L., Bacon, Francis L., and Keene, Charles H. *Foundations of Health*, pp. 163, 249-261.

Suggested Experiences:

1. Film: "It's the Brain That Counts", 20 minutes, 16 sec. Dramatisation of injurious effects of alcohol.
2. Committee make a source report on poisons found in tobacco.
3. Etc.

Part-VI: Where Can One Learn?

1. Where can one find good books to read on this subject?
2. How reliable are popular magazine articles?
3. Etc.

Readings:

1. Brace, David K., *Health and Physical Education for Junior and Senior High School*, pp. 80-85.

Suggested Experiences:

1. Bring in articles from the newspaper concerning alcohol, tobacco, and drugs. Evaluate these and separate the reliable sources from the unreliable. These articles should be judged in class.

In the foregoing units it should be noted that any physiological detail is taught in a meaningful connection with the development of the problem. It is not given as uncertain background but as useful explanation.

Units for Elementary Education

Naturally, units of instruction for elementary children are simpler, are less time-consuming, and require less use of resources in the community and less reading. They are not, however, less interesting, nor are they less pertinent to the daily affairs of the child. *The same principles of unit construction apply*— and not only to the unit outline which the teacher may follow but also to the reading which may be assigned. Furthermore, it must be recognised at once that *the instruction given in the classroom period is of less importance in the elementary school than are the things that happen to and for the child which bear upon his health.* It is of greatest importance, for example, to have the child immunised against all diseases where immunisation is feasible. Instruction about immunisation is of secondary importance.

The direct type of teaching might also call for a ten- or twenty-minute period in the day when children would read from one of the numerous health series readers or would discuss with the teacher health problems or behaviours of immediate concern. Or the procedure might even approximate the committee investigation and report technique used so profitable on the upper levels. The units should be kept simple and within the language boundaries of the age, should involve little if any anatomy or physiology (and then only in explanation), and must be meaningful in an immediate sense in order to sustain interest. There are many promising situations or problems out of which a learning experience may be drawn. They range from very simple things like teaching the children to use the drinking fountain to something more complex concerning their basic understanding of disease prevention and immunity. For example, classroom use could be made of the following:

1. The regulation of classroom temperature and ventilation.
2. The lunch the children bring or buy.
3. The annual or entering medical examination, its findings, uses, and meaning.
4. The use of the washroom and toilet; cleanliness.
5. The safety precautions to be taken in the corridors, gymnasiums, playgrounds, shops, assemblies, streets, sidewalls.

6. Bicycles, scooters, skates, cars, and their safe usage.
7. The rest period, rest at home, sleep and relaxation.
8. The children's teeth and toothaches, dental decay and candy.
9. Their eyes and glasses, reading and infections.
10. Their friends and groups, sportsmanship and courtesies; their tempers and angers.
11. Their play and skills, their courage and all of their social adjustments in play.
12. Their study habits and their concentration.
13. Their diseases and infections, their cuts and bruises.
14. Their weight and height and the meaning of variations.

As working examples of the psychological approach in action on the elementary level two units, somewhat reduced from the original, are reproduced here:

A. A breakfast unit for primary grades.

Finding the problems (Determining the need)

This unit resulted from an informal discussion on meals. We talked about the meals we liked best, and why these were favourites. The majority of the children mentioned either lunch and dinner, or dinner and supper. It was quite obvious that breakfast didn't seem to rate as either a very important or enjoyable meal. This left no question as to the need for improvement of the breakfast habits of these youngsters. An inventory revealed that many of the children needed to change attitudes.

Objectives

1. To eat a good breakfast.
2. To establish favourable attitudes toward better breakfast habits.
3. To know what foods provide a good breakfast.
4. To choose a variety of foods for breakfast.

Procedure (Motivation)

Interest was aroused by placing posters, pictures of healthy, happy children, pictures of food, food models, and illustrated booklets about the room for the children to examine and read. This led to such comments as: "I had this for breakfast", "I like this for breakfast", "I believe I would like this and this."

We talked about the need for a good breakfast, and what happens when we do not eat a good morning meal. We discussed foods which were appropriate for breakfast and how these helped build us up and give us energy. The children expressed a desire for these so each child made his own wheel chart and his height and weight were recorded. We also used a film on the eating habits of children. We talked about the morning eating habits of people, showing the difference between those of birds, animals, and people.

Problems and Questions (Things we talked about)

1. Why don't some children eat breakfast?
2. Why do we need a good breakfast?
3. What is a good breakfast?
4. Do the breakfasts we eat measure up? If not, what shall we do?

Activities (Things we did)

To help us understand the problem of time, the children suggested making clocks. We counted the hours between the evening meal and breakfast and found the approximate number for each child. The children were surprised that so many hours had passed between these two meals. We agreed that everyone should be ready for a good breakfast. We discussed the importance of getting up in time to eat a good breakfast before going to school. We discussed good things to eat and illustrated by posters and food models. These included fruit, cereal, milk, butter. Also suggested as an addition or substitution were: eggs, bacon, waffles, and hot cakes. Posters of a good breakfast were made by cutting pictures of food from magazines and arranging them attractively on coloured paper. Reading charts such as the following were made: I had a good breakfast, I had cereal, I had toast, I had milk, I had orange juice. (The foods were illustrated with pictures.) We discussed what these foods do for us and why growing boys and girls need them daily.

When the subject of cereals was brought up, it opened the way for a very interesting study. Since we live in a section of the country which produces much wheat as well as other grains, we associated cereals with the grains from which they were processed. Small amounts of these grains were brought by the children; they also brought empty cereal boxes and placed them in the proper grain section from which they were processed, thus indicating what foods could be made from each of the grains such as wheat, corn, oats, and rice. The last mentioned grain, of course, is not grown in this section but the children wanted to include it with the cereals. We talked about cereals which needed to be cooked and those which come ready to eat.

We also had a little store which was stocked with empty cereal boxes, egg and butter cartons, milk bottles and cans, bacon boxes, fruit juice cans, and break wrappers. Models were used for fruits. Playing cafeteria was a great delight for them. We used food models and attached a very small price to each. This provided some number experiences as well as experience in the use of money. We dramatised a conversation between a mother and her children during the planning of a breakfast; a scene contrasting the actions of a child who has had a good breakfast and one who has had little or no breakfast.

All of our activities and topics of discussion were the outgrowth of group planning. They resulted from reading, observations, films, pictures, and discussions of different foods and how they help us to grow.

B. A unit on "Growing Up" is here shown, somewhat reduced as an example of what might be done in the sixth or seventh grade.

A. The Problem—personal and emotional problems resulting from irregular maturation rates are common with pupils of junior-high-school age. Unless satisfactorily solved they can lead to serious maladjustment on the part of the child. Some of the chief methods for discovering the problems connected with growth and development are:

1. Observations of pupils in the classroom.
2. Questions and problems actually stated by the pupils themselves.
3. Observations of pupils during their play periods and at school recreation nights.
4. Written problem lists from each pupil.
5. Discussions at intervals with individuals and with groups.

B. Objectives:

1. To help pupils understand that growth problems are normal.
2. To help pupils understand that those who are "growing up" have new and puzzling problems and that there are ways of coping with them.
3. To help pupils understand that large height and weight gains are normal growth stages.
4. Etc.

C. Procedure

1. Approaches for arousing pupil interest.

(a) Soon after the class had met often enough for me to gain their confidence each child wrote out some problems. From these we compiled a list of "common problems". It was very interesting to see the similarity of their lists. Some of the problems were: Why am I so fat? What makes me clumsy? Will I be more attractive later in life?

(b) Class discussions were kept on a very informal basis with the result that they brought out many other questions.

(c) The pupils were asked to bring in pictures of children of all ages to illustrate growth changes.

2. Specific questions and problems

   (a) What stage of growth am I now in?

   (b) How can one tell what one's eventual height and body build will be?

   (c) How does the body grow and keep itself in good repair?

   (d) What is meant by the statement "growth is uneven"?

   (e) Why is one always hungry?

   (f) Are there any special physical requirements for success?

3. Activities selected and learning situations provided for helping pupils answer their questions.

   (a) The pupils kept a personal growth record during the study of the unit.

   (b) Charts were prepared showing weight and body build forecasts.

   (c) Pictures were collected to show that "Success and Fame Come to All Types of Body Build".

   (d) The pupils were requested to bring in snapshots to show how each had changed in size and proportion since babyhood.

   (e) Posters were made to remind others of ways to keep strong and promote growth.

   (f) Families were studies to discover what characteristics might be inherited.

   (g) The specific questions listed by the pupils were discussed in class.

   (h) Etc.

Summarising the Psychological Pattern

There is ample reason to believe that the psychological approach to the selection of material to be taught is more effective than others. It has the benefit of interest and motivation and is more readily adjustable to individual and group needs. Its outstanding characteristics are as follows:

1. The material is presented in functional sequence (see units), and structure is used to explain.
2. The material is selected in relation to an ongoing activity or interest in the life of the student and thus attention and motivation are commanded.
3. The generous use of activities, projects, motion pictures, field trips, committee reports, and discussion leaders assures variety and greater coverage than a single text or lecture.
4. The principal purpose of health instruction being the development of conduct, the emphasis must be on *doing* rather than *knowing,* and the psychological pattern strongly provides for action.
5. The learning proceeds from the specific, the familiar, the commonplace (see units) to the generalisation or conclusion.

OTHER ARRANGEMENTS

Specific health instruction as organised in school periods has not always been presented thus. The application of psychological principles to the teaching of health is a comparatively recent development. Most course outlines, syllabi, and textbooks written prior to 1945 were written in the antiquated pattern of "Get the scientific background first and then you can solve all your health problems." So many course outlines and texts have been written in this pattern that it is possible to discern four types of them. These are:

1. The Historical

The historical pattern always begins its unit, chapter, or lecture by tracing the history of the subject to be discussed. The student is introduced to the history of a problem as a means of giving him a perspective on the present status or importance of the matter. For example, from a college unit on bathing and cleanliness we find the approach to the subject to be through: "A. The bathers of ancient Rome; B. Bathing among primitive peoples; C. The development of modern types of bathing; D. Changing concepts of the need for cleanliness". Now it is highly doubtful whether such historical data are useful in getting the student to bathe or to be clean, and such information is, at best, pleasant material, providing possibly some interest and amusement but little else.

Or, in another series of health lecture outlines, the teachers begin the first day of the first week by opening up the subject, "Conceptions of Disease", with the demonic concepts, the four humours of Hippocrates, the theories of Sydenham and Pasteur, and the germ theory presented in their historical order. The order of development is chronological but hardly germane to the daily problems of the student.

2. The Etiological

The etiological arrangement is not seen as often in course-of-study organisation as in unit or single-lesson construction. It is the cause-effect pattern. A cause is given and the effects or consequences of the cause are described. It is likely to be used most frequently in studies of disease and its control. For example, a college syllabus begins its second lesson (after the introduction) by setting forth "the causes of death from natural and unnatural means". Here are discussed, of course, germs, accidents, old age, organic diseases. Next comes a consideration of germs, microbes, metazoa, and molds with full description of bacteria and cocci. From there the students study transmission of germs by air, water, milk, food, insects, and animals, and, if they are patient enough, they will eventually come to human carriers, typhoid Mary, tuberculosis, and cancer! A long and circuitous route!

3. The Anatomical-Physiological

The approach to lesson planning is the favourite among those who disregard student interests. For decades hygiene teachers have believed that all subjects should be introduced by laying the scientific foundations. Digestion could not be understood until the fundus of the stomach was located; and nervousness could not be discussed until the fissure of Rolando was explored! Libraries are full of hygiene textbooks, each chapter of which spends the first half on anatomy and the second on things in which the students are really interested. For example, it is the rare chapter on the nervous system indeed which does not begin: (a) structural arrangement of the nervous system; (b) cerebrospinal and autonomic; (c) the unit of the nervous system—the neuron; (d) the reflex. Then, after the anatomy has been laid down, meaningless and unrelated, the text may discuss emotional control, worry, nervousness, adjustment, fatigue, vocations, and other cogent and important considerations.

The following teaching outline on food is typical of this approach:

Food

I. Food as a source of energy:

  1. Nutrition and its part in digestion and assimilation.

II. Classification of food:

  1. Carbohydrates.
  2. Proteins.
  3. Fats.
  4. Minerals.

III. Vitamins:

  1. Vitamin A.
  2. Vitamin B.
  3. Vitamin C.
  4. Vitamins B, D, etc.

IV. The caloric values of food.

V. Good elimination.

VI. Indigestion.

1. Causes and remedy.

Students frequently lose interest when the course is overloaded with unrelated and extraneous details of anatomy and physiology. They ask, "Why do we have to learn all that when all I had in mind was discussing how to take school examinations without worrying myself sick?" Anatomical detail is useful only in explanation, never as unrelated and extrinsic background to be taught just because someone thinks it is good to know that the duct of Wirsung is in the pancreas or that there are so many main branches off the aorta. *The material is too far removed from an ongoing interest,* a need or a problem, and contributes only partially and then mostly by chance to the students' understanding of life. Such lifeless and meaningless teaching is responsible, in part, for the unpopularity of many hygiene courses and for the slight impact which many health books make upon the reading public. The psychological pattern, based as it is upon student problems, deals with needs and interests and thus has an advantage in affecting behaviour.

BUILDING A UNIT

A unit of work is a segment of the total syllabus or course of study and requires a comparatively short period of time, a fraction of a semester, to accomplish. It is frequently constructed by the teacher alone but is more meaningful to students if they can have a hand in its preparation. In preparing teachable units the following steps are recommended:

1. From the entire range of available problems or areas of interest to students and suitable for their age and grade, one will be selected after discussion with the class.
2. The teacher, with the group, will discuss the range and depth of the problem and its potential value and meaning to students for purposes of determining the objectives which might be sought. These objectives or goals should be stated in understandable and attainable terms.
3. The principal questions (ten to fifteen) which students would like to have answered in connection with the area should next be stated.

4. With the foregoing objectives and questions in mind, the teacher should then raise with the group the question of how to proceed. How can we get our questions answered? How can we achieve what we set out to achieve? Are there resources in school or the community we can use? How shall we organise our class to get this job done? An orderly list of these activities and procedures should be made, assignments to them agreed to, and the work on the unit begun.

5. Many units carry within their written form a listing of available films, reading materials, resource persons, field experiences, laboratory experiments, and other aids to teaching which might profitably be used.

6. It is likewise good to prepare a sketch of whatever evaluating devices may be used to test the worth of the unit. Suggestions for getting student judgment of worth, effect upon the class, success of the various activities, interest in the reading, resource persons, and other aids, and also notes of mistakes to be avoided next time can be prepared.

TEXTBOOKS

There are many school systems which prefer to adopt single textbooks for each grade in each subject. To meet this purpose there are several good textbooks or series of books written for health teaching purposes. All the books are not, however, of equal value. Some are very old-fashioned in their approach and organisation, some are scientifically inaccurate in spots, and some are excellent indeed. In order to help the teacher judge the quality of a textbook proposed for use the following criteria are suggested:

1. The contents of the book should be based upon the health needs and problems of the age group for which it is written.

2. The major emphasis of the text should be upon problems crucial to the pupils and important to the community in which the book is being used.

3. The content material must be scientifically accurate throughout and in thorough accord with the best available knowledge in the biological sciences.
4. The first chapter of the book should provide a good springboard for the year's programme in health instruction by appealing to the pupils' goals, such as interest in appearance, athletics, vocational success, and by pointing out the relationship which exists between the achievement of these goals and the satisfactory solution of the health problems contained in the remaining chapters of the book.
5. The book should be written in an interesting and readable style with the vocabulary on the comprehension level of the pupils who will use it.
6. The text should contain a glossary of difficult words.
7. The text should contain suitable and purposeful activities, participation in which will help the pupils solve their problems related to growth, development, and adjustment.
8. At the end of each chapter, there should be listed suitable references of books, pamphlets, films, filmstrips, and other audio-visual aids.
9. The charts, graphs, and tables contained in the book should be meaningful to the pupils.
10. All statistics should be accurate and up-to-date.
11. The illustrations should be attractive, accurate, and apropos.
12. The paper and print should be of a quality and size which will minimise eyestrain.
13. The authors should have sufficient training and experience to qualify them to write a satisfactory text.
14. The book should have an attractive cover, a suitable title, and a satisfactory index.

ADDITIONAL MATERIAL ON ORGANISATION AND METHOD

In Chapter 6 will be found additional suggestions for course organisation and teaching method inasmuch as many of the suggestions which can be made apply equally well to all of the three patterns of course organisation.

GRADE PLACEMENT AND TIME ALLOTMENT

When should hygiene be taught? There is no standard answer to this question. Many organisations, groups, and experts in school health education have made recommendations in this connection and a cross section or consolidation of these opinions is represented by the accompanying table:

Time Allotment and Grade Placement for Direct Health Teaching

Grade	Best	Next Best	Least Desirable
1, 2, 3	1 period a day	1 period twice a week	1 period once a week
4, 5, 6	20 minutes 3 times a week	20 minutes once a week	20 minutes once a week
7, 8	1 class period a day for the year	1 class period 3 times a week for a semester	1 class period once a week for a year
9	1 class period a day for a semester	1 class period 3 times a week for a semester	1 class period once a week for a year
10, 11	1 class period a day for a semester	1 class period 3 times a week for a semester	1 class period once a week for a year
12	1 class period a day for a semester	1 class period 3 times a week for a semester	1 class period once a week for a year

Any such recommendations must be adapted locally to the particular needs of the students, the curriculum and time schedule in vogue, and the facilities available. It must certainly be recognised that if any school becomes committed to giving direct instruction in health this cannot be done well on starvation rations. Time, space, and equipment must be provided and *no once-a-week arrangement or makeshift rainy-day sharing with the physical education periods will suffice.* If health is to be taught at all it must be taught well and that means consecutive class periods for a semester or a year uninterrupted by long waits between periods. If hygiene can be offered in the seventh grade, for example, it will not produce best results if offered once a week for the year. Twice a week for a half-year would be better and daily for a semester would be still better. Sharing a twice-a-week physical education schedule is not satisfactory generally nor is any form of once-a-week class meeting. Daily meetings for a shorter length of time will maintain interest at a higher level and be productive of better results.

Nor is there any unanimity on the problem of grade placement. It is fairly well agreed that in the first six grades some time each day should be spent on reading about health, discussing health activities, or doing things pertaining to health. Perhaps twenty to thirty minutes per day three times a week would suffice. As the grades advance, the health problems become more involved and the students more aware of them and articulate about them. It can be demonstrated that children in every grade from seven through twelve have problems in sufficient quantity and of sufficient importance to make a one-semester course every year worthwhile. Some fear that if so much health is taught in the curriculum the subject will be exhausted in the first three years or at least be spread very thin over the grades. There need be no fear on this score. Various studies have shown rather conclusively that there is enough to be taught for one semester of all six years of the secondary school. A teacher with imagination and resourcefulness could lay out such a programme with no fear of wastage of time or repetition. However, few schools are organised so as to permit so much teaching in this area. The next best allotment of time would then be a semester course in each of the seventh, ninth, tenth, and twelfth years, with the tenth year of these four omitted if one of them has to be. This arrangement would get students entering and leaving both the junior and senior high schools.

The very minimum would be a course for students at entrance and departure from the secondary school.

CLASS COMPOSITION

In the elementary grades there is no problem as to whether boys and girls should be taught about health together or in segregated groups. The question does arise in junior high school, though, and persists through the college years. There are many who prefer to have boys taught by themselves and by a man and girls in a separate class and by a woman. Others, however, see no important reason for segregation and believe that health problems germane to the high-school and college years should be discussed in mixed groups for best results.

Actually it is a problem of exaggerated importance. It has been well proved that mixed groups can be taught successfully and without embarrassment and by either a man or a woman. It has likewise been demonstrated that a woman can teach boys and a man girls. The issue of success depends upon the preparation, personality, skill, and approach of the teacher and not upon the subject matter. All but a few of the areas of hygiene are acceptable to both sexes in a mixed group. A teacher might have difficulty sustaining the interest of high-school boys on problems of child care and family feeding, and, likewise, girls might be bored with a discussion of training procedures for competitive athletics. Boys would profit some but not much from intimate instruction concerning menstruation, and discussion of the details of reproduction would, unless handled well, be potentially embarrassing to all. These areas are, however, in the minority and do not loom large enough in the total scene to justify the position that all hygiene should be taught in segregated groups.

On the college level there is still less reason for segregation. Usually merely administrative convenience keeps the courses apart, at least on the freshman level where the customary one-hour-per-week hygiene course is found. After the first year the elective courses usually found in college bulletins do not require segregated classes. In fact it is the experience of many who have developed the recently appearing "marriage courses" that a mixed group has a definite advantage in that ideas may be tested and contrasting points of view reconciled.

In summary of this point, either mixed or segregated classes are acceptable. The success of the instruction does not depend on the homogeneity of the group. If a class starts out mixed it should not be separated into boys and girls when the time comes to discuss "sex" or any other controversial area. Such temporary segregation only highlights the subject and distorts its importance and emphasis. Groups which start out mixed should remain so throughout the semester.

To teach about health in a specific course with a room and period, syllabus or text all its own is popularly the ideal way to attain the objectives of health instruction. To many it seems the best and most fruitful way to convey to youth the great lessons of science as they may be applied to the preservation and development of human life. As will be seen later in the general summary of the problem of health instruction, there are several techniques and points of view which *must be* observed or the teaching of hygiene becomes a boring and sterile thing. Teachers will do well constantly to bear in mind that the students in hygiene are not medical students. They are not even interested in science because it is science. They are interested in life in general, in their lives as they are being lived, and they will accept only a small amount of unrelated scientific data and *will reject that which is not pertinent to their ongoing interests and problems.*

The easiest way, by far, to teach hygiene directly, in a course set up for the purpose, is to divide the material by the great systems of the body, teach the anatomy and physiology of the systems, and then allow for a few questions of practical application if time remains. This is at once the easiest and the most sterile. Little happens to the learner beyond the temporary acquisition of some knowledge. What is desperately needed is *action, behaviour.* People need to *live* more healthfully, and cramming their heads full of knowledge will not guarantee favourable modifications in their living. The material to be taught must be chosen in relation to the living needs. The teacher must cultivate an insight into the students and talk to them. A college student one day expressed this point eloquently to one of the better teachers of hygiene when he said, "I have gotten so much out of this course because I have had the feeling all along *that you were talking to me*". When teachers can create *that* atmosphere, have their students *feel* the value of the material as well as learn the material itself, then the direct teaching of hygiene is justifying its existence.

But no tricks of rearrangement of anatomy or physiology or other basic sciences will do. Whether one begins with the fascinating activities of the cell and works outward, "dresses up" the anatomical detail "to make it interesting", or uses all the personality of a vaudeville performer, the course will still be largely wasted until and unless it deals intimately, helpfully, and understandingly with the problems of its students. The material must be chosen in relation to its intrinsic value, taught as living material, and students must be allowed some share in the whole process. The smug complacency of scientifically trained teachers who assume that they *know* what students should learn and then proceed to teach without seeking and getting an identification of the student with the material is deplorable indeed. There are health problems to be solved, living to be made happier and more effective, and lives to be saved. No teacher can afford to miss the opportunity, in a class of direct teaching of hygiene, to affect favourably the lives of students by dealing exclusively with material intrinsic to those lives.

4

Correlation and Teaching

Teaching health by correlating hygiene material with other areas of the traditional curriculum was once a very popular way of covering the field. The programme of correlation had strong advocates. They conceived of health instruction as a study of life, and as the curriculum in elementary or secondary schools covered all the aspects of life, it should be easy to teach in science, physical education, history, and all the other areas the health material that was appropriate. Conversely, if there existed a special health course in the curriculum an appropriate correlative relationship could be established whereby history or science could be taught with the hygiene material. The programme of correlation aims at the breakdown of the rigid barriers which separate the subjects and areas and seeks a co-relationship between health material and all the others. Technically, correlation means the relation of parts to parts—a co- or shared relationship between them. Applied to health education it means the relationship, within the curriculum, of health to the biological sciences, of health to music, of health to the social sciences. To correlate health with these other areas means to plan to include health material in the teaching of biology, English, social studies, and the rest.

POTENTIAL AREAS

Correlation does, of course, have some rich possibilities. There is such a close relationship, for example, between the biological sciences and the hygiene of living that correlation is inevitable and will occur whether planned or not. In fact, in many modern textbooks in biology the material has been chosen purposely to deal with human biology and with human health.

The correlation here is inescapable. Likewise the social sciences and physical education are rich in correlative possibilities for the teaching of health. Home economics and the physical sciences offer excellent opportunities also. These are the most likely areas. Correlation within these five fields comes easiest and is the most readily demonstrated. Other areas such as art and music have potentialities but not as many or as rich. Some of the outstanding topics or problems from health education which might reasonably be dealt with in other areas are as follows:

(a) With physical education:

1. Cleanliness, infection, bathing, skin infections.
2. First aid and care of injuries, protection against injury.
3. Clothing and weather.
4. Use of the physical examination, limitations and possibilities for activity, development of compensating activities.
5. Experience in participation in developmental and individually prescribed activities.
6. Experience in planning, decision making, social conduct, and emotional control.
7. Experience in choosing activities for current and later use and in evaluating results of participation.
8. Relation between vigorous and restful activities.
9. Fatigue, conditioning, "training", diet, and nutrition in relation to activity.
10. Safety precautions in all activities.
11. Experience in the development of a sense of achievement, in personal evaluation, and in self-direction.
12. Individual differences in size, strength, endocrine factors, and ability in relation to performance.
13. Sex differences in performance, organic and psychological development.

14. Experience in the appreciation of play, fun, and recreation.

(b) With biological sciences:

1. Development of the cell, influences for retardation, normal growth and development, cell needs.
2. Plant and animal sex development and reproduction, pollination, fertilisation.
3. Plants, molds, bacteria in relation to infection; disease-producing organisms.
4. Heredity, its operation in living things including man, facts and fallacies; evolution.
5. Biological anti-agents, communicable diseases and control.
6. Basic functions of digestion, assimilation, elimination, sensory activity, respiration, and irritability.
7. Adaptations of organisms to environment.
8. Mammalian structure and function.
9. Water, milk, and food protection and purification.

(c) With physical sciences:

1. Night ventilation and heating.
2. Vision, refraction, optics.
3. Disinfectants, germicides.
4. Chemistry of food, nutritional needs.
5. Weather, climate, and health and disease.
6. Water and food preservation and sanitation; food freezing.

(d) With social sciences:

1. Comparative health states on international basis.
2. Governmental health organisations here and abroad.
3. Functions of government relating to health of people.

4. Current issues of medical and health care.
5. Studies of environment, home and community planning, city planning.
6. School and community recreation.
7. The family, domestic and comparative.
8. Traffic control, automobile hazards, industrial safety, legal backgrounds.
9. Poverty, sickness, economic status, race, depressions, and disease.
10. Health in relation to rural and urban populations.
11. Growth of superstitions, fallacies, rumours, prejudices.
12. International relationships as they relate to health.

(e) With home economics:

1. Nutrition, food preparation, distribution and production.
2. Home management, recreation, personal problems.
3. Child care and development, home care of the sick.
4. Marriage problems.
5. Clothing.
6. Housing adequacy, ventilation, heating, planning.

In one area, history, some of the correlative health material may be shown in the following brief outline:

(a) *The Old World Background:* Greek medicine and Hippocrates, who is often called the father of modern medicine. He advocated the gymnasium system of educating the young to develop a sound mind and body.

Roman Empire, a great administrator of health affairs. Police officers supervised paying and draining of streets, inspection of weights and measures, maintaining of order, and provision of good-quality grain. Romans were provided with clean drinking water, and hundreds of public baths in the cities were supplied through thirty-four stone aqueducts.

Medieval medicine; cleanliness of spirit was stressed more than bodily cleanliness. Sanitation conditions and disease-control methods were sadly neglected. Principle of quarantining houses one important contribution. Beginning of the era of sanitation.

(b) *Settlement and development of the colonies:* Druggists came from Europe. First drugstore in Boston in 1646. Lack of food and health education hindered the development of the colonies. Bloodletting, a heritage from Europe. Benjamin Rush, professor of medicine, College of Philadelphia, called bloodletting "the sovereign remedy". He was bled to death by his own doctor in 1813.

(c) *Conditions of the colonies on the eve of the Revolution. Causes of the American Revolution. The War for Independence:* Two medical schools in colonies before Revolutionary War. Most practising physicians never attended medical school; served as apprentices to other physicians. Quacks were overrunning the country, and personal health was seriously affected by treatment from such quacks.

At outbreak of the Revolution, a good physician was Dr. John Morgan, chief physician of the Continental Army, who showed that pus came from blood vessels and not from solid tissue.

Sanitary conditions in army camps and hospitals during Revolution were almost primitive. Mansions of rich had no plumbing. Troops were ordered not to be quartered near swamps, as it was believed the "miasmas" from marshes brought disease. Soldiers were ordered to cut hair short. They were inoculated against smallpox. Typhoid, dysentery, and typhus took a heavy toll. Army lacked sufficient medical supplies. Ignorance of medicine, inefficiency and squabbles among doctors. Army sanitation just starting. Nine soldiers died of disease for every one killed by British bullets.

(d) *Political and commercial development between 1815 and 1845. The settlement of the territory west of the Mississippi:*

Communities started to organise their water supply, their sewage disposal, and their community health activities. Movement for development of boards of health and health officers accelerated. Officials did not know what steps to take to protect the health of the public.

Health education on the frontier was left to the family itself. Doctors few and far between. Health conditions far better than in the crowded eastern cities.

(e) *The industrial revolution. Effects of the industrial revolution upon American life:* The industrial revolution brought about an increased need for health education, community and personal health. It saw the beginning of sweatshops and crowded living conditions in the cities. Movement of people to the industrial centres created such crowded living conditions that disease and ill health were greatly increased.

Workers in sweatshops laboured under such poor conditions and for such long hours that they were old long before their time.

Sweatshops brought about an increase of injuries to workers because of poor working conditions. Homes were broken up through use of child and woman labour in sweatshops because they would work for such low wages.

More attention was being given to health activities in the cities because of crowded conditions. Municipal housecleaning phase.

Mr. F. A. Meier reports a study of the correlation between health instruction and general science in which he shows the health areas most and least frequently treated in general science textbooks. These are:

Most frequently treated: disease, eyes, food, heart and blood, air and sunlight, education for parenthood, general physiology, elimination, ears, nose and throat.

Least frequently treated: alcohol, tobacco, and drugs, teeth, posture, feet, exercise, first aid, mental hygiene, sleep and rest, safety, health agencies, home and family, clothing, and others.

Meier's investigation shows rather clearly how difficult it would be to rely wholly upon the field of general science to get the job done which is needed in health instruction. But it also shows how reasonable the correlation possibilities are between the two fields and how, if general science and health instruction are both taught in the same school, the teachers should familiarise themselves with their respective efforts in order to avoid any wasteful duplication and also in order to compare the nature of the material they are teaching.

From these most likely areas the others shade off to a point where deliberate correlation with health material becomes a laboured process. It would be difficult, for example, to write a very good play about the vitamins or to do acceptable poetry about the various molds and bacteria which are dangerous to man! The pattern of correlation eventually reaches the point of diminishing returns. It is apparent, however, that in literature discussions of organic, psychological, and emotional problems as may be revealed in biographies and a study of heterosexual relationships as related in biography, fiction, or history would be valuable. Likewise one cannot overlook the healthful experience itself which is the singing and playing of music. And actuarial tables, vital statistics, and population trends might as well be the subject of mathematical discourse or anything else. In these less likely areas there are possibilities but also real limitations.

ADMINISTRATION

Properly to develop and administer a programme of correlation the following conditions are necessary:

1. Some one person, or small committee, must become sufficiently familiar with all of the areas and with the wide area of hygiene to recognise where each could enrich the other, and be prepared to make recommendations for the inclusion of health material in the other areas.

2. The faculty must be receptive to the idea of correlation and ready to receive and use such recommendations as appear reasonable.

3. A programme of in-service training should be provided for the teachers involved so as to improve their ability to handle the acceptable health material.

4. Conferences should be held during the year as needed for the exchange of ideas as between, for example, the social science teachers and the health group. Such conferences would be useful in checking facts, exchanging teaching materials and ideas, agreeing on purposes, and setting directions.

PRECAUTIONS AND DRAWBACKS

As has been mentioned there are precautions to be taken and drawbacks to be noted in the development of any correlation plan. These are as follows:

1. The best-developed correlation plans will not reach all the students in school with all the material, nor will all the material from the broad area of healthful living be included even in the sum of the offerings of all the other areas. Many students will miss entirely the important contribution which home economics makes. Others will not have had much biological science. It can be demonstrated from studies on student needs that even after the absorbent powers of these other areas have been taxed to the limit there are still human health problems untouched. Correlation plans at best are never perfect; they never can cover the area of healthful living as it should be covered.

2. Teachers' qualifications vary so that a health coordinator should be rather chary about encouraging a social science teacher, for example, to deal with current issues of medical *care unless the teacher is adequately prepared to do so.* Biology teachers can make sorry mistakes in dealing with human sex life if they are relying only upon their knowledge of the birds and bees. Teachers must be well prepared to handle human health problems if they are to be handled at all.

3. Health material does not lend itself gracefully and conveniently to all areas equally well. The health content to be incorporated must never violate good standards in the host area. To draw a picture with a health motif may, and probably will, result in bad art as well as bad hygiene. Writing health

themes in English may result in inferior literature, and composing a song about vitamin A will be sorry music. No host area should be asked to use health material unless it is contributory to that area and hygiene alike, and in no case should health material be used if it violates the best purposes and standards of the host area.

4. When matters relating to human health are taught in chemistry, history, or other areas it is exceptional when the health material is taught in relation to goals of students or for the purpose of solving their specific health problems.

Correlation thus appears as the second of the three patterns for incorporating health instruction in the curriculum. Well conceived and executed it can contribute materially to the knowledge and understanding of students concerning their health. Improperly developed it can become a travesty on good teaching and do the cause of health education far more harm than good.

5

Role of Integration in Teaching

As education has moved through the years, changing its directions, clarifying its purposes, and refining its techniques, seldom has it developed a concept and a programme more controversial than that which it now seeks: "integration" in learning. The "integrated programme", the "integrating curriculum", the "project", the "resource unit", the "core curriculum"—these and other terms are used to describe facets of an important movement which holds great promise for the enrichment of education. For health education it presents an unusual opportunity for the development of an understanding of health in relation to contemporary problems in our society and the realisation of full personal development in terms of the "wholeness" of the organism.

Integration may be defined as the result of a process, a process of relating parts of a thing to the whole or to a single purpose. In a well-integrated "something", all of the parts are working smoothly together, with no friction, nothing out of step, and the "something" is thus able to function with maximum efficiency in the way it was designed to function. To integrate is to relate parts to the whole—it makes no difference what the "whole" or purpose is. A well-integrated automobile is one in which all parts—carburetor, spark plugs, tires, chassis, driver, battery, and all the other thousands of parts involved—mesh smoothly together to provide safe, economical, and pleasurable transportation. Let the battery go dead, the spark plugs become fouled, or the driver be intoxicated, and *dis*integration has set in. The "wholeness" of safe transportation is not achieved.

A well-integrated battle requires complete and efficient interrelationship among all branches of the service involved and a complete meshing of individuals within those branches. The price of disintegration in battle is lives. A well-integrated gang of thieves functions smoothly in their antisocial activities by having each member coordinate his activities with the others to the end that the big bank robbery goes off without a hitch. Integrating is a process, not a state of affairs, and it does not demand that its "wholeness" or its purpose be good or bad.

The concept of integration applied to school health education requires some study and considerable experimentation before it will become most fruitful as an educating process. To develop an integrated health education plan in today's schools requires time, skill, and imagination. Furthermore, in the confused state in which the whole idea of integration is held by some there is no clear application of the concept of the various phases of health education. The term itself is sometimes confused with "correlation" but *to correlate* and *to integrate* are not synonymous although it is equally true that they are not mutually exclusive.

"Integration", or the process of integrating, may be applied in health education in any one or all of four principal respects:

1. Integrating the individual, the child, the personality. One speaks of "the integrated personality". A well-integrated person becomes an object of admiration and respect.

2. Integrating the curriculum, the programmes of study, the things that go on in the classroom. Thus, one may speak of "an integrated curriculum", a "core curriculum", or an "integrated project".

3. Integrating within the course itself. Health instruction need not be a series of disconnected topics relating to the human body. Learning may be organised around large whole themes or problems.

4. Integrating the school programme, the entire experience of the child from the time he leaves home for school till he returns. One may thus speak of an "integrated

programme", or an "integrated health programme", and imply the marshalling of *all* the forces in school around a common objective.

Now these four applications or usages of "integration" are *not* mutually exclusive. They are related and there are some shadings and peripheral developments of each which might easily be thought of as belonging to another. Nevertheless, in the interests of simplicity one may make these four applications first and later think through the process of integrating *them!*

INTEGRATION AND THE INDIVIDUAL

What kind of children leave our schools? Are they well behaved? Informed? Stable? Well? Debilitated? Nervous? Strong? Smart? Socially well adjusted? Physically mature? Happy? What kind of children do we *want* to graduate from schools and colleges? These questions are important as one tries to think through the functions of education anywhere. If educators content, as many now do, that education is interested in the development of the whole child and not just his brain, or his memory, then teachers must look at all the "parts" of the "whole" child and determine what can be done for each and all of the "parts". A leading university reported a few years ago that its principal function was the "training of the mind", thus implying no responsibility for the rest of the complicated and potentially well-integrated organism that is man. To make such an assumption opened that university to two criticisms: (1) that it shared no interest with other modern schools and colleges in their devotion to the development of the "whole" man and (2) that it believed in the spurious and untenable possibility that man may be divided into mind and body for purposes of "training".

But this is not the place to cite the evidence for man's unity. It must be assumed here that man is an entity, that his best growth, development, and maturity depend upon a successful interrelation of all of his parts, that any neglect of any phase of his nature—physical, social, psychological, intellectual, emotional, or whatever—will leave its mark in disintegration of the whole. The school and college devoted to the development of the "whole" child must then give thought to the thing they are devoted to and answer the question, "What sort of *person* is to be produced by this institution?"

It becomes good sense then to try to describe the sort of person the school wishes to produce. Shall he be tall or short, lean or fat, smart or dull, courageous or cowardly? Shall he be effective or poor in language, socially minded or selfish, a snob or democratic, sick or well? Even though the school can do little or nothing about *some* of the personal characteristics possessed by its students, nevertheless, committed to the development of the whole child, it must *describe* a well-integrated child and proceed to work toward that end.

The first step in the integrated process applied to school health education is, therefore, the establishment of those characteristics of desirable personal integration which can be used as objectives and *toward which every influence in the school must contribute and none detract.* This is usually done by putting a committee to work on the problem and asking them to bring before the faculty of the school a set of characteristics of a well-integrated child toward the attainment of which the entire school may work. Frequently such committees find it helpful to ask, "What would the ideal child, in so far as this school can affect him, be like?" Committees at work on this problem have produced some interesting characterisations of the integrated person. Here follow some examples:

A. An integrated individual:

> If a man gave his best to the task at hand, if he enjoyed optimal harmonious function of his physiologic and psychologic processes and possessed a normal anatomical structure, if he mastered his environment so as to be unaffected by its social and physical adversities, if his intellectual curiosity served to satisfy his potentialities, if he gave himself to communion with the Supreme Power, if he loved life for its own sake and gave no false opinions to his friends and associates, then that man would represent a bona fide integrated individual. But as a recipient and instigator of the luxury and blinding rush of modern civilisation, modern man has made it rather difficult to reach that utopian level at which he could enjoy complete integration. In place of a calm, steady round of labour, with proper periods of mental and physical rest, he lives in and contributes to an age of ever-increasing hustle. He invents all sorts of worksaving devices, and

in speeding it up he sacrifices his nerves and his peace of mind. He has virtually become a slave to a machine. He avoids outdoor games, feels that having fun is a sign of weakness, because his subservience to his own creations causes him to forget that he has himself to serve also. But if he would only stop for a moment and take stock of the endless procession of broken-down individuals that surround him on all sides as they race to their graves, he would perhaps wonder if such a strenuous life is worthwhile. Perhaps then he would use his creations to his advantage instead of to his disadvantage—an ultimate defeat.

B. The integrated child:

The integrated child is an individual whose resources are in a constant state of mobilisation, ready to meet his physical, intellectual, emotional and social needs by an integrated response, or by an adjustment based upon an excellent set of values and on a democratic interpretation of himself in regard to his environment.

The integrated child is gradually achieving an understanding of himself and his relationships to society; more particularly family, age mates, community and state. This child is experiencing optimal growth and development toward correct thinking, feeling, relationships, and living both in terms of himself and his environment.

More specifically, the integrated child is healthy, vigorous and energetic; is able through skills, knowledges and attitudes, to meet his basic needs. He is ever extending and increasing his interests; has an ever maturing purpose in life and achieves objectives toward that purpose. He adapts more fully from day to day to the complexities of his environment and does so in a manner increasingly consistent with the elements of our democratic way of life.

C. The faculty of the University Schools at The Ohio State University has for many years been working toward a satisfactory and workable set of objectives. Through committee effort and later faculty action, the school is directed toward making whatever contribution it can to develop what the faculty has called "Characteristics of an Individual with Optimum Health". The essential points of this remarkable effort are produced here. They have served well in guiding the actions of the entire school personnel toward an improvement in the health of children:

Health in the Area of Personal Living

1. The individual is gradually achieving a consistent and unified outlook on life.
2. The individual's evident vigour and tone imply reserves of energy and power of initiative indicative of successful adaptation to environment.
3. His bodily parts function with harmonious integration and optimum efficiency in energy transformations.
4. The individual has a sense of achievement.
5. He is gradually achieving status as a person through growth in independence, in establishing security and in developing a sense of belonging.
6. He is gradually freeing himself from childish egoism, and evidences growth in social sensitivity and willingness to sublimate personal desires for the larger concerns of the groups to which he belongs.
7. He understands the wide range of variability that can exist within the concept of normality, and in so doing he is becoming more able to accept and to live more intelligently with his own personal variations.
8. He understands his sex role.

Health in Personal-Social Relations

1. He has status in family relationships.
2. He has status in the various groups and with his age mates of both sexes through his effective participation in several functional groups.
3. He is frank, communicative, and sociable, and he enters heartily and with enjoyment into the spirit of social intercourse.
4. He is considerate and helpful and is growing in his concerns for other people, their plans, their successes and failures.
5. He is growing into a satisfactory heterosexual adjustment.

Health in the Wider Social Relationships

1. The individual has a zeal for promoting more healthful living through social reconstruction.
2. He is achieving status in society as a contributor to the furthering of more democratic ways of life within the social order.
3. He is achieving status in society through increasing economic independence and through social competence.
4. He participates effectively in social institutions.

In the later situation the laudable objectives set forth become meaningful and alive. The school is alert to contributions to these objectives from all areas. The report of the Health Committee goes on to cite the contributions made by the many and varied aspects of school life to each of the individual objectives. There is no gap between their theory and practice, between their ambition and their effort. Objectives in child development are established and their attainment is sought.

The foregoing illustrate existing efforts to establish a set of objectives toward which a school faculty may work. Such objectives become more meaningful when they are the product of the group using them. There is no perfect set. Faculties should make their own, and then, when the wording is acceptable and the meaning clear, it should be obligatory on all to make every influence in the school *contribute to and none detract from* the attainment of these objectives for every individual child. If this programme can be put into operation regardless of its imperfections, the school at least knows where it is going, what its goals are, and what it is trying to do for the health of its children.

To help the child develop his capacities, to develop "normally", is the oft-stated commission of the school health programme. The concept of "integration" requires an enlargement of this statement to the point where the detail of it comes within the range *and understanding* of each member of the faculty. He will soon recognise that it is integration the school must work for—not *dis*integration. It can be made clear that an adolescent with tuberculosis, a child with an inferiority feeling, a boy with marked facial acne, or a girl ignorant of the best practice in menstrual care cannot attain better than a partial integration, cannot reach fullest capacity until the disintegrating factors are removed. Life becomes a constant struggle between the forces which would tear apart and those which would hold together. Where does the school stand? On which side is "schooling"? Do children emerge from their twelve mandated years in school better or worse off personally? Successfully to integrate the child would require the school to examine its programme, its personnel, its curriculum and make sure that "going to school" is an integrating and not a disintegrating experience.

The *process* of helping an individual become integrated requires a description of the characteristics of the state of integration and then a union of all efforts to attain it. It means direction, a focus for effort, a "whole" toward which all parts can, and must, work.

THE INTEGRATING EXPERIENCE

How much of "going to school" is responsible for the current toll of personality problems and general ill health is not accurately known. When a child is sent off to school at the tender age of six he is poorly equipped to deal with the overwhelming experience which will come to him. For five hours a day, five days a week, for thirty weeks a year, he will be exposed to the influence of teacher, classmates, administration, to curriculum, method, and environment. The experience is bound to leave its mark. We are all the victims or the beneficiaries of our school life. Schooling can be helpful or harmful, favour child development or retard it, be an integrating experience or frustrating.

The curriculum which a child undertakes is, perhaps next to the teacher, the most important element in the school bearing upon child life. The experience of studying, of learning new things, of tackling hard problems, of responding to the pressures for advancement, can be made an integrating thing if the child's interests and welfare come first. Perhaps the best description of this application may be taken from *Health Education* as follows:

> The curriculum should provide not only diversified experiences, but also unifying ones which integrate the individual. A person is not a composite of separate areas of functions, needs or interests. One area interrelates with other areas so that the person functions as a whole. The observation of a normal child indicates that his behaviour is concentrated, purposeful and whole-hearted. When these qualities are not present, the person is scatter-brained, inconsistent in belief and action, and compartmentalises belief and action. An extreme lack of integration gives rise to emotional instability and blocking, loss of orderly behaviour and physical incapacity.
>
> The programme of the school should, therefore, promote the development of a person who behaves consistently and orderly, is emotionally stable and who acts upon thinking. Integration is so much a unique quality of a person or a group of persons that it cannot be planned for in advance by interrelating the various parts of the curriculum, such as relating one subject to another. Such an "integrated curriculum" reflects the integration of the person or persons who make it but just as likely as not, may tend to disorganise and upset the learner, rather than contribute to his integration. The best which can be realised is regularly to provide enterprises for children which have an integrating influence upon their lives. Integrating enterprises may vary greatly from a dramatic performance to an extended trip, or to the making of a community health survey.

The following criteria can be used to determine whether an enterprise has an integrating influence. It has integrating values if it,

(1) requires an extended time from development to culmination, the amount depending upon the maturity of the children;

(2) holds a high level of concern for the children and the staff;

(3) requires socialisation: interaction among children; group participation for planning, for outlining appropriate action and for making an evaluation;

(4) utilises for the most part skills already acquired by the children; does not involve for its success the acquisition of essential and new skills;

(5) is scheduled so that large blocks of time can be devoted the enterprise;

(6) is sustained by leadership and participation which give it direction and maintain a high level of productivity;

(7) possesses normative elements: opportunities for making choices, for weighing values, for calculating consequences, and for making judgments;

(8) offers potentialities for spreading into other activities which children initiate or are carrying on at the time.

Certainly all teachers, particularly those of health education, should avoid teaching techniques and situations which thwart and disappoint, which produce insecurity and inferiority. The frustration attending the lecture because the student cannot "talk back", the blind-alley type of discussion, or the debate in which there is neither understanding nor concession must be avoided. These are, in themselves, non-integrating experiences. The health lecture may fail completely not only of its own message but as a wholesome and integrating learning experience.

INTEGRATION AND THE CURRICULUM

When the integrating process is applied to the curriculum, to the organised study plans of the school, changes take place in the traditional way of conducting the school day. Usually, two and sometimes more hours a day are reserved for the study of a particular and carefully chosen theme, a large living project, an agreed-to problem or aspect of life. Sometimes, to make this time-block possible, the time given to some of the traditional and compartmentalised areas like science, health, social science, English, and others is shortened.

The knowledge from these different traditional areas is not discarded; only the routine "one period a day for history, one for hygiene, one for biology" is changed. The knowledge from the field of hygiene, or history, or mathematics is brought to bear on the solution of a large problem, or theme. This may take weeks or months to work through and may require three or four hours per day during which the leader or teacher may need assistance from other teachers whose specialised knowledge applies to the problem.

Does this imply that the study of health or hygiene can be made without a special course for it? Can one learn anything about healthful living under the guise of studying the industrial revolution, for example? If there are not "subjects" to study, what are there? The best answer to these questions will be to set up several examples of such integrated studies, some carefully and formally planned, some informally marked out, some merely spontaneous—all of them, however, taken from real school situations.

Examples of Integrated Units

1. A fifth grade once spent a semester studying "The Pioneer". Three hours each morning were spent in the process. They studied his life, his diseases and causes of death, his trails and geography, his government; they made a Conestoga wagon one-fourth scale; they sang his songs, danced his dances, played his games, and wore his clothes; they studied his life from every aspect and in so doing made innumerable applications to contemporary life. They used the resources of library, shop, and laboratory. They learned of mathematics, engineering, geography, hygiene, music, science, *et al.* They studied all of these thing and yet they studied none of them. *They studied the pioneer.*

2. An eleventh grade chose to spend a year on "The Span of Human Life—its origins, developments, changes, and emphasis." This required three weeks of planning before the first wheels turned. The sweep of man's life was divided into the convenient periods of prenatal, infancy, childhood, adolescence, maturity, and senility. Committees were put to work studying these. The causes of sickness and death were explored, comparative life expectancies were gone into, and the actuarial problem became a fascinating study of the productive uses of mathematics. Factors influencing growth, growth spurts, relation of physique to intellect, to attainment, and to personality were all explored with the aid of science teachers, the school physician, and nearby specialists.

The project was alive with laboratory and experimental possibilities. The students did an inordinate amount of studying on the problems of human life and the interest throughout the year was at a high level. The amount of information acquired about human health was enormous, and if interested study predicts a transition to effective behaviour then the results were gratifying.

3. The following study of "Pioneers of the Stratosphere" is an example of a half-semester concentration requiring two hours per day and a leader who knows a great deal about the physical sciences. It is appropriate for any of the upper six years and, as reported by the teacher, was conducted as follows:

> The topic "Pioneers of the Stratosphere" was chosen because we are looking at air transportation more each day as a mode of travel. Every day the student sees huge planes flying through the air and he wonders about them. Aviation is an every-day problem which the child faces but seldom solves. The project was set up to give the student a better understanding of air travel from all its aspects. The historical, mathematical, scientific, psychological, physiological and futuristic aspects were studied.
>
> The project began with a study of the historical background of the airplane. Diagrams of early planes were made and models constructed. The relationship between the designs of the first planes and the anatomy of birds was shown. After this part of the project was completed the students then planned and showed the development of planes since the Wright brothers made their first flight. The students studied why planes fly. The structure of the wings, their design in relation to speed and altitude, and the effect of retractable landing gears on speed were explored. As planes flew higher, research was necessary to find the effect of the stratosphere on man. The oxygen mask was developed. Studies were made on diet and its relationship to body pressure. It was found that stomach disorders often resulted in air sickness. Pressurised cabins were finally developed. All these factors were related to the health of the individual. A study was made of the diet of the people who fly today by commercial air-ways, and body functions during flight were studied. Organic disturbances due to rapid changes in altitude were considered. The future of travel beyond the stratosphere offered an opportunity for research to try to determine what part the rocket may play.

In order to make the project of most value it was necessary that a wide variety of opportunities be opened up for the students. If they were required to expend too much time on a particular phase the whole project might have lost its interest. The project was planned by the students in ten days and after this period each student knew exactly where he was to go from there. The project itself did not take more than forty-five days. Individual differences and special interests were considered but the responsibility of each individual to the group was well established in order to further the over-all purpose of the project. Papers and reports were studied for grammatical construction and correctness before they were submitted.

From these three illustrations one can begin to see the shape of the kind of planning necessary to make these integrated study plans successful. Students and teachers together work on the plans, objectives are agreed to, a direction is set, work is accomplished.

Four more illustrations will be useful:

4. A learning unit on "Insurance, A Means of Security".

This learning unit was constructed for and by an eleventh-grade class. The class was composed of twenty-two boys and twenty-seven girls. The unit was carried out in full during their daily core meetings from 1 o'clock to 3.30 o'clock in the afternoon and whatever additional times were required to gain the fullest advantage of the unit purposes.

The first week of class meetings was devoted to suggestions for unit subjects and the forming of committees on the subjects suggested. There were eight such studies proposed that found the interest and approval of the students. Thus, there were eight committees formed, each member of the committee having interest in the respective study, and work was started on the organisation and outlining of the various studies for presentation to the rest of the class for the final selection of a class unit study. In addition, these committees outlined the tentative path that the class would follow if their subject were selected in the final analysis.

The following two weeks were devoted to committee planning. The members of the class met in their committees every day during the core period to organise, investigate, plan, and outline the unit subjects. On the fifth day of the second week of committee planning all had completed their work on their subjects and the first was presented to the class.

In the week to follow the remainder of the subjects were presented to the class. Each topic was thoroughly discussed by the class. By the end of the week the class was unified on their selection of the unit subject—INSURANCE, A MEANS OF SECURITY.

The fifth week of class was spent making additions, subtractions, and reorganisations of the selected study outline. An extensive list of class purposes was prepared and the total unit outline was completed. Student interest was high, they were ready to go to work. The following major objectives were established:

1. To meet the students' needs for a better understanding of the part insurance plays in the individual, family, and community life of our society.
2. To assist the student in his formation of definite attitudes in relationship to the need for insurance in America's democratic way of living.
3. To satisfy the interest of the students in their thirst for knowledge.
4. To stimulate the seeking of answers to any and all problems concerning insurance and security for the population.
5. For the students to make sound and stable evaluations of all findings in regard to social and economic standards.
6. To apply the facts of this unit to personal insurance problems.
7. To influence others through the students' findings, learnings, and practices.

The following large problems were investigated by small groups and discussed in class:

1. What degree of security can be achieve through insurance plans? Definitions of terms and presentation of tentative evidence on need for security in the family.
2. What insurance needs are recognised?

(a) What amount of security does the family and home receive from hospital insurances?

(1) How does hospitalisation insurance function and what does it cover? Discussion on illnesses and accidents within the community that necessitate hospitalisation.

(2) Relation of medical costs to other expenditures in the home.

(3) Number of people that need hospitalisation but are not financially capable of having this medical attention. Could they be helped through hospitalisation insurance? How would socialised medicine affect these people?

(4) What is community reaction to hospitalisation insurance? Attitudes of heads of families, hospital, management, medical societies.

(5) Conclusions.

(b) What does accident and health insurance mean to our security?

(1) Understanding the coverage of accident and health insurance. Critical discussions of policy benefits.

(2) Is there a need for accident and health insurance? Study of various hazardous community occupations. Number of working hours lost each year due to accident and health problems. What is the loss to industry? What is the loss to the working man? Number and types of accidents other than in industry resulting in loss of man-hours.

(c) Will life insurance give my home security?

(1) Whom does a life insurance policy protect?

(2) What is the average life span of today's American man and woman and how does it apply to life insurance?

(3) What advances has modern medicine made to increase the average life span?

(4) The effect of a lowered mortality rate upon life insurance.

(d) In what way does liability insurance affect my economic and social security? The laws governing non-payments of damages from persons convicted.

3. Study of present problems concerning insurance within our society and suggestions for possible relief of the problems.

4. The final evaluation of the unit.

(a) How far have we come in achieving our objectives?

(b) What improvements can we make in our next unit to improve its content over the unit just completed?

5. A unit on the American Indian.

The seventh grade core class in a school where I am teaching has discussed various units to be used for a year's period of study. The reasons for studying each unit were brought before the class by committees on each of the units. The committee working on the American Indian gave the following reasons why they thought the group should study that subject:

1. Indians were here before Columbus landed.
2. We imitate Indians when we play.
3. Some geographical names have Indian origins.
4. Movies and history books show Indians as bad men. Is this true?
5. Indians were good in athletics.
6. We wear Indian jewellery and leather goods.
7. We use Indian rugs and baskets in our homes.
8. Through our government we are supporting many of the Indians.
9. Some of us may have Indian ancestry.
10. Indians lived in our state.
11. We use some of the Indian means of transportation.

12. We follow customs today that have Indian origins.
13. Adobe which was used in making Indian houses is used today on houses in the southwest. Indian architecture is also used.

After thoroughly discussing each proposed unit, the class and teacher decided to study the American Indian. It was also agreed that the unit was broad enough to consume an entire half year of study.

The first job of the group was to plan the unit. The topic was divided into three sections of study: (1) the Indian before the arrival of the white man; (2) the effect of the coming of the white man; and (3) the Indian today. These sections were further divided into parts for study, and committees were formed to study each. The committees reported to the class information they had gathered. Members of the class could serve on any committee and more than one if they desired. New committees were constantly being formed as the need arose.

All faculty members cooperated to the fullest extent with the study, some relating their special courses to the American Indian, and others coming into the core class when their knowledge and experience were needed.

Field trips were planned and carried out when they were felt necessary. Evaluation of the field experience always took place afterwards.

A. The Indian Before the Arrival of the White Man.

(a) Relation to any other people in world?

(b) Culture similar to any others?

(c) Physical characteristics?

(d) What, when, and where were the first evidences of the North American Indian? Excavations, writings, and paintings on rock?

(e) Do all Indians belong to the same family?

Sources of information:

(1) Historian

(2) Archeologist

(3) Books

2. Location of Indian tribes in our country.

   (a) Evidences of locations.

   (b) Reasons for settling in certain area—climate, trade, transportation.

3. Indian homes:

   (a) Types—wigwams, hogans, pueblos.

   (b) Relation to tribes.

   (c) Relation of type of house to geographical location.

   (d) Size—length, width, area.

   (e) Building material.

   (f) Evidences of Indian type architecture in our homes today.

   (g) Ventilation.

   (h) Sanitation.

4. Transportation

   (a) Foot.

   (b), (c) Etc.

5. Making a living.

   (a) Agriculture—men's or women's job, food raised, implements used, plant diseases.

   (b) Products made, etc., etc.

6. The Indian at play.

   (a) Dances.

   (b) Games, etc.

7. Teaching and learning.
8. Tribal wars.
9. Dress.
10. Food and preparation.
11. Indian customs:
    - (a) Religious ceremonies—purpose, dances, costumes, songs, musical instruments.
    - (b) Etc.
12. Indian diseases:
    - (a) Leading diseases of Indians—smallpox, leading cause of death, causes, treatment used as compared with treatment for those diseases today.
    - (b) Medical facilities.
    - (c) Witch doctors—compare with quack doctors today.
13. Art and Literature.
14. Communication.
15. Trade.
16. Indian behaviour.

B. Coming of the White Man.

1. Why were whites and Indians enemies?
2. White-Indian wars.
3. What did the white man give the Indian?
    - (a) Firearms.
    - (b) English language.
    - (c) Diseases—smallpox and other epidemics; tuberculosis, sexual diseases, whiskey and attendant dissipation, removals from land, starvation and subjection to unaccustomed conditions, low vitality due to mental depression under misfortune.

4. What did the Indian give to the white man?
5. Famous Indians.
6. Intermarriage of Indians and whites.
7. US Government Department of Indian Affairs.
8. Indian trek west.
9. Decreased population.

C. The Indian Today.

1. Increasing population.
   (a) Better medical facilities.
   (b) Better educational opportunities.
2. Indian reservations.
3. Indian employment.
4. Famous Indians of this era.
5. National Indian monuments.
6. Indian villages.
7. Indian names familiar today.

In the reproduction of this unit it has been necessary to omit practically all of the material the group proposed to use as resources. Significantly, they had many suggestions about things to do, people to see, places to visit, and investigations to make to enrich this study of the Indian.

6. The following illustration is not given in full. The material has been selected from an outline of a study unit on the steel industry for purposes of highlighting the opportunities within the unit for the study of health.

The class, after hearing each committee report decided that their unit would be an investigation of the steel industry. The subject held a natural interest, for nearby was a large city containing many steel mills, also some of the students' parents, relatives and friends were employed in the industry.

The next step for class decision was to set up some specific objectives to guide them in their investigation. Following are a few of the students' suggestions:

1. To become acquainted with the various positions in the steel mill and the opportunities associated with this type of work.
2. To obtain information as to the process of making steel.
3. To secure a knowledge of the development and history of the steel industry.
4. To understand the principles of tonnage, percentage of raw materials used in the steel making process, bonuses, pay rates, shipping costs and freight rates.
5. To investigate the recreational opportunities afforded to the employees.
6. To obtain information about the cafeteria and the type of meals usually served.
7. To study about their emergency care programme.
8. To investigate the organisation and function of the union.
9. To determinate what type of insurance is provided for the workers.
10. To investigate the causes of so many accidents.
11. To obtain information relative to their safety rules and regulations.

The committee directed to deal with the many health implications of the industry decided to begin its work with an investigation of accidents occurring in a mill. They obtained material from insurance companies and other sources which calculated the statistics dealing with the type, cause and number of injuries incurred by steel mill employees. They noted these statistics computed on a nation-wide scale and then took a trip to a mill where they studied the accident statistics from the mill's records.

Several lectures were given by the mill personnel, such as the safety director and the first aid team, films were viewed, and cause and prevention of accidents was dealt with in detail. They visited the mill dispensary where minor injuries were treated by the mill's doctor or nurse; then observed the facilities and equipment; listened to the nurse and doctor lecture relative to the many aspects of their positions; witnessed a demonstration performed by one of the mill's first aid teams; and later these same men gave an interesting discussion of actual emergencies in which they were called upon to administer first aid. As a sidelight the first aid team presented a description of an accident and then questioned the group to determine just what they would have done in that particular emergency.

Following this an investigation was made into the medical care programme for the workers. Compensation was investigated as well as insurance for hospital care and benefits. A visit was made to one of the hospital wards where they saw actual cases of those benefiting from the insurance programme. They studied the advantages and disadvantages of all types of health insurance, and even discussed economic conditions of the home resulting from injuries that disabled the mill workers.

It was noticed in one of their visits to the mill that many of the workers took small white pills with regularity. This led to a discussion about salt tablets and the body demand for salt. Clarification of this question led to study of the anatomy and physiology of the body in respect to better explaining the body's need for salt. They studied about heat exhaustion, its treatment, prevention and symptoms. Burns were discussed, their degree of severity and treatment, which led to a further discussion relative to tissue growth, skin grafting and composition of the skin.

After noticing the large amount of dust in the air and the amount which collected on the worker's clothes the question of whether or not this dust would injure the worker's lungs was brought up. Breathing was discussed and it was found that the nose acted as a filter and passage-way to the lungs. Here the class touched on anatomy to discover this passage-way, its structure and function. The lungs were then studied relative to structure and function and it was decided that the dust itself would not be directly injurious to the lungs, but there was an indirect possibility it might be. Diseases of the lungs were studied briefly or thoroughly as indicated by their relation to the central study of the steel mill. Silicosis, however, was one condition which seemed pertinent enough to warrant a thorough investigation. . . .

7. There have been many excellent study units developed by workshop groups devoting considerable time to a complete exploration of one theme. An example is found in a mimeographed document entitled "Science: Servant or Master?" and prepared with the counsel of Dr. Harold B. Alberty, Professor of Education at The Ohio State University. Obviously the entire project cannot be reproduced here but enough of it will be given to show rather clearly the essential parts of the unit, its manner of construction, and some of its involvements of health material.

The Major Purposes of the Unit

1. To help the student to understand the meaning and significance of the scientific method in solving problems of human concern.
2. To develop in the student an appreciation of the scientific attitude and an ability and desire to use the scientific method in its generalised form (i.e., reflective thinking) in solving his problems.
3. To help the student to understand the problems which have arisen in all areas of living because of the growth of technology, e.g., health, social-economic life, morals and ethics, and on his own level to help solve these problems.
4. To help the student to realise the dangers of both utilising the fruits of scientific achievement for destructive ends and the possibilities of utilising them for the advancement of human living.
5. To help the student to develop consistent attitudes toward the problem of applying science to living.

6. To help the student to see the connection between the method of science and the method of democracy.

Alberty's group then devotes its Section 10 to a development of the meaning of science. With a good bibliography and ample footnotes, it presents its discussion by defining science, showing its evolution, presenting the differences between pure and applied science, showing the method of science, and applying the scientific method to contemporary problems.

In Chapter IV "The Scope of the Unit", there is a cogent discussion of the impact of technology and the scientific method on

A. Social living.

B. Economic living.

C. Religion, ethics, and morals.

D. Healthful living.

In this last section will be found most of the material which health educators look for when they seek to determine how their area is faring in an integration plan. In this instance health and hygiene fare rather well and only limitations of space prevent the illustration here of that fact. The following excerpts will, however, give a fair impression of how the area is handled:

V. D. Science and Healthful Living.

Introduction Early man lived in uncertainty and fear. His world was mysterious. Nature seemed unpredictable and undependable. Storms, famine, sickness, and death made him afraid. For these disasters, he blamed evil spirits and unfriendly gods. Sunshine, plentiful food, and health made him happy, and for these he thanked good spirits and friendly gods. The early Greeks were the first to break away from such superstitions. They began to ask the "why" and "how" of such things. Believing that nature was orderly, they tried to develop a new method of understanding her ways.

The rapid progress made in discoveries and inventions in

the nineteenth and twentieth centuries would not have been possible if the early scientists had not prepared the way. The magnifying lens, for example, has helped us better to understand the nature of all living and non-living things, and has brought to our knowledge the existence of a world of microscopic life unseen by the naked eye. This invention has had a profound effect upon the study of disease. Without our many inventions and discoveries we should still be living among the discomforts of the Dark Ages. With them, we have effective weapons for fighting disease and death. . . .

In spite of the advancement of science in the areas of health, many problems need to be solved before optimal health may become a reality in America.

Problems and statements of position First of all, there is a problem of the applicability of scientific method to the solution of *all* problems of health. There seems to be no opposition to the application of science to the improvement of livestock and plants, and great strides have been made in this direction, but when it is proposed that similar methods be utilised for improving human beings, many groups, particularly in the religious field, enter objections. The application of technology of birth control, eugenics, sterilisation of the unfit, and the like, are held to be contrary to the laws of God. These groups resist any attempt to interfere with "natural" processes. Thus there develop rival hypotheses which need to be carefully examined in the light of the supporting evidence. These conflicting positions may be stated as follows:

1. The scientific knowledge and techniques which have proved to be effective in improving plant and animal life should be applied without limit to the problem of improving the human race.

2. There are "higher laws" which control the processes of human reproduction, and the improvement of the human species, and these must not be violated. Science may be applied up to the point where it interferes with these "higher laws", but beyond that point it must not go.

Somewhat related to the above problem is the question of

the extent to which science should be applied to the healing of disease. . . .

A third problem has to do with the issue as to the extent to which healthful living for *all* citizens should be regarded as a public function. This is one of the most important problems confronting the American people today. Like the issues discussed above, there are widely differing positions bearing on this problem. The groups advocating each of these are made up of honest and sincere people who believe that they have the solution of the problem.

VI. Activities for Groups and Individuals

The following list of activities is designed to suggest to the teacher the wide variety of possibilities for making the learning unit interesting and worthwhile. Most of them are addressed to the teacher rather than to the student. This does not mean, however, that they are to be assigned in an arbitrary manner. Rather they should be discussed by the class to discover whether or not they meet the needs of the group. The resourceful teacher will think of many other types of activities, and students are bound to have many other fruitful suggestions. Out of teacher-student planning should come an initial selection of activities which may be supplemented as the unit progresses.

No attempt has been made to classify the activities as to the appropriate sequence in the development of the unit. This is a matter that can best be worked out in the local situation. It will be noted that many of the activities involve areas such as social living, economic living, health, and morals and ethics. It will be noted too that there is abundant opportunity to utilise material from fields such as science, social studies, language and literature, mathematics and the arts. The organisation of the curriculum in the school in which the unit is to be used will determine the areas which should be drawn upon. The idea, of course, is to utilise all areas that are pertinent to the problems that are being studied.

1. If a group is particularly interested the members might make a list of the commercials that are heard time and again

over the air. These might be analysed as to their scientific truth and the findings could be presented to the class. . . .

11. As an outgrowth of the study of recreational activities a discussion of hobbies based on some scientific principle or on the scientific method might develop. Students working on this might explain and show their personal hobbies to the class. . . .

19. The destructive usages of science in our daily lives might be studied. The class may, through reading and exchanging ideas, list the ways science has brought disaster, sorrow, and destruction to mankind. Possibly a group will be interested in making a mural or a frieze that depicts the way science has progressed in militaristic weapons starting with a sling shot or bow and arrow up to our modern war machines. The class could study and then discuss the questions—"War has always been inseparable from science", or "There is a relationship between the frequency of wars and the rise of science". A group of students might find it interesting to make a scrap book on the way science is used to destroy or retard civilisation. . . .

27. Many are aware of the present plight of American housing. It might be suggested to the class that there are real obstacles to any improvement. It seems that there are three tantalising questions which need special treatment. (1) Redevelopment of slum areas, (2) Government assistance for the lowest income families, (3) The advisability of home ownership. Someone may wish to take one or more of the tantalising questions involved in the problem and try to discover a solution. Scenes from Slum Land before and after in sketch, story, or play might result from this work. . . .

56. The students are quite likely to be interested in the superstitions held by members of the class. A survey of these might be made and some attempt to discover their origin might be of concern to the committee. These superstitions could be set up and examined just as the scientist tests his tentative conclusions. Some attempt to get pupils to examine their reasons for their superstitions might come about through examining stories like the following. A young lady named Susie

Q. always kept a good-luck charm in her automobile. But Susie Q. also took out insurance on the automobile. A committee or even the entire class might make a collection of stories similar to this and the following classification might be developed: (1) Common superstitions, (2) Rare or unusual superstitions that have their origin almost completely lost in antiquity, (3) Regional superstitions, (4) The farmer's superstitions, (5) Primitive superstitions. . . .

59. Some group in the class may be much interested in the broad health programme that is being considered as socialised medicine. A thorough study of the plan might be made and the definition of the term, "socialised", clearly stated for the class. A critical examination of all phases of the plan should be critically made by the group as it works so that when it presents its findings to the class both weaknesses and strengths would be pointed out. Countries that have tried socialised medicine or industrial concerns that have operated in part in this plan should be noted and the success or failure studied. Probably any group will be divided on this issue. The main purpose of an activity of this nature is to help get the facts before people for examination. Free and unhampered discussion on all phases should follow with no right answer in the minds of either the teacher or the group as the final answer for the whole class to accept. . . .

63. A study of the life and work of Pasteur and how he finished a piece of work and went on to the next, how he worked, and what tangible results he had to show for his work might help to give a student some insight into the scientific method of work.

64. The class might make a survey of the health facilities which are found in the community, the services rendered, number of people served. Some questions concerning how these agencies operate, who supports them, and how effective these agencies are in improving health in the community might be studied. Representatives of the various agencies might be invited to talk and questions which concern the group might be presented to the speakers. . . .

75. It might be suggested to the group that well informed

people see many changes ahead in the way we live and in our attitudes toward recreation, education, health, religious activity, use of language, family life and even in our thinking. These changes grow out of developments in air transportation, it is thought. This provides basic material for many investigations. If the group is divided in its thinking (as is quite likely) on this hypothesis, issues might be set up and round table discussions or panel discussions developed. A group should summarise its findings and suggest some action which the class might consider in the light of their acceptance of conclusions. . . .

Steps in the Development of Such Units

To develop such units and to alter the traditional curriculum in order to include them requires time, patience, a cooperative faculty, teachers and students willing and able to plan together, ample resources and freedom to use them, and a lively imagination and enthusiasm on the part of the teacher in charge. If such unit or "core" plans have never been used in the school before, care must be exercised to orient the students to the purposes and nature of the approach so they will be sympathetic to it.

The following steps are usually taken in the development of integrated study units:

1. A period of orientation of new personnel with the nature and course of the project is undertaken.
2. A discussion of criteria by which the final selection of the study unit will be made is held. The class will not want to select units willy-nilly. Such guides as these should be considered:

Definite criteria for unit selection should be discussed, presented, and then practice. Facts or problems like the following should be considered:

Does the unit involve the common interests of all?

Is the problem broad and important?

Will it make a contribution to the basic purposes of the school?

How much time does it require?

Will it be a continuous experience?

Will it require specialised laboratory equipment?

Does it require specific skills?

Are these resources available?

3. The class will have many suggestions of seemingly worthwhile problems for the year's (or half-year's) work. Freedom should be allowed all to propose problems for study.

4. After all suggestions have been received the class should then begin the process of elimination and combining until some six or eight of the most promising ones are left.

5. The class should then be organised to investigate these promising ones. Voluntary committees can be selected to present the virtue and nature of the experience which would be had if this one or that one were selected. These preliminary investigations are exploratory only and are for the purpose of revealing to the class what they would be in for in connection with each of the promising problems.

6. Eventually (after ample time has been given to consider the various proposals) the class will select one (which might have been unique originally, or it might be the result of a combination of two or more of the originals). This selection must be arrived at democratically and not as the result of a pressure group's arguing for its favourite project. The one selected should be selected on the basis of merit, interest, and potential contribution to the educational growth of students and in full light of the criteria previously agreed to.

7. After the selection has been made the class then goes back, and with the preliminary prospectus at-hand, amplifies its approach to the problem, making all plans for work upon it. This is a critical stage. Teacher and class together must work out the scope of the problem and their attack upon it. Things to be done, resources to be tapped, experiments to

make, literature to use, analyses to be made, issues to be explored—all these things need to be sketched out at this point.

"Group planning is an essential element in democratic living and at this time progress is likely to be slow. Teachers may think that time is being wasted, that the class is not getting any place and become impatient and so, hurriedly accept assumptions, values, issues, and problems that are not part of the unit or are . . . of minor importance or irrelevant".

8. Eventually the unit will be sketched out in detail sufficient to have work begun upon it. Students will be ready to make choices of individual or small group assignments and all-class activities will have emerged. Such assignments should be agreed to and work begun without further ado. Important at this point would be the formation of a tentative time schedule for the work to be accomplished. Such a schedule should include the sequence of development of the study, the tentative assignment of reporting dates for committees, field trips, special events, class group work and study.

9. The students now proceed to go to work. Each knows what he is to do either individually or with his group. If a high quality of thorough work is not required of each student the value of the study will be lost and the teacher might as well revert to the old page-by-page assignment method. Students should be expected to be thorough, careful, and diligent and to make their reports (written or oral) meet high standards in content and composition.

10. There is a continuous flow from the preceding step (9) to this one: work in class. Study and reports, field experiences and the use of resource people flow together as the unfolding plan requires. This is the crux of the study. What the students "get out of" the unit is determined by the quality of work reported back to the class for discussion and evaluation. "During this phase of the unit there will be much class discussion and many reports of progress of individuals and groups. *The teacher will need to plan with the class for sufficient all-group activities to protect the unit of the enterprise."*

11. Plans are made for closing the unit. "As the solution of problems begins to take shape, statements are clarified, ideas are refined, and certain behaviour changes appear, the teacher discerns that it is time to consider with the class the plan for closing the unit. A new period of planning begins and, as in the initiatory phase, it should be a teacher-class planning period. Evaluation, although a continuous process, is exceedingly important at this time for new students are in the stage of sizing up their own work and the work of other individuals, and groups, and of selecting the culminating activities."

12. "In order to make the learning experiences more effective and permanent, culminating and evaluating activities should be planned. The type of culmination should depend on the nature of the unit, the needs of the class, and the facilities and time for engaging in the activity. Worthwhile activities in bringing the unit to a close will give the students a sense of satisfaction and a feeling of completeness. Good culminating activities will provide further opportunities for the student to express himself through music, art, dramatics, writing, and other creative work of various types. . . .

"Culminating activities are of two kinds: one is the reporting, discussion, and arriving at group and individual attitudes, appreciations, and viewpoints in the classroom; the other one is the type of activity which calls for a reorganisation of learning experiences around a central theme or several central but related themes."

Such activities "bring to a head" the preceding weeks of work.

13. A summary is made and conclusions are stated. It is frequently helpful and illuminating to bring together at the end of the study statements, oral or written, which describe the highlights of the work: conclusions reached, issues explored, significant knowledge acquired, experiences undertaken.

14. "A final evaluation period after the culminating activity is completed should round out the continuous evaluation that

has occurred throughout the unit. . . ."

With these steps in view the teacher and class can proceed to the development of units of work.

This resource unit on "Science: Servant or Master?" has been presented in detail because it is a workable and accomplished unit. It presents ample opportunities for learning a great deal about healthful living and, as in so many of such units, the learning goes on in a meaningful and interesting setting.

The possibilities for unit titles or themes are virtually unlimited. Literally scores of themes have been developed in schools committed to some form of integrating process within the curriculum, and, depending upon the nature of the theme and the imagination of teacher and students, health information may be acquired and health behaviour developed from all of them. Among hundreds of available themes here are a dozen, in addition to the seven already presented, which are usable:

1. Healing Through the Ages
2. Contemporary Healing Systems
3. Superstitions and Fallacious Beliefs
4. Heredity as a Factor in Success
5. Home and Community Hazards to Life
6. A Farm
7. The Automobile Industry
8. The Vegetable Gardening and Distribution Industry
9. The Sea and Its Relation to Man
10. The Panama Canal: Its Building and Usage
11. Great Personalities in Science
12. The Control of Infective Organisms

"Integration", thus applied, becomes a process rather than a thing. It is a means of organising learning. It is a means of bringing some of the great lessons of science, of health and hygiene, into the consciousness and behaviour of growing students. It is not a "cause", something to be "for or against" or to be "believed in". It is a method, and a good one, of accomplishing learning. It is not restricted to uses in "progressive schools" alone. It appears in some very "traditional" schools and may appear quite within the boundaries of a subject curriculum. It has a wide range of application. For example:

1. In a subject-centered curriculum the teacher of chemistry may center attention for weeks on the use of plastics, or new developments in housing. The teacher of physics might spend a term on atomic energy including, of course, atomic energy and the healing arts.
2. In less rigid curriculum arrangements involving associated areas like the social or the physical sciences, units can be developed on projects or themes which would be of interest. These would cut across all associated areas and require joint planning and execution.
3. Or, in curriculums organised around a required "core", such a unit or units become an important part of the year's work.

THE DEVELOPMENT OF RESOURCE UNITS AND THEIR USE

Naturally, the school health educator is interested in the amount of understanding of health matters which can be developed from such integrating studies. As indicated earlier, the amount of material from hygiene and its related fields varies with the unit and with the teacher's skill and imagination. Teachers unprepared in hygiene will be less likely to give a full treatment to the possibilities for learning about health inherent in the unit. For that reason particularly many health educators prefer a separate course or a specific opportunity to teach health in order to cover the wide variety of informational needs exhibited by students at any age.

Where such integrated plans exist *the health educator should:*

1. Make available to core or area teachers suggestions for

problems rich in health material.

2. Assist all area and core teachers with the discovery of resources for data on the problem.
3. Suggest a wide variety of student activities of interest to the solution of the problem.
4. Arrange, if invited to do so, to bring resource people or paraphernalia to the school.
5. Be available himself for group leadership in the exploration of phases of the problem.
6. Assist when desirable with the development of the unit.

The health educator can be even more helpful if he will prepare in writing some material for the core teacher. This might be in the form of a resource unit complete with problems to be studied, resources including bibliographies for both teacher and students, and suggestions for activities. The following shows how such resource material might be presented:

A. A unit for a tenth-grade core class:

The tenth grade Core Group has selected a unit concerning: "Problems of Living in the Air Age".

As a health education instructor I will take this opportunity to present to them some source material to aid them in the area of: "Problems of Health in an Air Age".

This resource material will be in the form of:

1. Suggested Problems
2. Resource Readings
3. Suggested Activities

   1. Suggested Problems:

      (a) How can the spread of disease be prevented with the greatly increased air travel?

      (b) How can we bring about more health education here and abroad through clinics, lectures, films, public health services, etc.?

(c) What are some present international efforts to strike disease at its source?

(d) Discover how and why diseases spread to other populations and what and are some of the possibilities for prevention of this danger.

(e) Study the costs in prevention and cure of disease on an international level.

(f) Why is education and immunisation of air travellers, especially air pilots, so important?

(g) What effect will the air age have on the mental and emotional health of the people?

(h) What dangers await these air travellers in their journeys through the atmosphere?

2. Resource Readings:

Armstrong, H.G., *Principles and Practice of Aviation Medicine,* Baltimore, The Williams and Wilkins Co., 1939.

Grow, M.C., and Armstrong, H.G., *Fit to Fly: A Medical Handbook for Fliers,* New York, Appelton-Century Co., Inc., 1941.

Haggard, H.W., *The Science of Health and Disease,* New York, Harper & Brothers, 1938.

Kafka, M. Martyn., *Flying Health,* Harrisburg, Pa., Military Service Publications Co., 1942.

Van Liere, E.J. *Anoxia: Its Effects on the Body,* Chicago, University of Chicago Press, 1942.

Ward, Harold, *New Worlds in Science—An Anthology,* New York, Robert M. McBride & Co., 1941.

3. Suggested Activities:

(1) Use a globe to demonstrate existing airplane travel routes around the world. Point out the possibility that tse-tse flies could be carried to South America or North America and that infested rat fleas could be brought from the Orient. Also point out where and why bubonic plague is a menace.

(2) Discover how lice are related to the transmission of typhus fever. Show how rapid air travel might be responsible for rapid spreading of the disease.

(3) Discover what precautions are used to prevent infested mosquitoes from travelling from one country to another in airplanes. Discover what diseases are carried by mosquitoes.

(4) Discover why pilots must have excellent muscular coordination.

(5) Discover why an efficient circulatory system is a requisite of a good pilot.

(6) Find out why an airplane pilot must have perfect vision and other sensory perceptions.

(7) Discuss the training programme of an air cadet. (In these activities not only must the reading references be used but use must also be made of all the various community and even government sources of information.)

For Example:

There should be men who have done flying available in the community and even young men who are in or have gone through the Naval or Army Air Cadet Training Programme.

Likewise, are there many helpful materials available at airports and issued by various government agencies that can be of great help in this area.

B. This unit was prepared for a core class studying the steel industry:

Some questions which might be asked:

1. What are some diseases which are prevalent among steel workers?
2. What is the biggest cause of accidents in the steel industry?
3. Does the geographic location of most plants affect the health?

4. What has been done by the steel industry to reduce hazards?
5. Is silicosis dangerous to the health?
6. What are some safety factors which will reduce the incidence of silicosis?
7. What are some of the main occupational hazards in the making of steel?
8. Has the government done anything toward improving the health of steel workers?
9. Is good medical supervision available to steel workers?
10. Does working under extreme heat affect the health?
11. Does the melting of steel and iron ore produce any toxic gases which might be bad for the health of the steel worker?
12. Is the wearing of safety clothing such as goggles, shoes, helmets, etc., required by the steel industry?
13. Do the steel companies have their own safety departments or does the government do all that sort of thing?

Some Films which might be useful:

1. *Occupational Hazards in U.S. Steel.* Available for free use by sending to the U.S. Steel Corporation Public Relations Department, Pittsburgh, Pennsylvania.
2. *Medical Care in Industrial Establishments.* Available for free use by writing to the National Safety Council, Park Avenue, New York, New York.
3. *Stop Silicosis.* Ohio State Department of Education Film Library, Columbus, Ohio. Free.
4. *Health and Recreation.* Ohio State Department of Education Film Library, Columbus, Ohio. Free.

Some valuable references in Health in the Steel Industry:

1. Watkins, J.A., *Health Conservation in the Steel Mills,* U.S. Public Health Service, 1951.

2. U.S. Bureau of Steel., *Health and Safety of Steel Workers*, Washington, 1951.

3. *Industrial Health Series*, Metropolitan Life Insurance Co., New York, 1949.

4. Klemm, Margaret C., *Industrial Health and Medical Progress*, Public Health Service, Division of Industrial Hygiene, 1951.

5. *Industrial Hygiene for the Steel Mills*, U.S. Bureau of Mines, Washington, 1946.

6. *Occupational Hazards Eliminated*, Occupational Hazards, Inc., Cleveland, Ohio, 1950.

INTEGRATION AND THE SEPARATE COURSE

If a separate course for health instruction is established, then the better health teachers proceed to the organisation of integrated projects *within the course itself.* This method also holds great promise of improving the quality of learning about hygiene. Projects developed within the course itself, in which ideas, resources, and evidence are mobilised around a "whole", a theme or a problem, have the advantage of being meaningful, understandable, and integrated. There are many such problems now in use among which the following are good examples:

1. A Study of Marriage and Divorce
2. The Healing Arts and Frauds
3. Feeding the Nation
4. International Disease Control
5. Organisation of the Community for Health
6. Current Issues in Medical Care
7. The Control of Traffic
8. The Care and Distribution of Food
9. Health Insurance Plans
10. Local Problems of Disease Control

11. Food Adulteration
12. Dates and Dating
13. The Origins of Life
14. An Evaluation of Health Advertising

The development of such units of work follows the same steps as outlined for the core type of curriculum on page143. The hygiene or health instructor has precisely the same ends in view, namely, to guide the students in an undertaking of the study of a large problem and to make the study as rich as possible. Applying the process of integration to the separate course in health requires a sense for problems, or ability to develop with the class the various aspects of the problem and a capacity to resist chopping the course up into small fragments of anatomy and physiology for purposes of teaching these facts alone. On must resist the temptation to jump from unit to unit week by week in order "to cover the ground". If the class should choose to study, for example, "Current Issues in Medical Care" this could not be disposed of in a couple of days. It would have to be treated as a core project and several weeks of work would be involved in its planning and execution. Thus, the learning about health problems would be thoroughly accomplished with some problems being given careful attention. This would, of course, be thought by some to be a disadvantage if time is limited or if only one semester in six years can be given to a study of healthful living.

INTEGRATING THE PROGRAMME

If the extension of democracy is one of the goals of education, the school itself must be a democratic place in which to work and live. If health is a goal, all the influences within the school must lead toward and not away from the health of a child. Integrating the school health programme means that all personnel, all programmes of study, all environmental influences, all health activities performed contribute skilfully and in coordination to the best interests of the child. An integrated health programme, then, is one in which the physicians, nurses, teachers, administrators, parents, and public all coordinate their efforts to secure effective results in student health. None may retard the effort. All must agree on policy and programme and then in cooperation and coordination work toward the common end. In the perfectly integrated health programme there would be no safety hazards in the shop, no unguarded traffic corners, no unclean locker rooms, no neurotic teachers to influence susceptible youngsters, and no lack of nursing and medical service. There would be a well-developed disease control programme. A group of stable and healthy teachers would be working with the students. The classrooms would be clean, well lighted and ventilated. The school administration would be willing to invest intelligently in measures for the protection and development of the health of their students. A well-integrated programme would involve everybody, and every influence within the entire school would have to measure up to a high standard in its effect upon the lives of children.

REQUISITES TO ATTAINMENT

Such a completely developed programme as would be presented by integration in the perfect sense would require four major developments, each related to and interdependent with the others:

1. A faculty of the school aware individually of problems involved in child growth and development, and sensitive enough to the importance of the welfare of children to be willing to conduct their programme in relation to child health.

2. A programme of instruction which provides knowledge and experience in healthful living.

3. A programme of health activities and supervision aiming to do those things necessary to attain the objectives in child health agreed to by the faculty as they seek integration in the individual child.

4. A school-community relationship which (a) familiarises the public with the health problems within the school, (b) develops effective teacher-parent relationships, (c) takes the children into the community for a study of health problems,

and (d) utilises to the fullest the professional health personnel of the community.

ADMINISTRATION

A programme of this kind does not spring up overnight nor does it function without careful planning and determined effort. Many people are involved. Considerable work is entailed. Cross-purposes may develop. The administrative direction needs to be firm, thoughtful, and persistent. The following administrative arrangements have been found desirable in the development of a completely integrated health programme:

1. The establishment of a school-community health council.
2. The election of a chairman of the council who will serve as the operating agent in securing the effective development of a health programme in the school.
3. The operation of a series of committees with faculty, student, and public personnel to study and analyse the health conditions and programme and recommend improvements to appropriate authorities.
4. An effective programme of environmental control so that traffic, ventilation, custodial service, sanitation, nutritional services, class schedules, play fields, and other elements influence favourably rather than unfavourably the health of students.
5. Employment where possible of physicians, nurses, psychiatrists, dentists, and other specialised personnel to make their necessary contributions to the development of the child as described in the objectives.
6. A programme of physical education based upon individual differences and providing a programme not only for the normal or typical child but also for the handicapped and atypical.
7. The installation of modern, sanitary, scientific, and useful school equipment in classrooms, laboratories, and offices.

It is evident that a fully developed, well-integrated school health programme is a complex thing. Many persons are included and they must work harmoniously toward a common end. Many things need to be done. Many functions on and beyond the traditional classroom procedures must be instituted. The entire school atmosphere must be charged with the importance of attaining the agreed-upon objectives for each individual child. The concept of integration applied to health education is the most promising of the three existing patterns—direct teaching, correlation, and integration—from the standpoint of getting the complete job done. Only with integrated instruction and integrated programmes can good health permeate the programme entirely. Children can reap the best harvest from their educational opportunities only when every every phase and facet of their educational experience contributes to and none detracts from their best interests. Personnel, curriculum, administration, buildings, atmosphere, colour, field experience, *everything in the school environment* must fit together to the end that the student emerges with as well-integrated a personal development as the influence of the school can make possible.

6

Course Teaching

There are some problems of organisation common to all three patterns of health instruction. Whether the study of health is offered students in a specific course, or by correlation with other areas, or through an integrated plan, certain decisions have to be made concerning the organisation of the material to be used.

The principal problem in course construction is to know what material to select and to whom to teach it. There is much more material to be taught about human health than ever can be placed in the modern school curriculum. The storehouse of scientific information and of social problems is full and overflowing with teachable material only a fraction of which can ever find its way into the school and college experience of a student. The need is to select the most important, most useful, and most interesting problems for the age group being taught.

Furthermore, considerable boredom and wastage result when students are asked to learn material which they covered long ago, studied perhaps in another grade. The timing can be so faulty as to cause the material to be overly simple and repetitious, or so far "over their heads" that little understanding develops. To select and place material in a course of study so that it coincides with student readiness to receive it is a complex problem.

Some repetition, for instance, is desirable. It is implausible to believe that one can learn all there is to know about nutrition in one semester and need never reopen the study at a later year. No student can ever be taught all he needs to know about sex and social relationships in the tenth grade and have it safely assumed that he is then equipped to answer all problems the rest of his life. Health problems in life keep re-occurring, perhaps in a different form, perhaps with different intensities or meanings. They are continuous, furthermore; the child of ten or the adult of eighty has problems which are important to the age and need to be met. It is erroneous to assume that, having received a good one-semester course in the physiology of the human body in the ninth grade, students will thereafter be prepared to solve all their problems of normal and abnormal function even as much as a year later.

The course-of-study maker must realise he has to undertake two processes at the same time, to wit: he not only must choose new material to be introduced at the right time but also must skilfully handle repetitive material, expecting and getting a higher standard of performance from the older students.

The existence of the three patterns of health instruction—direct teaching, integration, and correlation—has further complicated course-of-study construction. A problem like medical care might be planned by the health teacher as something of interest to the eleventh grade in the special course in hygiene, whereas the social science teacher anxious to use the subject in a study of current social problems would find it acceptable in the eighth grade. Or a health teacher may have planned a unit of work on fads and fallacious beliefs as appropriate for the tenth grade only to find in the "core area" that the subject became a six-week study for the seventh-grade children. The human mind being the flexible thing it is and student avidity for the solution of problems being an ever present phenomenon, it becomes impossible, under any conditions, to develop a sequential course of study which would introduce precisely graded material measured out by some formula of interest or readiness and free of all repetition. Such a formula simply does not exist.

Nor will segregation of material into logical categories of relationships be altogether satisfactory. Some teachers have made a practice of thinking of the broad area of health as cut up into sub-areas like personal hygiene, community hygiene, industrial hygiene, physiology, anatomy, disease prevention, home care of the sick, and so on. Frequently courses are organised to cover each on these areas and then one course is offered each semester, either required or elective, until all the courses are "taken". The seventh grade, thus, might get anatomy and physiology "to lay the proper foundation for later understanding of health problems" when all the time that seventh grade was perfectly ready, able, and eager to deal with their contemporary problems of boy-girl friendships, or with their intensifying interest in public affairs. They would be ready to deal profitably with problems of community effort at disease control or recreational development.

As one "expert" put it many years ago: the seventh grade should have a foundation *(sic)* course in anatomy and physiology, the eighth grade human physiology, the ninth personal hygiene, the tenth general and public hygiene, the eleventh safety education, and the twelfth home nursing. Faith in such convenient arrangements is not held by one who knows children's needs and how they learn and who faces course-of-study construction with a modern point of view. The grouping of teachable material into those areas may be convenient for the teacher but causes it to lose much of its meaning and appeal for students. The categories are logical from the adult standpoint but divide the otherwise interesting material into too tight compartments.

Better to mass all the problems of the seventh grade into the seventh-grade course whether they refer to physiology, safety, public health, home nursing, or what not. If, more realistically, one "course" is offered in junior high school and one in the senior, then the materials of the course become those areas, problems, subjects, discussions, investigations, or experiences, regardless of their logical arrangement, which the students want and need at that age. If junior-high girls have need of knowing something about the home care of the sick they should not have to wait until their twelfth year to get it. If the twelfth-graders are studying, as they most assuredly will want to, the pseudoscientific aspects of the manipulative cults, then the need for studying the anatomy of the spine will be apparent. The teacher could not rely upon the anatomy learned in the seventh grade!

Definitions

Three terms need defining and differentiating in order to clarify the process of course-of-study construction: syllabus, course of study, and curriculum. A *syllabus* is an outline of *one course* usually prepared by the teacher or, better, by a process of teacher-student planning and used by students as they pursue their study of the subject. Thus a syllabus in health instruction would be a teaching outline, a guide, a series of units or problems with major areas or problems described and with appropriate suggestions of readings, activities, and other resources to be used. Such an outline generally pertains to a course lasting a semester or a full year.

A *course of study* is best thought of as a series of sequential syllabuses all within the same general area but dealing with new material in each syllabus. Health instruction is not one of those study areas which, when dealt with once, may be put aside forever. Problems of living are continuous and as people grow older they need to seek the solutions to new ones and also obtain better and more advanced information on old ones. Hence, health instruction is ideally offered not just once in twelve years but several times. If instruction in health is offered more than once in the elementary or secondary years, then the sum total or the aggregate of all the outlines followed represents the course of study.

Such a description of a *course of study* is sometimes used interchangeably with *curriculum*. However, the latter term is used more properly in connection with the series of related courses in high school or college which, grouped together, prepare a student for some very large purpose. We speak of the arts curriculum in college, or the curriculum in health education which prepares a person professionally for work in that area, or the college preparatory curriculum in high school, or the science curriculum. One does not ordinarily refer to the curriculum in health instruction and mean the series of instructional experiences a student may get in elementary or secondary school dealing with healthful living. *Course of study* would be a better term for that, and the arrangement of such a course of study is the subject of these paragraphs.

Selection and Placement

Modern health instruction, being principally concerned with the solution of health problems and with guiding the student into a scientifically ordered life, faces the task of finding the problems and dealing with them at the appropriate age. This is not easy to accomplish nor is there a pat formula for telling the teacher the problems to take up in any given year. However, if the teacher is willing to do a little investigating and to allow students to participate in the selection some guides can be mentioned:

1. Finding the Problems

There is no one who can reasonably say he has no health problems. They exist. The invitation to the teacher is to find them. Of these sources student questions are the most fruitful. If teachers will take the time and care to *ask* students what their problems are and what they want to learn about, the students will tell them. Or, by analysing contemporary health literature, radio programmes, books, and other vehicles by which the adult has expressed himself as to the nature of the problems which the public should be informed on, the teacher will get additional valuable suggestions. For example, Oliver E. Byrd of Stanford University has analysed over ten thousand scientific and public health articles appearing in various journals between 1942 and 1948. From the analysis Byrd is able to suggest twenty-one major problem areas with three hundred sub-problems divided over the twenty-one. The major problem areas listed by Byrd are as follows:

Interests of Three Thousand Secondary-School Students in Major Health Areas

	Major Area	Percentage of Students Interested
1.	Habit-Forming Substances	38.0
2.	Family Health	36.4
3.	Safety	36.2
4.	Mental Health and Disease	31.0
5.	Exercise and Body Mechanics	30.0
6.	The Care of Special Organs	29.0
7.	Health as a Social Problem	28.4
8.	Health and the Physical Environment	27.6

9.	Health as a Social Accomplishment	26.0
10.	Chronic and Degenerative Disorders	25.0
11.	Infection and Immunity	24.2
12.	Fatigue and Rest	24.2
13.	Nutrition and Health	24.1
14.	School Health	23.0
15.	Community Health Services	21.0
16.	Heredity and Eugenics	20.0
17.	Excretion and Health	19.0
18.	Health Services and Facilities	18.8
19.	Occupational Health	17.0
20.	Trends and Possibilities	15.0
21.	International Health	14.0

If teachers will consult this grouping of Byrd's they will be able to make appropriate choices for their classes.

2. Selecting the Problems

What problems out of the many hundreds available shall be selected and when shall they be taught? When is the appropriate time to discuss vaccination, say, or heredity? The few studies that have been made on the subject to date are helpful but inconclusive. They principally suggest the following:

(a) Student interests should have an important bearing upon grade placement. If a thousand student questions on health are collected and marked according to the age and grade of the one who asked the question, a sorting of these problems by grades will reveal differences. The differences will not be sharp—that is, any one question may appear over five or six grades—but there will be very real peaks of interest (as judged by frequency) so that the teacher can group other less well-defined problems around them and construct a unit.

(b) Students, if given an opportunity, will ask more questions concerning health than any teacher could possibly use. A selection of them has to be made, and the teacher's judgment as to which of them is important and therefore admissible to the syllabus or course of study is fallible. If a systematic collection of student questions has been made, the questions can then be placed in appropriate categories from which the teacher, using his own judgment, can select, say, forty of what he considers the most important or crucial questions. These can be arranged in mimeographed form so that other children can read and check for importance *to them.* A three-point scale—very important, important, and of no importance—can be used; or a five-point—very important, important, interesting but not important, of little importance, of no importance—can be used and from the results the questions can be ranked according to their cruciality and a place made for a discussion of the crucial problems in the course of study. It is hazardous to allow any one of four persons or groups—the teacher, the health education expert (including the physician, the public health worker), the parent, or the student—to have sole say over what shall be included and when. All could well be consulted, and best results for teaching will be obtained if student judgment is obtained first and then tempered or adjusted by adult opinion.

Two illustrations will show the wisdom of that point. In the study of 4,000 students giving 23,000 questions, there were many questions in two controversial areas—insanity and sex. Students were curious, and eager to learn and to express their problems. Some adult experts, however, strongly urged that neither area be included in the state course of study—too volatile. If the adult judgment had prevailed much of interest and importance would have been lost. Left entirely to students, the problems in sex and reproduction would have come too late to have done the most good. The questions were asked as they appeared in the life of the students. Experts looking at the questions, e.g., some of those relating to venereal disease, sex relations, pregnancy, were of the opinion that the problems they represented *should be taken up a year ahead* of the year in which the frequency peak appeared. It seemed good sense in such important matters to "jump the gun" by *anticipating* needs which would appear later. Much can be said for that point of view.

(c) If it is left entirely to adult or teacher judgment when certain material shall be taught, there is a great risk that the material will be too late and therefore simple, or of no interest, or both. Likewise, if students are allowed full say in selecting material they may miss some of the great problems of public or community health and perhaps some of the health problems of the adult years. Each group—students and adults—must supplement the other, with the student-selected problems taking precedence because of their higher interest and learnability.

(d) As a clue to the interests of secondary-school students the study by Joseph E. Lantagne is useful. We have already quoted his findings on the percentage of students interested in the major problem areas. Dr. Lantagne sought the interests of freshman-sophomore boys and girls, and junior-senior boys and girls with the following results and conclusions:

Ten items of Highest Interest to Freshman and Sophomore Boys

Juvenile delinquency	60 per cent
Atomic warfare	57 per cent
Sex instruction	57 per cent
Tobacco and human health	53 per cent
Hit-and-run drivers	52 per cent
How to report accidents	51 per cent
How to use a gun properly	51 per cent
Sports vs. apparatus activity	51 per cent
Causes of suicide	51 per cent
Cancer	49 per cent

Ten items of Highest Interest to Freshman and Sophomore Girls

Juvenile delinquency	69 per cent
Sex instruction	63 per cent
Safest age to have a baby	60 per cent
How to have good posture	57 per cent
Causes of suicide	57 per cent
Preparation for marriage	57 per cent
Cancer	56 per cent
Lifelong care of the eyes	53 per cent
Dangers of sleeping pills	52 per cent

Ten items of Highest Interest to Junior and Senior Boys

Sex instruction	63 per cent
Sweets and dental decay	60 per cent
Juvenile delinquency	60 per cent
Tobacco and human health	59 per cent
Atomic warfare	57 per cent
Causes of suicide	55 per cent
How to report accidents	52 per cent
Speed and accidents	52 per cent
Cancer	52 per cent
Hit-and-run drivers	51 per cent

Ten items of Higher Interest to Junior and Senior Girls

Sex instruction	77 per cent
Preparation for marriage	73 per cent
Juvenile delinquency	73 per cent
Causes of mental illness	66 per cent
Causes of suicide	66 per cent
Safest age to have a baby	65 per cent
Cancer	62 per cent
Pregnancy and health	62 per cent
Lifelong care of the eyes	59 per cent
Mental health and marriage	58 per cent

Some of Lantagne's conclusions and recommendations are pertinent to the problem of selection. These are:

Conclusions

1. There is a common core of health interests among high school pupils regardless of age or sex which should prove useful for curriculum construction.

2. There are negligible differences in health interests in respect to religion.

3. There are some variations in health interests between boys and girls; this information should prove useful for segregated classes in health.

4. There are some variations in health interests by grade placement, but these are relatively few in number.

5. Some health problems long considered by teachers to have little interest-appeal to pupils have ben shown to rank highly in student interest. Cancer is a good example of this.

6. Some health problems entirely overlooked by some health educators have been revealed as ranking highly in student interest.

Recommendations:

1. All curriculum directors and teachers of health on the secondary school level should explore pupil health interests as a basis for partial determination of curriculum content.

2. Health classes should not be segregated by sex, inasmuch as there is a fairly common community of health interests among both boys and girls.

3. On the basis of pupil interest greater emphasis should be given in the secondary school curriculum to the category of habit-forming substances which leads all others in interest quality.

4. On the basis of pupil health interests greater emphasis should also be given to family health, safety, and mental health and disease in the secondary school curriculum.

3. Arranging the Courses

There is no standard practice in American education regarding either the content of health courses or the grades in which they shall be taught. In elementary education some health instruction is usually given each year in terms of the needs and age of the children. But at the junior- and senior-high-school level there is a wide variation in practice. If there is a tendency discernible at the moment it is to arrange one course in the junior years and one in the senior. This seems to be an emerging pattern in secondary schools.

If such is the case then the teacher needs to distribute the consideration of problems over the two courses in terms of need and interest. There will be some desirable duplication or rather re-emphasis and, with only two semester opportunities, there will be many health problem areas ignored altogether.

Teachers face this problem locally, making their plans in terms of local needs and possibilities. State courses of study are helpful in suggesting areas to be covered by grades or ages.

One state course of study, for example, in an effort to show how various parts of a major problem area might be distributed over courses in the seventh, ninth, and twelfth grades, makes the following suggestions. The major area is "Keeping Well". The seventh-grade section would include the following:

1. Cause and spread of colds and sore throat.
2. Spread of bacteria—germs.
3. Specific diseases.
4. The heart: strength—phenomena of beating—fainting and dizziness.
5. Nature and use of first aid for burns and sprains, resuscitation, bites.
6. Effects of smoking tobacco.
7. Effects of drinking alcohol.

The ninth grade would take up these problems:

1. Symptoms and self-diagnosis.
2. Use of medicines.
3. Use of patent medicines.
4. Cause, prevention, and spread of the common cold.
5. Tuberculosis and influenza.
6. Further discussion of other specific diseases.
7. Inoculations and immunity.
8. Vaccination for smallpox.
9. Death rates from degenerative diseases.
10. Blood transfusion.
11. Traffic control.

And the twelfth grade these:

1. Advanced discussion of inoculations, immunity, allergic reactions.
2. Anemia, appendicitis, diabetes, nephritis, and other advanced diseases.
3. Constipation.
4. First aid for heat prostration, shocks, suffocation.

The above areas of study for the seventh, ninth, and twelfth grades do not represent all the material in hygiene which can be taught in the general category of keeping well. The material left out would be recommended for grades eight, ten, and eleven. A six-year graded course of study would cover the entire area. If six years were not available then the material would have to be condensed into the years which are being used.

Thus, the consideration of keeping well would be full—and graded according to the interests and needs of students.

4. Criteria for Syllabuses or Courses of Study

The experiences which students will have as they move through instruction in health should be worthwhile.

7

Teacher Preparation for Child Development

Until very recently colleges and universities have made no effort to provide curriculums for the health education teacher. For years the personnel has come from other fields, principally physical education, nursing, home economics, and the biological sciences. Occasionally, and mainly in colleges, the teachers of hygiene have been physicians. Two developments in recent years indicate, however, that in the future a health education teacher may have the adequate preparation the area deserves: (1) The four- and five-year curriculums for preparing physical education teachers are being materially strengthened in school health education, and (2) major curriculums are being developed specifically for the purpose of preparing teachers in school and public health education.

To teach successfully in health education, one needs to know a great deal. It is not unreasonable to point out that preparation in physical education *per se,* or nursing, or medicine, or home economics, does not equip one well to serve in a health instruction capacity. That is, there is no reason to believe that such specialised training *and nothing else* will suffice. Something more is needed before one can competently undertake to construct and use a course of study in school health instruction. This additional preparation could well consist of four areas of study:

1. The philosophy, principles, techniques, and evaluating procedures of modern education. Not just anyone can successfully teach any more than just anyone can practice medicine or nursing. Preparation is necessary, techniques

must be practiced, knowledge must be acquired. A point of view and philosophy need to be developed. Thus, anyone who teaches must be familiar with the professional aspects of education itself.

2. Hygiene: A preprofessional understanding of anatomy and physiology as may have been learned in undergraduate days is helpful and basic, but insufficient to enable the teacher to meet the many demands of modern hygiene teaching. Preparation of a thorough sort must be had in personal hygiene and in general and community hygiene.

3. Special Areas: Because much of the interesting and absorbing part of any course or course of study will deal with problems involved in immunology, sex, reproduction and marriage, nutrition, genetics, mental hygiene, and child development, the teacher should be especially well prepared in these areas. Not only should collegiate courses be undertaken in each of these spheres but the teacher-on-the-job should constantly read scientific material in these areas in order to keep up-to-date.

4. Personnel and Guidance: Because school health instruction is such a personal matter, because it deals so frequently with individual and highly personal problems, the teacher must be prepared to deal personally with students. They will come to him for all sorts of advice. They will seek counsel for their difficulties. It must be clear that the teacher is in no sense a physician (unless of course he is, in fact, by training) and must not pose as one in any way. He will, however, have many opportunities to give help in organising the personal regimen of his students and will need to have many resources ready to use in his referral and guidance work.

These are the four principal areas which need to be secured against oversight when one enters school health education from other fields. The curriculum which prepares directly for health education will undoubtedly contain adequate preparation in the physical and biological sciences, the social sciences, psychology, education, and principles and techniques of school and public health education. These areas studied in relation to thorough preparation in the many aspects of hygiene should provide one with sufficient background to undertake teaching in school health education.

IN-SERVICE PREPARATION

There is no field which exceeds school health education in its demand upon the teacher to keep up-to-date. To interpret to students the findings from fast-moving science alone requires constant study of scientific literature, constant attendance at professional meetings. To dispel the folklore and tradition, to eliminate the superstitution and quackery, to answer the thousands of simple daily questions related to healthful living requires constant and discriminating reading of professional materials. To know truth from fiction, fact from fancy requires the development of a sense of discrimination which can only be cultivated by a liberal and persistent reading of the literature from the scientific fields.

The teacher in service could well follow a programme of self-improvement involving something of *all* the following suggestions:

1. The acquisition of a professional library of standard works in hygiene and its special fields. The bibliography at the end of this chapter makes specific suggestions for such books.

2. The subscription to professional journals. From three to five weekly or monthly magazines are virtually indispensable to a teacher in health education. Articles on recent discoveries, new points of view, experiences of others are needed in the modern classroom. The bibliography has several suggestions in this category.

3. Attendance at lectures, institutes, conferences, workshops, and other such special events.

4. Graduate university training. It can well be recommended that teachers should return to the campus periodically for additional courses, perhaps in areas not previously explored, perhaps to acquire new information in familiar areas. Such study is highly profitable particularly in some of the special areas of school health education to which general courses have not given full treatment.

There is, of course, no substitute for personal interest and zeal for self-improvement. Health instruction is a live, vibrant field, deserving imaginative and enthusiastic teachers. It can be ruined by teachers who are still dispensing information a half-century old or whose conception of teaching is typically to have the students memorise the enzymes in the alimentary canal. It can be absorbing, however, if the teacher is alert to modern problems, is scientific in his hygiene and contemporary in his educational point of view, and is willing to keep himself abreast of the times by diligent and constant application to the best reading of the day.

SELECTED RESOURCES FOR TEACHERS

In addition to selected readings at the end of each chapter the following resources will be helpful to the teacher:

Resource Books on Personal and Public Health

Ackerman, Lloyd, *Health and Hygiene,* The Jacques Cattell Press, Lancaster, Penna., 1943.

Bauer, W.W., *Health Questions Answered,* The Bobbs-Merrill Co., Indianapolis, 1937.

Beck, Lester F., *Human Growth,* Harcourt, Brace and Co., New York, 1949.

Birkeland, J.M., *Microbiology and Man,* Appleton-Century-Crofts, New York, 1949.

Byrd, Oliver E., *Health Instruction Yearbook,* Stanford University Press, Stanford University, annual.

Cattell, Raymond B., *Personality: A Systematic, Theoretical, and Factual Study,* New York, McGraw-Hill Book Co., 1950.

Crow, Lester and Alice, *Mental Hygiene,* McGraw-Hill Book Co., New York, 1951.

Diehl, Harold S., *Textbook of Healthful Living,* McGraw-Hill Book Co., New York, 1941.

Dublin, Louis I., *The Facts of Life from Birth to Death,* Metropolitan Life Insurance Company, New York, 1951.

Erskine, Earl B., *Hygiene and Public Health*, Prentice-Hall, Inc., New York, 1949.

Hagman, Patricia (ed.), *Good Health for You and Your Family*, A. S. Barnes & Co., New York, 1951.

Harrowes, William, *Human Personality and Its Minor Disorders*, Williams and Wilkins Co., Baltimore, 1949.

Liebman, Joshua L., *Peace of Mind*, Simon and Schuster, Inc., New York, 1946.

Maxey, Kenneth F., *Rosenau's Preventive Medicine in Hygiene*, Appleton-Century-Crofts, New York, 7th ed., 1951.

Montagu, Ashley, *On Being Intelligent*, Henry Schuman, Inc., New York, 1951.

Rugen, Mabel (ed.), *The Physical Educator Asks About Health*, Report of the Joint Committee on Health Problems in Education of the National Education Association and the American Medical Association, Washington, 1951.

Scheinfeld, Amram, *You and Heredity*, Lippincott, Philadelphia.

Spiegelman, Mortimer, *Health Progress in the United States*, American Enterprise Association, Inc., New York, 1951.

Stolz, Herbert Rowell, and Stolz, Lois Meek, *Somatic Development of Adolescent Boys*, The Macmillan Company, New York, 1951.

Turner, Clair E., *Community Health Educator's Compendium of Knowledge*, C. V. Mosby Co., St. Louis, 1951.

Turner, Clair E., *Personal and Community Health*, C. V. Mosby Co., St. Louis, 8th ed., 1948.

Van Buskirk, Edgar, *Principles of Healthful Living*, Dryden Press, New York, 1948.

Vaughn, Wayland F., *Personal and Social Adjustment: Foundations of Mental Health*, Odyssey Press, New York, 1952.

Watson, E.H., and Lowrey, G. H., *Growth and Development of Children*, Yearbook Publishers, Chicago, 1951.

Williams, Jesse Feiring, *Personal Hygiene Applied,* W. B. Saunders Co., Philadelphia, 9th ed., 1950.

Williams, Jesse Feiring, and Wetherill, Lloyd G., *Personal and Community Hygiene Applied,* W. B. Saunders Co., Philadelphia, 1950.

BOOKS ON THE PROGRAMME OF SCHOOL HEALTH EDUCATION

American Medical Association and National Education Association, *School Health Services,* National Education Association, Washington, D.C., 1953.

Brownell, Clifford Lee, *Principles of Health Education Applied,* McGraw-Hill Book Co., New York, 1949.

Coops, Helen L., *Health Education in the Elementary Schools,* A. S. Barnes and Co., New York, 1950.

Fields, Morey R., and Edgerton, Avis E., *Teacher's Guide for Health Education,* Remsen Press, Brooklyn, 1949.

Grout, Ruth E., *Health Teaching in Schools,* W. B. Saunders Co., Philadelphia, 1953.

Lamkin, Nina B., *Health Education in Rural Schools and Communities,* A. S. Barnes and Co., New York, 1946.

National Education Association, *Health Education,* Joint Committee on Health Problems in Education of the National Education Association and the American Medical Association, Washington, 1948.

National Education Association, *Health in Schools,* Twentieth Yearbook of the American Association of School Administrators, National Education Association, Washington, 1951.

National Education Association, National Committee on School Health Policies, *Suggested School Health Policies,* Washington, 2nd ed., 1946.

Nyswander, Dorothy B., *Solving School Health Problems,* The Commonwealth Fund, New York, 1942.

Sharman, J. B., *Introduction to Health Education,* A. S. Barnes and Co., New York, 1948.

Turner, C. W., *School Health and Health Education*, C. V. Mosby Co., St. Louis, 1952.

Wheatley, George M., and Hallock, Grace T., *Health Observation of School Children*, McGraw-Hill Book Co., New York, 1951.

Williams, Jesse Feiring, and Abernathy, Ruth, *Health Education in Schools*, Ronald Press Co., New York, 1949.

RESOURCES ON CHILD GROWTH AND DEVELOPMENT

American Academy of Pediatrics Committee for the Study of Child Health Services, *Child Health Services and Pediatric Education*, Report of a Committee for the Study of Child Health Services, The American Academy of Pediatrics with the cooperation of the US Public Health Service and the US Children's Bureau, The Commonwealth Fund, New York, 1949.

American Council on Education, Commission on Teacher Education, *Helping Teachers Understand Children*, The Council, Washington, 1945.

Association for Childhood Education, *Healthful Living for Children*, Washington, 1944.

Averill, Lawrence A., *The Psychology of the Elementary School Child*, Longmans, Green and Co., New York, 1949.

Baruch, Dorothy W., *Understanding Young Children*, Bureau of Publications, Teachers College, Columbia University, New York, 1949.

Beck, Lester F., *Human Growth*, Harcourt, Brace and Co., New York, 1949.

Breckenridge, M. E., and Vincent, E. L., *Child Development: Physical and Psychological Growth Through the School Years*, W. B. Saunders Co., Philadelphia, 2nd ed., 1949.

Children's Bureau, *Your Child from Six to Twelve*, Department of Labour, Washington, 1949.

Cole, Luella, *Psychology of Adolescence*, Rinehart and Co., New York, rev. ed., 1948.

Dunbar, Flanders, *Your Child's Mind and Body—A Practical Guide for Parents*, Random House, New York, 1949.

Faculty University School, *How Children Develop,* The Ohio State University, Columbus, 1946.

Furniss, Austin, *Handbook of Child Health,* Sylviro Publications Ltd., London, 1950.

Gallagher, J. Ruswell, *Understand Your Son's Adolescence,* Little, Brown and Co., Boston, 1951.

Garrison, Karl C., *Psychology of Exceptional Children,* Ronald Press Co., New York, 1950.

Gesell, A. L., and Amatruda, C. S., *Development Diagnosis,* Paul B. Hoeber, Inc., New York, 2nd ed., 1947.

Goodspeed, Helen C., Mason, Esther R., and Woods, Elizabeth L., *Child Care and Guidance,* J. B. Lippincott Co., Philadelphia, 1948.

Hathaway, Winfred, *Education and Health of the Partially Seeing Child,* National Society for the Prevention of Blindness, Columbia University Press, New York, rev. ed., 1947.

Havighurst, Robert J., and Taba, Hilda, *Adolescent Character and Personality,* John Wiley and Sons, Inc., New York, 1949.

Jenkins, G. G., Chacter, Helen, and Bauer, W. W., *These Are Your Children: How They Develop and How to Guide Them,* Scott, Foresman and Co., Chicago, 1949.

Jersild, Arthur T., *Child Development and the Curriculum,* Bureau of Publications, Teachers College, Columbia University, New York, 1946.

Josselyn, Irene M., *Psycho-Social Development of Children,* Family Service Association of America, New York, 1948.

Keliher, Alice V., *Life and Growth,* D. Appleton-Century Co., New York, 1938.

National Research Council, *Physique, Personality, and Scholarships,* Society for Research in Child Development, The Council, Washington, 1943.

Olson, W. C., *Child Development,* D. C. Heath and Co., Boston, 1949.

Plant, James S., *The Envelope: A Study of the Impact of the World upon the Child,* The Commonwealth Fund, New York, 1950.

Symonds, Percival M., *Adolescent Fantasy,* Columbia University Press, New York, 1949.

Watson, E. H., and Lowrey, G. H., *Growth and Development of Children,* Yearbook Publishers, Chicago, 1951.

Williamson, E. G., *Counselling Adolescents,* McGraw-Hill Book Co., New York, 1950.

ON SAFETY EDUCATION AND SAFETY PROGRAMMES

Fishbein, Morris, and Irwin, Leslie W., *First Aid Training,* Lyons and Carnahan, Chicago, 1943.

Hyde, Florence Slown, and Slown, Ruth Clara, *Safety Programmes and Activities,* Beckley-Cardy Co., Chicago, 2nd rev. ed., 1938.

National Committee on Safety Education, *Safety in Physical Education for the Classroom Teacher,* National Education Association, Washington, 1952.

National Education Association, *Safety Education,* Eighteenth Yearbook of the American Association of School Administrators, National Education Association, Washington, 1938.

National Safety Council, *Safety Education Methods, Elementary Schools,* The Council, Chicago, 1940.

National Safety Council, *Safety Education Methods, Secondary Schools,* The Council, Chicago, 1940.

National Safety Council, *Safety Education in Rural Schools,* The Council, Chicago, 1939.

National Safety Council, *Safety in Physical Education and Recreation,* The Council, Chicago, 1941.

Olson, Lyla M., *Prevention, First Aid, and Emergencies,* W. B. Saunders Co., Philadelphia, 1946.

Stack, Herbert J., Siebrecht, Elmer B., and Elkow, J. Duke,

Education for Safe Living, Prentice-Hall, Inc., New York, 2nd ed., 1949.

RESOURCES ON SOCIAL AND FAMILY LIVING

Allison, Samuel D., and Johnson, June, *VD Manual for Teachers,* Emerson Books, Inc., New York, 1946.

Biegel, Hugo G., *Encyclopedia of Sex Education,* Stephen Daye Press, New York, 1952.

Bowman, Henry A., *Marriage for Moderns,* McGraw-Hill Book Co., New York, 1948.

Bundesen, Herman N., *Toward Manhood,* J. B. Lippencott Co., Philadelphia, 1951.

Child Study Association of America, *Parents' Questions,* Harper & Brothers, New York, rev. ed., 1947.

Christensen, Harold T., *Marriage Analysis,* Ronald Press Co., New York, 1950.

Corner, George W., *Attaining Womanhood: A Doctor Talks to Girls About Sex,* Harper & Brothers, New York, 1952.

DeSchweinitz, Karl, *Growing Up,* The Macmillan Company, New York, 1935.

Drummond, Laura W., *Youth and Instruction in Marriage and Family Living,* Teachers College, Columbia University, New York, 1942.

Duvall, Evelyn, and Hill, R., *When You Marry,* D. C. Heath and Co., Boston, 1945.

Good, Frederick L., and Kelly, Otis F., *Marriage: Morals and Medical Ethics,* P. J. Kenedy & Sons, New York, 1951.

Griffith, Edward F., *A Sex Guide to Happy Marriage,* Emerson Books, Inc., New York, 1952.

Groves, Ernest R., Skinner, Edna L., and Swenson, Sadie S., *The Family and Its Relationships,* J. B. Lippincott Co., Philadelphia, 1946.

Gruenberg, B. J., and Kaukonen, J. L., *High Schools and Sex*

Education, Government Printing Office, Washington, 1940.

Kinsey, Alfred C., Pomeroy, Wardell B., and Martin, Clyde E., *Sexual Behaviour in the Human Male,* W. B. Saunders Co., Philadelphia, 1948.

Kirkendall, Lester A., *Sex Education as Human Relations,* Inor Publishing, New York, 1950.

Klein, Robert A., and Schuman, B. J., *How to Have a Baby: Techniques for Fertile Marriage,* Hermitage Press, New York, 1951.

Mooney, Belle S., *How Shall I Teach My Child?* Cadillac Publishing Co., New York, 1944.

Mudd, Emily Hartshorne, *Practice of Marriage Counselling,* Association Press, New York, 1951.

Sadler, W. S., *A Doctor Talks to Teen-agers: A Psychiatrist's Advice to Youth,* C. V. Mosby Co., St. Louis, 1948.

Scheinfeld, Amram, *Women and Men,* Harcourt, Brace and Co., New York, 1944.

Stone, Abraham, and Hines, Norman E., *Planned Parenthood—A Practical Guide to Birth Control Methods,* Viking Press, New York, 1951.

Welshimer, Helen, *The Questions Girls Ask,* E. P. Dutton and Co, New York, rev. ed., 1949.

Whitman, Howard, *Let's Tell the Truth About Sex,* Pellegrini and Cudahy, Inc., New York, 1948.

ON NUTRITION

Bauer, W. W., Eat *What You Want,* Greenberg; Publisher, New York, 1942.

Bogert, L. Jean, *Good Nutrition for Everybody,* University of Chicago Press, Chicago, 1942.

Bradbury, Dorothy E., and Drenckhahn, Vivian N., *Good Food and Nutrition for Young People and Their Families,* John Wiley and Sons., Inc., New York, 1946.

Gillett, Lucy H., *Nutrition in Public Health,* W. B. Saunders Co., Philadelphia, 1946.

Hawley, Estelle E., and Carden, Grace, *The Art and Science of Nutrition,* C. V. Mosby Co., St. Louis, 1944.

Kilander, Holger F., *Nutrition for Health,* McGraw-Hill Book Co., New York, 1951.

Pfaffman, Mary, and Stern, Frances, *How to Teach Nutrition to Children,* Barrows and Co., New York, 1942.

Sherman, Henry C., *The Science of Nutrition,* Columbia University Press, New York, 1943.

Wilmot, Jennie S., and Batjer, Margaret Q., *Food for the Family,* J. B. Lippincott Co., Philadelphia, 1944.

Books on Community Health Organisation

Buell, Bradley, and associates, *Community Planning for Human Services,* Columbia University Press, New York, 1952.

Cavins, Harold M., *National Health Agencies,* Public Affairs Press, Washington, 1945.

Emerson, Haven, *The Selected Papers of Haven Emerson,* American Public Health Association, New York, 1951.

Ginsburg, Ethel L., *Public Health Is People,* The Commonwealth Fund, New York, 1950.

Gunn, S. M., and Platt, P. S., *Voluntary Health Agencies,* Ronald Press Co., New York, 1945.

Hanlon, John, *Principles of Public Health Administration,* C. V. Mosby Co., St. Louis, 1950.

Hiscock, Ira V., *Community Health Organisation,* The Commonwealth Fund, New York, 4th ed., 1950.

Johns, Ray, and DeMarche, David F., *Community Organisation and the Agency Responsibility,* Association Press, New York, 1951.

Paterson, Robert G., *Foundations of Community Health Education,* McGraw-Hill Book Co., New York, 1950.

Patterson, Raymond S., and Roberts, Beryl J., *Community Health Education in Action,* C. V. Mosby Co., St. Louis, 1951.

Shyne, Ann W., *Community Organisation for Child Welfare,* Montgomery Country, Pennsylvania, 1943.

Smillie, Wilson G., *Public Health Administration in the United States,* 3rd ed., The Macmillan Company, New York, 3rd ed., 1947.

PERIODICALS FOR THE TEACHER'S OR SCHOOL LIBRARY

American Journal of Hygiene, 615 N. Wolfe St., Baltimore, Md.

American Journal of Nursing, American Nurses Association, 50 W. 50th St., New York, N.Y.

American Journal of Public Health, 1790 Broadway, New York, N.Y.

Channels, National Publicity Council for Health and Welfare Services, Inc., 257 Fourth Ave., New York, N.Y.

Child Development, Society for Research in Child Development, National Research Council, 2101 Constitution Ave., Washington, D.C.

Child Study, Child Study Association of America, 221 W. 57th St., New York, N.Y.

Childhood Education, Association for Childhood Education, International, 1200 15th St., N.W., Washington, D.C.

Health Articles of the Week, The National Health Council, 1790 Broadway, New York, N.Y.

Health Bulletin for Teachers, Metropolitan Life Insurance Co., Health and Welfare Division, 1 Madison Ave., New York, N.Y.

Journal of the American Dental Association, The American Dental Association, 222 E. Superior St., Chicago, Ill.

Journal of the American Medical Association, 535 N. Dearborn St., Chicago, Ill.

Journal of Exceptional Children, International Council for Exceptional Children, Saranac, Mich., Michigan State Normal College, Ypsilanti, Mich.

Journal of Health and Physical Education, American Association for Health, Physical Education, and Recreation, 1201 16th St., N.W., Washington, D.C.

Journal of School Health, American School Health Association, 3335 Main St., Buffalo, N.Y.

Mental Hygiene, National Commission for Mental Hygiene, 1790 Broadway, New York, N.Y.

National Parent-Teacher Magazine, National Congress of Parents and Teachers, 600 S. Michigan Blvd., Chicago, Ill.

National Safety News, National Safety Council, 20 N. Wacker Drive, Chicago, Ill.

Nutrition Reviews, The Nutrition Foundation, Inc., Chrysler Bldg., New York, N.Y.

Public Health Nursing, National Organisation of Public Health Nursing, 1790 Broadway, New York, N.Y.

Public Health Reports, US Public Health Service, 19th St. and Constitution Ave., N.W., Washington, D.C.

Public Safety, National Safety Council, 20 N. Wacker Drive, Chicago, Ill.

The Child, Children's Bureau, Federal Security Agency, Washington, D.C.

Today's Health, American Medical Association, 535 N. Dearborn St., Chicago, Ill.

Understanding Your Child, The National Committee for Mental Hygiene, Inc., 1790 Broadway, New York, N.Y.

8

Administration and Personnel Relationships for Child Development

It is apparent to all experienced workers that the development and execution of a programme of school health education is not a one-man job. It requires the cooperative effort and effective coordination of several professionally trained people willing to pool their knowledge and ability for a common beneficiary—the school child. In its beginning the programme may have involved only a teacher of physiology who taught young people some of the great facts of life. Or it may have centred in a physician who came to the school to examine for vision and teeth and who considered the examinations of value only as a source of statistical summaries. In other situations the physical education teacher was the sole purveyor of health instruction and his work was devoted to the building of the muscular strength and coordination that might come from the exercises of the day. School health education in the nineteenth century was well intentioned but inadequate and was conducted chiefly by professional personnel working by themselves and without a planned relationship to each other.

In contemporary times the situation is wholly different. In a fully integrated school health programme the child as a whole takes the centre of the stage. Objectives in child development are agreed to and sought. His health and welfare, his psychological and social development, his safety and his immunity all become prime considerations along with his intellectual and academic advancement. It becomes imperative that all things which go on within the school experience contribute to and do not detract from the total development of the student. To bring this ideal to its fullest maturity obviously requires the highly coordinated effort of many persons, none working in isolation from the other but all within a master plan to the ultimate benefit of childhood.

SOME BASIC CONSIDERATIONS

Before dealing with administrative relationships it would be well to consider several matters basic to the attainment of such cooperative action as is needed in a well-rounded school health programme.

1. *Many talents are needed.* There is a place in a full health programme for physicians, nurses, teachers; special teachers of physical education, sight saving, speech reading, home economics; psychologists, dental hygienists, dentists, social case workers, immunologists, dietitians, sanitary engineers, school administrators, and some others of specialised and non-specialised ability. The talents of all these can be used. Their counterparts from the consumers' side are, of course, the children and their parents. Little can be done without some of these key professionals; likewise little can be done without the full participation and cooperation of these consumers. A school health programme is truly a huge experiment in group action aimed at the improvement of the life of a given child.

2. *The talents must be used in an atmosphere of mutual respect and professional confidence.* Success in school health education comes when each professional recognises the worth of the contribution of the other, refuses to usurp more scope or more credit than is his due, and shares in the thinking, planning, and execution necessary to get the job done. It is at this point that many school programmes have wavered and some collapsed. It is not always easy to get a group of individualists to work cooperatively. Sometimes the teacher assumes far too much prerogative in the guidance of a child or, worse, discounts the efforts of others as they try to affect the life of one of her classroom children. Sometimes the physical education teacher assumes far too much in the sphere of diagnosis or fails to make use of the best of scientific information in giving health

instruction. Sometimes the physician, prepared in a highly individualised professional tradition, finds himself unable to appreciate the work of others or, worse, insists that all school health work be considered his private reservation and all others subject to his direction. Such manifestations, in whomever they occur, are always unfortunate. They jeopardise the attainment of the objectives in child development.

Careful study must be made of personnel interrelationships, and personalities must be so geared as to allow for smooth operation with no friction born out of professional jealousy or mistrust.

3. *A programme of school health education should not be an object of charity.* Contributions to it should not be sought on that basis. In the early days many physicians and some nurses were asked to give their services free for examinations or screening. Others were urged to contribute books, equipment, or time. Private practitioners were asked to examine children and give the summary of their findings to the school. With rare exceptions this charitable approach to administration has been a failure. Physicians have their professional competence to sell. Others have specialised talent costing them years to develop. Such skills should be bought and paid for by the school if it expects to make good use of them. No part of the programme which involves any measure of *professional* competence should be performed without adequate compensation.

4. *A school health education programme is an educational enterprise—not a medical one.* It is *not* in competition with the practice of medicine. It is complementary to medicine, supports it, educates school children to patronise it, discovers individual needs for it, but does not compete with it. School health education has no aim eventually to substitute its services for those of the private physician.

There has been much misunderstanding here. There are some physicians and public health workers who have the misconception that the health interest of educators is a proprietary one. They are apprehensive lest the outcome of school health education be the destruction of the private practice of medicine and the substitution of some form of state medicine. Three things must be said in this connection. First, there is evidence to show that where complete school health education programmes have existed there is not less but more demand for the services of physicians and public health workers. Second, the school has a legitimate purpose in concerning itself with the health of the child. It realises that education cannot go on fully and constructively unless the child is in good health. It tries not to waste public funds attempting to educate children who are unfit to receive an education. Third, to teach about health, to organise experiences pertaining to it, and to carry on education in a healthful environment are all parts of the basic purposes of a school. The school must give its students control over the means of existence, over life. Certainly learning about health and living healthfully can be considered in no other way than as a means of furthering our existence and theirs within the scope of education. There is no infringement upon the province of the physician, the hospital, or the clinic. There is, thus, no ground for discoordination. A school health education programme deserves the cooperation of all professional personnel united to serve within it.

5. *The school is in no position to finance extensive curative or remedial medical or dental programmes at public expense.* Of course, exceptions are being made but in nearly every instance the exceptions are endorsed by the medical and dental groups in the community who appreciate the fact that only through these means will the children involved be properly cared for. Principally, however, the school acts merely as an interested community agency willing to stimulate others into finding the means to do a needed piece of work for the benefit of handicapped or ailing students.

It is well recognised that there are millions of people unable financially or unprepared intellectually to seek and get medical service. The school sees their need, at least in so far as the need is expressed through the children, and is in a position to encourage social and public agencies in their efforts to bring medical aid to them.

6. *The emphasis in school health education has moved from the mass to the individual.* This is a general trend in all of education.

It becomes no longer important to survey thousands and thousands of children in an annual physical examination unless within such a programme *each* child is given thorough attention and his individual status and needs are discovered and adequately dealt with. Just as physical education has moved from the former practice of marching thousands on the field for the same exercises given to all at the same time, to a programme of activities taught in small groups and in the light of individual needs, so also has school health education veered away from mass production. As Baumgartner expresses it: "For school health this [means] that finding what the individual child needs and building a programme to meet those needs comes first."

Thus, in all of school health education, as in all education, the workers must never lose sight of the fact that they are dealing with persons—with individuals. Neither the medical office nor that of the counsellors nor the physical educators can, in the light of this trend, ever become impersonal centres where so many cases are handled per day, and where the individuality of the student is observed with cold professional efficiency. Little of educational value and much of harm becomes the product when any phase of school health education loses the personal touch and becomes a mechanical thing.

ADMINISTRATIVE ORGANISATION

From an understanding of the foregoing six basic considerations, which underlie work in school health education, one can believe that administrative organisation would be somewhat complex. And yet, as state and local programmes have developed, it is true that certain agreements have arisen as to points of view and, although there is little standard practice in local organisation, some similarities in the placement of responsibility are beginning to appear.

In the Federal Government

It is generally well known that the federal government has little or no administrative control over local school procedures and programmes. Except in those instances when federal money is appropriated (e.g. for school lunches, for vocational agriculture) the government in Washington exercises merely an advisory and research function in relation to education in general and to school health education. Where federal money is appropriated for the support of educational enterprises. Congress has usually established minimum standards for local acceptance and left the enforcement of those standards to an appropriate executive branch. Otherwise, the tradition of local autonomy in education persists, and states are reluctant to give up their rights in determining the kind of education their people should have in favour of control from Washington. As time goes on, however, and the movement for equalising educational opportunity over the nation gains more popularity, it is entirely possible that the government will have increasing control over the administration of local programmes because of the use of federal funds in their support.

Furthermore, Congress may some day become interested in legislation specifically directed at school and college health and physical education and be willing to subsidise much of a school health education programme as it is now known. Such bills as may be drawn for that purpose will probably call for the acknowledgement of basic minimum standards in programme and personnel. Depending entirely upon the state and local administration thereof, such bills may, thus, have a salutary effect upon the extension of the benefits of school health education to more and more children.

There are many executive agencies in the government now having influence in school health education. Chief among these are the Office of Education, the Public Health Service, the Children's Bureau, and the Department of Agriculture. There are many others. At one time it was determined that over seventy bureaus or agencies within the government had something to do with the health or recreation of the people! But the above-named four are the principal ones. The Office of Education maintains an office for a Senior Specialist in Health and Physical Education and his staff, and from this office comes a great deal of assistance in the form of information, field consultation service, research data, and information on trends which is of use to local and state groups. The other three agencies are likewise of great assistance to local groups in providing information. The four operate together in giving suggestions on policy and standards which guide school systems over the nation in the development of health education. Teachers and administrators will find all four agencies available for consultation by field representatives or by correspondence.

In State Governments

Three-fourths of the states have active programmes in school health education operating out of state departments of public instruction or state departments of health or both. These departments are the instruments used by the state legislatures for the execution of whatever legislation is passed benefiting the health of the school child. It becomes exceedingly important to all personnel in school health and physical education locally to know the limitations and possibilities of programme development as established by state law.

State supervisory programmes not only interpret existing statutes for the benefit of communities but extend a great deal of consultative service as well. These programmes are ordinarily located in departments of public instruction and are thus under the administrative direction of the state superintendent. In some states, however, the office is located in the department of health and in others the two share the work. The most fortunate states are those that not only have such programmes established but have the two principal departments—health and education—working in complete harmony and in enthusiastic support of each other in their relations to school health education. Where friction or misunderstanding exists between these two departments the echoes of it are heard in disharmonies in state and local medical societies and educational associations, and between local physicians and educators.

In Cities and Smaller Communities

Below the state level is found an old, traditional standard practice in regard to school administration. The city, district, and country board of education has long enjoyed the privilege of determining its own programme and employing its own personnel subject only to the approval of the state department of education. Thus, a superintendent of schools assumes responsibility for all that enter the educational programme and is the administrative and executive officer of the school system.

With the development of a modern programme of health education including both health instruction and health service phases, this framework of administration has to be re-examined to see if the job of health education can get done within it. As soon as schools began to employ physicians and nurses, as soon as physical examinations, immunisation programmes, and screening and referral systems were established, the question arose as to whether all of that sort of activity did not belong under the administrative jurisdiction of boards of health rather than boards of education. Should physicians and nurses be employed as school personnel and work in schools and communities without any official relationship to the official health agency or should the local health authority supervise and conduct all of the activities going on within the school? Under whose banner should the *school* health service function?

The problem has never been solved universally in all our states. There have developed *two* patterns of administration—one in which schools operate their own health services and the other in which the health department operates the programme for the schools. Both patterns are probably here to stay; neither is wholly in error, nor is either wholly strong. The problem which confronts local authorities is one of getting the best help and counsel to the child with the least friction and wastage among the adults, who may be more concerned about jurisdictional disputes than they are about educating children.

But the local group must get the job done. They must organise both instructional programmes and health services. In thousands of small communities which are not health districts by themselves but are part of a country system they find it effective to invite the health authorities to assist them to set up a plan but proceed to administer that plan directly from the school offices. In many cities the board of education is reluctant to give up its jurisdiction over any part of the programme (Cleveland, Los Angeles) and hence operates the school programme from within the educational structure. In others (Cincinnati, Detroit) the local health departments take over and in cooperation with the educational authorities work out excellent programmes.

In virtually no instance is there any dispute relative to the administration of health instruction. That phase of the programme is recognised to be wholly educational in nature and needs health department service only as a consultant to the programme.

But there is much less agreement over the health service problem. In an excellent article summarising the important points of this controversy, Samuel M. Wishik, M.D., of the City Health Department of New York has presented the following:

Certain advantages in having the school health service administered by the school system itself have been advanced and rather generally accepted as being valid. They include:

1. There is usually greater efficiency and simplicity in the single administration.
2. There is usually better understanding of the school needs by the health service.
3. Greater interest comes from increased responsibility on the part of the school personnel.
4. There is better acceptance of the health programme when it is within the same agency.
5. More emphasis can be given to school health than when it is one among many public health activities.
6. There is closer integration of health service and health education.
7. Through the teachers the parent-teacher association shows better cooperation and interest.
8. Greater success in obtaining funds for school health services can be expected in the much larger educational budget.
9. There is usually less turnover of health personnel.

To a large degree the advantages just listed add up to a

higher degree of intramural integration and effectiveness of the school health services.

Advantages have been advanced and again rather generally accepted for the school health service being administered by a health department. They include:

1. A health service programme is more properly administered by health personnel in a health agency.
2. More appropriate definition of duties and use of the time of health personnel is likely.
3. Rotation of personnel through related health activities to obtain broader experience is possible.
4. In rural areas with scattered small schools part-time nursing service for each school is more easily obtained from the health department district nurse.
5. Greater likelihood exists of including the school in various community health activities, such as a tuberculosis control programme.
6. Health services are extended to parochial and private schools more easily under health department administration.
7. Health department administration results in more authoritative content of the health education curriculum.
8. By administering the school health service the health department is stimulated to encourage the development and expansion of community health resources for children and through its contacts with other agencies to assist in setting standards and improving service.
9. It is an economic waste to have multiple health administration in a community.
10. Health departments usually give greater emphasis to health supervision and selective examinations than to safety and annual examinations.

To a large degree the advantages just listed add up to attaining better extramural integration of the school health service with related health activities.

In this connection it is always helpful for school personnel to remember that the scope of activity for local health authorities is usually prescribed by law and thus their duties impinge upon the school population. Children are children first and school children second. Health authorities see children as part of the public for whose health they are responsible and thus it is entirely essential that school and health personnel cooperate so as to get *both* jobs done. School people should realise that health officers are charged by law to:

1. Enforce all state health laws and regulations.
2. Prepare and enforce regulations for the control of communicable disease.
3. Record incidence and instances of communicable disease.
4. Investigate all instances of disease, carriers and contacts.
5. Under some conditions, supply and administer vaccines and serums.

Those and many other legal and traditional functions of boards of health bring them in close contact with school problems.

At all events, regardless of where the final budgetary and administrative jurisdiction lies, the following features of a smooth-running and adequate school programme should be preserved and maintained:

1. Joint planning for school and community programmes between boards of education and health should be a constant feature of any system.
2. School personnel should welcome the advice and consultation of health or medical personnel at each stage of programme development.
3. Medical personnel should learn to work with school people, to understand their problems, and cooperate within rather than dominate the programme.
4. Health departments should be constantly ready to improve the in-service preparation of teachers.

5. School and community health councils should invariably carry adequate representation from both health and education administrative offices.
6. In any given school building the administrative authority of the principal over all activities, including health service, must remain.
7. Medical personnel (physicians, nurses) who have some preparation in the field of professional education have an advantage in working in an educational setting.
8. Boards of education, charged as they are with the responsibility for the education of the children of the community and recognising the basic *educational* character of school health education, can be encouraged to work cooperatively with boards of health on mutual problems without relinquishing administrative jurisdiction over any part of the educational programme.

Qualifications

Some localities and some states are perplexed over the problem of qualifications of the administrative personnel for the programme. Should a physician or an educator be chosen to administer, supervise, "head up" the programme?

There is no standard practice. Good work is being done under both. Whether a physician should head the school health programme or whether an educator should be its principal officer depends almost wholly upon the administrative skill and personal qualifications of the people in question. In cities or countries large enough to have a staff of supervisors or consultants at work in this field, the medical or educational background of the person is of less importance than his conception of the programme and his organising ability. In smaller school systems where there may be one supervisor of health education in a country or a small city or village, the possibilities are that the position will be held by a specialist in health education or in health and physical education. Physicians are rare in these positions not because they are disqualified on professional grounds but merely because there are not enough of them available to serve communities in that way.

These central office supervisors or consultants, working directly under the superintendent, are helpful in assisting elementary teachers with instructional plans and materials, providing teaching aids and demonstrations, aiding in the appraisal programmes, supplying new materials for teaching, coordinating school and community effort, and facilitating in every way the development of school health education in the communities, in the individual schools, and with the administration. In many rural areas the consultant becomes a travelling teacher and may be on the staff of six or seven schools teaching in each one and conducting health service activities in them all.

In Schools

What shall be the plan of organisation in a given school? Regardless of the size of the school is there a standard organisational plan which can be recommended? How will the various personnel involved fit into this scheme of things?

1. The Health Council

The formation of a school and community health council (or committee), with a council chairman chosen from available trained personnel, seems to be the best administrative plan for single schools. Experience is proving the soundness of such a plan. The council gives everyone concerned a chance to participate in the formation and conduct of the programme. It assures the various special interests concerned with child health an opportunity to be heard. The council and the chairman are mutually dependent and helpful, and under an able school principal many fine school programmes have come into being as a result of this cooperative effort.

In some places the council does not have community interests represented but confines its membership only to school personnel and its activities only to school matters. It serves in this way as a school committee on the health programme. Current thought, however, favours a broadening of scope to include community interests and thus gives tangible recognition to the fact that the health of the school child is the concern of many and not only of school personnel. The 1947 Conference on the Cooperation of the Physician in the School Health and Physical Education Programme voiced this opinion in its report as follows.

It was suggested that in establishing a school health programme:

1. There must be school and community planning by means of a Community Health Council composed of representatives of the schools, public health authorities, the county medical and dental societies and other organisations interested in and concerned with health.
2. Each school system and each school within that system should establish an advisory health council of its own to provide leadership and direction for its health service and health education programme and to cooperate with the community health council through duly appointed representatives.

There must be administrative leadership for each school system and for each school. This may be provided by a superintendent, assistant superintendent, principal, health coordinator, director of health services, director of health education and service, director of health and physical education or director of health and safety education; in short, there must be someone within each school who has a definite responsibility for the total school health programme and for cooperation and coordination with the medical and dental professions and with community health agencies, public and private.

And the Conference, in its "Principal Recommendations and Conclusions", made it clear that:

> In order that a school health programme may be kept continuously in proper relationship with public health services, welfare services, medical and dental services, and all the health resources of the community *it is essential that some form of community health council* bringing together representatives of all local groups with definite health responsibilities, be formed.
>
> Every *school system should have* an advisory *school health council,* every *school a health committee,* every local *medical society a school health committee.* In some instances such committees or council

can best be developed within the framework of an already existing plan of organisation.

Wide *recognition* should be given to the fact that in the schools and health departments of many communities *health education consultants* or coordinators have been found to be *very helpful in developing* the cooperative type of *school health programme* which succeeds in utilising all the resources locally available.

The health council or committee plan is adaptable to any school, large or small, rural or urban. *The work of each is planned in relation to local needs.* A survey may be made, needs established, and people on committees invited to undertake the work. The list of activities to be undertaken will depend largely upon the imagination, insight, and conscience of the members of the council.

The organisation of such a body either wholly within the school or joining forces with the community should remain as simple as possible for effective action. Its officers could well be only a chairman, a secretary, and perhaps an editor for whatever publications the council chooses to issue. Subcommittees can be appointed for continuous function and reporting to the council on emergency and accidents, the school environment, disease control, appraisals and screening, school-home relationships, athletics and physical education, research, or any other large area of health interest. The membership on committees and officers of the council could well be rotated every two or three years for variety and sustained interest.

The membership of the council should include persons interested in child health and willing to work cooperatively for its betterment. The list of potential members of such a council usually includes:

From the School	From the Community
The principal	Physicians
Physical education teachers	Dentists
The nurse	Ministers
The physician and dentist	A PTA representative
The psychologist	Representatives from service clubs
Teachers	

The custodian
Students
The dental hygienist
The guidance counsellor
The public health officer and nurse
Any appropriate civic leaders
The mayor or a councilman

Such a school and community health council could be small or it could be very large. If the latter, it should have a strong programme committee to guide the work, a competent chairman, and a well-conceived plan of action. Individual schools within the community where such large councils exist would want individual school committees chosen from school personnel only.

The best way to understand how health councils operate is to study the mechanism and accomplishments of some of them.

1. The Health Council of Clinton County, Ohio, began their work by seeking the needs of their population through a survey. Through committees and by consulting specialists they found the following needs, the answer to which has become the programme of the Council for several years to come:

Too many babies are miscarried or born dead.

Preschool children are not protected against diphtheria, tetanus, whooping cough, smallpox or typhoid.

Only 60 per cent of school children are protected against smallpox and diphtheria.

School children lack dental and medical examinations.

Many families do not drink pasteurised milk.

Wells, cisterns and springs could easily become contaminated.

The surface privy is the principal means of sewage disposal.

Undulant fever is an immediate problem.

Tuberculosis cases are not found early enough.

Cancer strikes heavily.

There are 643 persons who have recovered from typhoid, which suggests the likelihood of carriers present.

Rheumatic fever has claimed 234 victims.

Heart disease and diabetes are high.

There was no poliomyelitis problem during the survey.

Accidents and fires take a heavy toll in time and life.

2. From Hempstead, New York, the following achievements of the council are reported:

1. An environmental survey of our seven school plants and certain followup physical improvements.
2. The addition of a teacher of physical education in the elementary schools.
3. Freeing of another teacher for one-half physical education work in the elementary schools.
4. Increase in elementary school nursing service from one and a half to two full-time persons.
5. Better coordination of health and physical education and health service activities.
6. Establishment of a health service fund.
7. Improved coordination and public relations community wise.
8. A complete lighting survey of all school plants.

Plans for immediate future include:

1. Provision for a more complete medical examination at certain grade levels.
2. Extension and improvement of playground and playfield areas.
3. Addition of a second nurse at the high school level.
4. Improvement of classroom lighting in all schools.

3. A Council in action presents its programme.

An example of a school health council that is studying and dealing with health problems in a democratic and practical way is that of the Vallejo City Elementary Schools.

It has met regularly once a month since its inception three years ago. Its personnel, which has a wide representation within the school system, includes the school physician, as chairman, the director of elementary education, the supervising school nurse, and one representative (either a principal or teacher) from each of the fourteen elementary schools. A committee representing the secondary schools also meets monthly, both groups working closely together whenever the need arises.

The Elementary School Health Council is concerned with the health programme from nursery school level through the sixth grade. Its functions, therefore, are many and varied. As set up by the group they are to:

1. Study health needs of the Vallejo elementary schools in the light of the most modern thinking;
2. Advice the director of school health regarding the conclusions of the committee with recommendations on the implementation of these conclusions;
3. Carry back to the administrators and faculty of their own schools the findings and recommendations of this council;
4. Assist in every way possible the growth of health interest and health consciousness, in its broadest sense, within their individual schools;
5. Assist the director of school health in formulating recommendations for the ensuing academic year, these recommendations to be incorporated in the annual report of the Board of Education.

The democratic procedure and way of working of this health council have been very effective. Not only were health problems brought from the individual schools for consideration, but the school system as a whole benefited from the findings and study done by the group under the very able guidance of the school physician. Some of the subjects and activities carried on during the last school year included:

1. Study of health legislation.
2. In-service education for teachers.

3. Health recommendations for teachers; e.g., recommendations that all school personnel have chest X-rays each year. (Made possible by the Tuberculosis Association.)
4. Adaptation of school schedules to meet the needs and capacities of children.
5. Study and revision of pupils' health records.
6. Consideration by teachers of the effect of heat, light and voice.
7. Study of methods of "screening" children who have deviations from the normal.
8. Consideration of school lunches and food sold to children outside of school.
9. Discussions of use and value of rat feeding projects in teaching nutrition in the classroom.
10. Coordination with other agencies and organisations such as the parent-teacher association, tuberculosis association, country health department, and the State Department of Public Health.

4. From Bronxville, New York:

Chairman—The School Administrator

School Staff	*Community Interests*
School Physician	5 Private General Physicians
School Nurse	5 Pediatricians
School Psychiatrist	Parents' Representative
School Psychologist	Other Council Representatives
Physical Educator	
Teachers' Representative	

The council convenes for one hour quarterly during the school year. Well planned agenda presented in round table discussions expose the misunderstandings and misconceptions relative to policies and pave the way for the pooling of ideas mutually acceptable to the school and community interests. Subjects to be discussed are agreed upon in advance. Some have been—the rules for the control of communicable diseases, the physicial education programme, the part to be played in the improvement of posture, immunisation procedures to be advocated, the value of germicidal fluorescent lamps in schools, tuberculin testing, X-ray examinations in older children and school staff members, vision testing, the fluorine treatment in the control of dental caries, the school guidance programme. Specialists have been invited to participate in discussions as indicated by the subject. Letters to parents have been composed by the group, advocating annual health examination by the private doctor and acquainting parents with policies agreed upon relative to matters of health guidance. Parent-teachers conferences devoted to the presentation of subjects dealing with emotional development have been sponsored by the council.

5. Another council during the first year of its organisation (a) issued publications to parents on rheumatic fever, scarlet fever, diphtheria immunisation, preschool examinations, and poliomyelitis, (b) established a programme of communicable disease control, (c) established a programme of safety and emergency control, (d) examined the sanitary conditions in all school and community eating establishments, (e) obtained restricted parking areas on thoroughfares near the school, (f) encouraged the establishment of a course in health instruction for senior-high-school boys and girls.

The constitution and working policies of this particular council are reproduced in Appendix B.

2. The Chairman of the Council

The chairman will bear the lion's share of responsibility for the success of the council during his term of office. He will probably be selected because of his interest in child health and health education. The chairman should have a knowledge of school and community organisation, information about community resources, an ability to plan and conduct a meeting, and, above all, an ability to get along with people in an effective, cooperative manner. Through his own efforts and the work of his appointed committee chairman, he should discharge the following responsibilities:

1. Stimulate the work of the health council.
2. Be the agent for the health council on appropriate projects.
3. Confer and study with teachers on matters pertaining to curriculum development in health instruction.
4. Represent the health interests of the school before the administration and board as improvements are sought.
5. Arrange school and public meetings devoted to health problems.
6. Engage in such study of problems or research as may be needed to improve the local programme.
7. Arrange for whatever all-school surveys or studies may be made upon the request of the health council or any other authoritative body.
8. Extend helpful overall supervision of the health implications in the entire school programme and secure close cooperative working relationships between all the interests concerned with school health.

3. The School Administrator

Basic to the work of any council or programme is a sympathetic, interested, informed, and willing school administrator. Nothing can go on successfully in school without his support and consent, and, in turn, the administrator knows that he must accept the final responsibility for everything that *does* go on. Hence, many principals are cautious about the development of school health education until they are sure of their lines and of the merits of the programme.

The responsibilities of the school administrator in school health education have been the subject of considerable investigation. The National Conference for Cooperation in Health Education determined his opportunities to be somewhat as follows:

1. To direct and coordinate all phases of the school health programme under the school's jurisdiction.
2. To see that adequate funds are secured and budgeted for

the health programme administered by the school, and to cooperate with the health department in obtaining and budgeting funds for medical and nursing services which may be administered by that department.

3. To be responsible for seeing that all functions of the school health programme are performed.
4. To recommend for appointment physicians and nurses employed by the school and to assign their functions.
5. To make provision for in-service training of school personnel.
6. To give leadership and guidance in establishing and maintaining community understanding of, and relationships to, the school health programme.
7. To encourage cooperative and democratic efforts among school-employed personnel, parents, and others in the community in the operation of the school health service programme, and to help in establishing good working relationships between school personnel and health department personnel, if the latter are responsible for medical and nursing service.
8. To assume administrative responsibility for providing and maintaining a safe and healthful school environment.
9. To set up a health curriculum in which health education is coordinated with all other features of the school programme.
10. To set up a procedure for the continuous appraisal of the school health programme.
11. To establish sound understanding and sympathetic relationships between the school health programme and the health and educational programmes of other agencies in the community.
12. To assist the medical and nursing staffs in interpreting to the community the health needs of children.
13. In school systems in which no medical authority is available, the school administrator secures medical guidance through some other qualified source.

14. To assume a definite responsibility for acquainting the home and community with the school health programme.
15. To provide for an organised programme of parent participation in the school health programme, and of parent education in the field of health.
16. To develop understanding of the extent of the authority granted in existing laws regarding school health procedures and to make an effort to have these laws improved where necessary.
17. To assume administrative responsibility for providing an adequate school health service.
18. To provide the building space and equipment advised by the technical staff for carrying on health examinations and other school health services with due regard for privacy and hygienic conditions.
19. To be responsible with the physician and nurse in working out relationships with members of the local medical profession, public health agencies, volunteer groups, service clubs, and other community groups.
20. To provide for changes or adaptations in the school programme for children with special needs.
21. To cooperate with the physician in establishing procedures for the education of school personnel in the techniques of observing children.
22. To ensure the establishment and efficient use of an adequate system of health record keeping.
23. To cooperate in setting up a programme for controlling communicable diseases and accidents.
24. To see to it that adequate health service for school personnel is available.
25. To provide a safe and healthful physical environment for children and for the staff.
26. In planning the construction of a new school plant or the remodelling of an old one, to use the latest competent

advice so as to recommend the type of plant, including grounds and playgrounds, which will be in conformity with the best modern standards in sanitation, ventilation and lighting, safety features, and other conditions conducive to healthful living.

27. To provide an administrative plan or programme which subordinates administrative convenience to educational and health needs.
28. To provide a teaching staff which radiates good health, and a healthy custodial and lunchroom staff.
29. To secure and budget funds for the health education programme and to appoint the necessary qualified school-employed personnel for the health education programme and to assign their functions.
30. To encourage the development of health councils made up of school personnel, medical staff, and students, to plan and help to carry out the health education programme.

These are his basic responsibilities. He may allocate some of them to other people but in the end the success or failure of the enterprise comes back to the principal or superintendent. School health education can develop just as far and no farther than is agreed to by the principal administrative officer of the school.

4. THE MEDICAL ADVISER

In an ideally developed programme of school health education a physician serving the school is a requisite. Much of the success of the health activities programme revolves around him and his services. Originally brought into schools to examine for hearing and vision, the physician has now had the scope of his work enlarged to assure him a key position in the entire educational programme. His duties extend far beyond the routine and hasty examination of children and the compilation of statistics. He has become in every sense a member of the school personnel participating uniquely in the development of school health programmes. His potential duties have been described variously—they are many—and include:

1. Serving as the medical adviser to the entire school in all its activities.
2. Assisting in the establishing of sound school health policies.
3. Advising with school administrators with regard to health supervisory activities.
4. Coordinating school health services with community health programmes, both public and private, especially in the fields of health education, communicable disease control and medical and dental services.
5. Being responsible for formulating procedures in cooperation with the health officer and school administrator for communicable disease control.
6. Making medical examinations (1) to discover all structural or functional defects; (2) determining the fitness of pupils to engage in school activities including athletics; (3) noting any need that may exist for modification of the pupils' school environment or programme, including special programmes for handicapped children.
7. Advising parents as to the correction of defects through the utilisation of community resources.
8. Advising school authorities with regard to conditions which are conducive to the maintenance of healthful school environment.
9. Carrying out a health service programme which is educational in nature and acting as a consultant to school health authorities in the development of a vital, functioning health education programme.
10. Working with community groups to assure the availability of necessary professional health services for all children. One of the weaknesses of the school health programme has been the fact that school physicians have too often functioned as defect finders with no provision by administrators of the school system for adequate follow-through.

The Committee on Professional Education of the American Public Health Association supplements the foregoing list of duties by mentioning also these:

1. To assist in the establishment of policies and procedures for emergency control.
2. To direct teachers and nurses in systematic and continuous observation of the health of pupils.
3. To assist in the selection of pupils for special educational programmes such as speech correction, lip reading, modified physical education and others.
4. To offer professional advice regarding the health of teachers.
5. To supervise the conditions under which competitive athletics are played.
6. To supervise the conditions under which food is served in the school.

The unique position of a physician in an educational programme has not been easy to establish. Many years of experience and much careful thought have gone into the evolution of his present status. The idea of having a physician serve the school was not only readily acceptable to medical groups, and educators were prone to misunderstand his function and use him in a shortsighted way. The cooperation of medicine through physicians, nurses, dentists, and psychiatrists is today welcome and necessary in the better educational programmes, and the success of such cooperative effort depends largely upon the acquiescence to the following policies:

(a) Medical services should be paid for and not expected as a contribution from community physicians.

(b) Teachers must understand and function within the principle of privileged communication. Information from physicians about pupils must be held in confidence and used for professional purposes only.

(c) The physician serving the school should, with the school administrator, inform local medical and dental societies of the nature of the school problem and programme and utilise the judgment and resources of those groups.

(d) School medical personnel should be members of the local medical and dental societies.

(e) Parent should be advised and encouraged to have medical examinations performed by family physicians, and the record of findings should be transmitted to the school.

(f) Reparative treatment should be done by family physicians. In instances where it is not possible to make such arrangements the school authorities should arrange to have the work done through public agencies and clinics.

(g) The medical adviser should obtain all needed data on a child from the family physician's examination but in instances where these data are incomplete or the examination is of a type not helpful to the school programme, the medical adviser should make the examination as a part of the school programme.

(h) A great deal of the medical adviser's time could well be spent discussing with parents at school the health needs and development of their children. The adviser should demonstrate what good medical service is and assist the parents in the development of their own conception of the value and nature of adequate medical care.

The Second National Conference on Physicians and Schools agreed on certain conditions which, if acknowledged, will enhance the work of the physician who serves the schools. These are as follows:

The school physician should be a doctor of medicine officially designated by an appropriate authority to render specified services in one or more schools on a full or part-time basis.

The school physician will be in a position to make his optimum contribution to educational goals under the following conditions:

(a) When he has responsibility in his field as a recognised

member of the administrative staff of the school and is included in meetings of the faculty and the health council as well as staff meetings at the administrative level.

(b) When he receives compensation commensurate with his training and experience and the responsibility of his position.

(c) When he is given an appropriate place in the in-service education of teachers in health service functions, and as a consultant in the preparation of curricular materials in the field of health.

The school physician can best again professional status and command the respect of his medical and educational colleagues under the following conditions:

(a) When there is mutual understanding and agreement among both physicians and educators on the functions of the school physician.

(b) When he properly coordinates his programme with existing patterns of medical and educational practice.

(c) When physicians of the highest quality with the training and experience necessary to competently perform the many diverse public health functions required are selected as school physicians.

(d) When close cooperation with the private physicians in a community prevents misunderstandings from arising in school-family physician relationships.

(e) When school health services are made educational experiences for pupils, parents and teachers.

(f) When local medical societies devote some of their scientific programmes to the field of school health as presented by the physician serving the school.

The work of the school physician can be performed most effectively when:

(a) Adequate rooms for carrying on health services in privacy and dignity are provided.

(b) Teachers, nurses or technicians perform those phases of health services they can be prepared to do effectively, reserving for the physician those functions which only a medical advisor is qualified to do.

It is probable that less than one-quarter of all the schools in the nation have the services of a physician who is an employee of the board of education. Thousands of rural and village schools rely upon the local public health officer for whatever service they get. Still other thousands have no medical adviser, no physician serving the school at any time. Some state laws require the local health officer to serve the school if no school physician is employed. In such instances the school authorities should (a) establish a school health committee or council to (b) undertake as many of the proposed activities for such councils as possible with the limited medical help, and (c) institute proceedings early to obtain some form of assistance from local physicians or medical officials. With or without a physician as medical adviser to the school the need remains the same. Where no medical aid exists the school personnel should nevertheless undertake as much of the work as it can.

5. The Nurse

One of the major steps which any school can take toward the establishment of a complete and practical school health programme is to employ a nurse. It is estimated that one nurse can serve 1500-2000 students. She has become of central importance in the operation of today's educational programmes. Her functions and status are best described by the National Conference for Cooperation in Health Education:

The nurse serving the school may be employed directly by the school or by the health department and assigned to serve in the school. Her duties and responsibilities will vary according to the extent to which medical supervision of the children is available. In any case, she serves as an interpreter between school, home, and community. She understands the health needs of children and serves on the team which includes herself, the school administrator, the teacher, the parents, the physicians, and a wide variety of community agencies and groups in getting these needs met. . . .

Of all the individuals connected with the school health programme, the nurse usually has the most intimate relationship with the home. She interprets to the physician, the school administrator, and the teacher the conditions in the home which help to influence the development of the school child. She interprets to parents the health services of the school. . . .

The nurse assists the physician in preparing for and conducting the health examinations of school children. She cooperates with the appropriate school personnel in selecting those to be examined. . . . She helps teachers and parents to recognise significant departures from normal in their day-by-day contact with children so that medical attention can be received by those who need it. She gives demonstrations which will enable teachers to acquire the techniques and information necessary for testing visual and auditory acuity and for measuring and recording weight and height when teachers are made responsible for carrying out these procedures. . . .

The nurse serving the school assists in coordinating all available information regarding the health status, health behaviour, home environment, and progress of each child. . . . A large part of the nurse's time is spent in guiding and encouraging parents in their efforts to get their children's defects corrected or to provide the best possible conditions for healthy development of the children. . . .

She assists the physician and teachers in developing modified school experiences for children with special needs—for example, those with hearing loss, heart trouble, or emotional disturbances. . . . Working under the direction of the physician, she helps the school personnel to solve their health problems. . . .

The nurse in the school is familiar with standards for maintaining a wholesome school plant and works with the school staff, the children, and the parents to see that safe and hygienic conditions are maintained. . . .

The function of the nurse in the school in health teaching is chiefly advisory. She has a contribution to make in the planning of the health curriculum, in indicating source material for various areas of the curriculum, and in evaluating the health education programme. . . . She sees that the teachers are informed of personal and group problems affecting their children, so that such problems can be used constructively in health education. . . . She may teach home nursing and first aid if she meets the requirements for teaching in the particular school she serves. . . . The nurse may assist the teacher in planning field trips to community organisations.

The Michigan Department of Health describes an important function of the nurse as a liaison agent between home, school, and community agencies. She will be required to do a great deal of work with teacher groups, health communities, and councils, parent groups, curriculum committees, civic organisations, and student and faculty committees of various kinds. Her scope will involve all aspects of the health services, the health examinations, teacher observations, health records, accidents and emergencies, exclusion and readmission, counselling, and health instruction, and she will be consultant on health problems in the school environment. Hers is a responsible and important part of a total school health programme.

6. The Physical Education Teacher

The relation of physical education personnel to school health activities should be one of complete cooperation and interested participation. So closely allied are the health activities of the school with the conduct of a modern programme of physical education that frequently the physical education teacher is chairman of the council and the physical education programme becomes the central means by which the health of students is favourably affected.

7. The Classroom Teacher

The teacher is the central figure in any programme of school health education. She conducts the largest share of whatever teaching goes on. She sees the developing child for more hours per day than anyone else and thus has the best chance to observe the variations from normal as they occur. She knows more about the children than anyone in school and has in most instances the greatest influence on their behaviour.

Health programmes can stand or fall in terms of her interest and cooperation.

In terms of the school health service, the teacher's two-fold objective is recognised when she is informed of the findings of the school medical and nursing staffs so that she can use them in the instruction and guidance of students with health problems. In turn she can give valuable assistance to the physician and nurse in reaching their objectives. She is in a strategic position to observe changes in health status as they occur, and to give the continuous supervision necessary to meet the child's health needs as outlined by the physician. She is able also to make vision and hearing tests and to measure heights and weights at regular intervals, and thus have an opportunity for transforming rule-of-thumb, objective measurements into an educational experience for her students.

Most important of all, the teacher is able to supply the physician and the nurse with clues to guide them in doing their part in the health education of the child. She sees the individual differences of each student against a background of the behaviour and learning ability to be expected from the group of which the student is a part. To her the discovery of myopic vision, for example, explains why the pendulum of learning ability of a particular child describes a smaller are than the one which sets the tempo for the group, and to her its treatment is not so much the mechanical setting right of one thing that is wrong as it is an adjustment favourable for the child as a whole. The teacher who is sensitive to those relationships can help the physician and nurse to see them too, so that all three can work together for the individual child who is the direct object, stated or implied, of every process connected with public education in America.

The Research Division of the National Education Association summarises and specifies these functions to include innumerable responsibilities for the teacher in connection with:

1. Cooperative overall planning about the health needs of children.
2. Grasping opportunities for health teaching.

3. Helping each child to develop and maintain best possible health.
4. Making the school a safe and healthful place.
5. Using school health services and resources.
6. Using community health services and resources.
7. Cooperating with the home in promoting and maintaining good health.
8. Developing relationships among the school staff, parents, children, and community leaders which will contribute to the mental and emotional stability of children.

8. The Custodian

It is recognised that the school custodian is an important person in the school system. He not only carries a heavy responsibility in operating and protecting valuable school buildings, grounds, and equipment, but he is also a vital factor in promoting school health and safety. The school custodian promotes the health and comfort of pupils by:

1. Effective operation of heating and ventilating equipment.
2. Keeping floors, blinds, shades and furniture free of dust.
3. Cleaning walls, ceilings, windows, and artificial lighting fixtures to secure the best possible illumination.
4. Making certain that water pressure is kept up so that at no time will back siphonage occur to contaminate the water supply.
5. Providing tempered water on tap, liquid or powdered soap, and paper towels on hand at all times for hand washing.
6. Keeping every part of the building clean and sanitary at all times.

The school custodian promotes pupil safety by:

1. Systematically checking all playground equipment and keeping it in good repair.
2. Removing broken glass and other playground hazards.

3. Maintaining floors so that they will not be slippery.
4. Keeping all required exit doors and hardware in good operating condition.
5. Keeping all lines of travel to required exits free of obstacles.
6. Inspecting safety devices on boilers and pressure vessels to make sure they are always in good operating condition.
7. Periodically checking fire alarm systems and fire fighting equipment.
8. Assisting in the supervision of fire exit drills and traffic patrol activities.
9. Carrying on a continuous programme of fire prevention.

The work of the school custodian is no small task. In a large measure, the custodian, as well as the teacher, promotes appreciation for orderliness and cleanliness and promotes good health practices by pupils. Because of his close connection with factors in school health and safety, the school custodian should, obviously, be a member of the health committee. His understanding and appreciation of his responsibilities and his competence in doing work have a direct bearing on pupil health and safety.

9. Other Specialists

There are other professional workers who have a share in a fully developed school health programme. The work of a dental hygienist and a dentist has been described in a previous chapter, as has that of the psychologist. The nutritionist functions importantly in teaching and counselling on dietary problems and in supervising the school feeding programme. The speech supervisor renders important psychological service in straightening out emotional problems associated with speech variants. The sanitary engineer, the architect, the acoustical specialist, the lighting engineer are all of great value in planning new buildings or in remodelling old ones.

Each of these has a niche to fill. Each must fill it cooperatively and in relation to the best interests of children. A completely integrated programme requires their services but wants them in relation to the whole, not as independent specialists operating for other than the educational purposes.

LEGAL ASPECTS

Authorisation for any phase of school health and physical education must be established in law. Public money may not be expended for any purpose unless permission is granted or the expenditure is made compulsory in the laws of the state. Under the "states rights" principle established in colonial times each state reserves the right to conduct its own affairs educationally. Education is not basically a federal enterprise and, therefore, the federal government exercises comparatively little control over current educational development.

School law has reflected fairly well emerging philosophy and administrative practice over the years. Earlier the school and university took little if any interest in the health of students. A school was a place "to train the mind". No thought was given to the development of the health of that "mind" or to whether it was trained in isolation from the rest of the individual who owned it. As the point of view changed, a legal structure had to be erected state by state to permit the development of the instruction and services that constitute modern school health education. It had to be made permissible to employ physicians and dentists, to give physical examinations, to screen for tuberculosis. Some mandates were given to boards of education to offer health instruction, to "take due notice of health supervision", or to employ teachers properly prepared in health education. An entire legal structure for school health education has had to be erected. The laws cover a wide range of health matters from sanitation and safety provisions in the building to laws pertaining to the preparation of teachers. *Health in Schools* describes them: "(a) As provisions in both federal and state constitutions, (b) in statutes enacted as laws by state legislatures, (c) in municipal legislation in the form of ordinances, (d) in provisions contained in special charters granted to municipalities by state legislatures, (e) in regulations adopted by state boards of health, and (f) in case law handed down in court decisions based upon statutory and upon common law".

Federal Laws and Subsidies

The interest of the federal government in health and physical education is, of course, related to the interest of government in all of education. From time to time there have been serious proposals made to give the government greater jurisdiction in local education through appropriations to local systems meeting standards established by the government. In the fields of vocational agriculture, special education for the handicapped, trades and industries, and the school lunch, the appropriations from Washington are made on that basis. There seems to be something less than unanimous approval for such arrangements but, in the main, the results are good. Communities have profited from the programmes already established.

The Congress is constantly asked to widen the scope of federal participation in school health programmes. Some two dozen bills are usually presented in each regular session which bear upon the health of the child in school. So far the Congress has been very reluctant to approve bills which would withdraw from the state any of its prerogatives in determining the kind of programme it wishes. In the evolving social security programme subsidies are increasingly made for child health, maternal welfare, disease control, and numerous other health problems. These funds have been administered by the Children's Bureau and the US Public Health Service and given to state department of health for disposition in the states.

The funds have been used, in part, for school and public health education through the appointment of supervisors who have served communities. Several have been assigned to state departments of education to correlate better the health interests with the ongoing educational programme of the state. If the government in the future extends greater equalisation aid to state educational programmes, provisions will undoubtedly be made for the extension of health education in areas not now well developed. There are two principal ways in which this can be done—by equalisation funds paid directly to communities through their state departments of education or by the extension of supervisory service to communities to aid local groups in developing a programme with the resources at hand.

The latter is the less expensive of the two and retains a greater measure of local autonomy in the conception and development of local progrmames.

There are many who would resist the efforts of Congress to give the executive branch of the government, through the Office of Education, final authority in the development of the *curriculum*. Wartime experience, when schools and colleges had, sometimes, to teach according to set patterns, following set procedures and including only set material, has given many people sufficient impression of the undesirability of extending government control in either health education or physical education. The handbooks and manuals in hygiene and in physical education used by the services were difficult to adapt locally and allowed insufficiently for local modifications. Local autonomy in the development of the instructional materials and administration of a curriculum is to be preferred.

State Laws and Standards

The state is the principal controlling agent in education in the United States. State legislatures are responsible for the passage of laws and appropriation of money in support of public education. The agency which the state uses for this purpose is the state department of public instruction, or of education, as the case may be. In the operation of school health education that agency is supplemented in its work by the state department of health. The two work jointly in the development of school health education, frequently sharing personnel and extending joint services to communities in need of aid.

Such work as is done on the state level, emanating from state departments of health or education, is directed in forty-one of the states by a supervisory staff in school health and physical education. These supervisors and their assistants serve a variety of purposes, all aimed at the development of programmes in school health and physical education. They establish minimum standards for programme development, set standards for the training and certification of teachers and others who serve in school programmes, publish state courses of study for suggested use in communities, develop in-service improvement programmes for personnel, give direct aid to communities in programme development, and perform numberless other functions related to the promotion of the fields. The state laws require that such standards for programme and personnel be established by state departments and be accepted by the schools of the state. Thus it may well be said that the quality and quantity of local programmes will depend upon the leadership exerted at the state level.

There are contrasting ways in which the framework, within which this leadership can work, is set. Some states have extended laws specifying in great detail the character of the programme which is expected. These laws indicate how many minutes a week must be devoted to health instruction, the frequency with which examinations are to be held, which types of immunisation are mandatory and which optional, and in many other ways describe an optimal programme in law. Other states rely more upon state standards. The law will briefly declare that there must or may be programmes of health and physical education in the schools of the state and vest the authority for developing the details in the state department of education. This department then develops a programme of standards which is accepted by local schools wishing to become accredited. Such a plan allows for greater flexibility in the improvement of the minimum level of programmes in that standards may be altered by the official state agency without raising the complicated problem of legislative action. Furthermore, the acceptance of standards is, to many school systems, a more palatable process than adherence to law. Whether the state operates principally by law or by standards the personnel of a local system will want to know the full detail of what is expected of them and what the mandated and permitted features are in school health education in their state. There being no standard school law used in all states, a study must be made locally to determine the scope of the law or standards.

It is clear that the trend is toward centralising the responsibility for the supervision of programmes in state departments. As a recent bulletin from the US Office of Education indicates:

There is a definite trend in State departments of education toward establishing administrative responsibility for all phases of school health, physical education and recreation in one unit or division. This trend is also shown by board rulings and laws making health education, physical education, recreation, safety education, school lunches, and education for handicapped and exceptional children the responsibility of the director of the division of health and physical education. In some instances, the titles of the directors of the divisions have been changed to indicate the range of responsibility.

There is also a trend toward the establishment of specific administrative or instructional requirements through codes, standards, or rules and regulations. . . .

A third trend is toward the establishment of "Cooperative Arragements" between State departments of health and education in the various states.

Examples of State Laws and Standards

1. In examinations

There is local option in the matter of health examinations in California—boards of education are permitted to do as they wish. In Pennsylvania examinations are required regularly and costs are subsidised by the state through the health departments. Colorado requires that all teachers *must* have an examination before teaching, and Ohio gives boards the *right* to ask for an examination as a condition of employment. In nearly every state provision is made for the "conscientious objector"; i.e., parents with religious or other conscience scruples which make them unwilling to have the health of their children supervised in school may withdraw their children from the programme of examinations.

In Massachusetts the Department of Public Health prescribes and establishes regulations relative to the physical examination of school children. These regulations (1952) include the following:

The school committee or the board of health shall provide the services of a school physician to carry out health appraisals on such children as do not have this service performed by the family physician. He shall carry on other responsibilities of the school health programme including (1) interpretation of the child's health situation to the school personnel, (2) assistance to the teacher and nurse in meeting the health needs of the child insofar as this is possible in the school environment, and (3) interpretation of the school health programme to the family physician and parents. . . .

The school committee or board of health shall cause every child in the public schools to be separately and carefully examined by a physician duly registered in Massachusetts within six months before entrance and at intervals of either three or four years thereafter. . . .

The school committee or the board of health shall cause children in the public schools to be separately and carefully examined by a duly registered physician under the following circumstances:

1. Children returning after an absence from school of five consecutive school days or more due to illness.
2. Children referred because of frequent absences due to unexplained illnesses.
3. Children referred because of known physical defects that require repeated appraisal.
4. Children referred from teacher-nurse conferences because the child is not making expected progress in school or because of signs of illness noted by the teacher or nurse.
5. Children under sixteen and over fourteen years of age requesting employment certificates.
6. Children planning to participate in competitive athletics annually, previous to such participation. . . .

The school committee or board of health shall cause the vision and hearing of each child in the public schools to be tested in the first grade and every second year thereafter. . . .

The health appraisal shall be done with such care and detail as to command medical reșect and be a desirable educational experience for the child. . . .

Disabilities and defects found on health appraisal of an individual child shall be brought to the attention of the family.

The school or health department shall encourage the family to take the child with physical defects to the family physician or other source of care. . . .

In the matter of these health appraisals one can see all the variations of laws and standards from openly permissive to strictly required.

2. In Disease control

North Carolina requires immunisation against whooping cough and smallpox before the age of one year, and schools are not permitted to admit children who are not immunised. Ohio permits boards of education to require such immunisation as a condition of entrance, and one or two other states expressly forbid boards of education to impose such regulations. Most states allow either boards of education or boards of health to exclude children who have or were exposed to communicable disease, and boards of health, almost universally, may close schools in time of epidemics.

3. In sanitation of school plant

There is wide divergence in the area of sanitaton. Local schools are subject to the observance of a variety of rules, regulations, standards, and laws emanating from boards of education and health, city councils, country commissioners, and legislatures. The standards of the fire marshal, state architect, smoke inspector, and sanitary engineer must all be met, and local architects must be familiar with a vast detail of sanitary, safety, and building specifications.

4. In the employment of personnel

Michigan, Pennsylvania, Indiana, and most other states allow boards of education to employ physicians and nurses for school health work. Pennsylvania law stipulates what physicians shall do and establishes a minimum fee for their services. New Jersey stipulates what school nurses shall do. Several states have arrangements whereby local health officers may, or must, supervise the health of school children if boards of education have not employed their own physician.

5. For health instruction

Thirty-two states emphasise the teaching of health within

their laws and standards for health and physical education. There is great variation in the stipulations concerning the years of teaching and the time allotment. Special laws requiring the teaching of temperance and in the uses of tobacco and narcotics are to be found in some states. Idaho priovides for a state supervisor of narcotic education and appropriates $25,000 every two years for narcotic education work. Two full semesters of health instruction are recommended for high schools in Indiana, and Louisiana authorises a half unit of credit for such instruction. Massachusetts, on the other hand, has no state standards but complete local option. New York has mandatory laws requiring instruction in elementary schools.

6. In the health of employees

Maine requires all employees to file a physician's certificate annually showing the employee to be free of communicable disease. The costs of health examinations are borne by the state department of education. Maryland also requires such an annual certificate. The majority of states, however, have no such statutes.

The foregoing are but a few of the great many kinds of laws and standards which bear upon school health and physical education. Standard practice is only emerging. There are several "backward" states which have not yet given attention to health needs of school children and there are a few which have provided moist amply for it. Such variations are, in the main, desirable because they reflect the judgments of the various state groups as they see and solve problems of their relatively homogeneous groups.

LOCAL AUTONOMY

The system we have in American education gives virtual autonomy to the community in determining the kind and quality of educational programme it shall have. State departments of education lead, encourage, illuminate, and enforce minimum standards. Departmets of health can enforce state laws representing minimum standards of performance in sanitation or safety. As we have seen, there is, so far, a faint relationship between the federal government and the community. But by and large the programme in school health and physical education is a local matter and dependent almost wholly upon the willingness and ability of local administrators and teachers. To offer health instruction well, poorly, or not at all is in most states a local matter. To employ a physician, to organise special education for the handicapped, to install adequate lighting and sanitary facilities—these are local problems mainly. *School health and physical education is well or poorly done according to the extent to which local school, health, and municipal authorities exercise their prerogatives under the law.* The responsibility falls heaviest upon the local superintendent of schools. The quality of the health programme in the school reflects his professional attitude toward and skill in developing adequate programmes for the health of the children of his community. Others share with him but leadership can and should come from the chief administrator as he works within the framework of law and standards which his state and board have established.

DISTRIBUTION OF COSTS

It has been said many times that the American people will have the kind of medical care they are willing to organise and pay for. The implications of all such sweeping statements must be examined to find the hidden danger. Surely in this one there is an implication of oversight of the specialist—the medically trained who, because of his experience, knows a great deal about the way medical care *can* be best organised to get the best results from money which is paid by the public. There is nothing virtuously democratic about overlooking the expert in medical organisation for the sake of providing any kind of medical care which seems to meet popular fancy at the moment.

So it is with school health services and activities. Communities will have the activities they are willing to pay for. And yet, few activities related to the practice of medicine require the helpful hand of the expert more than does the development of these school services so needed by children. A community may, if it so pleases, cling to the ancient notion that the school is the place to train the mind and any effort to broaden its scope is foolish. If that point of view prevails there will be no health activities carried on and the toll in child health will be heavy. The community may believe, if it wishes, that *any* school health activity is an infringement upon the medical sphere and throws the school forthwith into the practice of medicine, in which it is professionally unprepared and ethically unsuited. Such a point of view prevails in many places and is developed in ignorance of enlightened medical and educational opinion. It also costs heavily in child health.

The public can be brought around to and is slowly developing the understanding that school health services and activities need *not* be infringements upon the medical province as long as they are guided by the enlightened principles of cooperative effort—as long as the experts from both medicine and education are allowed a voice in the policies. Allow the unguided voice of an uninformed public opnion, or the prejudiced voice of a segment of either professional group, to predominate and school health programmes will usually be missing entirely or be such that the ultimate beneficiary of them gathers little. There is room in today's schools for neither extreme view: the school health activities need not be organised as "state medicine" nor need they be absent altogether for fear of infringement. The public will have, eventually, about the kind it wants, and the expert, the informed educator and physician, should take the leadership in forming up the programme of the future.

Sources of support

One of the very simple and yet potentially complex problems concerning school health programmes is their financial support. Obviously, they must be paid for. It is out of the question to expect that they will be provided gratis by the medical, nursing, and other specialising personnel involved. It is rudimentary that the school organisation must provide on its budget for the services and equipment which it uses in protecting and developing the health of the child. Whether such necessary funds actually come from the school tax money is another thing. In the last analysis it matters only that they be a part of the general funds of the school and that their expenditure be subject only to the control of the school authorities. It is seldom wise to have two official agencies spending money within the school programme. Crossed purposes, duplication, and waste frequently result. Whatever funds are used and spent for school health should be subject finally and irrevocably to the judgment of those in schools responsible for the programme.

The problem becomes complex when one considers the numerous sources from which such funds may come. Not every dollar spent by schools has been raised by the local school tax. Some money has come from state and federal taxes and from more than one agency and bureau within the state and federal government. Some may have come from local, country, or state health funds. Some may have been provided by a nonofficial agency and *given* to the schools for some specific purpose. The following sources are apparent today:

1. FEDERAL ENACTMENTS

The Congress has from time to time been asked to appropriate federal money for school health purposes. The School Lunch Law is a case in point. In this instance states and communities are allowed to share in a matching plan the support of a lunch programme for children whose need can be demonstrated. Other proposals have requested federal subsidy for local physical examinations and immunisation programmes although they have not yet become law. As many as twenty or thirty bills related in some way to school health and physical education are presented to Congress each session, and although few of them ever are passed the trend seems to be toward federal subsidies for services on supervision.

2. STATE LAWS

Every state in the Union has some law or other pertaining to school health. Many states are rather fully provided with the legislation needed to operate a school health programme in the community. Education equalization laws frequently provide money for employing health personnel, and other laws permit the community to spend its income on such programmes and personnel as it deems wise. Some states have enacted legislation to provide money directly to communities for school health purposes. The current law in Pennsylvania is a case in point:

Pennsylvania's present school health law requiring health examinations of school employees and pupils is definitely a public health act. It finances the cost of the medical and dental examination. It does not subsidise any school district. It applies to all children of school age in the Commonwealth regardless of where they attend school, whether public or private, and to those who are home bound. It also provides for the medical examination of all school teachers and school employees. The legislature has seen fit to designate the number of examinations that must be made during the school life of a child, by providing that pupils shall be examined while they are or should be members of grades one, three, five, seven, nine, and eleven. It also requires that teachers and school employees be examined at least once every two years. . . .

It places the entire health programme under the administration of the superintendents of school in areas under their supervison. . . . It places responsibility for financing of this special programme on the Commonwealth through the Department of Health, and sets up a standard fee for the medical and dental examiners, in order to insure that a definite standard shall be adhered to. . . .

This programme, it should be noted, provides for medical and dental examination, and makes no provision for a follow up corrective programme.

3. Boards of health

Funds may be, in certain states, transferred outright from boards of health to boards of education for the support of specified health activities. Or, more commonly, such activities may be financed by the board of health. This situation requires a fine type of cooperation for efficient administration when public health personnel render service in the school or when public health money is spent in the school. The quality of service should be no less than if it were contracted for from private physicians. School authorities should not expect *good* service if they ask the local health officer to visit the school, perform fifty examinations an hour, immunise all the first-grate children who need immunisation, and do any other thing necessary at the moment. Such services rendered by colleagues in the public welfare should be given well or not at all and the school should exercise its right to refuse anything less than the best. The health officer should decline to perform the perfunctory job sometimes asked of him.

4. BOARDS OF EDUCATION

In the last analysis most school health funds must originate in or be disbursed from local boards of education. The budgeting for disease control programmes, special classes for the partially sighted, testing programmes, anything having to do with school health education must be done locally. Physicians and nurses must be paid for their work and will be listed as salaried employees of the board. Every element of a school health programme must be approved and paid for ultimately by the board of education. That is why school administrators must know a great deal about health education in order to supply the board with appropriate recommendations.

5. AGENCY FUNDS

A precedent has been set in recent years by such organisations as the National Tuberculosis Association, the Kellogg Foundation, and others in granting funds or providing services to schools. Books have been bought, salaries paid, indigents cared for, audiometers purchased, nursing and medical salaries paid, courses of study underwritten, scholarships provided by these organisations as they seek to improve the health of people through the medium of the school. Much of the pioneer work, the frontier development in school health education has been made possible by grants direct to local or state boards of education from these private agencies. The practice continues. School health educators should be familiar with such potential resources in their own communities.

Costs in Salaries

For other than teachers standard salary scales are generally not in vogue in school health education. School nurses, dental hygienists, and some others in larger centres may have fixed salaries, but generally speaking the salary costs for nonteaching personnel become a matter of offer and negotiation. The amount paid is in relation to the current supply and demand for such services. Nurses and physicians are best paid by annual contract in terms of a fair appraisal of the value of their time in relation to the services offered.

How many specialists should be employed? The answer to that question is uncertain but it has a great bearing upon the total cost of a health programme. Certainly one nurse to every 1500 elementary pupils, a standard sometimes given, is too high a ratio. One to every 1000 or less would be better. A psychologist on the same basis, a dental hygienist to every 2000, a nutritionist to every 1000, and a full or part-time dentist and physician, depending upon the scope and quality of work expected of them, would be not unreasonable standards. Costs can be figured only in terms of prevailing salaries.

Sick leaves for teachers

The serious problem of sick leaves for teachers confronts most boards of education. It is basic to the morale of the taching staff. What is an adequate arrangement to make for teachers who are ill during the school year? Can a system be devised which will neither penalise nor be abused by teachers? It would be well if teachers remained away from school when they have respiratory diseases or are otherwise seriously incapacitated. And yet, if such absences are costly to them in income many teachers will prefer to inflict themselves upon the children. If sick leave is financially attractive some malingerers will stay away longer than is their due. The American Association of School Administrators has this to say about the problem:

Sick Leave—Although it is humanitarian to provide sick leave for school employees, the primary justification for a liberal sick leave policy is the protection and benefits that accrue to pupils. Without sick leave provisions, classroom teachers and other employees who cannot afford to lose even one day's salary may remain in school in direct contact with pupils when they are suffering from illness. A teacher who is ill cannot do a good job of teaching, and if the illness is contagious it is a direct hazard to the health of pupils.

State laws creating minimum sick leave plans are becoming

more and more numerous. Half the states now provide a minimum number of days of sick leave with pay. Many local school boards provide sick leave even though they are not required to do so and many grant additional leave beyond the state's minimum requirement. In numerous school systems, however, sick leave provisions still are totally lacking or are far from adequate.

Where sick leave is authorised by state law or local regulations, the time allowed may vary from five to twenty days. Accumulated sick leave may vary from twenty to ninety days or more and school boards sometimes allow more than the stipulated number of accumulated sick leave days to teachers who have rendered long and faithful service. Although a few employees probably take advantage of sick leave provisions, the great majority do not avail themselves of the provisions as frequently as would be justifiable for both their own benefit and that of the pupils.

Medical examinations before school employees return to work after being ill are a safeguard to both pupils and teachers. Compensation for periods of absence frequently depends upon presentation of a certificate issued by a physician—a practice that appears to be justifiable.

Equipment and facilities

To buy scales, tongue depressors, first-aid equipment, biologicals for immunisation, and other equipment for health services and to provide books and laboratory equipment for instruction costs money. Such materials should be provided for on the school budget. Ordinarily discounts are given to schools by supply houses. It is the experience of many that best equipment is the best investment. Inferior quality equipment, like second-run sport goods, is in the end most costly because it depreciates so rapidly. Superintendents and principals should expect their health personnel to combine their requests into an annual asking budget with provisions made for replacement requisitions during the year. In that way all interests—instructional, nursing, medical, nutritional, and others—will see their requests in relation to others and better all-school planning will result.

9

Evaluation of Child Development

The term evaluation means "appraising something according to a set of values." To evaluate health instruction means to find out how effective it has been in the lives of students. If the classroom experience leaves little or no imprint on the ideas or behaviour of the students, then it has little value. If, however, the learning is such as to have a real bearing upon the way life is lived, then the instructional materials and methods may be considered good.

In evaluating health instruction the thing appraised is the total learning experience—the "course," the "subject matter," the methods of organising and presenting the material. The set of values to be used in appraisal must be the intended outcomes. If a man wants to evaluate—measure—the length of a table, he uses a foot rule or yardstick, or perhaps a metric measuring tool, depending upon whether his values are in feet, yards, or metres. If he wanted to evaluate fire power of a rocket he would, if seeking to measure its penetration potential, fire it against various thicknesses of concrete or steel. First, he would decide what it was he was going to evaluate: the penetrating ability of the rocket. Then he would establish his values: penetration into concrete or steel. Then he would appraise his rocket by measuring how far into the steel or concrete it went when fired from a certain distance under stable conditions.

Appraising health instruction is not unlike that. Values have to be set. What are we after in health instruction? What are the intended outcomes? Once values are set, then devices are constructed by which one hopes to teli how good the instruction has been at attaining them.

Their may be many intended outcomes of health instruction. They may be specific, like the intention that all the students will thereafter be vaccinated for smallpox, or they may be rather general, like the intention that all students will make better adjustments to life's problems, or have an attitude of acceptance toward scientific discoveries. The teacher can aim for certain outcomes phrased in this way and can list them ahead of time as guides in course direction. If such a procedure were followed, i.e., if the teacher listed the objectives of each unit of work, they would probably fall into one of the following four categories:

1. Health Practice or Behaviour

It is apparent that healthful behaviour, conduct, living, is the principal thing to be sought in health instruction. To get people to *live* according to the best in the scientific world is the ultimate goal. To *become* vaccinated, to *eat* adequately, to *live* successfully in marriage, to *meet* a crisis in life—these are goals of greatest importance. "What do you *do?*" "How do you live?" These are the prime questions to be asked of students as a result of instruction in health. The answers are an evaluation of behaviour or health practice.

2. Health Status

What people *do* is closely related to what people *are*. The common salutation "How are you?" is, in essence, a form of evaluation. If, as a result of instruction, a student changes in his *being*—if he is different, or feels different—if a health condition has changed for the better, then the instruction has made a favourable contribution to his welfare. This sort of thing is a matter of status, organic or psychological condition, and may be evaluated only by the application of a great many tests and laboratory analyses usually available only to the physician or technician.

3. Health Knowledge

Knowledge is the basis for much of behaviour and status. If a person does not *know* that a serum is available for diphtheria he may never become immunised. If he does not know about the value of X-ray examinations for tuberculosis he may never have such an examination. Knowledge is important although it must be clear that knowledge alone may have little bearing upon the improvement or protection of health. Many may *know* of the existence of immune serums but unless they *act* in accordance with what they know their knowledge is of little use. That is why health knowledge is third in importance, after behaviour and status, as a value in measuring the benefit of instruction.

4. Health Attitude

There is also the rather uncertain and somewhat tenuous value known as *attitude*. The dictionary defines an attitude as "an habitual way of regarding something." One may have attitudes, therefore, about quacks, or vaccination, or doctors, or about "taking care of oneself." Certainly the best motivation for getting things done, for living in accordance with the best scientific thought, is found if the regard for science is high—if the attitude is right. Again, however, it is not the attitude but the action that counts. A person may mean well toward vaccination, may have a fine attitude toward it, and yet *if he is not vaccinated* his attitude is valueless. Neither attitude nor knowledge then is an altogether reliable indicator of the value of an instructional programme. It is what a person *is* and *does* which, in the last analysis, truly counts.

METHODS OF EVALUATION

In seeking to evaluate the worth of health instruction the teacher can get an estimate or a measure of each of the four values just mentioned—health behaviour, health status, health knowledge, and health attitude. Health being the exceedingly complex thing it is, no one estimation in any of those categories will tell the whole story of the effectiveness of teaching. For example, in a one-semester hygiene class some students may do nearly perfect work when tested for knowledge and yet be maladjusted emotionally in their personal lives. Others may carelessly expose themselves to skin disease although their "attitude" is all against that sort of thing. Someone may have had an undiscovered tuberculosis, but studying about the disease will have no bearing on its treatment unless the class provides for the actual experience of the X-ray and other analyses.

Evaluating one's health is complicated business. Evaluating the outcomes of a course of instruction is only slightly less so. The products of teaching may not show up on the final examination. Outcomes or values may not be readily apparent. A college hygiene teacher once reported this occurrence as an illustration of deferred values: The teacher usually gave an interesting unit on marriage and family problems. Year after year the unit had been given with the usual examinations testing the knowledge of the students in the subject. Once, ten years after the teacher had left the college, he met one of his former students, who told him how much that course had meant. The former student mentioned particularly how the unit on marriage had eased many a problem of his own and had helped him establish a happy family life. Here are deferred values. No evaluation at the time of instruction would have shown these. About all one can do in evaluation with students at the time is to hope to get an estimation of immediate values. And even with that in mind it is difficult to tell what outcomes result from the course and what from other influences.

Nevertheless evaluations are attempted and the following may be helpful in each of the four categories of values:

1. Evaluating Health Practice

Health behaviour or practice (erroneously called "habits") may be evaluated by several different techniques:

A. The Health Practice Inventory

The health practice inventory allows the student an opportunity to record what he does. Frequently, as in the Johns Health Inventory, students record whether they always, frequently, sometimes, rarely, or never do certain specific things.

Or, in a booklet published by the Cattaraugus County School Health Service and developed by Dr. Ruth Grout, elementary children are given the chance to mark as follows:

Yesterday I did the things in the list below which I have marked "yes." Those which I did not do I have marked "no." Fill in the blank spaces.

.... 1. I had......hours of sleep last night.

....

.... 13. I was troubled with indigestion.

....

.... 15. I had a bowel movement during the day.

....

.... 34. I was troubled with a toothache.

....

.... 43. I greeted my schoolmates in a friendly manner.

These inventories may be made to cover the suggested activities of the whole course or of any given unit. Scoring should be done with caution in that there are so few health practices which *all* should do *always* and *none* should *ever* do. For example, to fail to have a bowel movement every day is no indication of faulty practice; likewise, crossing a city street at other than an intersection may frequently be acceptable practice. Absolute scores for rating students for grades in the course are difficult to get from these inventories and they are best used as bases for individual consultation and as points of departure for class discussion.

B. THE CONSUMER INVENTORY

The consumer inventory is similar to the health practice inventory but more limited in scope. It is constructed to deal with such questions as "What do you use?" "What do you buy?" Why do you buy it?" "Would you use . . . ?" "Do you believe . . . ?" For example:

1. Do you buy your toothpaste as a result of car card advertisements?
2. Do you believe the "medical" reports as cited by cigarette advertisements?
3. How effective do you believe Beto is in the treatment of diabetes? 100 per cent-75 per cent-50 per cent 0 per cent.

A great variety of such questions in the form above or as true-false or as multiple-choice statements can be constructed covering nearly all phases of health quacks, commercial psychologists, muscle-building systems, beds, food, vitamins, because nearly every aspect of healthful living has been subjected to the merciless treatment of commercial advertising. The limitations of such tests are the same as for the inventories, namely, they may not reflect what the student got out of the course, and they are not easily used, therefore, as grades.

c. Observations

A variety of observation techniques can be used effectively. For example, class discussion may stimulate the group to evaluate their own susceptibility to radio commercials. Each student may, for a week, make note of each time he listens to the commercial (preferably advertising something to do with health) and estimate the extent to which he believes or doubts the implications in the script. These observations can then be brought into class for discussion and checking.

Or individuals within a group may observe each other. They may, over a week or a month or some such period, keep notes on the other fellow's temper, his courtesy, his cooperativeness, his selfishness. Then, if the appropriate rapport can be established, the behaviours implicit in the observations can be evaluated.

Teachers and parents can make observations on such matters as sleep, rest, food, worry, friendliness, cooperation, boy-girl relationships, extroversion-introversion. These observations can be recorded on prepared forms if desirable and later made the basis for individual consultation.

The bibliography at the end of this chapter has a selected list of published evaluating devices in this area, and teachers intending to use such inventories would do well to secure them or model their own after existing and standardised examples.

2. Evaluating Health Status

There are so many ways to appraise organic and psychological states as to make it difficult to present here any condensed list or description of them. Most of the important ones are usable only by physicians or by psychologists. The teacher is limited in this category because to appraise a health condition usually requires diagnostic or other technical skills which educators do not have.

These evaluating procedures range from the simple administration of a vision test from an eye chart to the complicated diagnosis of tuberculosis from X-ray and sputum examination or to the interpretations possible only to the experienced cardiologist from his stethoscope and electrocardiograph. Teachers may form an impression of the social health of a student by giving a social distance test but a psychologist or psychiatrist would be needed to evaluate fully the psychic or emotional disorders attendant, say, upon a cancer phobia or an incipient schizophrenia.

For purposes of understanding this range more clearly these tests of organic psychological states may be grouped as follows:

A. Tests of so-called "Organic Efficiency"

Organic efficiency tests are legion and most of them are within the ability of the teacher to administer. They are sometimes called tests of "physical fitness" and are useful in a general way in appraising "condition" or muscular skill.

B. Medical Tests

Medical tests are all beyond the scope of the teacher and involve such tests as blood serology, urinalysis, the basal metabolism test, blood tests, the Mantoux, tests of reflexes, and many others used by physicians in diagnostic and interpretive practice. They reflect organic and psychological states usually of a specific nature and it would be unusual if changes noted on such tests could be directly and specifically attributed to the instruction given in a hygiene course.

C. Tests useful to teachers

Useful information about the development and status of children may be obtained by teachers by carefully and skillfully conducted appraisals of such elements as posture, vision, hearing, weight, height, and general tone and energy. With practice and experience a teacher should be able, not, of course, to make a diagnosis of condition, but to supply information which may be useful as he adjusts the child's educational programme.

3. Evaluating Health Knowledge

It is within the area of health knowledge that the teacher does the best work in evaluation. The tests are the easiest to administer. The results are most readily noted and the evaluating process itself is a useful educational tool. Knowledge tests, when gone over with the students afterward, help them understand their weaknesses and strengths in health information. When used prior to the course, the tests are useful in placing students in homogeneous class sections. They are useful as quiz and final examination material, and, when their results are analysed item by item, they help teachers and supervisors to determine where individual students need assistance and where teachers need to bolster their course offerings.

Perhaps their most frequent uses are at pretests, placement tests, and examinations in specific hygiene courses. In small sections as well as in larger groups, knowledge tests aid in determining the status of students and, because of the very nature of the tests, inevitably throw some light on the more important element of health behaviour and the less important element of health attitude.

There are several different kinds of knowledge tests, such as:

A. THE ESSAY

Students are asked to write on a subject at a length determined or undetermined, e.g., "Present the arguments for and against vaccination for smallpox," or "What significant findings concerning the health of the nation's man power resulted from Selective Service examinations in the Second World War?" or "Present the three principal anatomical discrepancies in the theory of chiropractic," or "What factors in the smoking of tobacco make smoking an unwise practice for young people?" There are unlimited possibilities for such essay questions. They should be chosen in relation to the material dealt with in the class; should reflect more of an ability to interpret and apply than to recall anatomical fact; should be marked for worth on their accuracy and logic and are always subject to the great weakness of all essay questions—their lack of objectivity.

B. *THE OBJECTIVE TYPE*

The more popular type of knowledge test is the objective type, and the resources at the end of this chapter should be consulted for examples of some standardised tests of this sort. Most teachers try their skill at working up the questions to fit their own courses, using the published standardised tests for placement in sections or for measuring the knowledge status of large groups. There are various kinds of objective tests: true-false, multiple choice, completion, matching, discrimination, garbled paragraphs, and others, and a teacher would do well to try them all and interchange them, from time to time, comparing their results. In making objective tests the teacher should consider the following suggestions: (1) The multiple-choice question with five reasonable alternatives (one being the correct choice) is perhaps the best kind of objective question. For example:

1. Conservative estimates are that the percentage of people in this country infected with syphilis is (a) 1/5 of one per cent, (b) 2 to 57 per cent (c) 10 to 20 per cent (d) 20 to 50 per cent (e) over 50 per cent.
2. We can be absolutely certain that every boy or girl that develops tuberculosis (a) inherited a tendency toward the disease, (b) drank raw milk, (c) has been exposed to some person with the disease, (d) has inherently weak lungs, (e) cannot be cured.
3. What we know concerning the values of drinking large amounts of water in the treatment of acute respiratory infections is that (a) water helps in the elimination of the toxic products of the infection, (b) the water acts as a very mild and wholesome cathartic, (c) the water increases the volume of the blood, thus aiding circulation, (d) it is founded on unproven assumptions, (e) life processes are carried on in solution and thus it is helpful to increase the efficiency of these processes.
4. The reason that influenza is such a dread disease and has led to many deaths is that (a) influenza causes a swelling of

the larynx and the patient dies of asphyxia, (b) influenza lowers the resistance to other diseases, (c) influenza injures the heart, (d) influenza is easily spread by droplet infection, (e) influenza is a violent general disease, whose toxins cause death.

5. In the light of present knowledge the best way to prevent one from catching a cold is to (a) take vitamin D in cod liver oil, (b) sleep and eat at regular hours, (c) take a laxative and purge the system when exposed, (d) use one of the various vapour treatments when exposed, (e) carefully avoid infection.

(2) The completion question is the least satisfactory. ("If a wound is bleeding profusely a . . . should be applied." The correct word might be "bandage' but students might also very reasonably write in "tourniquet" or "stitches.") (3) "Knowledge of functional significance rather than knowledge of terms should be stressed." (4) "Judgment and choice of conduct in problem situations is possibly of greater health significance than simple recognition of correct answers." (5) Considerable leeway in favour of the student must be given when marking because much of the material in hygiene is not so precise and clear cut as to lend itself readily to clear-cut answers. (6) Tests should always be marked and handed back with ample time given to study the errors. Derryberry suggests that a briefly written or even an oral explanation of the true version of each question will enhance the educational value of the test itself. The teacher should, by all means, explain the correct version of each item and if the question remains unclear or ambiguous he should not hesitate to discard it. (7) All objective test questions should be "tried out" on several fellow teachers or other adults before being given to the class. Ambiguous and otherwise faulty questions should be discarded. (8) It makes little difference whether the scoring is done by merely adding up the number of errors or by the more complicated systems of subtracting the "wrongs" from the "rights" or counting two off for every error and adding one for every "right." (9) Trick questions are always resented and should be avoided. (10) Objectives tests for health knowledge decrease greatly in usefulness below the seventh grade.

4. Evaluating Health Attitudes

As has already been pointed out, because of the intangible and tenuous nature of attitudes it is extremely difficult to obtain a satisfactory evaluation of them. If a teacher wants to determine the attitude of students toward religious healing, for example, or toward the vitamin fad almost any question asked or any observation made would deal with what the students *know* about the subject, or what they *do* about it.

How one feels about a subject or what "habitual regard" he has for it is estimated, in the last analysis, by what he does, knows, or says about it. The teacher can find out just about all he needs to by carefully evaluating knowledge and behaviour and from such an evaluation estimating the elusive attitude.

There have been, however, worth-while efforts to evaluate health attitudes. By using observations (again perhaps of behaviour), discussions and interviews, autobiographical records, and written tests, involving choices of the "right" or "best" thing to do, a teacher may find out something of how the students think about an issue. One of the best illustrations of this last type was conducted by Southworth, Latimer, and Turner, involving 15,000 students, and was called "Your Opinion, Please!" The following is an excerpt from Test III of this extensive survey of the health practices, knowledge, attitudes, and interests of students in Massachusetts:

Test III

Your Opinion, Please!

Directions: The following statements represent opinions about various phases of health and you are to express your own point of view about them. Indicate how you really feel about each statement immediately after you read it. Do not pause too long on any of them. Read each item and in the blank on the answer sheet corresponding to the number of the item, blacken the space as follows:

1. Under A (agree) if you agree with the whole statement.
2. Under U (uncertain) if you are uncertain about the whole statement.

3. Under D (disagree) if you disagree with the whole statement.

Examples:

	A U D
1. All children should be allowed to play with fireworks.	1--
2. Children should drink milk.	2--

Statement	Key	Percent of Correct Answers
1. If a person believes that any fat or starchy food causes his skin to be excessively oily, he should follow a prescribed diet.	A	51
2. The natural form of vitamins obtained from foods (balanced diet) causes the vitamins to be more effective in the body than when they are obtained from vitamin capsules.	A	87
3. There is no danger of disease from raw, unwashed fruits and vegetables.	D	86
4. If one is going on a diet, he should do so under a physician's guidance.	A	93
5. The only purpose of food is to develop a strong muscular body.	D	75
6. One should select a balanced meal when ordering food in a cafeteria or restaurant.	A	88
7. A high school student should play at least one sport which he will be able to carry on after school days are over.	A	64
8. A person who is well and strong does not need to give any thought to the kind and amount of food he eats.	D	92
9. If two people maintain that the use of certain foods produces different effects on the skins of different persons, one or the other or both probably made incorrect observations.	D	42
10. The peddler of narcotic drugs should be given a jail sentence.	A	73

In this particular section devoted to opinion, ninety such statements were given and although a student would know something about the subject matter involved in the statement and base his opinion on this knowledge, nevertheless these tests represent a fine attempt to discover the "habitual regard" for the problem.

Attitudes, thus, are listed as least important in the evaluation possibilities not because the point of view of the student toward health or toward science is unimportant but because to locate an attitude in order to evaluate it is nearly impossible, and because the reaction of a student to the health problem involved can be more easily determined by evaluating his knowledge and behaviour regarding it.

Rugen and Nyswander conveniently group health status, knowledge, and attitude as "understandings" and present the following summary of procedures available for evaluating them:

1. Observation of pupil behaviour and the recording of these observations in behaviour journals, in anecdotal records, or in other ways.
2. Self-appraisal by the pupil in terms of standards of behaviour previously agreed upon.
3. Check lists and survey forms based on accepted "standards" and used at periodic intervals.
4. Interviews with pupils, parents, other teachers, and community workers, including home visits and individual counselling.
5. Health-examination records and reports from physicians, dentists, and nurses.
6. Reports from local physicians, ophthalmologists, and dentists regarding the increase in medical and dental supervision of school-age groups .
7. Diaries and other autobiographical records of pupils.
8. Specially created situations within the classroom and school which give pupils opportunity to apply voluntarily what

they have learned.

9. Paper-and-pencil inventories aimed at application of principles and evaluation of sources of help.
10. Expression of pupil opinion which considers positive health behaviour the "thing to do," because the natural leaders in the school have accepted it.
11. Records of the sale of milk, salads, fruits, whole-grain cereals, enriched bread, etc. in the school cafeteria or in local food establishments, including dairies and stores.
12. Samples of pupil creative work, such as drawings, models, exhibits, photographs, motion pictures, or written and oral reports which show sound application of health principles.

5. Evaluating Instructional Programmes

To date little significant work has been done in comaparing the effectiveness of the three patterns of teaching—through integration, correlation, or a specific course. There are many experienced teachers who favour each of the patterns, claiming that their favourite produces the most lasting results in the development and protection of the health of the student. Those who favour the integrated programme contend that although certain specific knowledge of the anatomy and physiology of the body may not be dealt with, nevertheless students emerge from one of the larger core units with a better understanding of health and health problems than if they had studied a specific and single health unit. The meaning of things is understood because it has been taught in relation to a living, integrated problem of human affairs.

Those supporting specific dislike the alleged "diluting of health material" by teaching it in association with larger problems and prefer to produce results in knowledge and practice by seeking them directly and with no competition or diversion.

Well taught, it may be safely assumed that any progressive and scientifically sound course of study will be productive of results in the lives of students. There is evidence that both the integrated and the correlated plans have done well in broadening the base of student understanding in health matters just as there is ample reason to believe that a well-taught course in hygience is a useful and productive experience.

Not all courses of study, however, are equally good. They need evaluation. Any teacher should constantly keep his instructional programme, his course, and his teaching aids flexible enough to be receptive to criticism and improvement. Nothing can be more deadly than a health course ill conceived in the first place and taught the same way year after year with no thought as to whether it is interesting or productive of results in improving students' lives.

Health courses of study can and should be evaluated in both general and specific terms. They may be analysed as a part of a larger curriculum or they may be scrutinised specifically for their own value as a teaching medium.

For example, any health course of study, as a part of a larger curriculum might be evaluated in accordance with the Bruner criteria. These are divided into four parts: philosophy, content, activities and evaluation of pupils' work, and the criteria themselves are phrased in question focus with directions for rating the courses of study being evaluated. For example, such questions as

Is self-activity considered fundamental learning?

Is significance attached to pupil meanings and insights?

Will the materials help to broaden the social interest of the pupil?

Are the materials organised around broad areas of significant human experience?

Do the activities arise from real life situations?

Is there a sufficient range of activities to provide adequately for the various interests and needs of the group?

are useful in determining whether the course of study is meeting the needs of the students. These and others comprise the Bruner criteria and may be recommended for course-of-study evaluation.

More specifically, a single course not in relation to a course of study or to a curriculum can be evaluated by applying criteria to it and judging the materials and methods used in the course on the basis of their excellence. The following criteria are useful for this purpose:

1. The content material must be scientifically accurate throughout and in thorough accord with the best available knowledge in the life sciences.
2. The experiences should foster the concept of health as a qualitative result of the interdependent functioning of all the vital systems, involving the mental and social aspects of living as well as the physical.
3. The experiences should constantly interpret health from a social point of view, explaining health in terms of its social uses.
4. The experiences should be selected in response to data from student life which indicate the needs and interests of the learners, and not chosen solely in terms of what course makers believe should be included. The experiences should be drawn out of, identical with, or linked to the life of the learner.
5. The experiences should be arranged on an activity basis, giving constant opportunity for healthful practice, and aimed more at the development of conduct than at the acquisition of knowledge.
6. The order of thought presentation should be from the particular to the general, each new principle, abstraction or generalisation being developed thought intimate, concrete, individual experience before reaching its final form.
7. There should be an abundance of material of varying difficulty so as to admit of choice suited to the needs of the individuals who differ in capacity and experience.
8. The experiences selected should be progressively graded so as to provide for continuous growth in healthful living and, if possible, reliable instruments of measurement should be applied to note the progress of each learner.

9. Frequent periods for review should be interspersed throughout the course, and if examinations, quizzes, or tests are used they should be analysed afterwards with the class.

10. There should be provided in connection with each major thought division an up-to-date series of standard and reliable references, so arranged as to stimulate in the student a desire for a widening of his interest and knowledge.

11. The general tone of the experiences with respect to all controversial issues should be one of discreet judgment, free from prejudice or inaccurate content. The learners should never be coloured with emotional bias for want of scientific data.

12. The experiences should require a mastery of a minimum of scientific terminology, enough to handle the ordinary health processes intelligently.

13. The experiences should provide frequent and specific opportunity for correlation with other areas in the curriculum and with other parts of the health education programme.

14. The activities of the course should lead to cooperation and understanding between the school and the home and community.

Some of the thoughts contained in the foregoing criteria find expression in an evaluation schedule developed in Texas, excerpts from which are here reproduced:

A. Direct and specific health instruction:	Yes	No
1. The teacher of health		
a. continually studies health information.	...	...
b. is trained for this teaching.	...	...
c. possesses qualities of research necessary to determine children's health needs.	...	...

d. demonstrates methods of teaching and handling of instruction materials that satisfy the children's health needs.	...	...
e. is capable of handling the total health coordination.	...	...
f. is thoroughly interested in the school health programme.	...	...
g. possesses personal characteristics that promote the total school health programme.	...	...
2. Direct and specific health instruction is given in class periods set aside for that purpose in the school day.	...	...
3. The teacher uses objective means of determining the health habits, knowledges and attitudes of each child.	...	...
4. The health needs and interests of the child become the basis of all health instruction.	...	...
5. Pupils share in the planning of health instruction.	...	...
10. The teacher constantly evaluates the health instruction through		
a. conferences with students.	...	...
b. self-appraisal lists.	...	...
c. objective knowledge tests.	...	...
d. observation of health habits.	...	...
e. surveys and questionnaires.	...	...
11 Students display enthusiasm and continued interest in health instruction.	...	...
12. Health instruction		
a. is concerned with vial problems of everyday living.	...	...

b. is aimed at acquiring knowledge and establishing proper attitudes and behaviour toward these vital problems. ... ...

c. seeks the individual's cooperation in solving the vital individual and community health problems. ... ...

SUMMARY OF EVALUATION OF INSTRUCTION

Although it is apparent that to estimate the value of instruction is a complex and not altogether objective process, nevertheless teachers should attempt it. Each device mentioned in the preceding pages is useful in its own way and there is none that could not be improved upon. For those who attempt evaluation of health instruction the following principles should be observed:

1. *The objectives of the unit or course to be evaluated should be clearly stated prior to the evaluation.* The appraisal is made to determine the success which is met in reaching the objectives.
2. *All appraisals in which students are the respondents should be geared to their age.* There is no use asking a student for evidence if he cannot understand the question or phrase the answer.
3. *The results should be kept honest no matter how meager or discouraging they may be.* Teachers sometimes "pad" evaluation results to make the situation look better. Clean, honest evaluations are the only ones which are helpful.
4. *It is not necessary to have the results entirely in objective and tangible form.* Subjective judgments, opinions, "jury" judgments, personal testimony are all admissible (with understanding as to their worth) as evaluating instruments. They should be used.

THE EVALUATION OF SERVICES AND ACTIVITIES

To evaluate the worth of school health services and activities is like appraising instruction. One seeks to learn how effective the procedures are and what results they produce. The foregoing chapters in Part III have described many procedures used in school health education which, when taken as a whole, aim to determine the status of child health and to organise for its improvement. But how good are these procedures? How effective are they in accomplishing the objective for which they were designed? Do they produce satisfactory results in terms of improving the health of school children? Is what we are doing up to date? Should we be doing anything new?

There are three approaches to the evaluation of school health services and activities. (1) It must be determined whether the programme as a whole is complete—whether it has in it those features it should have. (2) It is necessary to find out whether the procedures used in the programme accomplish what they are suppŏsed to accomplish. (3) An apraisal should be made of the outcome of the action, usually in terms of the effect of the procedures upon the health of children.

To illustrate: It is generally agreed that a health programme would not be complete (1) without vision testing. The Snellen test may be the one used by teachers. It is highly possible that this is an ineffective means (2) by which vision deviates may be screened. An evaluation would find out. The vision problem is not solved, however, even with successful screening. The correction of vision handicaps must take place before the circle is closed (3) Results must be shown in improved child health. The latter, or course, is crucial. The efforts of the school may come to naught unless parents follow through on the school's recommendations.

To evaluate effectively all aspects of a school health programme requires, thus, many tests, surveys, checks, follow-ups, retests, and other devices. To date the field does not provide means to accomplish an evaluation complete in every respect. New techniques are continually being developed through research and experience.

Administrators should include in the annual budget provision for evaluation. A subcommittee of the school health council could well be appointed to conduct the various aspects of the programme of inquiry. *It will seek to establish principles, first,* and the following are recommended as applicable:

1. Evaluation should be continuous.
2. It should embrace all of the important functions of the school health programme including instruction and activities.
3. It should be concerned both with end products and the means to reach these ends.
4. It should touch upon all health aspects of the school including curriculum, administration, buildings, grounds, equipment, finances, and community relationships.
5. Evaluation should be cooperative. All those who are affected by the evaluation should participate in it—administrators, teachers, pupils, parents, physicians, nurses, dental hygienists, nutritionists and others.
6. Evaluation should be focused upon the important values which underlie the health programme of the school, and the success or failure of the programme should be judged in terms of how well it meets the values held.
7. A long range evaluation programme should be so planned that no one year would involve the school in a complete study of every aspect of school health education.
8. The collection of data and keeping of records in the school have no value in themselves. Only as the data aid in evaluating the true functions of school health education do they attain value.

Second, it will recognise that not all aspects of the programme should be evaluated the first year. An approach will be mapped out something as follows:

First year:

1. The disease control programme.
2. The hearing testing programme.
3. The environment of the school in relation to health and safety.

Second year:

1. The vision testing programme.
2. The programme of correlation of instruction.
3. The dental hygiene programme.
4. The frequency and causes of absenteeism among students and staff.

Third year:

1. The effectiveness of the nursing and medical services, including the examinations.
2. The growth and nutrition programme including the lunchroom.
3. The psychological services and mental hygiene programme.
4. The programme of direct teaching in health.

Fourth year:

1. The physical education programme including the care of athletes and the programme of athletics in relation to health.
2. The emergency care programme including first aid.
3. Community relationships.
4. The programme of integrated instruction as it bears on health.
5. The use of teaching aids in health instruction.

Fifth year:

1. The administrative and financial structure of the health programme.
2. The effectiveness of personnel.
3. The relation of the school programme to community practitioners and agencies.

4. The school health education programme as a whole—as a functioning unit.

Such a schedule of evaluations would be predicated upon a continuous study of the health needs of the children in school and the communities from which they come. Alterations in programme aimed at greater effectiveness can only come when needs are known and met.

Third, the committee, having agreed on basic principles and established a tentative schedule from which to work, *should then give some thought to objectives.* It should have before it the objectives of the school health programme as a whole so that the objectives of specific parts of it can be seen in relation to the larger problem. Emphasising the educational aspects of a school health service or activity programme, the committee might understand these to be the general educational objectives of the programme as a whole:

For the child:

1. A favourable attitude towards professional medical and dental care.
2. An appreciation of the value and importance of early medical advice and the dangers of self-medication and over-the-counter drugstore prescribing.
3. Information concerning the transmission of communicable diseases, methods of protection, and proper health behaviours relative to their control.
4. The development of good health habits. . . .

For the parent:

1. It should produce a better understanding of the child not only with respect to his physical needs, but also his mental and social needs. . . .
2. It should inform parents concerning the medical facilities of the community and how they can best be used. It should also teach both parents and children how to appraise the various types of so-called medical facilities, or, in other words, how to separate the quacks from reputable and acceptable facilities.

3. It should develop among parents a favourable attitude toward the school, so that they will think of it as a place where they can go for friendly advice concerning their child. . . .
4. From the programme, parents should develop a favourable attitude toward all preventive measures, such as, immunisations and vaccinations, early care of colds, etc. . . .

For the teacher:

1. A better understanding of the handicaps of children in general and her children in particular. . . .
2. An improved knowledge of the meaning of certain physical symptoms and behaviours which she may observe in her children.
3. A more thorough understanding of the home conditions of the children whose homes are visited by any of the school health personnel. . . .
4. A knowledge of how to utilise the services of the other members of the school health staff in understanding her own children. . . .

For the nurse:

1. An appreciation of the child as a personality to be educated as well as an organism with a defect of some kind.
2. That there are scholastic, social, and psychological problems which interrelate with the physical.
3. The nursing in education is an integral part of a whole and not a special unrelated service.
4. That records on children are a means to developmental ends and not ends in themselves.

For the principal:

1. An appreciation of the need for administrative adjustment for children who are deviates from the normal.
2. An appreciation of the limitations and possibilities of the school medical examination and related services.

With some such arrangement of general objectives in mind the committee could then turn to the consideration of specific objectives for the specific phase of the programme to be evaluated now.

What does the vision testing programme aim to do? Possibly (1) to get a preliminary but accurate reading on the vision of all children every year, (2) to screen out all children with 20/40 vision or worse, (3) to arrange teacher-nurse-parent conferences where necessary to recommend corrective or compensating action, (4) to secure corrections in every needed case, (5) to adjust room environment (seats, lighting, reflectors) for benefit of vision, (6) to indicate need of special slight-saving training.

The committee would proceed to get the answers to the question: "How near does the vision testing programme come to attaining these six objectives?"

Fourth, the committee would determine its evaluating techniques in relation to the element of the programme to be appraised. Techniques good for finding the answers about the vision programme would not be applicable, perhaps, in evaluating the school lunch. The committee would choose from statistical analyses, surveys, testimony of participants or observers, rating scales, or any other suitable device. It would make sure that the measurements attained were:

1. Objective. They must be so constituted that the results obtained by one evaluator will be the same as those by any other evaluator in the same situation.
2. The items must be indicative of the total objective rather than a measurement only of the particular item included.
3. The measurements used must be truly indicative of the degree to which the objectives have been achieved.

There are several useful check lists or survey forms which can serve well as models or examples for a committee wishing to develop a local evaluation programme. Presumably these may be secured at their sources. They are listed in the next few pages.

As an example of a typical check sheet or survey for evaluating a total programme the following excerpts from one now in use will illustrate the scope of the coverage.

EVALUATING YOUR HEALTH EDUCATION PROGRAMME

Organisation and Administration of the School Health Programme

.... 1. Do you have a health committee or council which plans the programme?

.... 2. Are parents and students represented on the planning group?

.... 3. Do you have written policies relative to emergency care, first aid, what to do in case of accident?

.... 4. Do you utilise the resources and materials that community agencies have available for helping to promote an effective health programme?

Health Service

Health Examination and Teacher Observation.

.... 1. Are periodic health examinations given to all students?

....

.... 3. Is the examination utilised for its educational values?

.... 4. Are periodic dental examinations given to all students?

.... 5. Does your school have available adequate equipment to administer screening tests for such fields as nutrition, vision, hearing, and teeth?

.... 6. Are teachers trained in the techniques necessary for administering screening tests?

....

.... 8. Are teachers trained to make careful observations of students for deviations from the normal in physical and mental health status?

.... 9. Are these observations of teachers recorded?

.... 10. Are health appraisal records kept up to date for each student and made available to all faculty members for counselling?

.... 11. Are all of the students of your school immunised against smallpox and diphtheria?

.... 12. Do you have an adequate and effective follow-up programme for securing the correction of remediable physical defects?

....

Provision for Safety and Health Protection.

....

.... 3. Do you have standard first aid kits and essential first aid equipment in your laboratories and shops?

.... 4. Do you have a member of your faculty who is trained in first aid?

.... 5. Are all pupils examined upon returning to school after a long illness?

.... 6. Are adequate hand washing and shower bath facilities provided?

.... 7. Are paper towels and soap provided for students?

....

Provision for mental health.

.... 1. Are teachers well-adjusted with a sense of personal security and adequacy?

.... 2. Is a school environment provided which is free from tensions, pressures, rivalries, sarcasm, and inconsistencies in the handling of children?

....

Health Instruction Programme

Organisation.

.... 1. Have adequate materials and equipment, such as books, charts, posters, health magazines, pamphlets, been secured for the class?

.... 2. Have arrangements been made to secure the necessary visual aids such as films and films strips for the class?

.... 3. Do you have at least a semester's work in health instruction—a special class?

....

In addition to evaluating services to determine their adequacy or personnel to get an impression of their effectiveness, it is frequently desirable to check up on the quality of the school environment. A guide for such an evaluation has been prepared by the Ohio Department of Health, Division of Sanitary Engineering, and the Ohio Department of Education and is reproduced by permission here:

Guide for the Evaluation of School Health Environment

Organisation:

1. Is there a staff of employees adequate in number and qualified in their respective assignments for maintenance and operation of the school plant?
2. Is there an advisory sanitation committee of the school health council made up of school officials, teachers, employees, parents, and various specialists and consultants on school building maintenance and operation?
3. Is there competent local health department sanitation personnel who can work effectively with school personnel?
4. Are the school and community organisations interested and active in environmental health matters?

5. Are consultants available on specific problems related to health, sanitation, and safety—persons who may be from official local and state health and education departments, fire prevention offices, safety departments, and many non-official agencies and commercial concerns?

Programme:

A. High Department Responsibility

1. Are routine official inspections of all school buildings and surrounding made at least twice each year—once during the winter and once during the summer months—by competent health department sanitarians?
2. Are additional visits and consolations made when needed?
3. Are consultations held with school administrators, employees, and teachers at the time of inspection with the purpose of the inspection and defects and recommendations fully explained?
4. Are the "School Building Inspection Form" and the "Inspection Form for Eating and Drinking Establishments" (supplied by the ODH) filled out in detail by the sanitarian at the time of the inspection?
5. Is there an official letter signed by the health commissioner outlining the conditions found and improvements needed sent to the board of education and the school administrator following each inspection?
6. Is the public health sanitarian used as a resources person to help school officials in obtaining needed information and services?
7. Is the public health sanitarian used as an adviser and consultant to community and school groups on all matters pertaining to the school environment?
8. Is there a continuous in-service training programme for school employees sponsored jointly by the health department and school officials?

B. School Responsibility

1. Does the school make use of the health, sanitation, and safety standards for school buildings as developed by the Ohio Departments of Health and Education, the National Sanitation Foundation, the American Association of School Administrators, and other state and national agencies?
2. Does the school make periodic requests for building inspections to local health, fire prevention, safety, and school officials—with provisions made for follow-up on their recommendations?
3. Is reliable information on building maintenance and improvements solicited from commercial concerns?
4. Are responsible school officials alert to defect in building maintenance and operation, and do they initiate action for necessary correction?
5. Does the school cooperate with the local health department in an in-service training programme for school employees?

C. Responsibility of Others

(Teachers, Parents, School Employees, Pupils, etc.)

1. Is literature on school facilities and operation available and used?
2. Are school facilities and their operation compared with recommended standards of the state health and education departments?
3. Are important defects discussed with associates, neighbours, the school administrator, members of the board of education, and in school and community meetings?
4. Are official agencies such as the local health department, district school administrator, fire prevention and safety departments, consulted for opinions on important defects?
5. Are conferences held with the board of education and school administrator about ways and means of making important improvements and changes?

In selecting the techniques for the local programme of evaluation the committee will want to make the distinction between tests used in the programme itself (e.g., the Wetzel Grid, the Masschusetts Vision Test) and other evaluating techniques in order to determine the efficiency of those tests as a part of the total programme. The former appraise students; the latter deal with the attainment of programme objectives in a larger sense. The choice of such evaluating techniques can best be made if the committee reviews the best in currently available plans and makes a selection to fit the local situation. The following represents a selected list of such evaluation plans, standards, or policies to follow:

The Evaluation of School and Public Nutrition Programmes

Making School Lunches Educational, Nutrition-Education Series, No. 2, US Office of Education, Washington, 1944.

A Yardstick for School Lunches, Nutrition-Education Series, No. 4, US Office of Education, Washington, 1948.

As the fifth and last step in an evaluation study the committee will wish to make a report to the health council or any other appropriate body. This report should include the following:

1. A clear description of the programme or programme element which was appraised.
2. A description of how the appraisal was made including complete revelation of the techniques and procedures used.
3. The detailed specific results, the findings, with the original data available (but not necessarily in the report) if the parent body wants them.
4. A statement of general results or conclusions from the evaluation. This will include a citation if necessary of the deterrents found such as lack of funds, lack of personnel, inadequate referral services, misinformed administration, parental indifference).
5. A series of clear recommendations for improvement of the programme arranged from the simple to the complex and from those possible now to those possible only in the future.

All such evaluations will be tried to determine how close practice is to objective. Where money is being spent, time is being consumed, and the health of children is at stake, the things done must be proved useful. They must be constructive elements in a programme with a clearly stated aim. As Gudakunst once summarised it, the aim of all school health programmes is to:

1. Produce a healthier group of children in the community.
2. Produce an educated group of parents and citizens.
3. Produce students who, when school days are over, are self-sufficient in health matters, able to seek and find their own way with scientific wisdom.
4. Produce a community able and willing to support the efforts of the school in health education.

10

The Creative Process in Child Development

The Creator' *par excellence* is God and whenever we create some new thing we feel we are God-like and achieving immortality. The Greeks were aware of the awesomeness, the double-edged nature of creating, for Prometheus who discovered fire was venerated as a benefactor of mankind, raised to the Pantheon, but also, having aroused the envy of the Gods, punished cruelly for his pains. In its most basic sense (to 'pro-create') creating denotes sexuality—of beast as well as man—and hence is charged with all the emotion, the complexes and inhibitions, and the mysteries surrounding our deepest biological urges. Small wonder then that 'creativity' (a word of American coinage, not found in the *Oxford English Dictionary*) is a word of power, prestige and prodigiousness that we all wish to appropriate. Creativeness confers power and distinction. To quote Bruner (1962):

> It is implied, I think, that the act of one creating is the act of a whole man, that it is this rather than the product that makes it good and worthy. So whoever seeks to proclaim his wholeness turns to the new slogan. There is creative advertising, creative engineering, creative problem-solving—all lively entries in the struggle for dignity in our time.

It seems best to start with a working definition of what we mean by a 'creative act'. Whilst later I shall examine in greater detail the nature and conditions of the creative act we can take as our starting point a simple, but all-embracing characteristic of the creative process that allows us to place it roughly in our universe, and no wording, I think, defines it most pervasive characteristic better than Bruner's 'effective surprise':

> What is curious about effective surprise is that it need not be rare or infrequent or bizarre and is often none of these things. Effective surprises. . . seem rather to have the quality of obviousness to them when they occur, producing a shock of recognition, following which there is no longer astonishment. (Bruner, 1962)

There are two implications arising from this characterisation of the creative act: firstly, creative quality can reside in any kind of human activity. Men can be creative not only in painting, writing poetry or discovering scientific theories, but also in cooking, carpentering, playing football or making love. Secondly, it is not only the genius who produces creative acts, but this quality can be present in many minor acts at many different levels of ability or intelligence. We should here recognise a distinction between an objectively and a subjectively creative act. The product of *objective* creativity must meet certain criteria so that 'effective surprise' is felt by the beholder. The first and most important is perhaps appropriateness: the product must make sense in the light of the demands of the situation and the specifications of the producer. It should call forth satisfaction, because it fits its context—it is not only right, but *just* right. (This is another way of expressing 'effective surprise'.) The second criterion is novelty: the product should be unusual as judged by appropriate norms, or should lead to an uncommon way of experiencing the world. Thirdly—and this is the highest standard—we may judge a creative product by its power to transform the traditional constraints of reality and to yield a radically new perspective. Some original thoughts bring about a radical shift in our approach to a whole field of knowledge. (Cf. Jackson and Messick, 1968, for a detailed discussion of these points.)

Subjective creativity is judged by different canons: it can occur when a person combines things in ways that are individual to him, when he does not simply imitate, but regroups given stimuli or data by means of his own thoughts or actions, irrespective of the effort his creation has on others. We cannot, for instance, deny the epithet 'creative' to the five-year-old who with all his might and enthusiasm has given us an image of the world as he sees it, littered with square cows and peopled with round-bellied, neckless mums and dads. When he has, out of his own powers, made this vision of the world his own he has been—subjectively—creative, even if thousands of others have acted similarly.

A well-known story tells how a class was given the problem of adding the series: 1+2+3+4+5+6+7+8+9+10. Everybody was working away, laboriously adding the ten separate figures, but one six-year-old boy, after only a few seconds' thought, announced the answer, 55, to the astonished teacher. He had discovered that there was a logical structure to the series, which could be looked on as consisting of five pairs of numbers, 1 and 10, 2 and 9 etc., each adding up to 11. This boy, who was to be the mathematician Gauss, had by himself discovered a property of a series and thus show considerable creativeness, as far as his subjective mental processes were concerned, even though the rule was known to most adults before him.

If we call 'effective surprise' the hallmark of the creative act, we are in effect setting up a psychological state as the criterion of creativity. And indeed creative acts, or at least the finishing of them, are always marked by states of relief, exhilaration, thrill for the creator so that the act makes a psychological impact on the doer and, in most cases, also on the beholder. While this is a corollary of creativity, it is, of course, not a distinguishing mark exclusive to it.

Imagination and intuition

Before we look at the creative process more closely we must discuss some other concepts that are often mentioned in connection with it: *imagination and intuition*. Imagination has a number of different meanings. Thus, we can say 'I can imagine what this house will look like, when it is finished' or 'Imagine the Roman soldiers standing guard on Hadrian's wall! ', and in these cases by imagining we mean calling up before the mind's eye images of things that are not actually present, that are to be in the future or that existed in the distant past. This meaning is codified by the dictionary as 'Power of forming mental concepts or images of things not experienced'. We do, of course, conjure up before the mind's eye not only possible things, but also things or events that are completely divorced from reality, that are simply 'figments of our imagination'. In the midst of winter, sitting shivering in front of a small fire, we might for instance imagine ourselves being wafted away to a fairy island of permanent warmth and sunshine where manna rained from the heavens to give us sustenance. When we evoke images of this kind we are using our imagination in a day-dream. From this day-dream, and from deliberate pretence and make-believe, it is but a small step to hallucinations or actual dreams, where we say that our 'imagination' gets the better of us.

Another use of the term is apparent when we talk of people 'thinking imaginatively', or of younger children 'playing imaginatively', or when we say that an account has been written 'with imagination'. Here we attach a positive value judgment to the term, meaning by it that the thing has been done inventively (though we do not approve of too much invention, since we use 'his imagination has run away with him' as a polite euphemism for a whopping lie). This use corresponds to another dictionary definition of 'imagination', namely 'artistically inventive or creative faculty' and here, quite clearly, creativity is implied.

'Imagination', indeed, always implies going beyond the given data. Thus, for instance, in young Gauss's problem, simply adding up to find the answer was not imaginative, but going beyond the immediately obvious facts and seeing the hidden structure was an act of imagination and, thereby, of creativeness. (Bruner 1962) suggests the term 'formal effectiveness' for the kind of thing that yuong Gauss did: 'It consists of an ordering of elements in such a way that one sees relationships that were not evident before, groupings that were not present).' Although we are able to imagine things that are unreal, that we have never seen and that are inherently impossible, these things are in fact always somehow tied to a part of our reality. It is notable, for instance, that in medieval pictures painted by German artists, scenes from the Holy Land show a remarkable resemblance to medieval German towns with their half timbered, gabled houses.

At first blush it would appear easy to contrast logical,

systematic thinking with imaginative thinking. A Harvard publication, for instance, states: 'Logical thinking is straight, as opposed to crooked thinking, and that of the poet may be described as curved thinking' (Contant 1945). Hutchinson (1949) differentiates between systematic thinking and insight. In systematic thinking, the objective, problem, and method are clearly defined, the process is deliberate, methodical, the problem is well within the range of abilities of the thinker. Awareness of logical relations and the application of the laws of associative thinking are emphasised. Such systematic thinking applies in situations where plans can be deliberately formulated, where the number of variables and hypotheses is not too large. Insight, on the other hand, according to Hutchinson, occurs in the solution of baffling problems and is accompanied by the emergence of the unexpected by feelings first of frustations, and then of apparently effortless integration, feelings of exhilaration, finally and accomplishment.

Hutchinson considers these two types to be the extremes on a scale of thinking and similarly Bartlett (1958) postulates a range of kinds of thinking, the extremes of which he calls 'thinking within closed systems' and 'adventurous thinking'. Now it is tempting, but would be very inaccurate, to identify imaginative or insightful thinking with 'adventurous thinking' and systematic thinking, lacking the imaginative touch, with 'thinking in closed systems'. Bartlett (1958) defines a 'closed system' as 'one possessing a limited number of units, or items, or members, and those properties of the members which are to be used are known to begin with and do not change as the thinking proceeds'. An example of an easy task within closed system would be the well-known Verbal Reasoning Test question, requiring interpolation of figures in a series, e.g.:

1 2 4 7 . . . 22 29

Extrapolation, too, where the direction which thinking is to take is predetermind, but the terminal point is not given, is of the 'closed-system' variety. Indeed, the difference between extrapolation and interpolation seems to consist mainly in the formal presentation of the given data, e.g. the above problem would not change in nature if it was given as:

1 2 4 7 11 16 . . . .

The characteristic of the 'closed system' is the presence of a structure of logical constraints which determine a limited number of possible solutions, but these solutions need not be either easy or obvious. Where the evidence that has to be used in arriving at a solution is disguised, the problem-solving process may, in fact, be very complex. Bartlett gives as example an addition sum:

```
 DONALD
 GERALD
 ______
 ROBERT
```

The data provided are: (I) D=5; (2) every number from 0-9 has its corresponding letter; (3) no two letters have the same numerical value. (The reader may wish to discover the elements of this 'closed system' for himself.) Another example of difficult thinking within a closed system would be the detective work of a Maigret who has to fill in the gaps in very incomplete evidence, though when all the data *are* available only one answer is possible.

When the conditions of a given problem have been closely specified the solution can be arrived at by one small step or by means of a step-by-step trial of a limited number of alternatives to determine which one will fit the specifications. A computer can easily be programmed to carry out this task. The sparser the data provided, the larger the gaps in the evidence to be bridged, the greater is the number of alternative steps that might be tried. The practically limitless welter of permutations of moves possible, for instance, in a chess-game will, however, be reduced to a more manageable choice by the 'initiative familiarity' of the good player with the strategies and possibilities of the game. Even within a closed system, then, in order to select the *right* combinations leading to effective solutions, a person needs to be attuned to the problem, to be sensitive to likely leads and have a sense of which facts or combinations are relevant (this is probably what is meant by *intuition* in a certain field—the process of attaining solutions without knowledge of all the relevant data, without going through a process of step-by-step logical reasoning). In other words, where steps are not closely specified, where gaps are large or many and links remote (which means most problems outside textbooks) an imaginative leap beyond the data is necessary as part of 'closed-system' thinking, if this is to be effective. On the other hand, where gaps are small or links obvious, thinking can be stepwise. Such steps for the mental mountaineer are, unfortunately, not normally provided in nature, but have to be hewn out of the rock of data by some pioneer thinker. In working out such steps—an essentially imaginative task—the pioneer will routinise and thereby facilitate subsequent effective thinking either for himself or for other, more routine workers. In a significant aside Herman Bondi, the well-known physicist, once said: 'Mathematicians are not specially good at thinking, they are good at inventing ways to avoid thinking.' The programmer will perform the same task for his computer by programming it with the necessary sequence of steps or strategies of search likely to lead to success and will thus routinise and give direction to a search that may require a very large number of steps and combinations of steps. By having 'intuitive familiarity' with a certain problem area built into it, the computer is in this way enabled to simulate the competent scientist or good chess-playing. It should be said, however, that so far, no chess-playing programme has ever been achieved that has been thought a worthy opponent by any, even moderate, human chess-player.

On closer analysis, then, we find that imaginative thinking is, indeed, often an important part of 'closed-system thinking' and the most crucial difference between systematic and imaginative thinking turns out to be one of size of step, though there may also be other differences, such as the level of consciousness at which the attempts at a solution occur. (The verification of a solution and its checking against criteria would, of course, again necessitate systematic thinking.)

Another way of looking at the distinction is to think of routine, systematic thinking as characterised by responses that are high in the stimulus-response hierarchy. A response that is strong or high in the hierarchy is more likely to occur in the presence of a stimulus, i.e. it is a common response. Original thinking, on the other hand, is typified by responses that are weak or low in the hierarchy, in other words, uncommon responses. Problem solving in this view (cf. Maltzman, 1955) involves the selection of responses, often weak ones, as well as of whole 'habit-family hierarchies'. However, this view fails to convey any sense of directiveness in the process of imaginative thinking.

At the opposite end of the scale to 'closed-system thinking' Barlett (1958) places 'adventurous thinking' and he finds this exemplified in experimental thinking, in everyday thinking and in the artist's thinking. He contrasts the two as follows:

> The thinker in the closed system is in the position of contemplating a finished structure. Very often this may be exceedingly complex and elaborate and the rules of its constitution difficult to appreciate. The thinker is, however, in the position of a spectator searching for something which he must treat as being in some way 'there' all the time. . . . The experimental thinker is in the position of somebody who must use whatever tools may be available for adding to some structure that is not yet finished, and that he himself is certainly not going to complete.

In 'experimental' or 'adventurous' thinking the gaps have become wider and the situation more loosely structured. The first main task has shifted from solving problems to formulating the problem in most effective way, or to asking the right questions. Whilst there is more need and scope for imagination inadventurous thinking' than in the 'closed-system' variety, clearly, imaginative thinking is not co-extensive with or confirmed to thinking in unstructured situations, but can occur in many different fields and contexts.

Creative moments

But let us return to the creative process itself—and, as we have noted, imagination in one of its senses ('inventive or creative faculty') is synonymous with it. At the heart of creativity lie the creative moment and the creative impulse, the most intensely personal experiences an individual is capable of. It is here that the 'I' experiences—for creating means perceiving as well as doing—and acts following out its own most idiosyncratic ways. By definition, it is producing a novel recombination which is not predictable from general laws. No scientific, testable theory has, as yet, come to grips with this phenomenon and the best approach available to us is still through descriptive, literary accounts.

After forty-odd years the analysis of the creative process that is most widely quoted is still that by Graham Wallas (1926) and it must, therefore, be assumed to have a certain intuitive plausibility and appeal to a large number of artists and psychological writers. Wallas is concerned mainly with novel thought in the mathematical and scientific are, but it can be seen that his ideas have application in other fields too. He suggests the process can be divided into four stages: 1. Preparation—the stage in which the problem is investigated from all directions and this 'includes what whole process of intellectual education' with its training in experimental and logical procedures, as well as the process of acquainting oneself with background facts and knowledge. 2. Incubation—this is the stage during which the individual is not consciously thinking about the problem, when it is simmering in him, although he may seek relaxation from conscious effort (examples will follow later). 3. Illumination—this stage is not confined to the 'flash of insight' but includes the psychological events that immediately precede and accompany its appearance. 4. Verification—the stage in which the validity of the concepts is tested and the ideas reduced to exact form.

This division can be criticised—on the grounds, for instance, that although no doubt all four are involved in the delivery of the finished product, only incubation and illumination, and possibly to some extent preparation, throw light on the creative process itself. The different stages are, in other words, of varying importance. A more fundamental criticism is the point made by Vinacke (1952) who concluded on the basis of reports by various creative writers and scientists that 'it is necessary to conceive of creative thinking in terms of dynamic, interplaying activities, rather than as more or less discrete stages'. However, this kind of critique can always be applied to any more or less artificial analysis into stages—the stages are, after all, superimposed on an ongoing activity and the author would probably quite readily admit that in any given case the simultaneity of the processes is quite as striking as their discreteness.

The beginning of creation is marked, as many writers confirm, by a hunch, diffuse excitement, the awareness of some ill-defined, half-conscious problem—and this may, indeed, precede the stage of 'preparation', of gathering the material. Stephen Spender writes of a 'a dim cloud of an idea which I feel must be condensed into a shower of words' and Alfred North Whitehead of 'the state of imaginative muddled suspense which precedes successful inductive generalisations'.

The need for a period of 'incubation' or gestation when ideas sink down to subconscious levels where all kinds of mental processes can get to work at them is almost universally recognised. William Blake is one of the few who does not acknowledge this stage in himself, since he claimed that some of his poetry came without any apparent premeditation, as if dictated to him. On the other hand, Bertrand Russell has remarked on the fruitless effort he used to expend in trying to push his creative work to completion by force of will before he recognised how much easier it was to await the result of the more organic process of subconscious maturity. Poincaré (1913), too, writes: 'Most striking at first is this appearance of sudden illumination, a manifest sign of long, unconsious prior work.'

It should not be thought, however, that the individual must be completely *unconscious,* in the literal sense of the word, of the processes at work within him. Consiousness is a matter of degree and there are intermediate 'regions' (speaking in topographical metaphors) between full 'focal awareness', as Koestler (1964) calls it, and the unconscious 'regions'. The intermediate areas have been called 'the pre-conscious' or, stemming from the analogy of vision, 'peripheral awareness' and Wallas (1926) writes of the moment 'when our fringe-conciousness of an association-train is in the state of rising consciousness which indicates that the fully conscious flash of success is coming'. The problem which 'bothers' the individual, with which he is preoccupied, will very often be present just outside the bright spot illuminated by the light of his fully directed awareness, and indeed the focus of awareness will often shift, so that at one moment it will direct its full glare on the problem and at others will leave it in the semi-dark or pitch dark outer regions.

The state of mind which has typically been thought propitious to creative work is the day-dream. For Freud, certainly in his early writings, creative work, in common with the day-dreams and play, arises from wishes that, because they violate society's prohibitions, have been repressed and seek their fulfilment in fantasy. Creative production is therefore a form of 'substitute gratification' and an extension of the child's play and the ordinary man's day-dream. Freud displays an ambivalent attitude to the artist. While he exposes the lowly origins of his inspiration, he allows himself at the same time an expression of unease about this implicit devaluation of the artist's standing:

> We are perfectly aware that very many imaginative writings are far removed from the model of the naive day-dream; and yet I cannot suppress the suspicion that even the most extreme deviations from that model could be linked with it through an uninterrupted series of transitional cases. (Freud, 1908)

Most other writers on the psychology of creation, including psycho-analytic writers, however, take a more positive view of the value of relaxation of conscious controls. Koestler, whose views will be more fully discussed below, for instance, writes (Koestler, 1964):

> The temporary relinquishing of conscious controls liberated the mind from certain constraints which are necessary to maintain the disciplined routines of thoughts but may become an impediment to the creative leap; at the same time other types of ideation on more primitive levels of mental organisation are brought into activity.

A celebrated example of the benefits of a temporary abandonment of the discipline of consciousness is the following report by Kekulé, a professor of chemistry at Ghent who describes an experience he had in 1865 :

> I turned my chair to the fire and dozed (he relates). Again the atoms were gambolling before my eyes. This time the smaller groups kept modestly in the background. My mental eye,

> rendered more acute by repeated visions of this kind, could now distinguish larger structures, of manifold conformation; long rows, sometimes more closely fitted together; all twining, and twising, in a snakelike motion. But look! What was that? One of the snakes had seized hold of its own tail, and the form whirled mockingly before my eyes. As if by a flash of lightning I awoke . . . . Let us learn to dream, gentlemen. (Quoted in Koestler, 1964)

The snake biting its own tail conjured up before Kekulé's dreaming eye the visual image, the model, which helped him to see the molecules of certain organic compounds as closed rings instead of as open structures.

But how, from amongst the multifarious elements of the semi-conscious day-dream or unconscious thought, are those images or ideas selected that will bear fruit in a new theory, experiment or work of art? How, in fact, is the day-dream translated into creative work? Poincaré, who was a mathematician, writes: 'To create (in mathematics) consists precisely in not making useless combinations and in making those which are useful and which are only a small minority. Invention is discernment, choice', and goes on to propose that in this selection aesthetic sensitivity plays a decisive role: 'The priviliged unconscious, phenomena, those susceptible of becoming conscious, are those which, directly or indirectly, affect most profoundly our emotional sensibility' (Poincaré, 1913). However detailed knowledge of the appropriate field is by no means irrelevant. To quote Bruner (1962): 'In each empirical field there is developed in the creating scientist a kind of "intuitive familiarity", to use a term that L.J. Henderson was fond of, that gives him a sense of which combinations are likely to have predictive effectiveness and which are absurd.' Pasteur epitomised it in the self-congratulatory phrase: 'Fortune favours the prepared mind.'

It is worth considering one of the few coherent theories of the nature of creativity available—the one evolved by Koestler and expressed most fully in *The Act of Creation* (1964). Koestler, whose conceptions owe a great deal to the school of psycho-analytic thought, places creativity in the context of the processes of life in general which follow certain rules designed to lend the organism coherence, stability, as well as some flexibility.

One of the recurring life processing is that of regeneration, when mutilated lower organisms, such as the flatworm, retrace the steps of their original development, as it were, and are thereby enabled to create themselves anew from small fragments. Examples of less radical reconstitution of parts of the body exist also in higher animals. Koestler detects in a similar pattern in the creative act: *'regular pour mieus sauter'*. In the creative act the mind 'regresses', i.e. gives itself up to the 'games of the underground', the inventive name that Koestler gives to the subconscious mental processes. In these 'games' the mind combines apparently incomplete ideas, turns up hidden analogies between cabbages and kings and once again possesses the fluidity of the primitive consciouness of the child for whom the world and 'I' are one.

Such mental states are common to the child, the psychotic, the dreamer and the creative mind. But, writes Koestler (1964): 'In pathological states the games of the underground play havoc with the disciplined routines of thought—a *reculer sans sauter*. But on rare, priviliged occasions they have the effect of liberating the mind from its straitjacket and releasing its creative potentials.' Kekulés dream, quoted above, is one of many possible examples.

In this way hitherto unrelated frames of reference may be associated and objects and ideas seen in a new light. In an earlier work (1959) Koestler expressed it thus:

> This act of wrenching away an object or concept from its habitual associative context and seeing it in a new context is, as I have tried to show, an essential part of the creative process. It is an act both of destruction and of creation, for it demands the breaking up of a mental habit, the melting down, with the blowlamp of Cartesian doubt, of the frozen structure of accepted theory, to enable the new fusion to take place . . . . Every creative act—in science, art, or religion—involves a regression to a more primitive level, a new innocence of perception liberated from the cataract of accepted beliefs. It is a process of *reculer pour mieux sauter*, of disintegration preceding the new synthesis, comparable to the dark night of the soul through which the mystic must pass.

In the later book Koestler coined the term 'act of bisociation' for what to him is the essence of creation, namely the bringing together of two unconnected matrices of thought. (A 'matrix' is Koestler's formula for a bodily function, perceptual skill or mental habit, or a system of these). This 'bisociative act' is, in fact, characterstic of creation in any sphere of human activity.

Thus poetry conveys not only meaning, but the patterns of the sounds evoke primitive echoes in us, and it is the two frames of reference of meaning and sound which interact. Koestler sees a similar bisociation of matrices in all other arts and all forms of art, Koestler suggests, serve man's 'self-transcending' emotions or participatory tendencies, i.e. the emotion in which the individual feels himself to be part of some larger whole. This can be aroused by listening to Mozart, seeing the Mona Lisa or kneeling in prayer.

The complementary emotions in Koestler's system are the self-assertive emotions through which a person's individual functions are affirmed. These find their expression in humour, the essence of which is the clash of two incompatible frames of reference. (Koestler provides a fund of entertaining examples.)

Scientific discovery is associated with neither of these two kinds of emotion. It is not neutral or bereft of all feelings, but Koestler thinks of it as well-balanced compound of passions into which both self-asserting and participatory tendencies enter in highly sublimated form. In Koestler's neat philosophical-psychological system, to the different forms of creation, accompanied by their varying emotions, there correspond also differing ways of joining hitherto separate universes of discourse: 'The result is either a *collision* of matrices ending in laughter; or their fusion in a synthesis providing new insights; or their *juxtaposition* in the raptness of aesthetic experience' (Koestler, 1964).

Koestler's theory has not remained without its critics, particularly from the scientific and psychological confrèrie, and it must be said there is substance to some of the criticism. Koestler seems to place the criterion of difference between a scientific theory and a work of art in the emotional state of their creators; whereas the distinguishing mark of a scientific theory is usually held to be that it will lead to predictions which may, by experimental observations, be tested, so that, in principle, the theory can be disproved. Koestler, essentially, leaves the act of verification out of account in order to concentrate on the moment of inspiration. His 'cosmology of the soul' is altogether too neat, systematic and all-embracing and it is difficult to see how it could be disproved by any experiment, In sum, it is a literary, not a scientific theory, a contribution to philosophical psychology.

But, this criticism aside, his account of the creative forces is a plausible one and supported by evidence from the self-observations of many creative individuals. The idea of the mind reverting to more primitive levels of operation in order to accomplish the fusion of the creative act derives from the concept of 'regression in the service of the ego', developed by the psycho-analytic writer Kris, and has been widely accepted. It is, at least, not incompatible with the little experimental evidence we possess (cf. Wild, 1965). Koestler's theory is a semantic interpretation and conceptualisation of experimental data and it will always be possible to generate several alternative interpretations. In the absence of a more truly scientific theory of creativity, however (if such a one should be possible), we can regard his theory of the creative act—though not of the nature of science—as a facet of the truth and can admire its creative elegance.

The poet's inspiration

What do poets themselves have to say about the moments of inspiration and about their methods of work?

Stephen Spender (1946) writes: 'Inspiration is the beginning of a poem and it is also its final goal. It is the first idea which drops into the poet's mind and it is the final idea which he at last achieves in words. In between this start and this winning post there is the hard race, the sweat and toil.' He tells us of a phrase, 'the language of flesh and roses', that once flashed into his mind and that may in years to come be the nucleus of a future poem, and he adds: 'My own experience of inspiration is certainly that of a line or a phrase or a word or sometimes something still vague, a dim cloud of an idea which I feel must be condensed into a shower of words.'

The most famous account of writing that dispenses with the 'sweat and toil' is contained in Coleridge's Preface to *Kubla Khan:*

> In the summer of the year 1797, the Author, then in ill-health, had retired to a lonely farm-house between Porlock and Linton . . . . In consequence of a slight indisposition, an anodyne had been prescribed (elsewhere Coleridge, called it 'two grains of Opium'!) from the effects of which he fell asleep in his chair at the moment that he was reading the following sentence, or words of the same substance, in 'Purchas's Pilgrimage': 'Here the Khan Kubla commanded a palace to be built, and a stately garden thereunto. And thus ten miles of fertile ground were inclosed with a wall.' The Author continued for about three hours in a profound sleep, at least of the external sense, during which time he has the most vivid confidence, that he could not have composed less than from two to three hundred lines; if that indeed can be called composition in which all the images rose up before him as things, with a parallel production of the correspondent expressions, without any sensation or consciousness of effort. On awaking he appeared to himself to have a distinct recollection of the whole, and taking his pen, ink, and paper, instantly and eagerly wrote down the lines that are here preserved. At this moment he was unfortunately called out by a person on business from Porlock, and detained by him above an hour, and on his return to his room, found, to his no small surprise and mortification, that though he still retained some vague and dim recollection of the general purport of the vision, yet, with the exception of some eight or ten scattered lines and images, all the rest had passed away. . . . (Coleridge, 1954)

Jean Cocteau stresses the nature of the unconscious work in the artist and the overpowering force with which it demands to find expression:

> These unknown forces work deep within us, with the aid of the elements of daily life,. . . . and, when they burden us and oblige us to conquer the kind of somnolence in which we indulge ourselves like invalids who try to prolong dream and dread resuming contact with reality, in short when the work that makes itself in us and in spite of us demands to be born, we can believe that this work comes to us from beyond and is offered us by the gods. (Cocteau, 1952)

But among modern poets the one who perhaps most strongly felt the primitive force of his inspiration that came, as it willed, and would not be commanded, was the German poet, Rainer Maria Rilke. He began the poems, that later came to be known as the 'Duino Elegies', with a line that came to him, seemingly out of storm, as he paced to and fro outside his residence in the winter of 1912. For many years he struggled with the elegies, writing now one, now part of another, endeavouring to create in them a vision of the world, not as humans see it, but 'as it is within the angel'. But it was not until 1922 that the labour was completed and he announced the end triumphantly in a letter to Princess Marie von Thurn und Taxis-Hohenlohe, the owner of Duino Castle where the elegies had their origin:

> At last, Princess, at last, the blessed, how blessed day, on which I can announce to you the conclusion—so far as I see—of the Elegies:
>
> *ten!*
>
> From the last, the great one (with the opening, begun long since in Duino : 'Some day, emerging at last from this terrifying vision, may I burst into jubilant praise to assenting angels. . . ') from this last one, which moreover, even then, was intended to be the last,—from this—my hand is still trembling! Just now, Saturday, the eleventh, at six o'clock in the evening, it's finished!—
>
> All in a few days, there was a nameless storm, a hurricane, in my mind (like that time in Duino), everything in the way of fibre and web in me split,—eating was not to be thought of, God knows who fed me.
>
> But now *it is.* IS,
>
> Amen.
>
> So I've survived up to this, through and through it all. Through it all. And it was this that was needed. *Only* this.
>
> (Rilke, 1939, Introduction by J.B. Leishman)

Here we have the emotional charge, the passion, of the creative moment. But there are also trivial conditions that may be necessary to it. Pure inspiration may come anywhere, but for the elaboration of this vision, for the hard work that makes the vision tangible and turns it into a work of art the poet or writer needs conditions that he finds conducive to concentration. Rilke, for instance, needed the quiet and isolation of country mansions. Other writers required various more mundane paraphernalia to jog along the tired muse. Schiller was aided by the smell of rotten apples hidden in his desk and by a liberal supply of coffee. Balzac needed coffee and wet towels round his head to help him write in the middle of the night. Dr. Johnson was said to work best with a purring cat and some orange peel near by and plenty of tea to drink. The requirements are as multifarious, odd and unpredictable as the writers.

The scientist's insight

Scientists, too, have vouchsafed us glimpses into the processes that lead them to a complete restructuring of their 'matrices' of thought, to creative idea in their own fields. Kekulé's dream has already been quoted. Such sudden illuminations usually seem to emerge after the scientist has already spent weeks living with the problem, 'worrying' about it on and off—the period of 'incubation'. Thus the mathematician Jacques Hadamard records :

> On being very abruptly awakened by an external noise, a solution long searched for appeared to me at once without the slighest instant of reflection on my part—the fact was remarkable enough to have struck me unforgettably—and in a quite different direction from any of those which I had previously tried to follow. (Hadamard, 1952)

Poincaré given us a vivid report of how he struggled with the problem of the 'Fuchsian functions' :

> Every day I seated myself at my work table, stayed an hour or two, tried a great number of combinations and reached no results. One evening, contrary to my custom. I drank black coffee and could not sleep. Ideas rose in crowds; If felt them collide until pairs interlocked, so to speak, making a stable combination. By the next morning I had established the existence of a class of Fuchsian functions, those which come from the hypergeometric series; I had only to write out the results, which took but a few hours.

Then comes the famous description of the inspiration on the bus:

> Just at this time I left Caen, where I was then living, to go on a geologic excursion under the auspices of the School of Mines. The changes of travel made me forget my mathematical work. Having reached Coutances, we entered an omnibus to go some place or other. At the moment when I put my foot on the step the idea came to me, without anything in my former thoughts seeming to have paved the way for it, that the transformations I had used to define the Fuchsian functions were identical with those of non-Euclidean geometry. I did not verify the idea; I should not have had time, as upon taking my seat in the omnibus, I went on with a conversation already commenced, but I felt a perfect certainty. (Poincaré, 1913)

In the arts the creative process itself is a long drawn-out affair. The execution of the original idea, the flash of illumination, requires further long-term creative efforts of a high order, because the detailed expression is an essential and difficult part of the creative endeavour. In science, on the other hand, what follows the moment of insight seems a very pedestrain process, a matter of verification and formulation and this may be a long, tedious slog or a quick routine job. For Einstein, for instance, the 'axioms' in which his relativity theory was expressed were only a matter of later formulation, after the real thing, the main discovery, had occurred.

> This was merely a later formulation of the subject matter, just a question of how the thing could afterwards best be written. The axioms express essentials in a condensed form. Once one has found such things one enjoys formulating them in that way; but in this process they did not grow out of any manipulation of axioms. (Wertheimer, 1961)

It would almost seem that the equivalent of the scientist's checking would be the writer's proof-reading or establishment of a book's index.

A particularly fascinating picture of science in the making has been drawn by James Watson (1968), permitting us a revealing insight into how revolutionary discoveries arise out of a mixture of immersion in a field, patience, dogged persistence, collaboration, competitive spirit, moments of lucid insight and, above all, pure luck. Watson describes how he, Francis Crick and Maurice Wilkins teased out the structure of DNA, a discovery which earned them the Nobel Prize. They had arrived at the knowledge that thier problem lay in the sequence of the chemical bases, the 'polynucleotide backbone' of the molecules of DNA and they worked on physical models of these in their lab. In between Watson went off to spend the afternoons playing tennis or to watch X category films. But, he reports: 'Even during good films I found it almost impossible to forget the bases. The fact that we had at last produced a stereochemically reasonable configuration for the backbone was always in the back of may head.' He and Francis Crick were spurred on in their efforts by the knowledge of the importance of the discovery, if they could only reach it, and by the desire to beat Linus Pauling, an eminent American chemist, to the award of the Nobel Prize. A little later a possible solution occurred to Watson which postulated that the DNA molecule consisted of two chains with identical base sequences so that adenine on one chain was linked to adenine on the other, guanine to guanine, etc., by means of hydrogen bonds. The idea sent his pulse racing—he thought he had found the solution. But a collaborate in the lab soon disabused him: 'My scheme was torn to shreds by the following noon. Against me was the awkward chemical fact that I had chosen the wrong tautomeric forms of guanine and thymine.'

After this disappointment the men continued playing about with the models as well as following other more light-hearted pursuits. Then, one day: 'I began shifting the bases in and out of various other pairing possibilities. Suddenly I became aware that an adenine-thymine pair held together by two hydrogen bonds was identical in shape to a guanine-cytosine pair held together by at least two hydrogen bonds.'

An almost accidental finding, but this time it was 'it'. The essential, fruitful illumination had come, the 'fusion of matrices' had occurred. It remained for them to check this arrangement of a 'double helix' against the known chemical facts, to make sure that all the stereochemical contacts were satisfactory and that the postulated structure accorded with the calculations based on X-ray data. When all this checking had been done they knew they were home and felt confident enough to send off their paper to *Nature*. A scientific discovery was complete.

11

Imaginative Expression

The types of activities discussed here are sometimes called "creative expression," "creative writing," and "self expression." Very often (and perhaps more satisfactorily) they are known as "imaginative expression." The activities may be either written or oral, but the written usually outnumber the oral.

The nature of the activities included here is rather clearly established. The objectives of imaginative expression have become reasonably well defined and are much alike in all language arts classes from kindergarten to high school.

Teachers generally agree that certain things are not part of a creative programme. Imaginative expression is not a search for geniuses in the average classroom. It is not thought of as an unbridled expression of excessive egotism or self-indulgence, or a way for pupils to escape the hard work of thinking and organising which composing demands. It is not an occasion for a teacher to encourage in the average pupil the hope of becoming a great author. But it is a situation in which many children find pleasure by generating imaginative ideas and expressing them in the best form that they can command. The experience is likely to be a pleasure even when an author shares his compositions with no one except his teacher or some other confidant. It may be valuable because of what it does for the composer rather than for what the composition does for the public.

The boundaries of this aspect of language arts are somewhat flexible because the imaginative or creative element shows itself in various ways. It can be either oral or written. Though generally associated with poems, stories, and plays, an imaginative touch or enjoyable phrasing often adds a refreshing quality to conversations and factual reports. The spirit of imaginative expression can enliven any form of speaking or writing when a pupil uses originality and colour. It functions likewise when a child looks at his environment and his experiences in an observant manner and with an author's eye, seeing new relationships, new configurations. Thus it enriches environment and events by encouraging perceptive vision.

Practical Results of Imaginative Expression

In the opinion of many teachers, imaginative expression is a very practical phase of language arts, yielding benefits for teachers as well as for pupils. For pupils it opens new interests in daily life, clarifies experiences, and sharpens perceptivity. It challenges the abilities of the most brilliant, yet has possibilities for the average child. In written form it gives the timid child a chance to express himself because be can, as teachers often say to such pupils, "tell it to the paper."

Imaginative expression makes profitable use of various traits and assets which children possess: memories of experiences; opinions on many things; a lively imagination; a feeling for qualities like rhythm, pattern, and concreteness; and the very fruitful urge to "try things out" and "see what can be done" with materials. Also it is an outlet for a pupil's tensions and worries—two ingredients likely to retard progress in some other aspects of language arts but very usable here.

Therapeutic benefits are likely. Creative activities are reported to have helped children reduce maladjustments and understand themselves. Occasionally they become a means of resolving a discipline problem. The teacher may resolve a problem arising from something like a child's fantasies or fibbing by having the child or the class convert the situation into a player or story.

The experience of composing verse, stories, and plays is considered one of the surest and quickest ways to increase appreciation of literature. This viewpoint appears to be growing. As a result of having tried to give literary form to ideas and language a pupil is almost certain to find greater enjoyment in what others have composed. He knows what to look for in a literary work. He has points of view unknown to most people who never tried their hands at craftsmanship.

For the teacher two practical benefits derive from imaginative expression. One is the rejuvenating effect of working with original composition and keeping alert to new ideas and techniques. The second is an understanding of children. This is gained through the self-revelations of children who compose.

All told, the testimony favouring imaginative expression is strong. It outweighs cynical comments like "there's too much self-expression already," "better discourage such expression rather than promote it," or "why encourage children, when the best that most of them can produce is mediocre?"

Pupil Background for Imaginative Expression

"Oh, I can't get anything out of that class; they have nothing to write." Occasionally one hears this lament. It implies that the children have no information, opinions, or experiences that can be organised into entertaining prose or verse. The teacher who utters it usually implies, in addition, that she must hasten to fill her students with a cargo of information in order that those young people may "have more interesting thoughts" before they begin to write.

Both implications appear to be ill founded. The former may be challenged as untrue. The latter, though probably laudable as an ambitions, is generally impractical for the teacher of written or oral expression because of lack of time.

Experiences and Observations. Every child who has lived long enough to reach elementary school has had thousands of experiences and has gained innumerable impressions of his environment. Each pupil knows much about at least one topic. Perhaps he knows more about some one topic than does anybody else in his classroom, including the teacher. The total mental capital of a child's experiences is huge.

A pupil may not be stampeding to express his ideas. He may need encouragement. Perhaps he must be stimulated to recall some of his experiences and impressions, made aware of his usable material, and given confidence in his ability to compose something original. But one can seriously question the truth of "they have nothing to write." What the teacher should say, more likely, is, "I haven't found a way to get them started," or "they don't yet have the skill to express what they know."

It is possible that a few children really lack material to express. But a study of the occasional child whose reticence is almost pathological is likely to show that he is inhibited by a fear of using language. He lacks confidence in speaking or in handling written sentences, punctuation, or spelling. Successful experiences with these tools of expression may clear up the inhibition. If the trouble really lies in lack of material to express, the remedy may be found in some of the activities suggested later in this chapter.

Gradual Acquisition. A world regarding the matter of filling the pupils' minds with "interesting ideas" before they try to compose: no school calendar offers enough time to accomplish such an endeavour. An instructor who attempts the project is likely to keep pupils so preoccupied with acquiring something to say (probably about topics fairly remote from the child's interests) that the would-be writers have little energy or time left for expressing anything.

Enrichment of the mental life should be promoted along with experience in expression. Pupils may begin to experiment at once with original expression, using whatever they can speak or write about understandingly and sincerely. With even the humblest material they can practice their best craftsmanship in writing and speech. A richer mental life can grow concurrently. Meanwhile the teacher should judge material from the pupil's point of view, realising that ideas which seem dull and trite to her may be freshly new in the child's young life.

Linguistic Play. Imaginative expression benefits from memories of the linguistic play which children have fun with in testing out rhythms and sounds. It is fortunate if pupils continue to find pleasure in playing with the elements of language because such pleasure is one of the strongest inspirations for writing.

Favourable Classroom Climate

Imaginative expression is a sensitive growth, delicately affected by its environment. If it is to flourish among a majority of the pupils, not only among the few who have an irrepressible urge to express themselves, it needs a favourable classroom climate. Factors generating such a climate differ from school to school but certain ones seem to be present in all classrooms where imaginative expression flourishes.

Personal Interest

One factor is the teacher's belief that although her pupils will earn their living by means other than creative writing, they will find life the richer as a result of school experiences in imaginative expression. Further, she believes that what a pupil feels and says really matters—that it matters enough to justify the effort of helping the child find good ways of expressing himself. She agrees with the teacher who said, "I see significance in everything a pupil says or writes creatively, provided I feel that he is sincere. Whatever is produced is somebody's cherished personal expression. It is part of the author's self and, as such, is precious."

Patience

The successful teacher is patient, waiting for the fruition of an idea that apparently is growing. She encourages pupils but does not expect results to arrive on a fixed schedule. She knows that the strange alchemy of imaginative expression cannot function by the clock and may not show growth on a given day. Conversely, if a pupil happens to be working rapidly under the momentum of inspiration she lets him record his ideas swiftly, with the expectation that errors of grammar and spelling will be corrected later. She also accepts fragments, especially from younger pupils. Such fragments may serve only as "studies" or experiments, without ever being completed, although some will be finished eventually.

Knowledge of craftsmanship

A teacher's acquaintance with literary craftsmanship is a key factor. The teacher should be able to recognise whether a composition is excellent, good, fair, or poor (taking into account the author's age or grade) and to give workable advice on how to improve a piece of verse or prose. At best she is a fellow craftsman with her pupils, "playing with the ideas" and "scrimmaging" with words.

Pupils response to such a teacher is strengthened by several factors: the practical way in which she talks about what is composed, the studio or workshop atmosphere which her viewpoint generates, and the workable advice she given to pupils who ask, "How can I make this better?" "What's wrong here?" or "How can I get the effect I want?" Writers like to have a short story discussed *as a short story,* a poem *as a poem,* or a play *as a play*. And, perhaps best of all, this teacher approaches imaginative expression earnestly but not solemnly; lightheartedly, not grimly.

Such stable inspiration is lacking if an original composition throws the teacher into excited confusion. Not unknown are remarks like "One of my children wrote a poem today! I guess it's a poem, but I don't know anything about poetry." Equivalent uncertainties have been expressed about stories and plays.

Tempered Enthusiasm

For continued success teachers do not depend heavily on an "intense" atmosphere or conspicuous "enthusiasm." The "glow" or "bloom" technique has its place and uses, but it cannot be maintained very long. In addition, it soon becomes cloying to some pupils and seems silly to others. Creativity can be sponsored by calm, steady interest. Strong emotion has a role as a driving power and a guide in imaginative expression, but it functions within the author.

Professional Confidence

Professional confidence between teacher and pupil is essential. A child must feel sure that he can give a true account of what he experienced or perceived without danger of having his ideas circulated in a manner that would harm him. As he reflects on what sometimes are called his "collisions with life" he should have a chance to make language say what really happened and how he actually felt rather than be obliged to state what someone else expects him to say.

If a teacher loses the confidence of her pupils or otherwise fails to establish a favourable classroom climate, young writers take their compositions to other people. Perhaps they find a teacher who is more sympathetic with their ideas or experiments or more approachable. There is a possibility that pupils will take their writings to someone who praises everything they do, however poor it may be. But few pupils follow this practice very long, if at all.

A Process of Transmutation

A child composes a story about a grandfather clock. In the story the clock moves from room to room in the house, talking to each member of the family. It speaks in a hollow, rattly voice, and its breath, the child says, "smells like my snowsuit did when I wore it the first time this winter."

Fantastic enough, but it was not made out of nothing. At a Halloween party this child had masqueraded as a clock, and in that guise had talked to her family and friends. In the child's home was a grandfather's clock, which had to be wound by hand, and the winding produced a hollow, rattling sound of cogs, chains, and weights. The clock cabinet contained a few strips of cedar wood, and the child, occasionally peering into the cabinet, had smelled the fragrance of cedar and remembered the resemblance between that fragrance and the door of her snowsuit, which had been stored in a cedar chest.

In the story, ingredients from that child's daily life appeared in new configurations and novel embellishments. Like the elements in many dreams, they were recognisable, though transformed. In the alchemy of a creative mind they had been transmuted and recombined.

Imaginative expression is not, as is often supposed, a process of making something out of nothing. At its best it produces something relatively new, and it may point out relationships and significances previously unrecognised. But always it is woven from information and experiences already present in the pupil's mind. This fact is an important one to remember in teaching because it helps everyone keep a clear view of creativity. It assures the teacher that children can do something with the material which they already possess. Correlatively it encourages her to help each pupil draw on the reservoir which is within himself.

Inspiration for imaginative prose and verse may come unawares. Something touches it off. Suddenly it brings from an interest, a bit of information, or an enthusiasm generated by school activities or by some experience outside of school.

From Class Activities

A fifth grade, having visited the state fair during the second week of school, developed the pattern of a fair in their classroom. Their "fair" represented in miniature the products and enterprises of the home town just as the state fair represented the products and enterprises of the state. Under the inspiration of this project two children phrased slogans for their fair, another child composed a theme song (words and melody) for the event, and five worked out a dramatic skit intended for use as entertainment on a stage in front of the grandstand.

A sixth grade had studied the history of writing, including the development of the alphabet and of printing. For members of the class became interested in dramatising that history.

Another sixth grade was well represented in the membership of the school explorer's club, and three of those members decided that they would impersonate great contemporary explorers and engage in a conversation as part of the programme for the next club meeting. As an alternative plan they thought of recording the dialogue on tape and using the recorded version for the programme.

Children from a centralised school district went to a country music festival in May. They heard the same selection (a composition with a well-defined melody) played six or seven times because each participating orchestra was to be rated on it. By the middle of the week following the festival one of the girls had composed a twenty-eight line poem (in free verse) on the melodic pattern of that orchestral selection.

A third grade planted a small garden patch near the school and also sprouted some seeds in cans and jars in the classroom.

In one jar grew a plant that the children called the "jack-and-the-beanstalk" vine. The class kept a "garden book" to record what the children observed each day as they watched seeds sprout, plants grow, and leaves and blossoms develop and change colour and shape.

Children took turns writing the daily record, but before an entry was copied in the "garden book" it was discussed by the whole class. Pupils and teacher tried to make each entry sound right and say interesting things in an interesting way. They also attempted to have the wording for each day a little different from that of the days just previous.

Before school closed in June a good many original compositions had been entered, in addition to the daily reports. There were poems about seeds, plants, sunshine, rain, insects, and birds. There was a story about a modern Jack and the Beanstalk. There were prose sketches in which plants told of their lives or talked with each other. In the classroom some pupils acted mimes showing the work of planting, caring for, and gathering garden crops. The whole class worked out a play having seeds, plants, insects, rain, wind, and the sun as characters.

From the Whole Curriculum

There is much thought stirring in a body's or girl's mind as a result of usual school activities, even in the minds of pupils who do not rank among the "studious." Stimulation comes from the whole curriculum. Sciences and social studies contribute ideas, situations, and people. Music and visual art provide a stimulus of subject matter too, but their great contributions are the kinds that social studies and the sciences do not commonly offer. The arts stimulate pupils by giving them examples of imaginative use of ideas, situations, and characters; illustrations of how raw material can be shaped into aesthetic form; and experiences with the general spirit of "expressing something." Language arts contribute subject matter and stimuli similar to those provided by music and art.

The fruitful stimuli from science, music, and visual arts are neglected too often. Many teachers look quickly to social studies for subject matter, and some look no further. The situation is in better balance when teachers encourage children to draw inspirations likewise from additional areas. Science promotes careful observation of man's physical environment (with which the pupils must live all their lives, just as truly as they must live with their fellow men, and from which they may derive pleasure—and also solace, should their human environment seen to fail them). The fine arts give children some notion of the aesthetic qualities which account for the differences between literary expression and pedestrian prose.

"What shall I write about?" is a question answered fairly easily by the pupils of the teacher who uses the many sources from which inspiration may come unawares. As a matter of fact, in her classroom that question probably will be heard rather rarely. It is likely to be answered before there is occasion for it to be asked.

Meeting Inspiration Halfway

To some pupils inspiration does not so readily come unawares. At any rate it does not seem to come at times when it is wanted. Such individuals then need a special incentive to get started. For them a teacher can arrange situations in which they may meet inspiration at least halfway. They can be given a start in a likely direction.

"We could have fun trying some original verse for the next few days," a teacher might suggest. "Just a short piece, but one that will be really yours, and on any subject you would like. Take a subject you have thought about often—something you know very well.

"For example, if I were going to write a little verse just now, I might try something about my shadow. I've had fun thinking about it. My first line might be one that has been running through my mind for a few days. I'll write it on the blackboard.

I wonder what my shadow thinks of me.

"I don't know exactly what my next lines would be. Maybe I'd have the shadow talking to me—perhaps about my making him go so fast sometimes and making him wait so long at other times. Also he might be teasing me because I can't change shape and size the way he can.

"I don't know how I'd finish it, but I believe it would be short. I can think of one line that I might use two times, or may be there. My shadow would be calling to me:

Hello, up there!

That would give me something to repeat in the poem. I don't believe I would use any rhyme. Some lines would be longer than others.

"This reminds me that two years ago a girls in this room saw these lines on the blackboard:

Tell me,
Is a clown's heart really gay?

A few hours later she came to me with three lines added:

Tell me,
Is a clown's heart really gay?
Tell me,
Does his face always stay that way?
Who knows how he feels at the close of day?

She said she had an idea for at least one more group of lines. Those were to tell about what was 'behind the clowns mask.' She said she would use rhyme in those lines, but rhyme them on another sound, not one 'gay'.

"Now why not try something yourself, on your own subject? Maybe you can just get a start today and think more about it until tomorrow. I mentioned those lines about the clown and my shadow to show what somebody else did or might do."

That was one teacher's way of starting a project in verse writing. Of course she might have done nothing more than suggest to the class that they "write a poem during the next two days." But in a class of twenty-five pupils a request motivated in the former way will win the wider response. And the likelihood is that the more dynamic start will also lead to better quality in what is composed.

Thus the approach to a project in imaginative expression makes a difference. With one type of opening the pupils are standing at the starting line, perhaps poised for action, perhaps not. Another type fires the starting gun and also adds enough inspiration to give pupils a momentum down the track.

Types of Stimulation

The varied items which a teacher can use may stimulate inspiration in either of two ways: An item, as given, may appeal strongly to a particular boy or girl and become, itself, the subject which the pupil develops. Or the mention of an item or type of item may start some children recalling experiences of their own. A pupil's thoughts begin to simmer. Presently something precipitates. Stimulated by what the teacher has offered, the child comes upon usable material from his own reservoir.

This may be an idea more or less related to the item the teacher has suggested. Or it may be a different idea phrased in a rhythm resembling that of a line of verse which has been given. Again, it may be a creation very different in both subject and form from anything which the teacher has presented, though it was brought out by the teacher's suggestion. This second type of result is frequent in well-directed imagination expression. A final composition may have little apparent connection with the agent that evoked it. Action has taken place in which the teacher's suggestion was a stimulant but did not actually participate. That suggestion became a catalytic agent in the alchemy of imaginative expression.

Evoking imaginative expression is not a penny-in-the-slot process, of course. The mere dropping of a catalyst into a child's thought is not a guarantee that a poem or story will be produced. But many pupils can be aided in discovering the motifs and convictions they already have within themselves. Their material, heretofore amorphous, needs to be crystallized. Passive knowledge must be activated. Unresponsive pupils generally are silent for reasons other than a lack of usable material.

Samples of Literary Catalysts

Catalysts which help a student meet inspiration halfway are diverse: a group of words, a picture, a type of character, the name of a character, a description of a place, a chance remark by the teacher. Teachers gain by having a variety of such items on hand for winning responses from different pupils.

Here are some catalysts that have served well. Many of them have functioned in both of the ways mentioned above—directly as topics for imaginative expression, and as catalytic agents to precipitate some other topic. A number of the suggestions in the next section, "Replenishing and Discovering," have proved useful as catalysts too.

A Single Word. Connotation is the catalytic force here. Words like the following start lively trends of thought.

seahore	brook	shopping
circus	spacecraft	flag
canyon	foghorn	cave
surprise	doll	eclipse

A Group of Words. A word cluster, considered as a unit, gathers thoughts of action and situations around itself. In the examples below, each column of five words makes a cluster.

fog	kitten	snowman	letter	castle
night	table	fort	night	drawbridge
sunrise	meat	battle	camp	jester
robin	jump	sleigh	lightning	feast
rain	flypaper	pancakes	rain	turrets

A Sentence to Begin a Story. Some sentences set a story action in motion with a few words. Pupils then can easily keep the action going.

"Sammy, you're stepping on fresh paint!"

It happened a mile from town.

"Long distance calling," said the operator.

It was a small advertisement, reading: "Wanted, a boy who is not afraid."

Three puffs of signal smoke arose at five-minute intervals.

A Sentence to End a Story. These sentences work in reverse. Pupils automatically think of action that could have led up to them.

The "ghost" was my pet calf, with a handkerchief tied to his tail. And that is the reason why butterflies are always searching, searching.

After that, the black ants and the red ants remained on opposite sides of the log.

The frog remained on the lily pad and, in his croaking way, seemed to give the "ha! ha!" to the floundering boys.

I must tell you the rest of it some other time.

Then Aunt Clara closed the book, and all of us went to out beds.

A Newspaper Headline. With compactness and action built into them, headlines sketch basic situations but allow much freedom in the development of stories built on them.

Baby giraffe finds walking difficult

Elephant proves her long memory

Monkey leads chase across three housetops

Parrot, perched in tree, defies police: captured after his perch is sawed off.

Exhausted pigeon halts busy traffic ten minutes

4,200 canaries arrive in hold of dutch ship

Bear robs honey from hives near village.

A News Item. A news item usually is a summarised rather than a dramatised statement of its material, but it is likely to contain action, conflict, and characters for a plot. Pupils using the news item as their motif should be free to change the circumstances of time, location, and people to get the narrative and dramatic effects they want. Also they probably should substitute fictitious names for the real ones.

Names for Characters. Suggestions may be made for individual names or groups of names. In the latter case the group might represent all the characters for one story or play.

A Description of a Place. Such statements set the atmosphere or suggest a kind of character or action.

It was a shady spot in the old south meadow near a creek.

There streets met there, and cars were coming down each of them.

I found the room filled with strange objects from all parts of the world. Elephant teeth, tiger skins, conch shells, and shawls crowded each other on the middle shelf.

This must have been the garden where the sugar plum tree grew. The flowers were bonbons on frosted stems. The toolhouse had stick-candy boards and chocolate-bar shingles.

A Picture. The pupil should consider more than merely what is happening *in* a picture. He can think about what might have happened *before* and what might happen *next*.

A Proverb or Slogan. A proverb or slogan may suggest situations, characters, and action. It also can be a title, probably symbolic rather than literal.

A new broom sweeps clean.
Haste makes waste.
Wishes won't wash dishes.

The "If it Had Happened Yesterday" Point of View. Scientific, political, and social events and all kind of expenditions suggests themselves for use here. They can be of local, national, or world interest. Important occasions in the history of music, literature, and visual art offer fine possibilities.

Suppose that these events happened only yesterday:

The Wright brothers' first flight in an airplant at Kittyhawk.

Noah Webster's first dictionary is published.

Sir Francis Drake returns to England from his voyage around the world.

Printing by movable type becomes possible in Europe.
For the first time an automobile appears in our home town.
The first man-made satellite is successfully launched.
It is discovered that bacteria can be killed by heat.

Imaginary newscasts, interviews, newspaper articles, and editorials are what most pupils compose on this type of motif. But there are possibilities for imagined advertisements, handbills, posters, and, of course, for ballads, stories, and dramatic sketches.

A Title. Once well headed, some stories and playlets seem half written. The same motif, named by a dull title, would seem harder to develop.

A Boston Boy of '76	A Ride on the "Clermont"
Walking Eight Miles	A Flight with a Butterfly
My Dime Speaks	A Seat at the Round Table
Sister Learns to Cook	Colours and an Easel

Geographical Names. Geographical names are starters for stories or plays.

Wave Crest	Mackerel Hill	Saddleback Mt.
Gallows Hill	Thistle Hill	Panther Mt.
Deathrattle Hill	Misery Hill	Mutton Ridge
Lost Village Road	Butternut Ridge Road	Sunset Trail
Sunrise Road	Old Toll Bridge	Covered Bridge
Mad Tom Creek	Grasshopper Point	Lonesome Bridge
Dry Creek	Scar Valley	Feather Hollow
Beaver Dam	Goblet Spring	Hawk's Hollow
Sand Eddy	Mosquito Point	Frog Hollow

Items on the Bulletin Board. Posted items may be copies of pupil writing, copies of work from other classes and other schools, or clippings relating to authors and writing.

A Line or Two to Begin a Poem. A rhythmic line may start a trend of thought and establish a line pattern.

I wonder what my shadow thinks of me
With mighty brush I stirred among the clouds last night
Do flowers enjoy the butterflies?
The lilacs told the secret

To the chirping, chattering wren
I need my little shadow
The railroad tracks look tried today
With lashing hand
The thunder slapped the sky

A Suggested Refrain. The refrain would be used as the last verse in each stanza of the poem. Examples are:

The clouds and I	Trippety, trippety, trip
Into the silent sea	Out of the big bass horn
My shadow and I	And night crept under the eaves

A Verse Read Aloud. Reading and rereading aloud a line from any part of a poem, pupils may respond to the rhythm, mood, or imagery. The line becomes a kind of pitch pipe or tuning fork for the class.

Communal Composition of a Poem. People have their sport with communal composing at parties or while riding on a train or bus. Pupils can have fun with it in the classroom. The experience gives some children momentum to compose verse by themselves.

Patterns of Verses. Patterns can be drawn on the chalkboard or projected on a screen. They my crystallise an idea or suggest a topic that could be expressed naturally in a poem. Also this experience encourages pupils to look for pattern as a feature to enjoy in a poem.

(a) (b)

(c) (d)

A Poem Read Aloud. Several hearing of a poem set a rhythmic pattern or suggest a form for an original poem.

Words to Supply. Discussions of rhythm, meter, mood, and meaning come up naturally when pupils try out words suggested as fill-ins for vacant spaces in lines of verse. From the experience a class learns about the ideas and craftsmanship of poetry. Also a few pupils build poems on the given lines. Lines like these can be put on the chalkboard:

Mr. Wind comes________by.
So I________my dolly to sleep.
The leaves are falling;
They look like________
________in the air.

The wind told________me.
My echo is a________.
The fog________into town.
The spider________across the windowpane.

Pupils' Explanations. Shoptalk and a studio atmosphere develop naturally when pupils talk about what they had planned to do in an original composition and how they did it. Such sharings raise questions of technique, stimulate ideas, and encourage experiments in composing.

The Pattern of a Programme. The plan of a radio or television programme may be convertible to a creative purpose. Often the main character in the programme is the stimulus.

Replenishing and Discovering

Pupils look out of a window which provides a view across a lawn, road, pond, and grove of trees. How can they, within the classroom, by observation alone, and without information from another person, tell that a gentle breeze is blowing? From the same window, at another time, how can they tell that a strong wind is blowing? Or that the direction of the wind has changed?

Down the hall a carpenter is driving a nail into a board. In what way do the strokes of his hammer change in sound and frequency as he proceeds? How can pupils tell when the nail is driven in almost all the way?

These may seem like extraordinary questions, but children can observe keenly enough to answer them, and in doing so will benefit in at least three ways, and probably in a fourth: they gain new material to use in imaginative expression, discover hitherto unrecognised aspects of their environment, and maintain an alterness of their senses. This is important during the upper-grade years when the senses are likely to lose some of their earlier keenness. It is also likely that in the process of making discoveries outside themselves, children may discover (or rediscover) things within themselves. Earlier experiences, temporarily forgotten, are now brought to mind by something else.

Replenishing and discovering are important because a child needs new material if imaginative expression is to continue. Fruitful motifs are numerous, and the activities connected with them can be fun and profitable for the teacher as well as for the pupils.

Ways to Replenish and Discover

Any motif serves well if it stimulates observation. It becomes more rewarding if it also encourages a child to reflect on what he has observed.

Observation Alone. This kind of activity was illustrated by the first two questions at the opening of this section. Here are additional examples:

From observation alone, without the aid of any information from another person, now can we tell that:

The morning is a cold one?

A group of people have a secret among themselves?

The man is wearing a new suit for the first time?

Snow has fallen during the night? (How can you tell this even without looking outdoors?)

The haystack in the field is a very old one?

How Something is Done. Children are expert in noticing how something happens or is done; for instance, the way:

A person carries a precious parcel.

Rain, beginning to fall, wets a slanting roof.

Rain quivers the leaves of trees and shrubs when the air is very still.

The rhythmic swaying of the tops of two tall elms blown by a strong wind differs from that of three comparatively short maples blown by the same wind. (How do the rhythms differ when the trees are bare? When full of foliage? When the foliage is wet?)

Colours in the western sky change at sunset; in the eastern sky.

A sandy slope wears away during a heavy rain.

Irrigation water works its way along a row of vegetation.

A tree mends a wound in its bark.

A fern unfolds from coil to frond.

A dog moves around to the rear of an approaching person.

The prow of a boat cuts the water.

Cormorants fly in formation.

A rocket blasts off.

A Particular View. Views that stimulate observation come to one's attention every day. For example, the view of:

A patch of clouds passing off the face of the moon

A roller-skating rink filled with skaters

The landscape seen through the rear window of a moving automobile

Reflections on water
A butte, from a distance
A mesa
An orange grove
A parade coming down the street
A satellite crossing the sky

A View Glimpsed Briefly. There are flash views like these:

Through an archway, into a yard or patio as one drives along a street

Down a side street, as the bus on which one is riding crosses that street

Into the kitchen of a restaurant when a waiter pushes the door open to pass through

A Particular Time. There are special details characteristic of time:

The day after the first frost in autumn

The time when all shadows are long because the sun is low

A clear winter night

The day the ice goes out of the lake

A night of dense fog

Certain Types of Places. There are characteristic features in places such as the following:

A road over a mountain pass	The rim of a butte
A national park camposite	A shopping centre
The shore of a stream in a forest	An automobile dump
The place where there roads meet	The bottom of a canyon
Along the edge of a cloud	On the continental divide

Buildings. Each of these building or parts of building has distinctive features:

The interior of a bird store	A pagoda
A photographer's studio	A pueblo
A mountain ranger's cabin	An adoble house
The lobby of a post office	A plumber's shop

Why Certain Things Happen. By observing analytically a person can figure out why:

Kites fly
The sand on the ocean floor tends to be smooth
Maple keys swing and spin when falling to the earth
Aspen leaves "quake"
Tumbleweeds "tumble"
An eddy develops in a brook
A snow drift forms where it does

A Familiar Object Viewed as new. Pupils may develop an ability to view a particular object as something unique, not merely as one more specimen of a kind of thing they have known a long while. If they succeed, they rediscover details like size, colour, texture, shape, and the fitness of the design for the purpose which the object serves.

Pupils can try the experiment with some familiar object:

milk bottle	watch	shoe
ice cream cone	typewriter	nail
pineapple	wheel	cup
apple	cloud	leaf
hand	spoon	book

The Sense of Hearing. Any wakeful hour abounds in opportunities to train the sense of hearing:

On a summer evening in the country, what is the faintest sound one can hear? What is the loudes?

Tell what sounds one hears from a city street when one cannot, at the time, see the street.

When hearing a few different sounds at the same time, pick

out three of them, describe each one, and tell the direction from which each comes.

Compare the sounds made by approaching and departing locomotives, automobiles, horse-drawn vehicles, airplanes, people who are singing, people who are in conversation.

With eyes closed, try to tell the source of every sound you hear. Try it indoors in a house, waiting room, store, schoolroom, factory, office, library, post office, or barn and outdoors in a meadow, forest, street, park, public square, market place, or on the bank of a stream.

Walk around the source of a sound at some distance and try to decide from what direction the breeze is blowing.

See how many echoes can be heard after a loud, clear sound in a cave, a large and cavernous building, a valley lined by series of cliffs and hills, or in hilly wooded country on a quiet evening.

Study the pitches and rhythms of peals of thunder.

Pick out the sound of one instrument in a band or orchestra and follow that sound while the group is playing.

The Sense of Smell. Of the numerous experiments that are possible here are five suggestions:

Final a place where two varieties of shrubs or fruit trees stand close together and are in bloom. Pick out the fragrance of each and then find the spot where there is a division between the two fragrances. This is especially interesting when done on the leeward side of the blossoms.

Tell, by the odour, the stage of curing that mown grass has reached: newly cut, half cured, thoroughly cured, or overexposed to the elements.

Describe the fragrance of fresh laundry that has hung outdoors.

Try to describe the odor of smoldring wood.

Identify the smells characteristic of the first five minutes of rain on hot, dusty earth and vegetation; on hot, dusty sidewalks and streets.

The Sense of Touch. One can note the feel of:

The surface of the bark on various trees: maple, elm, shagbark, hickory, white oak, pine, sycamore, eucalyptus, beech, redwood

Water: lake, river, ocean

Summer breezes on the face

Zero-temperature air on the face

Rain on the arms

Sleet hitting the face

Criticism of Original Compositions

How to point out defects in a creative composition without discouraging the author is a universal problem. The situation is more personal and sensitive than in criticism of letters, reports, and other utility writing and speech.

Teachers have various solutions. They may get a pupil to compare his present works with something (perhaps of better quality) which he had done before, or with something from another author who had used a similar topic. Some like a pupil to compare the better portions of a composition with the less successful parts of the same composition. This latter plan works fairly well because most pieces are partly good, partly mediocre. One or two sparkling words may be lodged among a dozen uninspired ones or a single line or phrase may be far superior to all others. Recognition of those good features may stimulate the pupil to judge and revise the weaker portions.

A lapse of time usually brings an objective view and makes criticism easier. Therefore, teachers may defer critical comment a few days. As a variant they may ask the pupil to read his work aloud a number of times over a period of several days, sometimes with main attention to the thought, sometimes to how the thought is stated.

Good results often come from having the author tell what he wanted to do in his composition and how he tried to do it. This quickly leads to an objective discussion of the craft. Usually this discussion occurs between pupil and teacher, but a good many pupils are willing to tell their classmates about their work.

When the writer knows that his composition will be presented before the class, posted on a bulletin board, or published in a school paper he generally welcomes criticism. Many teachers consider this the most fruitful type of situation for giving criticisms.

A pupil is entitled to have the teacher judge the content of his work on the basis of what it means from the author's point of view. But if he wants something read before a large group or published, he should be willing to have it judged frankly on the basis of its probable interpretation.

Group criticism can be promoted by having a "contribution box" in the room. Anything found in that box is discussed by the whole class. Most contributions come in anonymously.

Efforts to improve a composition that a young student considers finished can be overdone in the art of language, as in other arts. This is especially true in precollege years. Having written out an idea the pupil is likely to be looking ahead to his next creation. He may therefore be more interested in how he can make the next one better than in revising a recent one. The situation resembles that of a motorist who has driven through one (green) traffic light; he is thinking of the next traffic signal rather than of the one he has just passed.

Efforts to Make the Next One Better

The thought of making their next poem, story, or playlet better than previous ones appeals to children. This interest opens a way for instruction in techniques.

Only the simplest points of craftsmanship can be suggested to pupils in the grades. Yet this must be done if children are not to continue floundering in shapeless, ineffective composing. Fortunately some very constructive techniques are fairly easy to explain.

The major recurring weaknesses in children's poems, stories, and plays are easily recognised types. About eight or nine types reappear in poems, six or seven in stories, and nine or ten in dramatic sketches. The checklist below offers suggestions for remedying most of them.

When writing verse

The points of craftsmanship needing attention in poetry can be discussed in terms that pupils understand. Discussions should be forthright and businesslike.

The Strength of the Last Lines. Many poems start well enough but fade into thin wordiness towards the end. Some last lines add little to the idea of the poem or needlessly emphasise a "lesson" or moral. Often they sound more like prose than like poetry. The end of a poem is a critical spot.

Such weakening at the end is less probable if young writers are assured that it is all right for a poem to be short. Five or eight lines make a better poem than ten or fifteen if the author had said what he wants to say.

A person usually writes a poem on a topic that he has thought about and probably brooded over for some time. Therefore he is likely to start vigorously, putting much in the opening lines. Soon he has said most of what he had on hand to say. At this point he ought to stop. If he continues just because he wants to make the composition longer he is not likely to improve the poem. He is working beyond his original material and cooling off on his readers when he should cool off on his wastebasket.

On this point the amateur writer of verse contrasts with the amateur writer of reports, interviews, and similar prose. The writer of utility prose tends to compose thin paragraph at the opening while warming up to his subject. He should warm up on his wastebasket.

Poetic Quality of the Idea. For poetry the ideas should differ somewhat from the ordinary matter-of-fact things people talk about in prose. A reader of verse expects a special turn of thought and some touches of imagination, even of symbolism.

If a pupil finds that his ideas are very ordinary he may decide that no poem is possible. The trouble, though, may be less in the topic than in what the author found to say—or didn't find to say—on it. Almost any subject has poetic possibilities, but an author must find them.

Words Evoking Sensory Impressions. A good many of the words in a poem should make a hearer or reader recall memories of things he has seen, heard, felt, smelled or tested. Concrete and specific nouns and action-suggesting verbs accomplish that. A poem or line that is weak on this point may contain too many abstract or general nouns and static verbs. Such words can be replaced.

A Minimum of Words. Poems are likely to be overloaded with modifying words, especially adjectives. One can substitute concrete nouns and action-suggesting verbs to do the describing.

Perhaps the number of articulating words like *the, an, a, have, has,* or *had* can be reduced. Those words excite no hearers or readers. And conjunctions like *therefore* and *because* suggest prose rather than verse.

Natural Word Order. Contemporary poets try to compose in the natural word order of English. They would not attempt to get "poetic effects" by saying "went they over the hill" instead of "they went over the hill." Pupils occasionally imitate the unnatural word order found in earlier poetry.

Current Diction. Contractions like *don't* or *I'll,* if used in normal conversation, are acceptable in poetry. But poets now avoid *'its, 'twere, 'twas* and other contractions which rarely occur in everyday talk. Children find these latter ones in earlier poetry and occasionally use them. The same is true of obsolete words like *ere.*

Inconspicuous Rhyme. Rhyme is pleasant but it should not steal the show. The author ought to be the master of it, not the slave. The poem should not give the impression that the poet changed the trend of his thought just to follow wherever rhyme led him. Oral readings provide pupils their best check.

Contemporary hearers and readers generally like rhymes three or four lines apart rather than in lines next to each other. Few poems now have **couplets** throughout, except for humorous verse. Yet children still tend toward jog-trot couplets made up of lines containing four beats each. They are influenced by earlier poetry and out-of-date and misguiding exercises on verse writing and rhyming found in some textbooks for the grades.

Nowadays, more than previously, free verse contains some lines that rhyme. But the rhymes seem casual and do not occur at regular intervals from line to line.

Lines in Accord with Each Other. All lines ought to have approximately the same kind of beat or rhythm. If most of the lines have regular beats (meter), as in Eugene Field's "Wynken, Blynken, and Nod" or Rachel Field's "Taxis," then perhaps all lines should have such beats. If the poem tends toward irregular rhythm (free verse), as in Carl Sandburg's "Fog" or Elizabeth Coatsworth's "The Mouse," then all lines should be more or less in that pattern.

All lines do not need to be the same in length, especially in a poem having irregular rhythm. Again the lines of "Fog" are examples. Poems with regular rhythm also may have some lines shorter than others. Short lines often occur at the end of a poem or a stanza. "Wynken, Blynken, and Nod" and Vachel Lindsay's "The Mysterious Cat" illustrate this.

A Plan or Design. The beginning of a poem ought to seem like a beginning, and the end like an end. All parts should be recognised as belonging where they are.

A poem's shape on the page often reveals the plan. This is especially true in poems that have regular rhythms and are divided into stanzas. Free-verse poems like Sandburg's "Fog" and Eleanor Farjeon's "Circus" have lines of various lengths and are not divided into stanzas, and therefore do not make very regular patterns on a page. But it is evident that each of these poems is composed according to a plan.

Total Effect. There should be an over-all harmony in a poem. Repeated oral readings tell much about the concord of rhythms, words, line grouping, and combinations of sounds.

When writing stories

Dialogue, conflict, and presentation of situations through action and talk head the list of points that come up for discussion in story writing. They have their equivalent in real life, and therefore are easy for children to understand.

Use of Dialogue and Action. The most important happenings ought to be resented through talk and action. Pupils often merely say or report that a character said or did something, even though what was said or done is very important for the story. Likewise they merely report that something important has happened. Such episodes should be dramatised through dialogue and action. Summarised reporting is not vivid enough.

Characters through Words and Deeds. On this point, as on the one just above, pupils often neglect the words and action. They merely actors in action and hear them talk so that he can form his own idea of what kind of people they are.

Animal characters too should be shown through action.

Conflict and Struggle. In the story there shold be people or animals that are in trouble or trying to do something which is difficult. Hearers and readers then become interested and wonder how the conflict or struggle will work out.

The Sequence of Events. Pupils should arrange the events in a story so that there is suspense over what might happen next. The order of telling—what is told first, what second, what third—is important in establishing suspense.

Pupils must check against the danger of letting the narrative wander off into matters which are not actually part of the story.

Convincing Details. Details—even very small ones—can make a character or situation seem real: how a person swings his left hand when walking, for instance, or the kind of pie he likes best. In daily life, children are good at seeing such details. They can be encouraged to use them in stories.

But a story has no place for details that do not help, just as it does not accommodate unnecessary talk.

Good Opening Sentences. The first three sentences ought to win the favour of a hearer or reader and also get the story under way. Children understand the former function of openings better than the latter.

When composing for dramatics

Discussing original playlets, teachers and pupils often find themselves talking about maintaining a conflict and developing important scenes more fully. They also try to heighten the dialogue so that it will be worth listening to.

Conflicts Early in the Play. Soon after the curtain opens somebody should be wondering what to do, looking for somebody or something, or wanting very much to get something that is hard to obtain. Or two or more characters (people or animals) might be opposing each other.

Conflict Sustained. The worry, fight, or desire that sets up the main conflict should run through most of the play. Spectators lose interest when no trouble or struggle is apparent on the stage. The problem of sustaining the main conflict is one of the most troublesome that they face when composing in dramatics.

Suspense. Conflict, action, and dialogue should be so arranged that spectators wonder what will happen next. Sequence is very important. Events presented in one order can be exciting; told in another order they seem dull.

Happenings on Stage. To show conflict and develop suspense the pupil must make events happen on the stage. People or animals must *do* things. There should not be merely talk about doing things or about what was done. Action connected with struggle or conflict is the heart of stage entertainment.

If dialogue is very witty or funny the physical action may be less important. But good dialogue, itself, constitutes a form of action—mental action.

Economy in Dialogue. On a stage, even more than in a story, every word should count. Conversation must stay on the main issues of the play, not drift off from one topic to another. Spectators do not like to spend time listening to dialogue which doesn't seem to be getting anywhere or which is getting somewhere too slowly.

This, of course, does not mean that a child should not use abundant words. The writer might make some scene better by having it longer, provided he thinks of additional relevant things that could happen and be said. The caution refers to needless words which make a dialogue thin.

Development of Episodes. Many potentially good scenes remain undeveloped in children's plays. Too often an episode comes on stage and is over in about a minute, before spectators get clear impressions of what is happening. Such scenes might be much more entertaining if developed to last three or four minutes.

A playlet in a fourth grade was supposed to show the actions and talk of two boys cutting pumpkins for Halloween. But the whole performance was over in two minutes. The audience scarcely knew what was supposed to be going on. The writers had not thought of the many interesting remarks that children make and the varied problems they must solve when carving jack-o'-lanterns.

Short Dialogue Units. On stage, as in daily talk, dialogue units shold be short. Characters should not speak very long without a break.

Stageable Scenes. Pupils should think about the practical matter of whether the scenes they are planning can be staged with the facilities at hand. Some kinds of action can be shown on a stage; some cannot. Actors can do many things but not everything. Possibilities differ according to whether the scene is intended for a regular stage, a puppet stage, or a situation using no special stage and no scenery. An animated cartoon strip is able to present almost any situation or idea.

Of course practically anything can be staged if the people watching it use enough imagination. And juvenile spectators are good at imagining.

Ease of Speaking. Pupils ought to give their lines a series of oral tests. In that way they can tell whether there are words or word combinations which should be dropped because they would be hard for an actor to pronounce or to project to the audience. The oral test shows also whether the dialogue sounds reasonably natural.

Discussion of Literary Techniques

The controversial matter of teaching techniques in connection with imaginative expression has no perfect solution. But it must be faced. Ultimately and somehow a pupil must practice a degree of craftsmanship if he is to produce anything that will please other people or even please himself. If he does not acquire some elementary techniques his works remain shapeless. Slovenly composing can throw a school's whole imaginative expression programme into disrepute.

As long as composing is going well there is little occasion for discussing techniques. When subject matter and form seem to come easily together, almost spontaneously, creativity is, more or less, an unconscious process—a dip into the unknown, supported by techniques probably unrecognised at the time. Then the unconscious dynamics of the creative process are working well. But when a young writer meets compositional difficulties, when his story, play, or poem does not seem so effective as he had expected, or when he feels like experimenting with new forms, he confronts matters of craftsmanship.

Even "touch-it-not" teachers, who say that nothing should be changed in what a child composes and insist that technique must never be brought up lest it "stifle" creativity or "curb" individuality, reveal their personal use of technique. They reveal it (probably unknowningly) when they "edit" their pupils' writings for the school paper or assembly. Sometimes they help the authors edit them. "I just shifted words around at a few places," they confide to a friend, or, "We substituted a longer word in this line to make the line come out right." Or they might tell the writer, "Start a new paragraph here," or "Omit your first paragraph." These are technical matters, every one of them.

A few hints on technique will not stifle a child who wants to improve his compositions. This can be assured if a teacher maintains the atmosphere of a studio, using informal and forthright shoptalk on topics like those discussed in the preceding pages.

Children pick up impressions of technique when reading or hearing what other people have done. A pupil active in composing might like to see writings from pupils of previous years.

There are additional sources of technical aid. One of them—rich, but widely neglected—is the store of relevant impressions gained through activities in the other arts. When drawing, painting, or modelling clay, pupils hear and talk about design, rhythm, emphasis, contrast, selectivity, and related elements. They meet similar matters of technique in music, dancing, and gymnasium activities. In addition, in all those arts they see ideas being developed with imagination and fancy. Such contacts illuminate creativity in language.

Sharing Original Works

When a pupil composes a piece of imaginative writing, should the teacher arrange to have the work heard or read by other members of the class, and, perhaps, by the public?

This insistent question has three aspects: Is the quality of the product such that the piece should be shared beyond the writer and teacher? Do the circumstances connected with the composing of the piece favour such sharing? If the piece is one that should be shared, is it of such length or nature that it can be read, staged, or published with reasonable convenience and economy?

These questions are complex, and a teacher's manner of answering them has great effect on the development of imaginative expression in her classroom. Sharing with someone else is a normal ambition of a person who has expressed himself in imaginative verse or prose. Such sharing completes the cycle of communication. The teacher, too, is happier when her pupils have an audience. A majority of the prose and verse that pupils write should be shared, and the authors deserve the satisfaction that comes from such sharing.

But for some writings publicity is questionable. Poems and stories may be so personal that public display of them would embarrass the author. Some writings are too imitative or borrow ideas or form too obviously from other sources. There may be compositions from pupils who are likely to become vain or otherwise "difficult" if their work is publicised. And many writings are weak in content or craftsmanship or in both.

There is also the question of sincerity. "Insincerity" may be difficult to detect. A teacher's knowledge of the author will help her decide. Language that is inflated or too facile may be a clue to insincerity. Yet, in playful moods a pupil may compose something which may seem insincere but which, in its playfulness or even mockery, has serious intent.

Even though a work is not widely shared, the author may feel rewarded. At least he has a chance to share the composition with his teacher, who should give it a sympathetic reading or hearing and a commentary that is as appreciative as the work justifies. Also by the very act of expressing himself, quite apart from any considerations of a public, he has gained the personal clarification that accompanies self-expression. Even when no one happens to share his creation the author of imaginative prose or verse does not usually feel the bitterness of the "theme" writer who thinks he is "just writing for the teacher's wastebasket."

Media for sharing original works are numerous in a modern school. Opaque projects offer a quick way to show anything written. Choral-speaking groups and a ready-at-hand puppet stage accommodate poetic and dramatic pieces. Sharing should be done without undue publicity.

Pupil Activities

The preceding pages gave suggestions that pupils can experiment with individually or in groups. Additional motifs offered here may stimulate facets of imagination and perception not directly challenged by previous experiments. A teacher can think of more and adapt them to children's aptitudes and interests.

1. Four or five people seeing or hearing the same thing are likely to have different feelings or thoughts about it. Try to guess the feelings and thoughts of these people about a

rainstorm:

Farmer
Classroom of pupils who had planned a picnic
Weather forecaster who had forecast rain
Policeman
Taxi driver

Of these people about a jet plane in flight:

Pilot of a propeller plane
Motorist
Hiker
Child

Of these people about Halloween:

Little girl
Policeman
High school senior
Merchant
The owner of a house

You can make up new ones that friends will enjoy.

2. One might wonder what people did or said when for the first time in history they saw somebody carrying an umbrella. What do you think they did or said?

Make guesses like that about what people may have said or done when they first saw:

A ferris wheel
A carbon paper in use
An image on television
An animal hitched to a wagon
A mirror
A gun being fired
A photograph
A curved lens focusing the sun's rays

3. The pupils and teacher of one room were composing a poem about the sunset. One of their lines told about a slender

steeple that stood in the west and was almost lost from sight in the glow of sunset.

The line was first written with these words: "The steeple was seen in purple light." But one pupil did not like the expression "was seen." She thought that a word like "stood" might be better. The teacher then wrote the line this way on the chalkboard: "The steeple stood in purple light." Everybody liked this wording better than the first one.

The other pupils suggested changes. After about ten minutes they had more than a dozen different ways of telling about the steeple:

rose
glowed
melted
dissolved
faded
shimmered
disappeared
"The steeple vanished in purple light."
was clothed
was wrapped
towered
was haloed
floated
swam

Which one of the suggestions do you like best? Which do you like second best? Can you think of additional words that would be better than "was seen"?

4. Early on a summer evening four boys walked across a meadow that lay near the base of a long cliff. One boy called loudly to his dog, Spottie. All four were surprised at hearing the name echoed, and each began to shout and listen for the sound of his words to return.

"That sounds like somebody mocking me," one boy said. "Yes, but it makes me think of a bouncing ball," said another. "An echo is like a boomerang," said a third.

These boys were using their imaginations. Their ideas were like ones we might find in a poem about an echo. What they said was much more interesting than if they had just called an echo "a funny thing."

Many people enjoy thinking ideas like these. They make a kind of game of the imagination out of it. Here are a few imaginative ideas that young people have thought of: "a jet plane is a big vacuum cleaner," "trees are the giants of the earth," "a ticking clock is the heartbeat of time," "the tide is the scrubber of the seashore."

You can have such fun, too. Start with anything you are interested in. For example, what might you say about fog? About a needle? About lightning, clouds, a cricket, goldfish in a bowl, or a refrigerator?

5. A poem might be written on any one of the subjects names below, and perhaps sometimes you will write on one or more of them. But for the present think about only an opening line—the first line—for a poem on one of the topics that you like.

My Cat	My Tractor
Canary Song	Soap Bubbles
Today We Planted Maple Trees	The Big River
My Dolly	Rain
A Field Mouse	Canyon Walls
A Cloud	The Vacuum Cleaner

After you have written the opening line for one of the subjects you might wish to do the same for several others.

6. What do you suppose are some of the things people think about first when they hear the sounds listed below?

A knock at the door
The noise when an airplane breaks the sound barrier
The ring of the telephone
The sound of a pencil writing
The screech of automobile brakes

7. A motorist has a flat tire along a busy highway on a Sunday afternoon in summer. He is taking two guests (his

brother and the brother's wife) to the bus station. How does each of the three feel about the mishap? What does each do and say?

Three young girls are looking for four-leaf clovers. One finds a specimen. What does each think and say?

Study Activities for Teachers

A teacher should keep up her literary training. To that end she might benefit from checking occasionally to see how many of the following she has done:

Said to herself (or to someone else) "that is an idea for a poem" or "that would be a plot for a short story" and then thought about how the poem or story could be developed.

Recorded, for possible use, some unusual ideas, observations, or situations

Clipped and saved news items that seem usable for stories or plays. Composed original verse or prose.

Speculated about resemblances and contrasts between expression in language and expression in other arts.

A teacher need not try to complete every experiment that she undertakes. Professionals in all the arts have desks or studios full of sketches which they started, worked out with care up to a certain point, and then left unfinished. They may not intend to finish them. They think of them as "studies"—exercises or experiments in various phases of their arts. For the artist it may have been a study of the trunk of a leafless tree or the colours of a yucca bloom; for the composer, an experiment in counterpoint; for the writer, a trial run on a dialogue between a Louisiana Creole and a tourist from Quebec, or on the sound and action of a hurricane for a verse.

There is a growing list of very readable books on how to write poems, plays, and stories. Some are included in the bibliography of this volume.

General Experiments

1. Someone wants to show that a girl walking up the street is happy. This he wishes to do by implication or inference

rather than by direct statement. Instead of saying that she is happy or looked happy he might imply her feeling in the way she walks, the way her curls bounce in response to her springing step, the twinkle in her eyes, and the way her mouth appears ready to laugh.

Experiments like this help one understand how authors achieve their descriptions.

For further fun in this direction, one might show by inference that:

The after-dinner speech was boresome.
The three-year-olds are having a good time.
The person going down the street is worried.
The dance band is playing a lively number.
The little lad is happy to go back to school after a week at home with measles.

2. How well does one's ability to visualise situations and actions help him to do the following?

Mentally trace the movement of the shadow of a bird or of an airplane over a specific landscape. Try this either while looking at the landscape or when recalling it. Interesting variations arise with different kinds of landscapes: flat terrain, rolling and wooded areas, mountainous country.

Also trace in imagination the transit of an automobile over a high-way in a familiar neighbourhood. Then trace the vertical movement of an automobile that is crossing a mountain.

3. We hear of eccentric people and places. Some such people really exist, if news reports are to be believed. As for the places, most are in a land of make-believe. But whether real or imaginary such characters and places stretch the imagination of anyone who lets himself go, fancy free, in speculating about their chief characteristic that fashion may get the impression that such direct statement are normal in poetry?

Find some poems that are improved *as poems* by omission of the moralising lines. Can you find many such poems among standard verse composed since 1920?

2. There is profitable fun in recasting verses that for various reasons do not fit into the poem. A line may have rhythm that doesn't harmonise with the other lines of the poem; it may contain syllables or sounds that are awkward to pronounce together; it may sound more like prose than like verse; it may have too many abstract words or needless articulating words.

A teacher meets many such verses when pupils come to her saying something like "I can't get this line to sound right" or "this line doesn't seem to go with the rest of the poem." In addition there are some unsuitable lines which children do not detect. These the teacher should identify.

A pupil wanted help on two lines of this poem:

My little cat is inky black,
His eyes are yellow moons,
And when I try to sleep at night
I hear him singing strange cat tunes.

By day he'll sit upon my lap
Or chase a spool for play,
At night he's a shadow in the dark
Going his own cat way.

The author felt that the last line of the first stanza did not "fit in." She also said that the third line of the second stanza "didn't sound very good." After various trials and readings the pupil decided on this for the last line of the first stanza:

He's singing strange cat tunes.

This gave the line the three beats which is needed (instead of the original four) to fit into the pattern of the whole poem. It also gained directness.

The other line was revised also, but its change required adjustment in the line following it:

At night, a shadow in the dark,
He goes his own cat way.

Thus the line became more compact by removal of unnecessary words, became easier to say because the *s* sound was dropped, and fitted the particular rhythm that the meter of this poem called for, since *he's* in the original version was an extra syllable.

In another poem the line "The wind, like a kitten, frisks here and there" was revised in several ways to make it seem less like prose:

"The wind, a kitten, frisks here and there"
"The kittenish wind frisks here and there"
"The wind's frisky kitten. . . ."

One young poet worked with the line

The Christmas tree, the last bouquet of autumn.

The seemed reasonably good as it was, but to make the line fit into his poem he revised it to read:

The Christmas tree, autumn's last bouquet.

Examples of harsh sound combinations and also of abstract words are conspicuous in the following line which a teen-age girl brought in for revision. It was from a love poem.

Your presence is as essential as breath.

Here the inappropriate hissing effects of six or seven *s* sounds, the phonetic difficulties of speaking the line, the proselike rhythm of the line, and the abstract nature of the words *presence* and *essential* all called for attention. No fully satisfactory solution was found at the time, but the author tried such variants as:

"Your presence is as breath to me."
"Your presence is as breath to life."
"Your presence is as breath to man."
"Your presence is a vital breath."
"You are as breath to me."

3. When stimulated, a class can push imagination quite far on a topic that has poetic possibilities. This is illustrated by the following sequence, developed after a class had spent several sessions on revising weak lines of verse. Someone had brought in two free verse lines:

Time, you serve as a swift broom
And sweep away every day.

Very soon "serve as a" was struck out as being proselike and wordy. Someone who did not like the phonetic combinations in "away every day" suggested "each day." By that time the version stood as:

Time, swift broom,
You sweep away each day.

That was considered a great improvement over the original. But several other revisions followed. One changed "swift broom" to "worn broom."

Just when the discussion seemed to be ending, two students spoke up, giving the two versions below:

Time sweeps each day
Under the rug of Eternity.

Time, swifting each day,
Like a broomish servant.

Some class members did not at first like the second version, but after a little reflection they accepted the bold derivatives of *swift* and *broom* and became very fond of the lines.

Imagination leaped as the original version developed into those final lines. The creative mind had acted. In fact the entire evolution of the first crude lines into something much better makes a good study in the creative mind at work. The evolution demonstrates also what a class can do if it has some knowledge of poetry craftsmanship.

Can you arrive at additional versions by experimenting with those original lines?

Experiments related to stories

1. Notice how skilled, writers use exact items and details to make situations in their stories believable. "They left by plane on flight 302 at 10:35 yesterday morning," is likely to seem more convincing than, "They left by plane about half past ten yesterday morning." So, too, there appears to be something

more real about: "He liked to click his heels on the pavement when he walked," when you add, "especially his right heel."

2. Story dialogue usually is more compact than exchanges in everyday life. Thin dialogue seems even thinner on paper than in actuality. Fictional talk also stays on a topic more consistently than daily conversation. A story has no time for talk that rambles aimlessly from one thing to another, unless such rambling is part of the characterisation, situation, or purpose.

Perhaps you will have a chance to test this by comparing stenographic transcripts or tape recording of ordinary conversation with literary dialogue.

Viewpoints to Emphasise Through Teaching Aids

Poems, plays, and stories from recordings and books or on the stage provide some of the best audio-visual inspiration and guidance for imaginative expression. They are heard, seen, or read. They may come from professional writers or amateurs, provided they are good samples of their art. For many children they provide both an inspiration to attempt something original and technical guidance in how to compose it.

Exhibits of all kinds—art, science, flowers, historical, and library—help too. They suggest ideas, extend the pupils' experiences and observations, and leave some impressions of craftsmanship.

1. *Every day we see, hear, or read about things that would be interesting to use in poems, plays, or stories.*
   - (a) Mounted or projected camera shots of various scenes and situations. Caption: What would you have seen, had you been there?
   - (b) Newspaper clippings with marked items that might be starting points for stories or plays. Mount or project the clippings.
   - (c) From a school window a few pupils watch outdoor events and situations. What different things do they see? How differently do two or more pupils see the same thing?

2. *A story, play, or poem is organised into a plan or pattern.*

   Audio-visual experiences to reinforce this fact are found in the sections on literature in following chapters.

3. *Our poems, plays, or stories probably can be improved by revisions.*

   (a) An exhibit of revised manuscripts from present or former pupils. Changes can be marked in colour.

   (b) An exhibit similar to *a*, above, but showing revisions made by well-known authors.

   (c) A series of drawings done in the manner of animated cartoons, showing words dancing into place. At first there is a blank space in a sentence or poetry line, or there is a word or phrase that doesn't seem satisfactory. Several words or phrases come dancing along. When the most suitable one comes it clicks into place and all is fine.

   (d) Additional aids on this point are in the audio-visual section, "Constructing Ideas with Language," and of following chapters on literature.

4. *We can learn by seeing how other writers composed poems, plays, and stories.*

   (a) Bulletin-board and poster displays of good specimens. Portions of poems and stories can be marked in colours.

   (b) Sometimes, to exhibits suggested in *a*, above, there can be added the statement: Which of these makes you say, "I like that, I'd like to write something like that myself"?

5. *Some kinds of words serve better than others in stories and poems.*

   (a) Poster, chalkboard, or projector showing of poems and passages from stories, with unusually effective words (particularly nouns and verbs) marked to indicate that name words and action words are highly effective in creating a situation and in describing it. (Excessive reliance on adjectives can be reduced. Also children note that *very, awfully, wonderful, pretty,* and *beautiful* do not rank among the effective words.)

(b) Chalkboard, poster, or projector showing of effective poems and good passages from stories. Question: Which words would you mark as best here?

6. *The position of a word, phrase, sentence, or paragraph in a poem, story, or play helps determine the effectiveness of the work. Position influences meaning, sound, and rhythm.*

(a) Direct readings or tape recordings test the effects of moving words or groups of words to several positions.

(b) Additional aids on this observation are in the audio-visual section, "Constructing Ideas with Language," and "Poetry."

7. *Poetry enjoy reading and hearing original compositions.*

(a) Tape recording of comments that people made after having heard or read original compositions by pupils.

(b) Letters containing comments similar to those of *a,* above.

Problems and Inquiries for Students

1. When children draw they exaggerate the size and prominence of what they consider especially important—the birthday cake, mother, themselves. Do you see any evidence of similar exaggeration in their poems, plays, or stories?

2. Can you note any decline in curiosity and alertness regarding their environment on the part of children when they reach the fifth or sixth grade, compared with the outlook of children in the earlier grades?

3. Observe how a topic can grow in a classroom, gradually becoming very live and then inspiring some pupils to imagination expression.

4. You will find it easy to help pupils who *can* compose originally and *want to,* but what will you try to do for those

who *can* but *don't want to,* or *can't* but *want to,* or *can't* and *won't?*

5. How many times during the last three months did you try to write original verse or prose?

6. What kind of circumstances or experiences are most effective as catalysts to start you composing something original? To start some of your friends composing?

7. How does your reading around from good prose or verse stimulate your creativity?

8. Associational (or emotional) logic and institutional logic are considered influential in literature and the arts. Do you find that they are strong in children? How are they related to the spontaneity of children's expression?

9. In imaginative expression, to what extent are creative moments impulsive and criticising moments analytical? Have you found that fine ideas are obscured by poor form and that good form is hollow if it lacks fine content?

10. Imaginative expression offers literary values and therapeutic values. Think about the differences between the two.

11. A child feels certain relationships between himself and his group and between himself and his teacher. Observe how those relationships influence his degree of frankness in imaginative expressions. Do they affect his sincerity? In your life, how does a knowledge of the way ideas will be received affect what you say or write?

12. Even after they can write stories independently, children tend to dictate their verse for the teacher to record rather than write it themselves. It this tendency related to the fact that poetry is primarily a spoken art? Can you think of other reasons for the situation?

12

Teaching Children to Think Constructively

Imagine the following situation: You have a week's vacation. You've been looking forward to this vacation for months, you've planned a number of outdoor activities, and of course you expect the weather to cooperate. The week finally arrives, and it rains five out of the seven days. Now, there are a number of responses you could have to this situation. You might think, "This is just my luck. It's not fair! My whole vacation is ruined!" You feel miserable the whole week and return to work stressed out. On the other hand, you might say to yourself, "Well, I'm disappointed with the rain, but I'll make the most of it. What other activities can I do to make good use of my vacation time?" And despite the weather you enjoy your week off. When you return to work, you feel refreshed and ready to get back into the routine. What is the difference between these two responses? The difference is in how you choose to construe the situation.

The great Greek Philosopher Epictetus said, "People are disturbed not by things but by their view of things." And Shakespeare made the very same claim in *Hamlet:* "There is nothing either good or bad, but thinking makes it so." The import of these famous statements is that personal control derives from the way an individual construes what's been seen, heard, or felt. In other words, it's the perspective we take and the appraisals we make of people and situations that primarily determine our emotional and behavioural reactions. The fact that you choose to look at the rainy vacation as an opportunity to do other things allows you to make the most of your time off.

Although there are a few inborn reflexes (e.g., a startle response to a sudden loud noise), there is ample evidence of a bidirectional influence between thoughts, feelings, and actions. Thoughts are in some cases the antecedents of emotions; in other cases thoughts are affected by emotions. Likewise, behaviour often follows from our assessment of a situation, but sometimes our assessment of a situation is influenced by what we are doing (Lazarus & Folkman, 1984). What's important to remember is that we can consciously and deliberately alter the cycle by examining and directing our thoughts. When we do, we typically feel different and act differently.

For example, Dweck (1986) taught children who were doing poorly in math to think differently about their failure, to interpret failure as a signal to try harder: the children who were instructed in this way persisted on math tasks longer than they did before and improved their grades. And therapists who work on helping children change the way they think (cognitive behavioural therapists) have observed a decrease in anger and aggressiveness in these children (Braswell & Kendall, 1988). Learning to identify negative thought patterns and replace them with realistic, constructive thoughts and images reduces anxiety and enhances performance (Deffenbacher, 1986; Hunsley, 1987; Meichenbaum, 1985). Finally, modifying destructive beliefs has a positive effect on both physical and mental health. Constructive changes in thoughts have helped Type A personalities (Friedman & Ulmer, 1984) and cancer patients (Taylor, 1991); change to constructive thinking is also a major ingredient for mental health and good coping skills (Lazarus & Folkman, 1984). The implication of all these studies is that thoughts can be put to good use and direction, even when the objective situation is bleak.

In the scenario with which this chapter began, the two different evaluations of the rainy vacation resulted in two very different states of mind of the vacationer returning to work. Granted, a rainy vacation is not an earth-shattering or life-threatening situation, but the kind of flexible thinking required for this irritating situation is exactly the kind of skill required for resilience in more difficult times. And it's not the case that constructive thinking eliminates the hurt. It does not. It simply allows us to channel the hurt or disappointment into constructive alternatives. Constructive thinking empowers us when mental muscle and coping skills are needed to deal effectively with a stressor. When we are able to think constructively, we are happier and better able to deal with stress and adversity.

What influences how we think about things? Researchers in the fields of cognition, social psychology, and clinical psychology have identified six major influences:

1. Language (specifically, words)
2. The opinions or beliefs we hold
3. Thinking errors (what experts call "cognitive distortions")
4. Age and maturity
5. Certain aspects of a situation or event
6. Attributions (i.e., the causes people ascribe to events)

I will discuss each one of these influences in the hope that the discussion will help parents and teachers identify and change faulty thinking and notice and reinforce constructive thinking in children.

LANGUAGE, THINKING, AND YOUR CHILD'S BEHAVIOUR

Language is the basis of thought and perception. It is the instrument we use to think about our experiences. It is also used to control behaviour and communicate needs. To get a feel for how powerful language really is, consider the following statements used to describe a person who reacts in an unruffled way to a wide variety of situations: "She is even-tempered"; "She is indifferent.". If we use the word "even-tempered" it results in a very different evaluation of the person than if we use the word "indifferent". An even-tempered person is viewed as calm, predictable, and in control. Someone perceived as indifferent is considered to be uncaring and unfeeling.

Our reactions to a person are guided by the labels we assign to them (Scheff, 1975). If the label is "even-tempered," we might trust, approach, and respect that person. If the label is "indifferent," we are likely to avoid or shun the person—or, at the very least, be cautious about what we disclose. Likewise, a child who is persistent in pursuit of a particular goal can be labelled as either "stubborn" or "strong-willed." The label given influences the adult's response to the child: the evaluation "stubborn" usually results in a more punitive approach to the child than does the term "strong-willed".

It is not only the evaluative label that has an impact on our reactions; word intensity does as well. The difference between "furious" and "disappointed" or "ecstatic" and "pleased" is the intensity of the emotion the words express. If I say I'm disappointed, I'm likely to react less strongly than if I say I'm furious. So not only do I have to watch the labels I use, but I also need to be cognizant of the words I use to express what I'm feeling.

Language also controls behaviour directly. The Russian psychologist A. Luria (1961) and the American psychologist A. P. Copeland (1983) have discovered that people use self-talk (also called private speech, internal dialogue, and automatic self-talk) to regulate their own behaviour. We literally talk to ourselves! We are not always aware of our self-talk, but it's always going on. It's particularly apparent when we are learning a new skill or engaging in a new activity of some kind. Do you remember when you were first learning to drive? Most people learning to drive think through the routine out loud: "Adjust and fasten seat belt, adjust mirror, make sure emergency brake is off" and so on. Eventually, the person does not have to repeat these steps out loud, but the self-talk continues internally.

Very young children do not use language to regulate behaviour. This is because language develops over the course of the first two years and because the ability to regulate one's own behaviour using language develops in three stages. In the first stage the child relies on the speech of others to control and direct behaviour. Children under the age of three require this kind of intervention. They do not have the cognitive maturity to self-talk. During the next stage children begin to use language to regulate behaviour, but in order to do so they have to talk aloud to themselves. When the self-talk becomes internalised, the child has reached the third and final phase of self-talk control. This third phase occurs around the age of five or six for most children. Children in this phase no longer need overt verbal guides for behaviour; they can talk to themselves quietly, just as adults do (Luria, 1961).

Parents and teachers can make direct use of language to reinforce those attitudes and beliefs compatible with resilience. They can do this by using expressions that cannote resilience and encouraging their children to do the same. In the following paragraphs are examples of statements that promote traits associated with resilience and productivity. Such statements serve to guide children's thinking and beliefs.

Statements That Promote Internal Control and Proactive Problem-solving

1. I can take charge of my (specific feelings).
2. It's up to me to try my best.
3. It's my responsibility to———
4. I can control my behaviour.
5. I'm responsible for how I act and behave in a situation.
6. I may not be able to control someone or something else, but I can always control my own reaction to whatever happens.
7. I accept responsibility for my experiences.
8. The best way to escape from a problem is to solve it.

Statements like these establish the centre of control in the person, not someplace else.

Statements That Promote a Sense of Challenge

1. I can handle a little at a time.
2. Even if I feel————, I won't feel this way forever.
3. Who knows, maybe something good will come from this.
4. I can manage.

5. I know what I can do.
6. I can stand it.
7. I may feel a little uncomfortable, but I'll survive.
8. It may hurt a little, but the hurt will go away.
9. Every experience in life is an opportunity to learn and grow.
10. Every problem is an opportunity.
11. Failure is success if we learn from it.
12. All things are difficult before they are easy.
13. When one door closes, another one opens.

Statements like these take the sting our of threats and allow the person to see change or adversity as manageable. Statements like "It's awful" or "I won't be able to stand it" serve only to exaggerate the problem and may lead to the perception that it's impossible to handle.

Statements That Promote A Sense of Commitment

1. I'm going to stick with——until I get it done.
2. It is my goal to——————
3. I believe in ——————
4. I'm sticking with this so that I can accomplish my goal.

These statements clearly establish a sense of goals and direction. They also convey the notion of persistence, which is so important for commitment.

Statements That Promote an Orientation toward Others

1. I can see your point of view.
2. I want to help you.
3. I want to cooperate with you.
4. I'm not the only now who——
5. You see things differently from me and that's okay.

6. I'm concerned about (name of person).
7. I care about (name of person).
8. I want to help (name of person).

These statements help children become "other-oriented."

BELIEFS, THINKING, AND YOUR CHILD'S BEHAVIOUR

Researchers and clinicians in the fields of cognition and cognitive behaviour modification have various ways of defining a belief. I have chosen to define a belief as an underlying assumption or opinion that people hold about themselves and their world. Beliefs filter our thoughts and form the basis for expectations. For example, if I believe all people act in a fair and just manner, then I will expect you to behave in accordance with my belief. The belief predisposes me to evaluate you positively if you act fairly. If you fail to act in a way that I perceive as fair and just, then of course I will view you negatively—unless I find good reason for why you behaved unfairly.

Beliefs are learned. Family, school, church, community, and society are the early teachers of beliefs. Personal experience influences beliefs as the child moves toward adolescence and adulthood. Because our beliefs are so fundamental to us, we are not always aware of them. And unless there is a problem, there is usually no need to question them.

Beliefs are either constructive or destructive. Constructive beliefs promote constructive thinking and lead to productive emotions and behaviour. Conversely, destructive beliefs produce destructive thinking, which in turn results in counterproductive feelings and actions.

Constructive beliefs

Constructive beliefs are moderate, reasonable, and realistic. Compare the following statements: "It is my hope that people treat each other in a fair and just manner"; "People must treat others fairly and justly." The first statement suggests that fairness is a desirable goal but not necessarily a natural condition. The second statement sets the stage for a very different expectation, namely, that all people will act fairly and justly at all times. The first statement is a constructive belief, the second a destructive one. Why? Because the first is realistic and prepares children for the possibility that people will not always treat them or others fairly whereas the second is unrealistic and ignores the many situations when individuals are treated in an unjust fashion. Children who are prepared for the realities they are lily to experience are better able to cope with them. Unrealistic beliefs about the behaviour of others do not provide children with the same kind of preparation. Generally speaking, beliefs that contain extreme and demanding language lead people to unrealistic expectations. Albert Ellis (1962) suggests that words like "should,", "ought", and "must" lead people to think destructively. He calls the persistent use of this language "musterbation."

Constructive beliefs fit the objective qualities of the situation. What this means is that what I hold to be true needs to be verifiable-unless the belief is a matter of faith. (And when it's a matter of faith, an individual needs to realise that the belief is an opinion, not a fact, and that it is true for some people but certainly not for all people.) Beliefs that are not a matter of faith can also be opinions, but they have some objective reality. For example, a child's belief that she or he is the best math student in the class is constructive if the objective evidence supports it (e.g., the child has the highest math average in the class). Similarly, the belief that Susie loves chocolate ice cream is also verifiable, by means of her response to chocolate ice cream. But the belief that chocolate ice cream is the only flavour worth eating (and that all individuals holding a contrary opinion share a defective belief) is destructive. There clearly is no objective base for such a position. The person who holds this belief has transformed an opinion with no reality base into a dogmatic doctrine.

Constructive beliefs promote goals and behaviours that are healthy for the individual and society. The belief that it's important to try to reach one's goals is a constructive belief because it prompts resilient attitudes and behaviours. The belief that it's easier not to even try is destructive because it supports the hopeless, helpless attitudes and behaviours that are observed in nonresilient individuals.

Destructive Beliefs

Destructive beliefs, like constructive beliefs, have certain characteristics. There is, for example, a demanding quality to them. They are filled with "shoulds," "can'ts," "musts," "have to's," and other extreme language. Destructive beliefs communicate the idea that people or situations need to be a particular way or need to be different from the way they are. Demanding beliefs are destructive because they often seek to change other people or situations. Other people and situations are not always influenced by what we have to say or by what we do. Besides, other people respond rather poorly to demands; they do better with requests.

Destructive beliefs are often cop-outs (Anderson, 1981), which place the responsibility for change on someone else. A copout is the belief that someone else is responsible for why I feel the way I do or why something did not get done. "He made me angry"; "It's her fault that I failed"; "He makes me feel so good!"—these are all examples of cop-outs. Others cannot make us feel this way or that; they do not control how we interpret or evaluate a situation. Someone else's actions may have prompted me to think a particular way, but ultimately I have control over the way I think, and therefore the way I feel. Cop-outs are destructive because they encourage people to think and behave as though they are externally controlled. In other words, cop-outs discourage people from assuming control for themselves.

Destructive beliefs have catastrophic themes (Ellis, 1962). Destructive beliefs often paint a "doom and gloom" picture of reality when things do not go quite the way we would like: "When I don't get an A, it is awful"; "When John calls me a name, it is terrible"; "I'll just die if I don't get first place." These are all examples of beliefs that distort a person's perspective and lead to negative feelings and behaviours. The catastrophic self-talk makes a challenge orientation nearly impossible because it discourages a person from coping with the situation. When we evaluate a situation in extreme negative terms, we may actually create a scenario that is worse than the reality of the situation.

Destructive Beliefs of Children and Adolescents

There appear to be three major categories of destructive beliefs that affect children and adolescents. The destructive beliefs discussed in the following paragraphs were identified through interviews with children and adolescents (Ellis & Bernard, 1983; Waters, 1982).

"I must excel in everything I do and get the approval of everybody all the time or else I am worthless." This is a destructive belief because it promotes an unrealistic set of expectations. It also leads the child to believe that all mistakes are awful things with irreversible consequences. In reality, people can learn and perfect their skills through mistakes. The difference between winners and losers is not that winners win; many winners were losers in past competitions. Rather, it's that winners learn from mistakes and losers don't. Losers are immobilised by mistakes and tend to give up when they make mistakes. This belief is destructive to the positive challenge orientation and willingness to persist that are so important to resilient children and adults. Moreover, a person may not excel in every area. Very few people do. Believing that you are worthy only if you excel at everything you do is destructive. Your natural abilities may vary across areas, making you more or less proficient in those areas. For example, your athletic ability may be far less than your intellectual abilities. Believing that you are a worthwhile individual only if you are good in sports and academically inclined is unrealistic and likely to result in a negative self-evaluation.

Negative self-evaluations reduce our sense of self-efficacy and compromise our ability to hold resilient and productive attitudes. Likewise, the belief that we need the love and approval of everybody all the time is equally destructive. It is the unusual person who is approved of by everyone all the time. Believing that this kind of continuous approval is a prerequisite for self-worth is therefore unrealistic and unnecessary. Besides, one has to differentiate between approval and unconditional love and respect. I may not approve of your behaviour, but that does not necessarily mean that I don't love or value you as a person. For example, there are plenty of occasions when I disapprove of my children's inappropriate behaviour, but this does not mean that I don't love or respect them as individuals. In a similar vein, adolescents and some adults often interpret disagreement as rejection. I may not agree with your opinion, but it does not automatically mean that I don't respect and care for you as a person.

Finally, there may be occasions when others do reject you as a person. While this may be disappointing and perhaps hurtful, it doesn't mean that you are worthless. People dislike others for a multitude of reasons. You may be rejected for the colour of your skin or the religion you choose to practice. Or you may be rejected because your interests and values are incompatible with those of others. Whatever the reason, rejection from some people some of the time is inevitable for most of us. The good news is that we need unconditional love from just a few people for a positive self-concept. Teaching children to understand that occasional rejection from others is common and to be expected helps them maintain a healthy sense of self when encountering negative responses from others.

"I must have and acquire what I want or else I will be miserable." How many times have you heard this one? Plenty, I'm sure. Children who believe that they have to get their own way are vulnerable because such a belief sets up unrealistic expectations in them. Again, the real world cannot always assure that they will get what they want all the time. If they truly believe that this is the only way they can be happy, they are bound to be miserable, as it's impossible to always get what one wants. Besides, sometimes what children think they want is not at all what they want.

"I must always feel happy and life should be easy and fun." Again, the expectation implied by this belief does not correlate well with what happens in real life. To expect no discomfort in life and to expect that things will be fun and easy all of the time is to expect too much. Discomfort and sadness are just as much a part of the human condition as comfort and joy. We have to be prepared to accept the range of life's conditions if we want to be happy, productive, and resilient.

Thinking Errors and Your Child's Behaviour

Destructive beliefs and language are not the only reason people come up with faulty evaluations. People also make errors in the way they process the information they receive. Researchers refer to these errors as cognitive distortions. Let's examine what they are and how they influence the way an individual thinks. Aaron Beck, a well-known American psychiatrist, has identified seven kinds of thinking errors, or "cognitive distortions." These distortions create problems because they result in faulty and maladaptive evaluations, which are threats both to self-esteem and to resilience. Let's look at and examine the common kinds of errors that both children and adults make.

Overgeneralisation

When people overgeneralise, they draw a conclusion based on one event and assume that it will be true for all other similar (and sometimes dissimilar) circumstances. Children who believe that because they have failed one spelling test they will fail all other spelling tests, and perhaps all other school tests, are demonstrating overgeneralisation.

Selective Abstraction

When a person takes something out of context and at the same time ignores all other pieces of information, he or she is committing the error of selective abstraction. Here's an example of selective abstraction, which is a little like selective attention: Suzie gets her report card. She receives all A's and one B. The B is in gym. Suzie concludes that she is a poor student. When she talks to her parents about the report card, she reports only the B. She has ignored the rest of the grades and has also failed to tell her parents that the gym teacher gave only one A and two B's. You can see the havoc that this kind of distortion has for self-esteem and resilience.

Arbitrary Inference

When a person comes up with an evaluation that is not supported by fact and acts upon it as if it were true, he or she has made an arbitrary inference. Some of the destructive beliefs that we discussed earlier provide the basis for arbitrary inferences. Consider this example: Jill concludes that her father does not love her anymore because he does not kiss her as he enters the house (he happened to be sneaking in her birthday gift). Jill's conclusion is based on her father's failing to kiss her this one time. An obvious example of arbitrary inference! There are less exaggerated examples as well: "I don't like you because you play the piano and I don't like the piano." Another person's piano playing is an arbitrary piece of information on which to base an evaluation of his or her character.

Magnification

Magnification happens when a person exaggerates one aspect of an event. A child who reports, "The teacher yelled at me all day" when the teacher simply pointed out an error on an arithmetic paper is guilty of magnification.

Minimisation

A person who plays down the importance of a positive event, for example, the teen who believes that the A on the chemistry final was a fluke, is demonstrating minimisation.

Dichotomous Thinking

One of the most common thinking errors stems from the belief that people and things are either good or bad, black or white, right or wrong. People and situations don't always fit in one or the other category. Most of us are good bad, smart dumb, pleasant unpleasant, and so on. To categorise ourselves or others in a restrictive one-category box is to miss half of the full picture! Thinking in a dichotomous fashion restricts flexibility. Flexibility is a must for problem-solving and for a challenge perspective.

Personalisation

The thinking error of personalisation involves the tendency to assume personal responsibility for things and events in your environment that go wrong when there is no rational base for doing so. For example, the child who believes that she caused the teacher to get a headache because she happened to disobey her by talking in the library is guilty of personalisation.

Thinking Errors of Young Children

Another common error that children make is to believe that everyone else thinks as they do. A corollary to this error is the belief that others should "know" what's on their mind and what they need. Young children are more likely to think like this because they have not yet developed the ability to see things from another's perspective. They are egocentric by nature and frequently process information about others falsely because of this bias. For example, Mary is upset with her big sister Jane because Jane didn't ask her if she wanted to go ice-skaging. Mary believes that Jane knew she wanted to go ice-skating! This is a perfect example of an egocentric processing error. Children, of course, are not the only ones who make this error. This kind of processing error interferes directly with social skills and interpersonal relationships.

Age, Maturity, and Thinking

The egocentric processing error in particular draws attention to the necessity of looking at the effect maturity has on thinking, especially as it relates to thinking constructively. Developmental psychologists study how people change as they age and mature. They have identified changes in almost every area of development. The areas that are of most concern to our discussion are the changes in language and intellectual abilities. These changes are important to know because they set the other limits on how people—and children specifically—come to understand their world.

Newborns are limited in terms of what they can say and think. That picture changes rapidly over the course of the first two years of life. Moving into toddlerhood, a child becomes increasingly able to understand simple language. In fact, children understand language before actually producing it. Between 10 and 15 months, the child begins to use single words to communicate a number of different things. The two-word sentence emerges around the age of 18 months. These two-word sentences are telegraphic in nature and contain content words only. Descriptors like "in" or "mad" are missing from the child's vocabulary. As the child approaches the preschool years, there is a dramatic increase in vocabulary and in the ability to use and understand grammar. By the time children are five or six, their speech and language approximates that of adults. However, there are still important differences in language capacity between young school-age children and older children (ten and eleven) and adults (Hetherington & Parke, 1986).

Young children have difficulty communicating about absent objects and about feelings (Shatz, 1983). This does not mean that they can't; it simply means that we cannot take this ability for granted when dealing with young children. They also have difficulty with semantically complex sentences. For example, the sentences "Jane likes to please" and "Jane is easy to please" have two very different meanings, but the word "Jane" is in exactly the same spot in each sentence. In one case Jane is the doer of the action, and in the other case she is the recipient, or is what linguists call the logical object (Chomsky, 1969). Young children get confused by sentences like the second one. Similarly, young children have difficulty picking up on subtle feedback (e.g., sarcasm, slight changes in nonverbal expression); by age seven, they are much better at this, although clear, direct communication is superior in every case. The ability to use and analyse language improves with age. Four-year-olds have difficulty understanding that sounds make up words. They also have trouble analysing their own language for clarity and meaning. Seven-year-olds are much better, and ten-year-olds are better yet (Hetherington & Parke, 1986).

Closely tied to language proficiency are cognitive, or intellectual, abilities. As with language, there are definite developmental changes that occur in the child's ability to understand and reason, changes that impact on the way children think.

Preschool children engage in what psychologist Jean Piaget called "preoperational thought". The major accomplishment of the preoperational child is the development of language. Preoperational children use language to represent objects and to control and regulate behaviour, but they have a number of limitations. For one thing, children of this age have difficulty reasoning and concentrating on more than one aspect of an object or situation at a time. For example, if you have two glasses filled with milk and one of those glasses is tall and thin while the other is short and fat, though each contains the same volume, prepoprational children generally perceive the tall, thin glass as bigger. They do this because of an inability to focus on the height and the width of the glass at the same time. This inability to "decenter" contributes to the preoperational child's egocentricity. Children are egocentric when they have difficulty seeing a situation from other than their own perspective. Third does not mean that they are selfish or inconsiderate. Piaget's writing is very clear about this point. Children of this age have difficulties thinking about more than one aspect of any situation at the same time; they have trouble decentering in the social area just as they do in nonsocial areas. The older preoperational child (three of four years old) can be taught to think in a less egocentric way.

Preoperational children are also animistic; that is, they attribute humanlike qualities to inaninate objects. For example, our son Alex had to make sure that his stuffed Dalmatian dogs were snug and warm at night before he would even consider falling asleep. Other children attempt to feed their pet rocks or favourite stuffed animals, believing that they have human needs. And, of course, stories and cartoons reinforce the child's animism when they portray animals and objects with humanlike characteristics.

Preoperational children have difficulty thinking about how they think (Flavell, 1979). Unlike older children, they do not ask the question, "Now, how did I figure that out?" or "What was I thinking when I did that?" The implication of this for the discussion at hand is that one has to present errors in thinking in a different way to young children. The implication of this limitation is that younger children have to be directed by adults to think about what they need to think about. I will be discussing just how to do this shortly.

At about the age of seven or eight children move into what Piaget called the "concrete operational" period. During this time children develop the ability to reason. They can process more than one piece of information at a time, and they can reflect on how they are thinking. Their major limitation is that the kind of reasoning they do has to do with concrete topics. For most children it's not until the age of 11 or 12 that they can reason in abstract terms. By the time children reach adolescence, their thinking is quite similar to that of adults. They lack the experience and the knowledge, but the basic cognitive structures are in place and ready to be used.

In summary, children's cognitive maturity determines the kinds of thinking they do and how they evaluate the world. The maturity of the child will also determine the way parents and teachers instruct him or her on the techniques of constructive thinking.

The Influence of the Situation on Thinking and Behaviour

Certain aspects of the situation interact with a person's temperament and influence how that person thinks and reacts. Stress researchers Richard Lazarus and Susan Folkman (1984) examined a number of studies and concluded that the following features exert the most influence:

1. *Event uncertainty,* or the extent to which you know if something will take place and when.
2. *Event novelty,* or the extent to which a situation is a familiar one.
3. *Event ambiguity,* or the extent to which you know what is expected of you in a situation.
4. *Number of event changes,* or the extent to which change has taken place over a given period of time.
5. *Event severity,* or the extent to which harm has been done.

For some people, knowing whether and when something is going to happen is far less stressful than being unsure whether it's going to happen. Thus, a scheduled test, no matter how unwelcome, may arouse less anxiety in some people than the possibility of a pop quiz. Recall the two brothers, George and Alex. George would perceive a pop quiz negatively, at least initially, whereas Alex would be less inclined to think of it this way. Similarly, some students may prefer to know their test results, even if those results are disappointing, than to remain in a state of uncertainty. Not knowing leaves some people wondering and perhaps imagining the worst possible scenario; knowing mobilises them to think of solutions for the problem. In other words, the reason George and others are bothered by event uncertainty is that it interferes with their ability to predict and prepare for the stressor. This need for predictability also explains why event novelty and event ambiguity may also be distressing.

When a situation is novel or when the rules and expectations are unclear, you don't know what is or will be expected of you. The newness and ambiguity make adapting to the change difficult. A person who has trouble adapting to change has to use purposeful effort to think positively about a novel situation. On the other hand, for a person like Alex, the novel situation represents a challenge instead of a threat. New situations temperamentally fit Alex, who likes change and novelty; novel situations seem to occupy his thoughts whereas familiar and routine events are sometimes perceived as distressing because they don't hold his interest or attention.

A similar set of circumstances exists when there are a number of event changes in a short span of time. Let's use George and Alex as examples again, and let's assume that they have just moved to another state. The move necessitated a change in school districts, a change in their living environment, and a change in friends. By nature, George would find it difficult to accommodate to so many changes in a short period of time. But Alex would perceive the events as exciting. Why? George needs time to adapt and Alex does not. The essence of what I'm saying is this: differences in temperament influence the way we think about the situations we experience.

Finally, the severity or negativity of a situation influences how we think and react. The death of a parent, grandparent, or favourite person is distressing to anyone. People react differently to these stressors, but there is no doubt that losses such as these affect everybody in some way. Children or adults who are subjected to a number of negative events may begin to think in a rather depressed and negative fashion. This is certainly understandable. This does not mean that they have lost all resilience. They may require support and help from others in order to maintain a reasonable perspective. In fact, resilient people recognise when they need help, and they take the necessary steps to get it.

Attributions, Thinking, and Behaviour

When people achieve a goal—for example, when a child learns to read or when a parent receives a promotion at work or when 16-year-old Shannon Miller earns several medals at the 1992 Olympics—what do you think they are thinking? Social psychologists have studied this question and have discovered that people automatically think, "Why? Why did I do well?" In fact, people question all sorts of actions and outcomes: "Why did he lose his temper?"; "Why did she do that?"; and so on. Attributions are the names given to the reasons ascribed to actions and outcomes (Heider, 1958). When Suzie believes that the A on the reading test is because she is a good reader, she has made a personal attribution. She sees herself as the cause of her success. But Suzie could make a different attribution: she could think that she got the A because the reading test was simple. In this case, Suzie has made an external attribution; that is, she perceives the situation, or some factor external to herself, as the cause of her success.

As you can imagine, the kind of attribution Suzie makes will influence what she thinks of herself as a reader and what she might do in the future about reading. If she thinks she has the ability to read, she is unlikely to shy away from reading assignments. But if she thinks she is a poor reader and can do well only if the test is easy or if someone helps her, then she will give up on a reading test that challenges her even a little.

There are four basic casual attributions (Heider, 1958). That is, we can attribute the outcome of an event to (1) some trait or ability in the person, (2) the effort the person extends, (3) the situation or someone else, or (4) luck or chance. Suzie, for example, can attribute her success to her ability only or to her ability, her effort, and the situation. If there is more than one cause assigned to an outcome, the observer (in this case, Suzie herself) has to decide the importance of each factor. Is it more ability than effort, or is it a little ability and a lot of effort? The end result is a weighted casual attribution, which then leads to a host of other judgments and behaviours.

Children (and adults) are observers of themselves as well as of other people. Often the attributions we make of ourselves are different from the ones we make of others (Jones & Nisbett, 1972). The difference in attributions sometimes contributes to communication difficulties. It's therefore necessary to make our thinking clear to others and to not assume other persons view situations as we do.

Thus far, I have discussed the factors that influence thoughts, feelings, and actions. This information provides a base for understanding how to teach children to think constructively. The pragmatics of constructive thinking come largely from the field of cognitive behaviour modification. They involve teaching children the dynamics behind the thinking-feeling-behaving connection.

The Pragmatics of constructive Thinking

The pragmatics behind constructive thinking are largely geared to instructing children how to be mentally resilient. There are two major objectives associated with this goal: (1) understanding how thoughts, feelings, and behaviours influence each other and (2) taking charge of a destructive thought-feeling-behaviour cycle by changing thoughts.

For children to understand the thought-feeling-behaviour connection, they need to be able to recognise feelings, recognise thoughts, and see the connection between thoughts, feelings, and behaviour. To break a destructive thought-feeling-behaviour cycle, children need to be able to

1. identify destructive thoughts
2. redefine situations by modifying verbal labels
3. redefine situations by modifying destructive beliefs
4. redefine situation by generating solutions
5. redefine situations by generating alternative perspectives

   (e.g., "How can I get something from this situation?" or "How can I time-limit the pain?").

Because children vary in maturity and because developmental maturity influences how they think, it's necessary to adapt the instructions to the child.

Instructing Young Children (Ages 3 to 6)

Young children first need to learn how to recognise and correctly label feelings in themselves and others. They need to know the external and internal indicators of emotions. External indicators are those things that show "on the outside". A smile, a scream, a cry, a stern tone of voice, sagging shoulders, and a straight, open posture are all examples of external indicators. Internal indicators, or "inside clues," indicate physiological arousal. A queasy stomach, clammy hands, and shakiness are some of the physical symptoms experienced by the individual.

There are a number of ways a young child can learn the ABCs of feelings. A good way to start is to use stories and pictures. By pointing out different emotions and the different ways they are expressed by the various characters in a story, we can help the child learn the basic components of an emotional experience. There are other equally good avenues a parent might use to help children become aware of feelings, for example, playing a game of emotional charades or constructing a collage of magazine pictures depicting people expressing different emotions. Once the basics have been mastered, parents and teachers can help children understand how others might be feeling or how the children themselves are feeling. Helping children understand that they have feelings and that those feelings get communicated to others in certain ways enhances their social skills and their ability to think constructively.

The second step in the process of helping young children understand the thought-feeling-behaviour connection is teaching the child the various labels that can be used to describe an emotion. Giving children an emotional vocabulary will ultimately help them learn to direct emotions appropriately. So, for example, describing feelings as "disappointed" or "a little upset" gives children some verbal leverage to use when they need to cope with a negative situation.

Teaching young children about feelings is only part of

what's needed to think constructively. Children need to know what thinking is all about the how it's connected to feelings. Since children are such concrete thinkers at this age, it's helpful to give them concrete definitions and examples of what constitutes constructive and destructive thoughts. I often use the TA for Kids programme and vocabulary to introduce the notion of constructive and destructive thoughts and the connection between thoughts and feelings (Freed & Freed, 1977). TA for Tots uses "warm fuzzies" to describe good feelings that come from thoughts like "I like you," "I can do it," and "I'm proud." "Cold pricklies" are bad feelings that come from thoughts like "I can't do this," "It's not fair," and "I want my way". I find that younger children can easily understand these terms and can then use them to describe other thoughts and feelings they experience or read about in stories.

To help them think constructively the adult must supply children with appropriate self-statements and effective problem-solving strategies, because children at this age are not capable of generating them themselves. I will illustrate how this might be down with an example involving five-year-old Jane, who is most reluctant to attend the first day of school. Jane wakes up the day before school starts with a stomachache, which intensifies throughout the day. Jane does not want to go to school, and when her mother insists, she begins to cry hysterically. Jane is obviously fearful about going to school. To help her deal with this new situation, it will be necessary to teach her how to think constructively about the first day of school. To do this her mother would take the following steps:

1. Help Jane identify fearful feelings.
2. Help her understand that the fearful feelings are the reason why she has a stomachache.
3. Normalise her feelings about the first day of school.
4. Help her understand that her thoughts are connected to her feelings.
5. Help her think differently about the first day of school.

The dialogue might go something like this:

Mother: Jane, I think you're a little scared about going to school tomorrow. Sometimes when we're scared we get stomachaches and our faces look very worried.

Jane: I'm not scared. I don't want to go to school.

M: You know, I was scared the first day I went to kindergarten. Yup, I remember I had a funny feeling in my stomach. It was like having butterflies in my stomach. I remember telling Grandma that I did not want to go to school. I told her I'd go next year!

J: What did Grandma say?

M: She said I had to go to school and that those butterflies would go away. And they did.

J: I don't want to go to school. I'm scared.

M: I know you are, honey. Maybe we can put our thinking caps on and figure out how to take the scared feelings and turn them into warm, fuzzy feelings.

J *(crying):* I don't want to go to school.

M: Cold prickly alert! I heard a cold prickly. I heard you say, "I don't want to go to school." (Mother says this in a gentle, lighthearted way so that the child understands its supportive nature). Now, Jane, tell me what you think kindergarten is going to be like.

J: I don't know, Mommy, I just don't want to go.

M: Some people are scared of kindergarten because it's new and they don't know what happens. That's a scary feeling. That's why I was scared of kindergarten. Other people are scared because they'll miss their moms or dads when they are in school. There is good news, though!

J: What is it?

M: You can help yourself feel better. Do you know how?

J: No. How?

M: You can put warm, fuzzy thoughts in your head, and then do you know what will happen?

J *(smiling):* I'll have warm, fuzzy feelings?

M: Right, right, right. So let's think of some warm, fuzzy thoughts in place of the cold, pricky thoughts.

J: Okay, Mom. This is going to be fun.

M: Good. I just heard a warm, fuzzy thought—"That is going to be fun!"

The parent then helps the child replace the worrisome thoughts with positive thoughts and gives the child other strategies to use. In Jane's case the dialogue continues as follows, with Jane's mother helping her generate positive thoughts and images:

M: Let's draw a fun picture of kindergarten.

J: Okay, Mom. I'll draw my teacher.

M: Super thinking! I love it. She looks like a nice teacher.

M: Jane, there are a few other tricks you can do to help yourself. You know the butterflies you feel in your stomach?

J: Yeah?

M: Well, tell yourself, "The funny feelings I have in my stomach are because I am excited." And now let's think of all the fun things you can do in kindergarten.

Jane's mother helped her identify the feelings and thoughts behind her fear of kindergarten, something Jane was unable to do by herself. Most children her age have the same difficulties. In fact, untrained older children and adults have similar troubles. They are not consciously aware of their destructive thought patterns. Jane's mom needed to help her identify what those thoughts and feelings were; then she helped Jane change the pattern by giving her alternative statements and images (the pictures Jane drew) to concentrate on. Jane's mom also helped her see that her feelings were shared by others and were therefore normal. This is sometimes very reassuring. I Jane's mom suspects that Jane is having difficulty the next morning before going to school, she can help her by repeating the positive thoughts out loud with her. She might also send the pictures Jane drew to school with her to give to the teacher. Sometimes a plan of action makes a child better able to deal with the ambiguity of a new situation. Giving the teacher the pictures might help Jane feel more comfortable with the new teacher.

Parents can reinforce this coping strategy by using guided imagery or any of the other techniques mentioned to deal with physiological arousal. They may also want to give the child the opportunity to visit the school and meet the teacher. These are all problem-solving strategies that are useful to the child and that build on constructive thinking strategies.

Instructing Older Children (Ages 7 to 10)

The strategies discussed for young children apply to older ones as well. Children aged seven to ten need to understand the language of emotions and the relationship emotions have to thoughts and behaviours. What is different is how these are explained and the kinds of verbal handles used by the child. For example, instead of "warm fuzzies" and "cold pricklies," you might use terms like "positive," and "productive" to describe helpful thoughts and "negative" or "hurtful" to describe destructive thoughts. In addition to using a more sophisticated vocabularly, children of this age are also capable of identifying positive and negative thoughts in themselves and in others. They can come up with positive thought substitutes themselves, but they occasionally require some prodding and direction from adults. The oldest children in this age range become somewhat capable of disputing their own erroneous beliefs and ideas. This is because they are beginning to develop the capacity to reflect on their own thinking (metacognition).

Stories are a great vehicle for teaching children the process of constructive thinking, especially those stories that address the influence of destructive and constructive thoughts on behaviour. For example, in the story entitled *The Recital*, by J. Joseph and E. Short (1992), a young boy, Oliver, attempts to master a piece of piano music for an upcoming recital. He becomes quickly frustrated when he finds himself making numerous mistakes. Instead of persisting, Oliver wants to give up and quit the piano altogether. His grandmother intervenes by helping him think differently about the mistakes. Oliver decides to continue with the piano and finally masters the piece of music. The message in this story is very explicit: Winners think about mistakes as opportunities to improve, as challenges.

Once children have the basic idea that destructive thinking is associated with negative feelings and behaviours, adults can help them apply the process of rethinking to their own problems and lives. To do this a parent can follow these steps:

1. Help the child identify positive and negative feelings.
2. Help the child identify the positive and negative thoughts that are connected to feelings.
3. Identify features of the situation that are important and/or troublesome to the child.
4. Help the child take a constructive perspective by helping him or her modify destructive beliefs and ideas.
5. Identify and apply constructive self-statements to the situation (words that communicate resilient attitudes and ideas are particularly important here).

To illustrate how these steps are applied, I will use a scenario involving competition and disappointment, issues that are especially troublesome for today's youth.

Angie, age eight, wants to compete for a particular role in the annual *Nutcracker* production. The number of roles available for children is limited, and the competition is fierce. Angie is at first reluctant even to try because she feels that she will "never get the part." Her parents take this opportunity to teach her about dealing with competition. Here is the verbal exchange that takes place between Angie and her father:

Father: I think that you're hesitant about trying out for the *Nutcracker*. I'm glad to talk to you about it because I know how hard it is sometimes to try out for something you want when there are a number of other good, talented kids trying out at the same time.

Angie: Thanks, Dad, but I don't want to talk about it. I don't think I want to try out, okay?

Father: Do you want to be in the production, Angie?

A: I really want to, but I'm scared that I won't get a good part. Maybe I won't get a part at all. There are a lot of girls trying out.

F: The only person you need to compete with is yourself. What counts is trying. If you don't try, you'll never know whether you can do it or not. Trying to do your best is the real challenge, Angie. It's hard, I know. But that's what all the famous actors, actresses, athletes, and dancers did. By trying, they gave themselves the chance. They took charge of their feelings. If you don't try, what happens is that your negative thoughts take charge of you.

A: But what if I don't get a role? Or what if I get a stupid part? I'll feel awful and stupid, I just know it.

F: Yes, Angie, you'll surely feel awful and stupid, but not because you don't get the part. No, Angie, that's not why. It will be because you think that not getting the part makes you look stupid. And that's not true. There are other reasons why people don't get parts. And those reasons don't necessarily have anything to do with a person's talent.

A: Like what, Dad?

F: Like size or colour of hair—sometimes people get parts for reasons we don't know. Sometimes it seems so unfair, and sometimes it is. The point here, Angie, is that thinking "I'm dumb if I don't get the part" just makes you feel bad.

A: Okay, Dad, I'll try out, but if I don't get the part, don't expect me to be happy about it.

F: I think you're making a good decision to try. If you don't get the part, I surely would expect you'd feel disappointed. I certainly would. But, honey, that disappointment will go away because you can make it go away.

A: Okay, Dad.

Angie did try out but she did not get the role she wanted, although she did get a role. At first, Angie seemed devastated, but again her parents took the opportunity to teach her how to constructively manage an emotion:

Angie (*sobbing*): I don't want to be in the *Nutcracker*. I don't want to dance. I hate everyone.

Father *(after letting Angie cry for a while):* I know. We know you're very disappointed, but we're proud of you and we're glad to sit down and talk about this.

A: I don't want to talk. I should never have auditioned. I knew it. I got a stupid part, a part for kids that can't dance.

F: Angie, you think the part you got was for kids who can't dance?

A: Yes, that's what I said!

F: But you *can* dance. Maybe there's some different way of thinking about this.

A: I said I didn't want to talk about it!

F: Understood. We'll leave you be. If you want us, we're right here.

(Angie goes up to her room and comes down five minutes later.)

A: It's just not fair. I worked hard and I got the worst part.

Mother: Listen, honey, I know you're disappointed, and I know that if I were in your position, I'd be just as disappointed. But maybe we can talk about it. Somethings talking about it gives you a different way of looking at it. First of all, I found out that there were twice as many children trying out this year than there were parts. Is that true?

Angie: Well, yes.

M: And I understand that the little girl chosen to be Clara is older than you and had your part last year.

A: Well, yes.

M: Then one thing you can do right now is give yourself some credit for getting the role. The second thing that would be helpful is to stop saying you got a stupid part—because it looks like you did very well—and the third thing you need to do is see how much fun you can make this part. Sometimes we can make something that looks uninteresting really exciting just by having a positive attitude. Angie, put your positive thoughts to work.

A: Okay, Mom, I'm feeling a little better.

Angie goes to rehearsal. She takes on a positive attitude and finds that the role is not as bad as she had first imagined. In fact, she likes the role now and enjoys herself. Her parents take the opportunity to reinforce how she chose to deal with her disappointment:

Mother: Angie, Dad and I are very proud of the way you chose to think about your role in the *Nutcracker*. I know you were initially very upset, thinking that it was a bad part and that you must be a bad dancer to get such a part. But you did think about it for a while, and you were able to see things differently. You took on a positive attitude, and now you're doing a great job.

If you were to analyse what Angie's parents did, you would find that they helped Angie label and reliable her feelings. Using a combination of active listening and constructive communication, the parents were able to direct Angie to think differently about the situation. They helped her identify the errors she was making in sizing up the situation and provided an alternative interpretation for her. They were very careful to allow Angie to defuse first, always respecting her feelings. As a result, Angie was able to rethink the situation and handle it quite well.

There are a number of ways parents and teachers can prompt children to think about their thinking (Waters, 1982). Here are some of the more common strategies:

1. Direct questioning (e.g., "What did you say to yourself when that happened?").
2. Situational charades (a game in which the child is asked to guess what kind of thoughts people are having in the situation being pantomimed).
3. Thought bubbles (Bernard & Joyce, 1984) (a technique in

which the child indicates what the characters in a story are thinking and saying by drawing them with "bubbles" of dialogue above them).

4. Story-telling technique (Elkins, 1983) (in which the parent makes up a story or uses an existing story and asks the child to think about all the things that the characters might be thinking or children are asked to tell their own personal stories and explain what they are thinking).

Once parents determine what their chils's pattern of destructive thinking is, they can proceed to help the child learn to think constructively by using these very same techniques. For example, the parent can use the story-telling or thought bubble technique to illustrate positive thoughts and to communicate resilient ideas. In addition, there are existing stories that address these issues quite directly. Publishers who address the issue of constructive thinking for children are as follows:

1. Stories designed to help children deal with destructive beliefs and ideas associated with competition, peer relationships, and academic problems are published by

Young Set Learning Associates
45, Fountain Street
Clinton, NY 13323.

2. The adventures of Pumpsey the dragon, and how she uses her clear mind to think about any number of situations common to school-age children, are offered by

Timberline Press, Inc.
Box 70187
Eugene, OR 97401.

3. *Colour Us Rational*, by V. Waters (1979), is a series of pamphlets for parents, designed to help them teach their children to think constructively, and stories about constructive thinking for children that is published by

Institute for Rational Living
45 East 65th Street
New York, NY 10021.

Instructing Preadolescent and Adolescent Children

Generally speaking, children as young as ten or eleven have the cognitive capacity to think about what they are thinking and to reason in a way that goes beyond the grasp of younger children. When children reach this stage of development, they are able to rationally debate and analyse their thoughts.

Parents of preadolescent and adolescent youngsters can approach the topic of constructive thinking in a more sophisticated fashion. Here are the steps suggested by clinicians who work to correct faulty thinking in adolescents (Bernard & Joyce, 1984): Instruct adolescents on the relationship between thoughts, feelings, and actions (if such instruction has not yet been provided). Explain that one way to control oneself (internal control) comes from directing one's thoughts in a constructive way. This entails the following: (1) recognising destructive thought patterns in oneself, (2) recognising the situational cues that prompt them, (3) understanding the underlying beliefs that support them, (4) understanding the errors in thinking that support them, (5) disputing destructive thoughts, and (6) generating realistic and constructive thoughts and self-statements. Teach adolescents to assume a balanced perspective by helping them learn to (1) focus on a small aspect of the problem at a time, (2) find information that will give them the most objective view possible of the problem, (3) think about the "worst thing that could happen" as a way of objectively rating the negative impact of the situation, and (4) think of how the negative situation can be used to their benefit.

To help adolescents recognise and change destructive thought patterns parents can have them ask themselves, "What am I thinking?" and then have them say or list any of the thoughts that come to mind. Parents can encourage adolescents to consider each thought and ask, "Is this constructive?" (using the criteria for constructive beliefs) or "Is this destructive?" (using the criteria for destructive beliefs). If a thought is recognised as a destructive one, the adolescent should be encouraged to identify which beliefs or errors need to be corrected. Finally, parents can have adolescents ask themselves, "What constructive thoughts can I think that will help me handle this situation?"

To illustrate how these steps might apply, I will discuss a situation involving a 15-year-old. Carol is bright and very responsible. Her day-to-day performance is outstanding. She participates in class discussions and is always well prepared, and her assignments are always well done. Her problem is that she cannot take tests. She seems to freeze even during tests in her favourite subjects, and her anxiety about a test starts the day before. Carol can feel her heart pounding; sometimes she actually feels nauseous and gets a headache. Carol's parents can help her. They can explain that the physical symptoms she is having are a sign of destructive thinking and that the destructive thinking might in fact be a major reason for why she freezes on tests. The dialogue might go something like this:

Mother: Carol, are you feeling anxious about the biology test tomorrow?

Carol: Yes, Mom. It's already started. I feel shaky and nauseous I'm scared to death that I'm going to bomb out on this test. It seems there's nothing I can do. I study and study. But when it comes to taking the test, I just freeze.

M: Yes, I get the picture. It's clear to me that you have worked very hard this year and that you actually know the material. I have an idea about how you can change the outcomes here (internal control message). I've been reading that people can help themselves by systematically changing the way they think about situations. Now, you're feeling anxious because you're thinking you're going to bomb another test.

C: Well, Mom, that's been my pattern.

M: I know, Carol. Would you like to change it?

C: Sure, I'd do anything!

M: Okay. Let's start with listing all of the thoughts you have about the upcoming test.

C: Okay, but what do you mean?

M: Just stop and think about what is now going through your mind. What thoughts do you have about the test?

C: Well, I think I'm going to fail. I think that I won't be able to remember anything tomorrow. If I don't get an A on this test, I'll never get into a good college and I know how stupid I'm going to feel!

(At this point Carol is visibly upset.)

M: Why do you think you're going to fail?

C: Because I traditionally screw up on tests.

M: Why do you think you have trouble with the tests?

C: Because I freeze and then I can't remember anything!

(Carol's mother now attempts to help Carol correctly identify the nature of the problem and the connection between her thoughts and both her anxiety and her performance).

M: Think about what you just said. What's the reason for your poor performance on the test?

C: I said that I freeze on tests because I get so anxious. *(Carol is suddenly struck with insight about the problem with her performance.)* Oh, I see what you're getting at, Mom! My anxiety is my problem.

M: Right! The real problem is not the test but your anxiety.

(Here her mother helps Carol put the problem in the right perspective.)

C: But what can I do about the anxiety?

(Carol's mother can now help her problem-solve by encouraging her to find an alternative label for her arousal feelings and adopt an alternative strategy for reducing the arousal, identify the destructive self-statements feeding the anxiety, generate more constructive self-statements.)

M: Two things. You need to address the physical aspects of the anxiety and you need to take care of what is causing the anxiety. To take care of the physical part of the problem, remember that anxiety is excitement that gets labelled negatively. To reduce the excitement, you can start now by doing some of the relaxation exercises on the tape I have in my room. You listened to them the other day and thought they were pretty good. Once you feel more relaxed, you can start desensitising yourself by actually forcing yourself to do the exercise to reduce the anxious feelings. I'll show you how to do it in just a few minutes. But remember, Carol, the excitement you feel is a sign that your body is preparing for the test. Think about the physical sensations you feel as excitement. Talk about them as excitement instead of anxiety. To determine what's causing the anxiety, think about the thoughts you told me before. Remember you said, "I'm scared, I'm going to fail, I won't be able to remember, I will feel like a fool if I fail, I'll never get into a good college."

C: Yes, I remember.

M: These are what the experts call irrational beliefs. They are destructive. Do you see why they might be destructive?

C: Sort of.

M: Well, first of all, assuming that you're going to do poorly tomorrow because you have done poorly in the past is not necessarily true. It's an overgeneralisation. *(Mother is helping Carol identify irrational beliefs and errors in thinking.)*

C: But I've had trouble on every single biology test.

M: Tomorrow is another day. Remember, it's not the test that's the problem, it's the anxiety. And you can do something about that. *(Mother is empowering Carol by again helping her keep the problem in perspective, she is providing her with a constructive way to view the problem and reminding her that she can make efforts to solve her problem.)*

You have more control than you think.

C: I can say that I'll do great, but I don't believe it!

M: Right, in which case it won't work. Besides, you also think that if you don't get an A on this test, you won't get into a good school. That's not exactly true; it's another good example of those errors in thinking we talked about earlier. Now what can you think and say that is believable and at the same time helpful?

(Here Carol's mother is helping her identify her destructive beliefs and replace them with more constructive self-statements.)

C: Well, for starters, I could say I may not do as well as I would like, but I'm not going to fail. I'll just do a little better this time and a little better the time after that so I can eventually get my A. Getting a B is not going to stop me from getting into a good college. I can live with it. The real test is dealing with the enxiety.

(Carol is now generating her own constructive statements.)

M: Well done. Let's go work on your anxiety.

Carol's mother then helps her desensitise herself to the physical aspects of the arousal. She does this by having Carol relax away the tension caused by just thinking about the biology test. Every time Carol thinks about the test and begins to feel any of the physical discomforts associated with anxiety, she is instructed to take a deep breath and do any one of the short relaxation exercises. In addition, she is taught to remember and rehearse the described constructive self-statements that she and her mother generated.

SUMMARY

To a very large degree we are what we think. When we think constructively, we make better decisions and, consequently, are more productive. Constructive thinking contributes to the effective management of change and adversity. It is an important component of effective problem-solving, a topic that is discussed in the next chapter. Conversely, destructive thoughts result in poor decisions, unproductive and frustrating attempts to accomplish tasks, and poor problem-solving. Because thought affects these critical areas, it impacts on our self-esteem and coping skills. Constructive thought contributes to positive self-esteem and resilience whereas destructive thought erodes the self-concept and makes the person more vulnerable to change and adversity. Age, maturity, situational factors, and attributions influence thought. Parents and teachers can help children of all ages learn to think constructively.

13

Teaching for Transfer: Sequencing Specific Capabilities or Encouraging Productive and Creative Thinking

All education aims for the future. Instruction is best when it has maximum transfer or carry-over from one course or level to another or from school to life, but how is this to be achieved? The discredited theory of formal discipline held that the influence of what is learned can be very widespread. It was believed that a person could strengthen his mind by difficult exercises. He would then be equipped to excel at almost any task. Several school subjects—for example, mathematics and the classics—were said to have special merit in this regard.

Formal discipline and massive general transfer were rejected after a series of studies by E. L. Thorndike and his students in the early part of this century. Thorndike found that transfer appeared to be very specific and limited to a narrow range of situations which were clearly similar to those of the original learning. He proposed a theory of transfer by "identical elements" in the learning and transfer situation. There is no doubt but what we do learn many specific things in school which we use in essentially the same form when they are needed later.

A third theory of transfer, which may be subsumed under that of similar or identical elements, states that transfer occurs through generally useful principles. This is usually attributed to C. H. Judd.

The two authors whose views are presented here have little faith in any more-or-less automatic transfer. Both believe we must plan for transfer by the use of content and methods which are directly related to our objectives for the future behaviour of students, but they suggest quite different objectives and methods.

In his article on the issue "Global Learning vs. Discovery," Shulman described Gagné as a conservative on the matter of transfer, and contrasted his views with those of Jerome Bruner. Gagné advises planning for transfer among skills required for the performance of a given task. He would not, however, expect much success in attempting to teach for broad general transfer from one subject area or field to an entirely different one. Unlike either Bruner or Crutchfield, the author of the second article presented here, Gagné is not optimistic about efforts to teach students "how to think," or to be superior discoverers or problem-solvers in any general sense.

Gagné's article on the present issue emphasises the sequential nature of learning and transfer when simple capabilities are combined directly in more complex ones. The entire article is about theory and evidence for sequences or hierarchies in learning. He states that knowledge about hierarchies leading to desired performance objectives is sorely needed, and suggests that this may be the same thing as saying we need more knowledge about transfer.

Crutchfield believes intellectual skills of high transfer value should be a major objective of the school. He finds such skills neglected, but denies that they cannot be trained. Then he describes the skills which he believes should be emphasised and summarises several results of some attempts to teach them.

What Crutchfield calls "productive thinking" here he has called "creative thinking" in other writings. Independent problem-solving may require one to put together the products of previous learning in new ways, perhaps imaginative or unique ways. This is certainly what many persons mean by creative thinking.

Thought Questions

How do Gagné's approach and recommendations differ from those which you might expect from Thorndike's early theory of transfer by "identical elements"? What similarities do you see between Gagné's approach and Judd's "principles" theory?

How do you respond to the statement that Bruner's view and that of Crutchfield are based on a return to the outmoded theory of "formal discipline"? Or, is it possible that these authors are recommending methods of instruction, especially of inquiry, which are the "identical elements" of method or the "generally useful principles" needed by students in the future? Which earlier theory does their approach resemble most, and what is really new about their views?

In your opinion would Crutchfield or Gagné be more optimistic about the value of school studies, if properly taught, for the solution of pressing social problems? What do you think the possibilities are for helping students with a wide variety of future problems different from those studied in school? If you take a positive view, contrast schools you would expect to be most effective and schools you would expect to be least effective in preparing students for the future. If you answer negatively, try to defend the continued existence of schools for other purposes.

Learning Hierarchies

A few years ago, in the course of studies of the learning of tasks resembling those learned in schools (Gagné 1962), I used the term "learning hierarchy" to refer to a set of specified intellectual capabilities having, according to theoretical considerations, an ordered relationship, to each other. It was possible I stated, beginning with a clear statement of some terminal objective of instruction, to analyse this final capability into subordinate skills in an order such that lower-level ones could be predicted to generate positive transfer to higher-order ones. The entire set of ordered intellectual skills formed a hierarchy which was considered to bear some relation to a plan for effective instruction.

In the framework of instruction in "modern math," children learn two distinguishable terminal capabilities: one of these, shown on the right, is simply finding sums of positive and negative numbers; a second, shown on the left, constitutes a demonstration of the logical validity of adding any pair of integers, using the properties of the number system to effect this demonstration. For both these tasks, an analysis revealed a set of subordinate capabilities shown in the figure, some in common and some not in common, ranging down to some relatively simple skills which the children were presumed to possess at the beginning of their instruction.

What I should like to do at this point is to tell you some things I have learned about learning hierarchies in the last couple of years. In part, these things have been learned by additional research, both mine and other people's; and in part, from the various reactions I have received about them from many sources. I need to say, surely, that critical comments have most certainly caused me to re-think and clarify, at least in my own mind, what the nature, characteristics, and uses of learning hierarchies may be. Since such hierarchies contain elements of theory, I am most eager to alter or augment these elements to provide improved prediction, if that is possible. What I am likely to be most obstinate about changing, however, is the basic idea of the feasibility of predicting optimal sequences of learning events.

Characteristics of Learning Hierarchies

What are the characteristics of a learning hierarchy? How does one know when he has one, and what precisely can be predicted from it?

To find initial answers to such questions, one can review the kind of study which first gave rise to the idea. This was a study derived from an investigation of the learning of a task of constructing formulas for the sums of number series (Gagné, 1962). In the original study using programmed instruction (Gagné and Brown 1961), individual differences in learning from the programme were of course highly evident. One could have attributed them to differences in "intelligence," and let it go at that. But it seemed to me these differences in learning performance were more likely attributable to certain identifiable skills which were not directly represented in the programme itself, but which were needed along the way in doing what the programme demanded. They were activities that the learners could or could not do, and which the programme was accordingly more or less successful in teaching them to do.

The next step was to figure out what these "subordinate skills" might be: Beginning with the final task, I found it was possible to identify nine subordinate capabilities, related to each other in an ordered way, by successively asking the question concerning each task, "What would the individual already have to know how to do in order to learn this new capability simply by being given verbal instructions?" It is probably of some importance to note that the kinds of capabilities identified in this manner did not directly pertain to number series, but rather included such skills as the following:

(a) identifying the location of numerals in a tabular array by means of letters giving their row and column location;

(b) completing statements of equality by supplying missing numbers in equations containing mixed arithmetic operations;

(c) identifying the numbers or letters in a tabular array which formed certain spatial patterns represented by lines connecting at 90^0 and 45^0.

I emphasise that the subordinate skills so identified are not related to number series in a logical sense; what they are related to, psychologically, is the kind of behaviour the learner has to engage in if he is going to be successful at *figuring out* from a tabular array of number series properties, how to formulate an equation for their sum.

Having identified a hierarchy of capabilities in this way, the next step was to test its validity. First, a test was made on a number of subjects to determine which of these subordinate tasks they already knew how to do. Two subjects could do all of the subordinate tasks but not the final one; two could do all but two; one all but three; and two all but four. Each of these learners was then taught to do whichever subordinate tasks he couldn't initially perform. Then, having completed this learning, each was given verbal directions about how to do the final task, without any practice on it. Six out of these seven subjects then proceeded to execute the final task of making a formula for four number series which he hadn't seen before. Additional evidence showed that a similarly marked change in capability was brought about in these learners at each "level" of the hierarchy for which instruction had been given.

Certain patterns of responding to the tests of subordinate tasks also were revealed in this study. Specifically, those who got subordinate skill number 1 correct, also got all the skills lower in the hierarchy correct. Those who got number 2 correct, and missed number 1, got all the skills lower than number 2 correct also. In other words, in these seven learners, there was in fact an ordered relationship (similar to that displayed in a Guttman-type scale) among the subordinate capabilities measured.

On the basis of this brief review, I should like to consider the question of what a learning hierarchy is. What properties of the learning hierarchy were either postulated or revealed in this study?

1. First, the question by means of which the analysis is begun, namely, "What would the individual have to know how to do. . . etc,". implies that one is searching for subordinate tasks which will transfer positively to the learning of the task in question. The criterion for such transfer is a stringent one—it is desired that the subordinate skill or skills facilitate the learning to such an extent that it will occur when only verbal instructions, and no further trials of practice, are given. It is evident that choices are being made here, since there are perhaps a number of kinds of subordinate skills which would, under suitable conditions, exhibit some degree of transfer to a given learning task. The method doesn't imply that all of these are searched for, but only those that will meet this stringent criterion. It is fair to say, therefore, that a subordinate capability identified by this method is a skill which is hypothesised to exhibit a substantial amount of positive transfer to the learning of the skill in question.

Second, how does one know if the order assigned to the skills in the hierarchy is correct? To specify this order, one depends first of all on the application of knowledge about transfer of learning, which comes from a great number of sources. A general guide to such ordering is the one I have described (Gagné, 1955), in which simple responses are subordinate to chains or multiple discriminations, which in turn are subordinate to classifying, which in turn is subordinate to using principles or rules. But this of course is rather general guidance, and does not begin to account adequately for the specific choices that must be made in any particular instance. Sometimes one is not sure about the location of a subordinate capability, particularly as to whether it is truly subordinate or merely at the same level.

Empirical tryout of the series of hypotheses represented by a hierarchy seems to be a reasonable approach to this problem. On the basis of such a tryout, one can in effect determine whether a particular skill transfers positively to another, or whether they are independent, or whether perhaps they covary in their transfer effects. I have in one paper made some suggestions about how these determinations might be made (Gagné, 1967), but I perceive these to be very unsophisticated compared with procedures I can only dimly imagine. An example of a successful tryout of this sort is in a study by Cox and Graham (1966), using a task of elementary mathematics. They were able to show that an initially hypothesised order was incorrect, according to their results. When the hierarchy was rearranged, the existence of an order of subordinate skills was confirmed. Thus it seems to me reasonable to suppose that many individual hypotheses about transfer represented in a hierarchy may have to be checked by some empirical means. If they turn out to be wrong, the conservative conclusion surely is that something is wrong with the specific hierarchy proposed. To the contrary, however, it does not seem reasonable to conclude on the basis of such evidence that *all* hierarchies are wrong.

A third characteristic of hierarchies seems to be of considerable interest. Do they represent a sole learning route to the learning of the final task, or perhaps even a most efficient learning route? Must each individual learner necessarily proceed to acquire each subordinate skill in order to enable him ultimately to learn the final task? By reference again to the method of analysis by means of which the hierarchy is generated, it is quite apparent that the answer to this question is no. Nothing in the method of analysis tells us about the capabilities of the individual learner. A given individual may be able to "skip" one or more of the subordinate tasks, just as a given learner may by able to "skip" parts of an adaptive programme of instruction. Another individual may be able to bring to bear on the learning of any given skills some capability which comes from quite a different domain of knowledge, which is not even represented in the hierarchy.

A learning hierarchy, then, in the present state of our knowledge, cannot represent a unique or most efficient route for any given learner. Instead, what it represents is the most probably expectation of greatest positive transfer for an entire sample of learners concerning whom we know nothing more than what specifically relevant skills they start with.

A related point needs to be made about what a learning hierarchy represents, and what it does not represent. Perhaps the best way to say this is that a learning hierarchy does not represent everything that can be learned, nor even everything that *is* learned, within the domain it attempts to describe. In particular, a diagram of a hierarchy does not represent what is perhaps the most important result of learning, the potentiality for transfer which is generated. I have spoken of the events reflected in a learning hierarchy as *cumulative learning* (Gagné, 1968). The cumulative effects of such learning show themselves, in a minimal fashion, by the occurrence of positive transfer from one level of skill to another. But beyond this, there is the fact that each new capability that is learned may generalise to many other situations and domains which cannot possibly be represented on a single chart. In considering, for example, how a child who has learned the skill of volume conservation in rectangular containers, and the skill of conservation in cylindrical containers, may then learn to "conserve" volume in irregularly shaped containers (Gagné, 1968, p. 187), I have pointed out a number of particular subordinate skills from which positive transfer may be expected. The new task can be learned much more quickly than the old, not because the latter is subordinate to it, but because there are many common subordinate skills from which positive transfer may be expected.

According to this reasoning, there are latent consequences of cumulative learning, which are not directly represented on a diagram of a learning hierarchy. Were they to be represented, one would have to draw lines of transfer, somewhat as indicated in Figure 13.1. Depending on particular circumstances in the individual learner, there may be transfer from a lower level, in other words, "skipping". As another possibility, transfer may occur from quite a different domain of knowledge, as when one uses a skill at identifying number series patterns to solve a problem in classifying patterns of letters. Still a third possibility, which should not be overlooked, is the atypical combinations of subordinate skills which, while they may seem conceptually very different, may in the case of an individual learner be able to combine to yield a rather unexpected source of learning transfer. A learning hierarchy cannot, in any practical sense, represent all of these possibilities. Yet to deny their existence would be wrong, and in fact quite contrary to the basic conception of what cumulative learning is supposed to accomplish.

Intellectual Skills

I turn now to one of the most important characteristics of learning hierarchies, and one concerning which I myself have been inconsistent in part writings. The question is, what exactly are these entities, sometimes called capabilities, that make up a learning hierarchy? The answer I would now give is the following. They are *intellectual skills,* which some writers would perhaps call *cognitive strategies.* What they are not is just as important. They are not entities of verbalisable knowledge. I have found that when deriving them, one must carefully record statements of "what the individual can do," and just as carefully avoid statements about "what the individual knows."

I believe that my previous formulation of these entities is misleading, when it deals with what are called "concepts" and "principles." I should prefer to substitute for these, words emphasising capabilities for action, such as "classifying," and "rule-following." This is more than a nominal change, however. I mean that what learning hierarchies describe is, in computer language, subroutines of a programme; what they do not

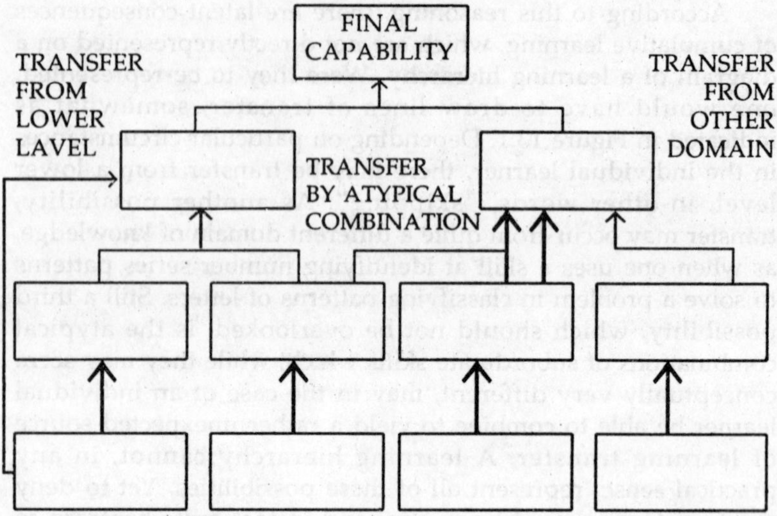

Figure 13.1. The latent consequences of cumulative learning, indicated by sources of positive transfer to the learning of advanced capabilities.

describe is the facts or propositions retrievable from memory as verbalisable statements.

Why do I emphasise this distinction, and what has led me to make it? First, it is surely noteworthy that the original hierarchies were developed in connectior with mathematics tasks. If one stops to think about it, the substance of mathematics is largely a set of skills for manipulating numbers. They differ in complexity, of course, and also in specificity. But they are always intellectual skills, and they are not (and probably should not be) verbalisable knowledge. In the original study using number series (Gagné, 1962), for example, what was being learned was not "knowledge" about number series, but a set of particular *skills* of forming relationships among sets of numbers displayed in a systematic array.

You may recall that I incautiously attempted to generalise the ideas of learning hierarchies to such subject matter fields as the social sciences (cf. Gagné, 1967). In doing this, it is quite easy to fall into the trap of describing "knowledge" entities rather than skills entities. For example, some time ago one of my students worked out a learning hierarchy on weather prediction, with my help and acquiescence. The idea was to teach fourth graders how to predict weather from a weather chart superimposed on a map showing terrain features. The subordinate entities of the hierarchy had a high degree of plausibility, and appeared to describe what the child needed to *know* if he was going to predict the weather. When a teaching programme based upon this chart was tried out, with much good will and persistence, the results can most succinctly be described by saying that it didn't work. The children did not learn much when a sequence of instruction based upon this chart was followed. Under these circumstances, little or no evidence could be seen in the data that positive transfer was occurring from one level of the hierarchy to the next.

I believe that the fundamental reason for this lack of success was that this was not a learning hierarchy for the task of predicting weather. It did not present the intellectual skills the child needs to possess in tackling the job of figuring out from the "weather chart" how to make a forecast of the weather. I haven't yet made an analysis that satisfies me, but I suspect the intellectual skills which should be included are such things as these: (1) from general descriptions, formulating relevant propositions in syllogistic form; (2) making a systematic review of the effects of specific factors on an air mass; and (3) constructing specific statements describing weather at designated future times. What should be noted is that such skills as these were not represented in the original formulation. They represent intellectual operations that the child can *do*. But they are not descriptions of what he *knows* (that is, of what he can recall in the sense of non-verbatim verbal propositions).

Then there is the evidence about the effectiveness of certain kinds of sequences of instruction, or in instructional programmes. First I should say that I am not sure that a learning hierarchy is supposed to represent a *presentation sequence* for instruction in an entirely uncomplicated way. Presumably, there should be some relation between an ordered set of intellectual skills and an ordering of a sequence of presentation of a set of frames or topics in an instructional programme. Results like those of Payne, Krathwohl, and

Gordon (1967), however, surely serve to give added emphasis to the distinction between verbalisable knowledge and intellectual skills. The painstaking study conducted by these investigations showed in a most convincing way that sequence of presentation, so far as reasonably mature adult learners are concerned, does not affect what is learned. The authors of this study suggest that, even when frames or topics are presented in scrambled order, the adult learner is able to make them into a coherent and meaningful internal arrangement, and to learn from them. Accordingly, one is led to believe from this study, and others like it, that a learner may acquire certain intellectual skills from a presentation that is quite disorganised when viewed as a sequence of verbalisable knowledge.

It is conceivable that this line of reasoning also applies to the study of Merrill (1965), who found no advantage to review and correction following each topic of an instructional programme on imaginary science, as opposed to a condition of no review and correction. While I am by no means highly confident of this interpretation, I believe it might be examined within this general context. To summarise the point, it is that learners can acquire verbalisable knowledge, and even intellectual skills, from sequences of presentation that are altered in various ways from what may be considered "highly organised." The hypothesis I should like to reaffirm, however, is that regardless of presentation sequence, if one is able to identify the intellectual skills that are learned, he will find them to generate positive transfer in an ordered fashion.

Another line of thinking which I believe reinforces the distinction between intellectual skills and verbalisable knowledge comes from an analysis of the kinds of tasks described by Guilford (1967). While I have not undertaken an analysis of all the tasks Guilford describes, I have done some of them, and enough to lead me to believe that in most cases they are sampling both these kinds of entities. The performance being measured, in other words, typically samples the stored verbalisable knowledge the individual has available; and it also samples the intellectual skills that can be brought to bear upon the task. Consider a rather simple example, shown in Figure 13.2.

Which of these letter combinations does not belong with the rest?

PXNO	VRIM	AQES	GUVC
1	2	3	4

Answer: 3, because it contains two vowels.

"Which of these letter combinations does not belong with the rest?" The answer is 3, because it contains two vowels.

What kinds of intellectual skills does the individual bring to bear on such a task? I have suggested what I think they might be, in the hierarchy of Figure 13.2. They include such things as (1) making hypotheses which are tried and discarded, without repetition; and (2) distinguishing various features of letter combinations, such as vowels and consonants, location of letters in the alphabet, symbol repetition, and so forth. But it is equally apparent, is it not, that the individual who can solve this task also brings to bear some stored verbal entities: he must know what the vowels are, what the consonants are, what the alphabet is, and what the letters are. Both intellectual skills and an elementary kind of verbalisable knowledge are required in performing the task. But any hypothesis is that they are learned in different ways. The skills have an ordered relation to each other, such that subordinate ones contribute positive transfer to superordinate ones. But I do not suppose that the verbalisable entities necessarily have this relationship to each other. Stated in overly simple fashion, one does *not* have to learn consonants and vowels first in order to insure greatest transfer to learning the entire set of letters; and one does *not* have to learn the letters first before learning their position in the alphabet.

This example is admittedly an elementary one, and I should not want that fact to obscure what I think to be the generalisability of this distinction. Consider another task, that of solving five-letter anagrams. The work of Mayzner and Tresselt (1965) and others has shown that such a task derives positive transfer from an identifiable set of intellectual skills, pertaining to the formulation of hypotheses regarding probabilities of letter combinations, probabilities of initial letter occurrences, and others. But it is equally evident that an individual learner who is successful at solving anagrams must have a store of verbalisable knowledge to call upon, which in this case is words. In solving a set of anagrams, the individual will show greater success if he knows a large number of words, besides having mastered the intellectual skills involved.

These are the major reasons, then, why I am led to think that learning hierarchies are descriptions of the relationships of positive transfer among intellectual skills, but that they are not descriptions of how one acquires verbalisable knowledge. Obviously, in solving any given problem, both kinds of retained entities must be brought to bear. And it seems equally true that, when a new intellectual skill is being acquired, knowledge must be available to the learner, since the skill cannot be learned "in a vacuum." I do not, in other words, wish to say that either kind of entity is the more important for learning. Both are essential. What seems to me most evident is that they need to be distinguished, and that the conditions governing positive transfer to them are probably very different.

To complete this account of the distinction between intellectual skills and verbalisable knowledge, it is of some importance to point out that this matter has possibly profound implications in its relation to the curriculum. Most educational psychologists, to be sure, recognise the distinction and clearly state that both intellectual skills and verbalisable knowledge must be learned in the schools. Ausubel (1968), for example, acknowledges the difference early in his text on educational psychology. Skinner (1968) draws a distinction between behaviours to be learned for dealing with particular classes of events, and precurrent self-management behaviours, which are more general in their applicability. Rothkopf (1968) distinguishes mathemagenic behaviours from the substance of what is learned. But the importance of each of these types of learned capability for curriculum design and planning would doubtless be estimated differently by these theorists, and probably still differently by me.

I should be inclined to entertain the notion that the most important things learned in school are intellectual skills, and not verbalisable knowledge. The major reason is, very simply, that

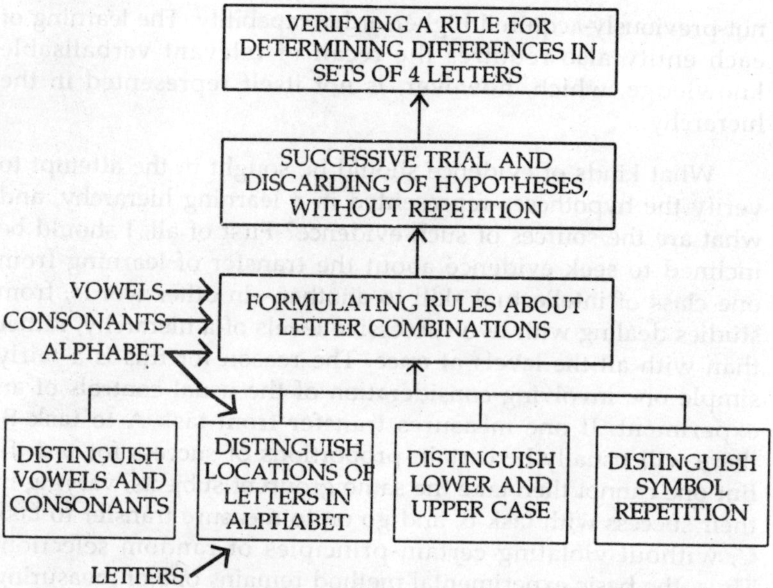

Figure 13.2. A learning hierarchy for a task of letter combination, indicating the contribution of intellectual (skills boxes) and verbal knowledge (circled entities). (Example is from Guilford, J.P., *The Nature of Human Intelligence*. New York. McGraw-Hill, 1968, p. 42.)

one can always look up the knowledge, but the skills have to become "built-in." I can obviously not do justice to this very weighty question at this time. The curriculum implications are such as to lead to a heavy emphasis on what is often referred to as "process," in contrast to content. In elementary science, for example (cf. AAAS Commission on Science Education, 1967), this line of thinking leads one to prefer teaching children the intellectual skills involved in classifying, measuring, and predicting, rather than the verbalisable knowledge of the accomplishments of science.

Evidence Relevant to Learning Hierarchies

Now I must return to the major theme of learning hierarchies. To characterise them briefly, they represent an ordered set of intellectual skills, such that each entity generates a substantial amount of positive transfer to the learning of a not-previously-acquired higher-order capability. The learning of each entity also requires the recall of relevant verbalisable knowledge, which, however, is not itself represented in the hierarchy.

What kinds of evidence should be sought in the attempt to verify the hypotheses represented in a learning hierarchy, and what are the sources of such evidence? First of all, I should be inclined to seek evidence about the transfer of learning from one class of intellectual skill to another—in other words, from studies dealing with two successive levels of a hierarchy, rather than with all the levels at once. The reason for this is a fairly simple one involving consideration of the usual controls of an experiment. If one measures transfer from task A to task B, there will usually be certain proportions of success for task B. But one cannot then take the same group of subjects, varying in their success with task B, and go on to measure transfer to task C, without violating certain principles of random selection. Thus, the basic experimentai method remains one of measuring positive transfer from task A to task B; or alternatively, from task B to task C.

There is quite a good deal of evidence concerning positive transfer from one class of intellectual skill to another. For example, in the verbal paired-associated learning field, the evidence reviewed by Battig (1968) is to the effect that the learning of paired associates is typically facilitated by prior discrimination learning on stimulus-terms and response-terms, as well as by prior learning of stimulus coding responses. When one looks at categorising skills (or concepts) like those exhibited by children in performing reversal-shift tasks, recent investigations such as those of Tighe (1965), Smiley and Weir (1966), and Johnson and White (1967) clearly demonstrate the importance of relevant prior learning of dimensional discriminations for transfer to the reversal task. Similarly, the different sort of classifying required in transposition tasks is shown to derive positive transfer from prior discrimination learning in the studies of Beaty and Weir (1966) and Caron (1966).

The importance of prior classification learning for positive transfer to rule learning is shown in a number of studies dealing with conservation tasks of a type derived from the work of Piaget, Beilin, Kagan and Rabinowitz (1966), for example, found prior classification training to transfer to the task of water-level representation in children, to a greater extent than verbal training. In this field of interest, a study of particular relevance to the present discussion is that of Kingsley and Hall (1967). These investigators made a specific analysis to derive a hieararchy of subordinate skills in conservation tasks. They then tested each child to determine which of the subordinate skills he knew, and proceeded to train each of the missing ones. The method, in other words, resembled that employed in "The acquisition of knowledge" (Gagné, 1962), and substantial amounts of positive transfer to the final conservation tasks were obtained.

There are also a number of recent studies verifying the general idea of positive transfer to problem-solving situations from prior learning on subordinate relevant rules DiVesta and Walls (1967), for example demonstrated positive transfer from relevant "pre-utilisation" training to the Maier two-string problem. Davis (1967) showed the effectiveness for transfer of previously learned verbal rules to switch-light problems, and a similar theme is developed by Overing and Travers (1966, 1967) in their studies of the problem of hitting an underwater target. In problems concerning mathematical groups and combinatorial topology, Scandura and Wells (1967) demonstrated positive transfer effects from prior learning in concrete situations involving relevant rules.

In this brief sampling of relatively recent studies, one can see repeated many times the general affirmation of the hypothesis that the learning of each particular category of intellectual skill depends substantially, in a positive transfer sense, on the previous learning of another particular category of intellectual skill. In brief, problem-solving draws positive transfer from prior rule learning, which is contributed to in the same sense by prior classification learning, which is in turn strongly affected by prior discrimination learning, and so on. I should say, therefore, that I look for verification of the learning hierarchy idea in studies of positive transfer from one intellectual skill to another. In studies of this sort over the past few years, there is a good deal of confirming evidence.

The major type of study from which evidence about learning hierarchies may be derived is one which attempts to try out a total hierarchy, applicable perhaps to a limited topic, but in which the various levels of intellectual skill are to be learned in a single instructional sequence. The collaborative studies I did on the learning of algebraic equation solving and adding integers (Gagné and Paradise, 1961); Gagné, Mayor, Garstens and Paradise, 1962), for example, are of this sort. The results one first obtains from such studies may indicate that some incorrect hypotheses were made concerning predictions about positive transfer. Specifically, a capability thought to be subordinate to another may turn out to be superordinate, or even coordinate. Such a finding calls for the rearrangement of the hierarchy, as was done, for example, in the previously mentioned study by Cox and Graham (1966) dealing with the addition of two-place numbers. Following such a step, the new hierarchy can then be tried out, in order to seek evidence of positive transfer from one "level" to the next.

I need to mention that methods of analysing data from such a study are not at all clear. Various possibilities have been tried beginning with Guttman scaling techniques, but none seem entirely satisfactory at yet. It is highly encouraging to know, however, that the measurement techniques needed for such analyses are apparently being worked on by a number of highly competent people. Hopefully, these will contrast with the rather crude methods used in the study. Just to remind you what these were, what we attempted to do was to find the probability of achieving Task 1 for those learners who had learned an immediately subordinate capability, Ia, and to contrast this probability with that for learners who had *not* learned the same subordinate capability. The findings were 73 per cent for the first set of learners, and only 9 per cent for the second set. In other words, there was indeed substantial positive transfer. Similar confirming findings were reported for all of the comparisons possible within the learning hierarchy.

My present estimate is, then, that there are two major kinds of study which are likely to provide evidence concerning learning hierarchies. One investigates only two "levels" of a hierarchy at a time, and in effect becomes a more-or-less traditional study of positive transfer between categories of intellectual skill. The other type attempts to construct a hierarchy which applies to longer sequences of instruction, and which after first establishing a suitable order for the capabilities to be learned, seeks a measure of the dependence (in the positive transfer sense) of one learned entity on another.

Concluding Statement

It will surely be apparent from this restatement and possible clarification of a theoretical view, that in one sense the notion of a learning hierarchy reduces itself to the notion of positive transfer. The question remains, what transfers to what? My answer has been, and still is, that the "what" of this question can be answered in terms of different varieties of learned capabilities. In particular, specific responses transfer to discriminations, which transfer to classifications, which transfer to rules, which in turn may transfer to more complex forms of rule-governed behaviour, such as that exhibited in problem-solving.

The entities that are affected by positive transfer in this manner deserve to be called intellectual skills of strategies. But it seems important to distinguish these from verbalisable knowledges. While the learning and retention of the latter entities must surely have a theoretical rationale of its own, as for example, Ausubel's (1968), it seems to me to differ in respect to the properties of positive transfer which are applicable to intellectual skills.

When one says, therefore, as I am inclined to say, that we need more evidence about learning hierarchies, he may simply be repeating something that has surely been said before: we need more evidence about positive transfer. Despite the encouraging signs from recent studies I have mentioned, it appears that there is an enormous amount still to be known about this subject. Perhaps reducing "learning hierarchies" to such familiar terms will encourage more investigation and more systematic thinking about this phenomenon, which is so obviously of central importance to education.

NURTURING THE COGNITIVE SKILLS OF PRODUCTIVE THINKING

One of the cardinal aims of education is to develop cognitive skills, the skills of acquiring, understanding, creating, and using knowledge. In pursuit of this aim, traditional schoolwork has concentrated mostly upon the simplest of these skills, those concerned with the sheer acquisition of subject matter. Relatively neglected, and often ignored, have been the higher-level skills of productive thinking and problem-solving.

Traditional curricula are so heavily weighted with the learning of specific subject matter content that there is little room in the programme for anything else. Since the skills related to this kind of subject matter acquisition have been regarded as much more easily developed than the more advanced skills of thinking, there has been in elementary schoolwork a preoccupation with the former kinds of skills and a temporary putting aside of the latter. Yet this postponement has more often been permanent than temporary; for secondary schools make no more than minimal efforts to deal with the skills of productive thinking, and even institutions of higher learning do very little in this regard. (Notice that they are not called "institutions of higher thinking".)

Underlying this comparative neglect of the training of thinking skills seem to be at least two implicit assumptions, both ill-founded and mutually incompatible. One view is that these skills *cannot* be trained. The other view is that they *do not need* to be trained. The first view—that productive thinking and problem-solving are simply not trainable—is based on the assumption that the marked individual differences found at all ages in ability to think and solve problems are a function of basic intellectual abilities of a deep-seated kind not readily susceptible to modification. There is gradually accumulating evidence that this assumption is wrong. A number of quite different approaches are showing success in direct attempts to facilitate the productive thinking and problem-solving performance of studies at all ability levels. Some relevant evidence of this kind will be presented later in this paper pertaining to the successful promotion of such thinking skills in the upper elementary grades.

The second view—that the highly advanced skills of productive thinking and problem-solving do not require direct training—is based on the assumption that they will more or less automatically develop as the student learns more and more subject matter; in short, the higher-level cognitive skills are assumed to be merely an extension and elaboration and adding together of the simpler cognitive skills. It is very doubtful that this assumption is correct. There seems no good reason to suppose that the higher-level mental skills can be counted on to emerge automatically out of the simpler ones. Productive thinking and problem-solving are complex processes which require direct attention in and of themselves. They are not just the additive end products of simpler cognitive processes.

Indeed, the view we present here is quite the opposite: In their fullest sense, *all* cognitive skills, even the simplest of the skills of acquiring information, are properly to be conceived of as integral parts of the more general processes of productive thinking. Productive thinking should not be conceived of as something special, rarefied, and removed from the usual mental activity of the individual. It is what goes on, or should go on, whenever the individual is engaged in cognitive work. And that it true equally of the young child and the mature student. Viewed in this way it becomes artificial to separate cognitive skills into simpler ones which do not require thinking and more complex ones which do. At every age and at every level of complexity, the training of cognitive skills should be seen as the training of productive thinking.

As we have said, the simplest cognitive skills have to do with the acquisition of information. A major part of the student's schoolwork in the traditional educational setting is the exercise of this function: He memorises facts, and he regurgitates the facts on command. Put thus baldly, it would appear that the individual's cognitive task in acquiring information is straightforward and uncomplicated and that the requisite skills are simple and few. Certainly there would seem to be nothing involved in the way of productive thinking. Indeed, the only "problem" to be solved in this kind of schoolwork seems to be that of passing the test or of otherwise satisfying the teacher that the facts have been learned. Viewed in this way there would seem to be little of significance to add to what has already been said repeatedly by educational psychologists about the best ways of training for the skills of efficient memorisation of facts, e.g., repetition, distribution of practice, and use of incentives.

The Acquisition Process

What is at fault here is a misleading description of the acquisition process. This process has been too narrowly conceived in much of traditional educational practice, being viewed mainly as one of sheer intake and output of unmodified information. It could properly be thought of in quite a different way—as a process of *assimilation,* in which the incoming information must be operated upon by the individual, restructured and transformed and fitted meaningfully into his pre-existing conceptual world. It is this problem of assimilating the new information into what is already there which requires productive thinking by the individual whenever he learns subject-matter content.

Reformulated in this way, it becomes clear that the requisite cognitive skills for assimilating information are by no means mundane; indeed they are essentially *creative.* For the problem posed by the intake of a given piece of information is unique to each individual. He must seek to assimilate the new information in a way which successfully fits it into and reshapes *his own* conceptual world. And since no two individuals possess an identical conceptual world, his solution must be to some degree distinctive and innovative.

Figuratively speaking, the person must make the fact his own. In becoming "part of himself," the fact has necessarily been changed in some degree. It is no longer the "same" fact that it was, nor is it now the "same" fact that exists in other people's minds. He must render the fact relevant and meaningful, and he must do this through a process of directed mental activity which has as its end the complete ingesting, metabolising, and incorporating of the fact in such a way that it becomes widely "distributed" throughout the diverse reaches of his conceptual system.

When we consider the customary manner in which facts are taught and learned in school, the foregoing description of the essential cognitive process occurring in the assimilation of new information may seem overly elaborate, exaggerated, or even downright wrong. Yet that is because what we customarily have in the classroom is the routine acquiring of trivial facts, or of potentially significant facts that are taught and learned in a trivialising fashion. What the school should be dealing with, instead, are clearly non-trivial facts--those which have widespread implications, those which can (if the student will but think) connect with and modify many diverse parts of his ideational world. And what the school should be concerned with is the presentation of such potentially significant facts in a non-trivialising way. Each significant piece of information, properly presented, constitutes a problem for assimilation. The student should be brought to attack the problem—to engage in productive thinking about it, to analyse the information, to consider its many implications, and to see how and where it fits, or fails to fit, with his other knowledge. Though the necessary hard, elaborative, cognitive work can be aided by the teacher and facilitated by class discussion, it must in the last analysis be done by the individual student himself.

The effective training of any skill, such as this skill in assimilating new information, requires methods of assessing the progress and outcomes of the training. For evaluating the sheer acquisition of unmodified facts as customarily required in the school, the method is a simple testing of how accurately the student can regurgitate and reproduce the memorised facts. But for assessing the outcomes of the productive thinking process involved in assimilating new information in the way described above, the evaluative approach must be both deeper and more comprehensive in scope. Evidence must be sought that the new information has indeed made a discernible difference in the individual's mind, in diverse and widely ramified aspects. Evidence is needed that the given fact, in the process of being assimilated into the total belief-system of the student, has produced changed in other contexts and structures of his belief-system, especially when the new fact is in some degree inconsistent with his preexisting beliefs.

Evidence is also needed on the extent to which the newly assimilated information has come to assume a proper salience in the individual's mind. This might be obtained, for example, by determining the ease with which the information appears "spontaneously" in a variety of mental contexts in the absence of explicit direction, and by determining the threshold for retrieval of information under conditions of direct inquiry. This foregoing account of the extensive requirements for an adequate testing of how well a piece of new information has been assimilated by the student brings into sharp relief the distinction between this kind of productive thinking process and the commonplace, low-level process of sheer routine acquisition of facts.

The purpose of this lengthy excursion into the nature of the skills of assimilating information has been a substantiate the earlier assertion that all cognitive skills, simple as they may appear to be, are properly to be conceived of as requiring the exercise of productive thinking and problem-solving. It seems perfectly clear, therefore, that the school must concern itself directly with the training and nurturing of productive thinking and problem-solving skills in all students and at all levels. The remainder of this paper will consider the nature of the thinking skills which are involved in problem-solving and what can be done to train and nurture these skills.

The Skills of Problem-Solving

We should make clear at the outset that in this discussion of problem-solving skills the term "problem" is meant broadly, pertaining to all kinds of subject matter and all domains of human activity. Both simple and highly complex problems must be included; so must precisely stated and well-structured problems as well as those which are loosely defined and weakly structured. The spectrum of problems must include the briefest, lasting but a few seconds, and those which stretch out over prolonged periods of time with many sessions of work by the individual. And problems may not only be fixed and static in nature, but may also be such as to undergo constant changes in structure and conditions as they are worked on.

Problems include those for which there are unique solutions

as well as those for which there are multiple solutions; those with partial solutions and those with complete solutions. Problems differ in the type of solution sought: some pertain to the achievement of understanding, as in the assimilation of new information described previously; others pertain to explanation, as in the accounting for puzzling phenomenon in science; others pertain to the creation of an innovative way of accomplishing an end, such as in resolving a conflict in human relations.

Although problems are usually defined and evaluated within an objective framework common to all individuals, they sometimes must be viewed within a purely individual and subjective framework. Some problems can be defined meaningfully from the perspective of the person himself; the success of the artist who seeks to construct on canvas a painting that "fits" what he has in mind can be judged only from his own frame of reference. How successfully he communicates to the viewer what he has in mind is a quite different, more objective, problem. Whether or not the solution to a problem is judged "creative" will depend in part upon the particular circumstances of the individual, how much relevant information he possessed, and how much he knew of other people's prior solutions to the problem.

For all of these diverse types of problems—simple and complex, brief and protracted, partial and complete, objective and subjective—the problem-solving process involves a large variety of thinking skills. We shall first discuss each of the specific skills and then consider the manner in which they are organised and integrated through the operation of a master thinking skill. We conceive of these various skills as *generalised*, that is, as transcending any particular kind of problem or subject matter. The importance of the role played by any specific skill will vary, of course, depending upon the particular problem and subject matter. Some problems will require a relatively large amount of attention to clarification of the questions, others a great amount of analysis of data; some problems will require a relatively large amount of idea generation, others a large amount of testing and checking out of ideas. But to some degree all these, and the other skills, will enter into virtually every problem.

Problem Discovery

One main set of skills has to do with *problem discovery and formulation*. The individual must, in the first place, somehow become aware of a problem—either through recognising a problem which already exists, or by creating a novel problem out of his own incessant mental activities.

The crucial stage in the productive thinking process tends to be short-circuited or completely omitted in the typical problem-solving which the child does in school. For example, a mathematics problem or a science problem is usually given to him in an already neatly packaged and labelled form. The relevant terms and conditions of the problem are clearly and specifically stated, and the question to be answered is explicitly put. Obviously, under these special circumstances, the student is not called upon to exercise or train in the important skills having to do with detecting and defining problems. But these special, and somewhat artificial, circumstances are not representative of most of the "real life" problem-solving in which the individual engages. In most cases he is not the passive recipient but rather the active seeker and discoverer of problems. And in most cases the problems he discovers are not clearly demarcated and explicitly defined but are imprecisely structured and difficult to formulate.

As the individual experiences and copes with complex situations and phenomena, he seeks to make some kind of sense of them. In so doing he may detect something puzzling, something which demands explanation or accounting for. He may notice an apparent inconsistency among several facts, an incongruity of some kind, something strange which violates what is to be expected, a casual gap. The accomplished problem solver has a sharpened sensitivity to such puzzling things and is adept in narrowing down and pinpointing the source and nature of the puzzlement.

Although such skills are especially in demand during the origin and initiation of problems, they are also germane at all stages of the problem-solving process. The total problem may need to be broken up into several sub-problems, each of them requiring separate specification. Moreover, at any point during work on a problem the person needs to be open to the discovery of wholly new problems, arising unexpectedly out of the old problem, and leading into entirely different directions. It is, indeed, one of the hallmarks of the truly creative thinker that he has this continuous set toward problem discovery—a readiness to find problems everywhere, to be puzzled by the obvious, to see the extraordinary in the ordinary, to make the familiar into the strange.

For a problem to be discovered is, of course, the first essential. Yet to attack the problem effectively requires that it then be *formulated* in a meaningful way by the individual; he must state the problem to himself in a form which points up the crucial issue to be solved and which avoids a misleading set. For example, the problem should not be stated in a way that implies a certain answer or range of answers to the exclusion of other possible answers. This skill in problem formulation is a difficult one and requires a great deal of training. The individual must be able to counteract a strong disposition toward conventional or traditional ways of stating the issue. A problem that has been worked on by others may prove intractable just because the individual too readily falls in with formulating the problem in the identical terms previously used. New solutions to old problems often occur because the new formulation of the problem is a more appropriate or powerful one. The inexperienced problem solver may not realise how much scope there generally is for alternative formulations of an issue. Part of the training he needs is to be shown the various possibilities and to be given practice in discriminating and choosing among these alternatives.

Processing Information

A second broad set of problem-solving skills has to do with the *organising and processing of problem information*. Having formulated the problem for himself, the individual must now get the essentials of the problem well in mind. He must identify the boundary conditions of the problem and the circumstances which govern it; he must get an overview of the facts, and must put the facts into some orderly form; he must distinguish the relevant facts from the irrelevant; he must recognise gaps in the available information and specify what other data are needed to fill these gaps.

The organisational and analytical mental skills involved in these various requirements are fairly obvious ones. We shall not dwell upon these skills, partly because they have been given disproportionately large emphasis in traditional work on thinking which concentrates most heavily upon logical reasoning, critical thinking, and analytical functioning, rather than upon the kind of productive or creative thinking which concerns us here. However, it should be mentioned that the manner and degree in which these skills are called upon in problem-solving depend heavily upon the type of problem. In the highly structured problem exercises that the student is often given in school, e.g., in mathematics or science, the problem information is substantially "predigested" for the student; the problem conditions are rigorously specified, the relevant facts are clearly stated, and all irrelevant facts are omitted. Obviously in these cases the student requires little use of the skills we are here describing. It should also be noted that this manner of problem presentation is highly artificial and unrepresentative of the kinds of problems customarily encountered in the everyday thinking of the person. In more realistic circumstances, problems are "messy" and cluttered with confusion and irrelevancy. A crucial part of successful problem-solving in these cases is the adept use of skills in organising and processing the information.

Another point is that problems vary widely along a dimension of sheer complexity. Simple problems are likely to involve a small amount of information; complex problems tend to be embedded in the context of very large bodies of information. In the latter, the problem solver must be able to exercise skills of rapid mental and perceptual scanning, of flexible deployment of attention, of efficient categorizing, and the like.

Idea Generation

A third broad set of problem-solving skills has to do with idea generation. Having formulated the problem, having gotten the relevant information well in mind, the individual must now come up with possibilities for solutions, directions to be investigated, hypotheses to be tested. These skills of idea generation are the very core of the problem-solving process. It is what happens at this fateful point, perhaps more than anywhere else, that determines whether the problem solver will succeed or fail in his quest. And what does happen here depends heavily upon the level to which these idea generation skills are developed in the individual.

In light of this, it is especially significant that of all cognitive skills, the typical school does *least* with the nurturing of idea generation. Depressingly little attention is given to stimulation of ideas in most schoolwork at most levels. This is partly because of the deadening influence of the conventional curriculum and teaching methods with their heavy stress upon the "authority" of established knowledge. Also, it reflects an uneasiness in some teachers about being able to cope with classroom creativity. It also stems from an implicit assumption on the part of many educators that "ideational fluency," "creative thinking," and the like, are deeply-rooted individual traits not at all susceptible to training.

It is certainly true that we do observe enormous individual differences in these idea-generation skills at all ages from young children to adults. Yet we also find evidence from many sources that these skill *are* subject to training, that the individual can be made better able to think of productive ideas. Studies of so-called "brainstorming" are but one such example. The successful use of "inquiry" methods in some of the new curricula is another example. Later we shall offer additional direct evidence on the point.

Part of the strengthening of idea-generation skills depends upon sheer repeated practice in thinking of ideas, something of which we have said the schools provide too little. Such practice is made meaningful by the learning and use of certain *strategies* of idea generation. One such strategy, for example, is the sequential scanning of the elements of the problem and the systematic listing of attributes of each element as a source of ideas. Another strategy is the orderly exploration of the ramifications of "idea-trees," by proceeding from the enumeration of general possibilities to the spelling out of specific ideas. Another strategy that the individual can learn to use is that of analogical and metaphorical thinking. Through searching for parallels and similarities with other perceived phenomena he can often come to discover whole new sets of ideas relevant to his problem.

Still another strategy is to plumb systematically the rich source of ideas which lies in what he has previously experienced and stored away in memory having to do with related phenomena, and with potentially applicable facts, concepts, and principles. How readily accessible these are to him as he works on a problem will—to revert to our earlier point—depend heavily upon the skill with which he has originally assimilated and stored them. Here we see a particularly compelling example of the way in which the various cognitive skills are inextricably interrelated.

The most creative ideas usually derive from some sort of *restructuring* of one's conception of the problem. The earlier way of looking at the problem must be abandoned and a wholly new perspective discovered. Tacit and misleading assumptions and rigid preconceptions must be overcome. A questioning and even skeptical stance must be assumed. These skills in insightful mental reformulation are perhaps the least studies and least understood. Yet there is every reason to believe that they, like the other skills of thinking, are susceptible to training. Some evidence on this will be mentioned later.

Evaluation of Ideas

The final set of problem-solving skills which we will mention has to do with the *evaluation of ideas*. This is, as some would call it, the stage of hypothesis testing. What is required of the individual here is a fairly high-level kind of critical and logical thinking. He must check to determine how consistent his idea is with respect to the detailed requirements of the problem. He must engage in a process of inferential thought in which the consequences or implications or likely outcomes of his idea are explicated. He must decide what specific evidence would be relevant to the confirmation or the rejection of the idea. Eventually, he must gather and marshal the evidence and come to a decision about the validity of the idea—whether it is to be accepted, modified, or abandoned as a solution to the problem.

In simple problems having clearly defined solutions, the skills of idea evaluation are relatively straightforward. The correct answer may be immediately evident once it has been thought of, or it may easily be checked in a rigorous and unambiguous way against the problem statement. Yet in complex problems involving a great amount of data, incomplete information, and the possibility of multiple alternative answers, the evaluation process may be considerably more difficult. The correctness of an answer or the validity of an idea may only be ascertained after a considerable amount of work. And in many cases, perhaps most cases, the evaluation cannot be made with complete certainty. Often the best that can be said is that a particular answer or idea is "likely" or "unlikely." In short, the individual must have the skill of weighing evidence and coming up with a probable decision. In the face of overwhelming complexity and unresolvable uncertainty, the superior problem solver may have to be able to exhibit an intuitive "feel" for the rightness or wrongness of a tentative idea.

For convenience in exposition we have chopped up the total process of problem-solving into the skills of problem formulation, information processing, idea generation, and idea evaluation. But this gives a false picture of the actual process. Problem-solving does not always, or even usually, proceed in these tidily ordered stages. Typically, the stages are overlapping and interwined. The process does not necessarily begin at the beginning and end at the end. Often an idea occurs to the person *before* he has adequately stated the problem; a period of information processing may precede rather than follow the emergence and formulation of a problem; an answer may wander in search of an appropriate question. There may be direct insightful leaps from problem to solution with the intervening steps of logical thought not filled in until after the fact. Moreover, for complex problems which involve many facets and many steps, the individual will often be working on several different subproblems simultaneously, each at a different stage of development.

In short, the problem-solving process is not a cut-and-dried sequence of steps executed in the orderly manner of the preestablished programme of a computer. This is not the appropriate model for either the student thinking productively in the classroom or the scientist experimenting in the laboratory. It should be noted that despite the venerable dogma of the "scientific method," much testimony agrees that productive thinking by scientists proceeds very differently from the "textbook" accounts of it. Creative thinking of scientists, like that of other creators, is often a wild and even chaotic process whose history is retrospectively tamed and rectified so as to fit better the stereotyped image of rational scientific thought.

It is clear that the process of solving problems is highly complicated, involving a great number of separate but interrelated cognitive skills. Whether or not the individual succeeds in solving the problem depends heavily upon his ability to marshal these skills in an effectively coordinated way. He must know which step to take at a given point, which plan of attack to adopt. He must know how to employ sensible "stop strategies", for instance, to be able to decide when it is time to stop collecting information and to start generating ideas, when it is time to stop generating ideas and to start evaluating them, and when it is time to abandon one direction of thought and to embark on another. He must be able to balance and harmonise the often contradictory demands which arise in the problem. For as we have seen, at times he needs to be rigorously analytical, at other times freely unconstrained and imaginative; at times he needs to be intensely involved in the problem, at other times capable of detachment from it to gain perspective; at times he may need to give free rein to an impulsive jumping to conclusions, at other times a patient reflectiveness is required.

A Master Thinking Skill

The ability of the individual to manage all these diverse and disparate requirements in the problem-solving process has been termed the *master thinking skill*. This is a metaskill which enables the effective coordination, integration, and utilisation of the many specific skills we have already enumerated. Without this overall master thinking skill, an individual may be able to accomplish some parts of the process, but not others. He may be capable of an outpouring of ideas but be unable at the same time to distinguish the good from the poor. He may be able to see the flaw in the evidence but utterly unable to come up with a new conception of the issue. On the other hand, in possessing a sufficiently developed master thinking skill, the individual will be enabled to make progress toward problem solution in all these interacting functions. The ultimate objective criterion for an adequate degree of development of this master thinking skill is, quite simply then, the person's success of achieving *solutions* to problems.

The educational implications of these comments about the master thinking skill are clear. If we seek to nurture the student's ability to think, then we must give him appropriate training on the many specific skills we have described. But in order to do this most effectively—so as to practice these skills in a mutually reinforcing way and to make for optimal transfer—we should train them simultaneously in the context of whole problems which have considerable scope, complexity, and meaningfulness. In this fashion the student will practice using his productive mental processes in the integrated way they must be used for genuine problem-solving in his school studies and in other "real life" situations.

To practice one of the specific component skills without reference to its place in the integrated performance pattern would be analogous to a pianist exercising the pressing of the foot pedal without any reference to the synchronisation of the hands on the keyboard, the visual input from the music sheet, or the auditory feedback from the sound of the keys. The pianist's purpose is to produce music, and his skill in using the pedal is but a single part of the organised whole; as such it must constantly be coordinated with all of the other specific skills of the whole performance. Similarly, the thinker's purpose is to solve a problem by using many specific cognitive skills. These skills must be effectively coordinated with one another if the problem-solving process is to go forward to a successful conclusion. The perfecting of one of these specific cognitive skills is thus as much a matter of learning how to integrate it with the other concurrently operating skills as it is a matter of practicing this skill by itself. In short, what is required is the development and strengthening of the master thinking skill.

The Training of Cognitive Skills

The educational feasibility of this kind of direct, integrated approach to the training of cognitive skills is attested to by a number of recent school studies making of *The Productive Thinking Programme*. This 16-booklet set of self-instructional lessons, plus supplementary exercises, is designed to train thinking skills in fifth- and sixth-grade children. Each booklet presents a complex problem to be solved, requiring the handling of a considerable amount of information, the asking of questions, the generating of many diverse ideas, and the relating of the ideas to the facts. By means of the programmed structure of the lessons the student is led systematically through the entire problem-solving process, being given periodic feedback to his answers and, through a succession of carefully planted cues, being led, eventually, to discover the solution for himself.

Also, at various places in the lessons he is given direct exposition concerning the nature of the thinking process, a number of explicit strategies for generating and checking ideas, and general information designed to increase his understanding of how to use and enjoy his mind. The booklets are cast in a semi-cartoon form. A story-line running continuously throughout the 16 lessons depicts the problem-solving adventures of two children who are intended to serve as positive identification figures upon whom the reader can model his own thinking performance. The problems are devoted to mystery and detective puzzles calculated to interest and involve the child. Included are such problems as these: to figure out how a large sum of money disappeared during a boat trip; to explain why a trial dive of a new deep-sea rescue vessel went seriously awry; to account for a series of mysterious and apparently unconnected occurrences in a "haunted" house.

The cognitive skills taught in these lessons are intended to be highly general ones, applicable to all the various subject-matter disciplines of the school curriculum. In order to facilitate the student's transfer of the skills to thinking tasks in these diverse areas, supplementary exercises have been prepared to accompany the basic lessons. These supplementary exercises provide additional opportunity for practice of the skills, and the exercises present problems which are somewhat more directly concerned in content with issues relevant to curriculum and society than are the basic lessons. For example, the student works on problems such as these: to think of new and more constructive ways of looking at the problem of coping with the huge volume of waste materials produced in our cities; given only the evidence of a complex pattern of animal tracks left in the snow in a small forest clearing, to figure out what must have happened there; to think of kinds of economic activities suitable to a fictitious small, developing country, given certain facts about its natural resources, possible markets, etc.

These instructional materials, like any materials which purport to teach skills, need to be assessed for their effectiveness by some objective test instrument. Accordingly, a battery of productive thinking tests has been constructed which can provide measures of many of the main dimensions of problem-solving performance. In the school studies using *The Productive Thinking Programme,* this test battery has been administered immediately following the training period, both to the trained students and to carefully matched control samples of untrained students. The effectiveness of the training has then been determined by comparing the score profiles of the two groups.

In very brief summary, the consistent findings of such school studies carried on with many hundreds of fifth- and sixth-grade children during the past several years are that the trained children significantly surpass their matched controls in virtually all of the measured variables of productive thinking performance. For example, the trained children excel in being sensitive to puzzling facts, in asking relevant information-seeking questions, in generating ideas of high quality, in seeing problems in new ways, in planning a systematic attack on problems, in evaluating ideas, and in achieving actual solutions to problems.

The magnitude of these training increments is indicated in Figure 13.3, which shows comparative distributions of thinking scores for a sample of 25 trained fifth-grade students and a sample of 25 matched control students.

Each individual's score is his total on a 23-variable composite of thinking performance based on eleven problems. Note that, whereas 72 per cent of the trained students score above the combined median, only 24 per cent of the controls do so, a three-to-one superiority. It appears, moreover, that the entire distribution of scores for the trained children is translated more or less uniformly upwards, an indication that the training benefited children regardless of their initial level of performance. This point is confirmed by further analysis of the data showing that the significant gains in thinking skills as a result of the training occur for children of average and somewhat below average IQ as well as for higher IQ children. Indeed, despite the substantial initial correlation found between productive thinking performance and IQ, the effect of the training is such that *trained* children of average intelligence (mean IQ of 99) come to score virtually as high on the productive thinking tests as do the *untrained* children of high intelligence (mean IQ of 124).

These positive results would seem to offer persuasive evidence on the feasibility of training of productive thinking skills. This is not, however, to imply that entirely new skills have been developed. Considering the brevity of the training—32 hours in all—it is unlikely that the basic thinking capacities of the children have been altered. Presumably what has happened has been a *sensitising* of the student to the availability of mental capacities which he already possesses though rarely uses, and, through practice, a strengthening and sharpening of his ability to *use* these skills in an effective fashion.

Nor should it be concluded from these results that the particular training materials and methods used in these studies are necessarily the best ones possible. Indeed, it should be stressed that these gains in performance have occurred when starting from the distressingly low absolute levels of thinking which are manifested by most elementary school children.

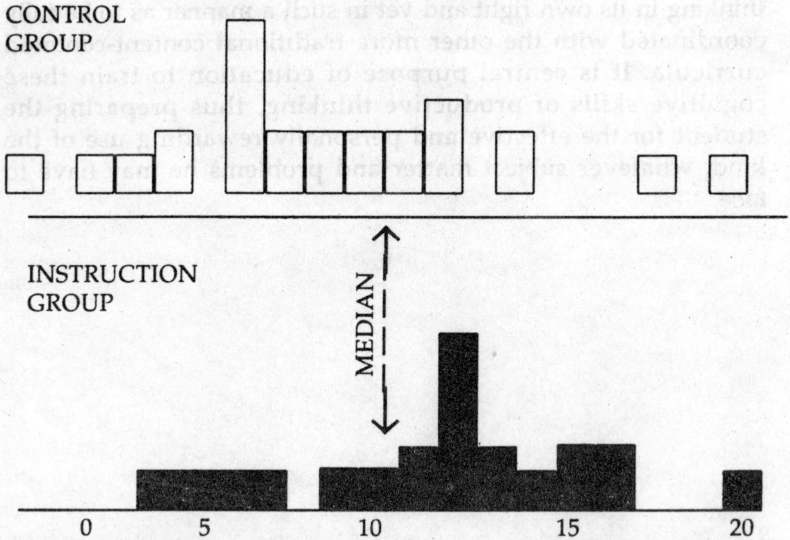

Figure 13.3. Distributions of 23-item productive thinking composite scores for instruction and control groups. The median of the combined groups is shown.

There is good reason to suppose, therefore, that any type of reasonably intelligent, serious, and direct effort to teach thinking skills is likely to yield similar positive outcomes.

Yet, as we have said before, schools now do very little in the way of such direct teaching of thinking skills. True, some of the new "reformed" curricula in mathematics, science, and social studies are giving a larger place to learning through thinking and problem-solving, but theirs is an indirect and subsidiary rather than a direct treatment of thinking skills, and as yet it is by no means clear how effective these new approaches will be.

The nurturing of the cognitive skills of productive thinking should assume a central place in the curriculum. Teaching of these skills should not be subordinated to the overriding demands of subject matter acquisition, as at present, but should be dealt with directly. What we need, in short, is a "cognitive curriculum," one which nurtures the process of productive thinking in its own right and yet in such a manner as to be fully coordinated with the other more traditional content-centered curricula. It is central purpose of education to train these cognitive skills of productive thinking, thus preparing the student for the effective and personally rewarding use of the kind, whatever subject matter and problems he may have to face.

14
Teaching Children to Make Good Decisions

Ann decides to save the five dollars she earned, Rachel decides to spend hers. Julia decides to cheat on a math test, Maria decides against it. Sherrie decides to give in to peer pressure and stay out all night to party, Justine decides to keep her curfew and come home. Decisions, decisions, decisions! We make them all the time. Some decisions, involve choosing between innocuous options, and some have to do with selecting the best solution for a personal, moral, or interpersonal dilemma. Sometimes the decisions we make have a major impact on our lives, sometimes they don't. Being able to make good decisions is a must for productivity and resilience (Spivack & Shure, 1974). Why? Because good decisions lead to success and effective coping.

The Decision-Making Process

The way we make decisions can vary, depending on the kinds of choices we have to make. To simplify matters I am going to discuss the decision-making process for three different kinds situations: (1) practical personal situations (e.g., how to spend an allowance, what courses to take in school); (2) problem situations involving moral and interpersonal issues; and (3) self-control issues involving delay of gratification, impulse control, resisting temptation, and low frustration tolerance.

Practical Personal Situations

Learning to make good choices begins with deciding between options that affect us personally. Practical personal decisions require the child to make a choice between two or more alternatives, and sometimes between alternatives that have different long- and short-term gains. Deciding how to spend an allowance, whether to study for a test or visit a friend, whether or not to do what a parent has asked, or what to do about a poor grade—these are the kinds of practical decisions I am talking about. The steps involved in practical decision making include the following:

1. Determining the nature of the need, want, or problem
2. Determining the options available
3. Determining how the options fit with one's resources, interests, personal characteristics, temperament, learning style, and physical makeup
4. Determining the costs and benefits associated with each of the options
5. Making a choice
6. Implementing the choice
7. Evaluating the choice

Here is an example: John, age ten, is having difficulties in school with English and social studies. He has never had difficulties in the past with these subjects and has no known learning disability or problem. John's parents sit down with him to explore the problem and some possible solutions. John willingly sits down with them to problem-solve. His parents explore with him the reasons for his difficulties in these subject areas and together they determine that John has trouble fitting study time into his busy schedule. The problem is defined as a busy schedule that precludes study time. The next step is to determine John's options. During the evaluation of John's options, several factors are considered, including the relative pleasure his activities give him, the possibility of pursuing some activities at alternative times, and the relative drain on John of doing the various activities. Dropping study time from the schedule is not an option because academic performance is highly valued. The following is a written summary of the decision-making process conducted by John and his parents:

1. *Problem:* Failing English and social studies.
2. *Reason for problem:* Insufficient time to study.
3. *Options:* Drop piano lessons; drop football; drop paper route.
4. *Analysis of options:* Piano lessons and football are good stress relievers for John and a good balance to the stresses and strains of school. The paper route provides an additional source of revenue for John but takes a large chunk of time out of his schedule.
5. *Choice:* John determines that while he would miss the revenue of the newspaper route, the time it requires is too costly. He figures he can reduce his extracurricular expenses and manage with his weekly allowance. The time saved would result in additional time for study.
6. *Implementation:* John arranges for his friend and neighbour to assume his paper route.
7. *Outcome:* Three weeks after the new schedule change, when John evaluates his decision to drop the paper route, he feels that it was a good decision because his grades have improved and he is feeling a lot better.

The scenario presented is an example of what can and often times does happen in homes. However, not every situation is so easy to solve. For one, children may not perceive the problem, or they may not perceive the problem in the same way their parents do. If this is the case, the first step is to find a way to define the problem so that both child and parent can agree. For example, if John had not been bothered by his poor grades in English and social studies, his parents would have had to make them a problem for John either by making involvement in sports and piano contingent upon academic performance or by finding an alternative incentive for good grades. When there is a good relationship between parent and child, often (not always) a conversation is sufficient to establish a mutual agreement about the nature of the problem. Sometimes parents have to re-evaluate their own view of the problem and accept the child's perception of it. For example, the parents of a child who is being excluded from an activity of his or her peer group may find this a very distressing situation. However, the child may not be motivated to change the situation, because he or she is not concerned about being excluded. In this case, the parents have the problem, not the child, and they would do well to reconsider their perception of the situation.

How do parents know when to redefine their own perspective of a situation and when to encourage their children to adopt their view? The answer to this question is not simple or straightforward, but the rule of thumb is to ask themselves the following questions:

1. Does the problem represent a major threat to my child's life or well-being?
2. Does the problem represent a major threat to my child's sense of values?
3. Does the problem represent a major threat to other people?
4. Will my child be harmed permanently if he or she refuses to accept the view that there is a problem?

If the answer to any of these questions is yes, the parent needs to proceed with efforts to have the child view the problem as a problem. If the answer to all of these questions is no, then the parent may want to reconsider or back off. As hard as it is, it is sometimes necessary to let children err so that the resulting situation will motivate them to problem-solve. For example, Mrs. Smith is bothered by the fact that her 14-year-old daughter, Jamie, leaves assigned projects to the last minute. Mrs. Smith attempts to get Jamie to deal with her procrastination, but Jamie refuses. Mrs. Smith decides, quite prudently, that she will allow Jamie to find out for herself the consequences of procrastination. She tells Jamie that it is up to her to decide when to do her school projects but that if she receives less than a B on a project, she will need to agree to work on other assigned projects in a more timely fashion. Jamie agrees. She does poorly on her next project because of her procrastination and decides to work out a different schedule for doing the remaining projects of the year.

In addition to a possible disagreement between parent and child on the definition of a problem, there is also the question of partially effective alternatives and of how much help the parent should give to the child during the problem-solving process. Sometimes the available alternatives will not completely solve the problem for the child. For example, suppose dropping the paper route results in only a partial solution to John's problem. Then John would need to pursue additional alternatives. As for the question "How involved should a parent be in the child's attempt to problem-solve?" the answer is, it depends. It depends on the cognitive and emotional maturity of the child (I will address this issue shortly) and on the nature of the problem and how skilled the child is at problem-solving. Initially, children and adolescents may need assistance. As they become more proficient at problem-solving, they require less direct intervention and more moral support. Complex or difficult problems may require more direct input. Including the child in decisions that affect the family, whenever possible, is good problem-solving training. If you recall, this is what democratic parents do; it gives children the opportunity to learn how to make good decisions and it gives them practice making decisions.

Not all practical decisions involve problems. John, for example, could follow the same steps in deciding what to do with his allowance. The decision process might look something like this:

1. *Issue:* Should I use my whole allowance to purchase an arcade game video tape?
2. *Options:* I could spend my whole allowance and purchase the tape, or I could forgo purchasing the tape and save my allowance.
3. *Analysis:* I would like to purchase the tape, but I don't absolutely need it; I would need to use my whole allowance if I decide to purchase it.
4. *Cost-gain analysis:* If I purchase the tape, I will not have the money I need to go on the class trip, and I really want to go on the class trip.

5. *Decision:* I will forgo the home video arcade game tape for now and buy it later.

6. *Implementation:* I will put the allowance away for use on the class trip.

This scenario is also a good example of self-control. In this case the self-control involves choosing a long-term goal (class trip) over an immediate goal (videotape). Children who lack self-control require specific instruction (procedures developed by Meichenbaum are discussed later in this chapter) on how to delay gratification.

Moral and Interpersonal Situations

Decision making is also required in situations that involve basic moral dilemmas, for example, keeping rules, telling the truth, keeping promises, and honoring friendships, and in situations that involve interpersonal dilemmas, such as deciding what to do when you don't agree with a friend and managing conflict with others. The skills necessary to deal with moral and interpersonal problems develop over time and involve the following steps (D'Zurilla, 1988):

1. Problem orientation
2. Problem definition and formulation
3. Generating alternatives (brainstorming)
4. Evaluating alternatives
5. Choosing an alternative
6. Implementing the chosen alternative
7. Evaluating the outcome
8. Changing or reinforcing the plan

During the problem-solving orientation stage, the emphasis is on getting the child (or adult) to have a positive mental set about solving the problem. This means recognising that there is a problem, viewing the problem as solvable, holding realistic expectations about the amount of effort and time needed to solve the problem, and believing that you can do something about either solving the problem or managing your reaction to the problem.

To define the problem, children must be able to understand the situation not only from their own perspective but, when appropriate, from another person's perspective (social perspective taking). They are taught to think constructively about the problem when conceptualising it. They are also taught to view the problem as the discrepancy between what currently exists and what realistically might exist. Children also need to learn how to make a distinction between problems they can fix directly (problem-focused formulation) and problems that require an emotional adaptation to a situation (emotion-focused formulation; see D'Zurilla, 1988). (This relates to the distinction I made between problem-focused coping and emotion-focused coping.) A problem-focused formulation means that the problem can be resolved. For example, homework is a solvable problem because one can re-arrange one's schedule or do whatever else is necessary to handle the problem directly. On the other hand, if the problem is parental divorce or death of a loved one, then the best one can do is learn to live with the situation by constructively thinking about the problem. To sum up, if a problem situation is changeable, then a problem-focused formulation is in order. If the problem is perceived as unchangeable, then an emotion-focused formulation is required. In many cases, both problem- and emotion-focused formulations are required.

Another important part of the problem formulation is what psychologists call "social perspective taking" (Selman, 1980). Social perspective taking is, basically, seeing the problem from someone else's point of view. It is being able to understand how another person thinks and feels in a given situation. Understanding that another person's perception may be different from our own has important implications for solving interpersonal conflict. Conflict management and negotiation skills require social-perspective-taking skills.

Problem definition is also influenced by moral beliefs and cause-effect reasoning. Small children who believe that getting what they want is fair and right, independent of any other factors, think that not getting their way is a problem. Conversely, an older child or adult is inclined to consider a number of factors before concluding that a situation represents a problem. Younger children also differ from older children and adults in how they view moral situations. For example, younger children view any kind of rule breaking as a moral problem. Older children and adults are inclined to consider other factors, such as the rule breaker's intent, before they make a judgment about the behaviour. Identifying the antecedents of a problem is important for problem formulation. This is especially true in situations that involve strong emotions because feelings influence problem perception and solution choices. How we reason about a situation will influence the problem perception, the problem formulation, and the kinds of solution alternatives that are generated.

Once the problem has been defined, it is necessary for the child or adult to generate alternative solutions to the problem. These need to be concrete and realistic. D'Zurilla (1988) suggests generating as many relevant solutions as possible (the quantity principle) without initially judging appropriateness, feasibility, or utility (the "deferment of judgment" principle). He also suggests considering different kinds of alternatives (the variety principle). The ability to generate alternative solutions is positively correlated to social adjustment and can even be found in young children (Spivack & Shure, 1974).

Once the list of alternatives is generated, it is necessary to evaluate each one. Consequential thinking (Spivack & Shure, 1974) is used to determine what the consequences of choosing a particular alternative might be for oneself and for others. Children are encouraged to judge each alternative in terms of (1) the anticipated benefits; (2) the resources, actions, and plans necessary to carry out the alternative; (3) the possible obstacles; (4) how well it fixes the problem; and (5) how many other problems it is likely to cause.

The problem solver is then in a position to plan out the solution and actually execute it. Once the solution has been executed, the child needs to evaluate the solution and make the necessary changes. At this point, parents can help children by encouraging them to reinforce themselves or a job well done. I'm sure that by now you may be thinking that problem-solving is time consuming. You are of course right. But some of the most significant problems children and adults face are around for a long while and require this kind of careful consideration. Besides, once children get into the habit of approaching dilemmas in this way, they become efficient problem solvers.

To illustrate the process of problem-solving, I would like to use a scenario that involves both a moral and an interpersonal issue: resisting negative peer pressure. Andrew, age 12, has been getting into trouble at school; he has had five detentions in school in the past two weeks. At home Andrew is very irritable and oppositional. His parents decide to sit down and discuss the situation with him. Utilising some of the constructive communication techniques, Andrew's dad learns that Andrew feels torn between his friends and his own moral standards. He is particularly bothered by the fact that his friends have recently found great sport in tormenting John, one of the unpopular boys in the class. They push John into mud puddles, call him unkind names, destroy his homework, steal his lunch or lunch money, and "rough him up." Andrew is a sensitive and caring person. He himself was harassed by the same group of boys the year before, and John was one of the few kids who refused to join in. Instead, John befriended Andrew and even helped him with homework assignments. And now Andrew feels he has turned on John. Andrew is truly in a bind. He is going along with the group because he fears that if he doesn't they will resume their attacks against him. Andrew feels that he is "between a rock and a hard place"; he does not know what to do.

The first step in the problem-solving process is to help Andrew see that he can choose differently. The dialogue between Andrew and his dad might go something like this:

Dad: Andrew, I feel there is something bothering you. I need to talk to you about the school detentions and what I feel the problems are at home.

(The message is direct and constructive. The parent then discusses the school detention and specific examples of problems he perceives at home.)

Dad: The detention notices the school sent home indicate that there is a problem with John. I am interested in hearing your side of the story.

(Andrew proceeds to relate the story to his father. His father listens passively and then summarizes what he has heard.)

Dad: I get the feeling you want to support John but feel that if you do, the group might once again torment you. I guess if I were in your situation, I would feel pretty trapped, too. The question is, do you have alternatives?

Andrew: I don't know, Dad. I don't think that I have very good choices.

Dad: I think you have more choices than you think. I would be glad to help you brainstorm if you would like.

Andrew: Okay, Dad.

Andrew and his dad sit down and brainstorm some alternatives. Here is a summary of the whole problem-solving process:

Step 1: Andrew recognises the problem and comes to see that he can choose to behave differently.

Step 2: Andrew recognises his need to

a. resist peer pressure,

b deal with the negative feedback received from his peers for taking a stand,

c. give John some support while at the same time minimising the costs of such action to himself.

Step 3: Andrew generates the following alternatives:

Alternative 1: Seek out Peter, leader of the peer group, and talk to him privately about how John is being treated.

Alternative 2: Leave situation alone and continue as is.

Alternative 3: Redirect group when they begin to badger John.

Alternative 4: Walk away from group when they begin to badger John.

Alternative 5: Publicly state disapproval of the group's action and offer John an opportunity to engage in an alternative activity.

Alternative 6: Choose a few other kids in the peer group who may feel the same way about the situation and devise a plan with them to redirect the group when it begins to badger John.

Alternative 7: Choose a few other kids in the peer group who feel the same way about the situation and plan an activity that includes John.

Alternative 8: Walk away quietly when the group is badgering John and seek John out later to plan an activity with him. At the same time, look for other more socially appropriate friends.

Step 4: The alternatives are evaluated:

Alternative 1: Andrew feels uncomfortable with this alternative, believing that Peter is likely to badger him as well as John.

Alternative 2: Andrew (much to the relief of his parents) does not feel comfortable with this alternative. He is bothered a lot about how John is being treated and is not pleased with his own behaviour or the resulting consequences.

Alternative 3: Andrew is not sure he has the skills or confidence to redirect the whole group, especially with Peter as the leader. Andrew feels that peter has a strong influence on the group and that his influence could not easily be diminished.

Alternative 4: Andrew feels that he could quietly walk away when the group badgers John. He sees that walking away would certainly address the first problem, since it would provide an avenue for resisting peer pressure, and would also reduce the probability of negative feedback, although it certainly would not eliminate the risk altogether. He recognises that the one drawback to this alternative is that it is not visibly supportive of John.

Alternative 5: This alternative represents a mixed bag of costs and benefits. Publicly stating his disapproval of the group's behaviour toward John is supportive of John, which is clearly a benefit, but the potential costs are great. Andrew feels that Peter would certainly be angered and would retaliate with a vengeance.

Alternative 6: Andrew can identify two other kids in the group who he thinks might feel as he does. But he is not sure and feels that if he is wrong, this approach would not solve any of the problems.

Alternative 7: The same drawbacks identified for Alternative 6 are true for Alternative 7.

Alternative 8: This alternative has all the advantages of Alternative 4 and would give John some support, too. There is still the chance that Peter might find out and badger Andrew again.

Step 5: Andrew chooses an alternative. He decides on Alternative 8. He then has to figure out what he needs to do in order to execute the alternative. He contacts John and makes plans to play chess at his house. He also explains to John his dilemma and tells him that for now he is going to walk away if the group starts bothering him. Andrew's father congratulates him on his analysis of the situation and takes the opportunity to suggest a few other more emotion-focused solutions as well. He shares with his son some personal stories of similar situations and what he learned from them. He also suggests that Andrew prepare for attacks from Peter, since Peter is very likely to find out that Andrew is not going along with the crowd. He recommends establishing a new group of friends and encourages

Andrew to use constructive thinking to deal with peer rejection and harassment.

Andrew's father was hoping that Andrew would choose Alternative 5 and stand up to Peter on principle. Andrew was clearly not ready to do this. The alternative chosen was, from the father's point of view, a good compromise and a good start toward a more assertive stand against social bullying. What happened in the end was that Peter did notice that Andrew was not joining in with the group when they were attacking John. He also found out that Andrew had befriended John. Peter, as you might have expected, started to attack Andrew once again. This time Andrew was prepared. He was able to stand up to Peter assertively and, as a result, won the support of the other group members. Andrew's father reviewed the whole situation with him, praising him for his choices and highlighting the aspects of problem-solving that were useful to him. If the scenario had not turned out as well as it did, Andrew would have had to either generate more problem-focused alternatives or move to an emotion-focused perspective that would make use of constructive thinking strategies.

Self-Control

A dollar today, or do I wait and get five dollars tomorrow? Do I take the five dollars out of Mom's purse, or do I wait to ask her? Do I jump at the first answer on the arithmetic test, or do I carefully think through all of the choices? Do I give up when I encounter an obstacle, or do I persevere? Self-control is the ability to make the better choice in situations such as these. It involves being able to delay gratification; resist temptation; and respond in a reflective, rather than impulsive, way to situations or choices.

Donald Meichenbaum (1985) is a researcher-clinician who has investigated ways of teaching children self-control. He used Luria's findings, showing the influence of internal language on behaviour, and those of Walter Mischel (1983), who studied delay of gratification, to formulate his strategies. There are various self-control training techniques. Most of them include the following steps (Hinshaw & Erhardt, 1991):

1. The parent demostrates the decision-making process or behaviour by verbalising out loud the strategies he or she is using.
2. Verbalising the steps for the child, the parent then has the child go through the task.
3. The child then performs the task while verbalising the steps out loud in the presence of the parent.
4. The child performs the task again, this time whispering the instructions.
5. The child then performs the task, verbalising the steps internally.

To illustrate this strategy, I will apply the steps to a situation where a parent is teaching an impulsive child to think before acting: Brenda, age 12, does poorly in school. Brenda's parents are quite concerned and seek out a professional evaluation. The evaluation reveals that Brenda's poor performance is due entirely to her impulsive response style to multiple choice questions. Brenda's mother then obtains a copy of a social studies exam. She goes through the exam with Brenda, telling her exactly how to think about the problem:

> Brenda, listen to how I think about the problem. I'll read the first question and then I need to read each of the possible answers. *(She goes through and reads each alternative out loud.)* Next, I ask myself, which of these answers is the best right answer for the question? *(She then thinks out loud about each alternative.)* Now, Brenda, you do the next question. Read the question out loud and then read each possible answer.

Brenda reads the next question and each of the possible answers. Then her mother instructs her to think out loud as she evaluates each alternative. Brenda's mother has her repeat the process for the next five questions. After that she instructs Brenda to whisper her thoughts as she attempts to answer the question. Then Brenda practices the strategy several times while verbalising all her thoughts internally.

This same self-control strategy can be used for other kinds of impulsive behaviour. For example, in the scenario used to illustrate a practical personal situation, John had to delay gratification in order to save enough money for a class trip. If John were an impulsive spender, his parents might help him by discussing with him how to think through his choices. They could do this by verbally modelling the decision-making process described under "Practical Personal Situations." They could have John list his alternatives and verbalise reasons for holding off on his purchase. They could brainstorm with him to determine other strategies that might help him delay gratification. For example, they might suggest that he keep the announcement of the class trip on his desk as a reminder of what he is working for. John could rehearse out loud why he decided to hold off on buying the home video arcade game tape and to save the money for the class trip. He could then review his decision steps, this time whispering them to himself. Finally, he could review the decision-making process by verbalising each step internally.

Self-control training of this sort can also be used to deal with aggressive behaviour and low frustration tolerance. Children are taught to identify their own physical cues of arousal (a knotlike feeling in the stomach and sweaty palms are examples of physiological arousal). A good strategy for teaching children to do this is to point out indicators of arousal in yourself and others, as well as in the child; for example: "I know that I am getting angry or frustrated because my stomach gets to feeling really tight and my hands and arms feel the very same way." Discussing the physical aspects of arousal sensitises the child to cues that are associated with destructive thoughts and feelings. Catching ourselves early in the arousal cycle increases the probability that we will maintain control. Once people are highly aroused or upset, it is much more difficult for them to maintain self-control or to problem-solve effectively. In situations where children or adults are highly aroused, it is better to allow them to cool off before attempting to deal rationally with the problem.

Children can be taught to identify the kinds of thoughts that are associated with anger or frustration; for example: "Anger is the way I feel when I feel scared" or "I feel like giving up when something looks hard." The parent who is teaching this skill to a child would first model it out loud for the child. The parent might say, "I get angry when I think you aren't listening. When do you think you get angry?" Or: "I feel like giving up when I have to do something that I don't know how to do. When do you feel like giving up?" Children can also be taught to identify the situations that tend to induce the anger or frustration response in them. The parent might start out by disclosing to the child their own situation triggers: "I find myself getting angry whenever Mr. Adams blames me for his own mistakes. What kind of things do you get angry about?"

Once children have learned to identify the thoughts, physical body sensations, and situations that are associated with their feelings of aggression or frustration, they are then taught to use these cues as signals to stop, think, evaluate, and act:

1. *Stop:* Parents can teach children to use some verbalisation or visual image that signals them to calm down and reflect before acting. "I need to calm down" or "Freeze!" or simply "Stop!" are appropriate verbal cues; visualising a red light is equally appropriate for children who think more in terms of images.

2. *Think:* Parents can teach children to think about what's happening and to determine what they need to do to think constructively and act appropriately. "What's happening here?"; "What am I thinking?"; "Let me think about this in another way"; "What can I do?"—these are all examples of sentences that can prompt children to think.

3. *Evaluate:* Parents can help children think about the consequences of selecting various alternatives and decide on one that is socially appropriate. "What will happen if. . . ?" and "If I do this, then this is likely to happen" are examples of the internal monologue a parent can encourage.

4. *Act:* Parents can help children learn to evaluate the efficacy of their actions: "All right, did my plan work the way that I thought it was going to?"

To show you how such instruction might work, I will describe a situation with a 13-year-old girl who has a quick temper and a short fuse. Karen is an attractive adolescent with many fine qualities. Her one major problem is that she tends to get very angry when a situation fails to go her way or when she feels her rights have been violated. Recently, Karen has had difficulties with her cheerleading coach. Karen feels that the coach does not particularly like her and that she blames her for everything that goes wrong. Karen's immediate response is to mouth off to the coach, which of course only hurts Karen. Karen's parents would be wise to help her learn techniques of self-control. They might, for example, help Karen recognise and channel her angry feelings:

Mother: Karen, I know that you have some difficulties with the coach.

Karen: Well, the coach is always picking on me. She hates my guts and treats me poorly. If she is going to treat me that way, she deserves what she gets.

M: I know that you feel the coach treats you poorly, and, quite frankly, Karen, I have seen her treat you unfairly on occasion. I don't blame you for being upset with her. I know I felt angry with her as well. What concerns me is how you choose to deal with your feelings. The coach is in a position to kick you off the team. What I am willing to do is to brainstorm with you on ways to express your frustration to the coach so that you don't get into trouble. Are you interested?

K: No, I don't think so, Mom, but thanks anyway.

After another practice in which Karen has a run-in with the coach, the coach gives her a warning and tells her that if she does not shape up, she is off the team.

M: My offer, Karen, is still available if you want to talk.

K: I'm ready. I really can't stand the coach.

M: Okay, what about the coach triggers your anger?

K: It's the way she looks at me and the way she talks to me. She always claims I'm not paying attention when that is not true. If something goes wrong, she blames me. If I make a mistake and someone else makes the same mistake, she picks on me only.

M: How do you physically feel when you get angry? Can you feel your stomach muscles tightening up or your heart pounding?

K: Well, I'm not sure, maybe both of those.

M: Good enough. It might he helpful in the future to pay attention when you are getting upset.

Karen and her mother then brainstorm on ways that Karen can "stop, think, evaluate, and act" when she feels herself getting angry with the coach. Karen decides that she will think of a brick wall that separates her from the coach and she also decides on the statement "Chill out, Karen, she can't get to you." With some help from her mother, Karen figures out the following strategy for accepting negative feedback from the coach:

1. Face the coach.
2. Maintain eye contact.
3. Say nothing while the coach is talking.
4. Reflect back, as accurately as possible, what the coach has said; for example: "Excuse me, coach, let me make sure I understand what you said. You think I was. . ."
5. State own side of the story if it is different from the coach's.
6. Apologise to the coach, if warranted.
7. If an apology is unwarranted, go along with the coach and see her later about the disagreement.

With encouragement from her mother, Karen reviews the plan. They role-play it several times before the next cheerleading practice. As expected, the coach does reprimand Karen for not paying attention. To her credit, Karen follows through with the plan. The coach is very surprised and refrains from criticising Karen for the rest of the practice. The assistant coach observes the entire episode and makes a point of talking with Karen after the practice. She congratulates Karen for controlling herself and admits that the coach was unfair in her accusations. Since Karen responded so well, the assistant coach offers to talk to the coach on Karen's behalf. Karen has no other problems with the coach, and the rest of the season goes well.

Karen was fortunate to have an assistant coach willing to stand up for her. But this happened only after the assistant coach saw that Karen was making a concerted effort to control herself. Karen's mother also handled the situation well. She used a constructive parenting approach with Karen: she validated her feelings about the coach without condoning her behaviour or solving the problem for her. As a result, Karen learned a valuable lesson in self-control.

Developmental Changes in Decision-Making Capabilities

For children to make good choices they have to be able to generate alternative solutions to problems, think about the consequences of those alternatives (consequential thinking), view the situation from another's perspective (social perspective taking), and think about how to implement the alternatives to effect a solution (means-end reasoning).

Researchers George Spivack, Jerome Platt, and Myrna Shure (1976) have found that young children (ages four and five) can (1) generate alternative solutions for age-appropriate problems (e.g., wanting something someone else has); (2) verbalise the potential consequence of various alternatives (e.g., asking for a toy versus grabbing for it); and (3) predict what will happen to a child who engages in a particular alternative. As a general rule, children of this age are unlikely to take the perspective of another (although there is evidence that they can be taught to), nor are they proficient with means—end reasoning. However, the general predictor of overall adjustment for children this young is their ability to generate alternative solutions. Parents and teachers need to help most young children understand the other person's perspective and identify the plan and steps required to realise the solution to a problem. Most young children, then, require assistance to solve problems in moral, interpersonal, and self-control situations.

As the child matures and enters middle childhood, existing skills are refined and new ones are added. Four interpersonal thinking skills have been identified by Spivack and his group:

the ability to conceptualise alternative solutions, means-end planning (cause-effect thinking), consequential thinking, and social perspective thinking (i.e., the ability to take in the perspective of others and to recognise that a situation can be interpreted differently by different observers or participants). Some perspective taking allows children to infer motives and to explain their own behaviour and the behaviour of others in terms of those attributed motives.

Children in middle childhood are generally capable of generating alternative solutions to problems and articulating the sequence of steps necessary to carry out solutions. Children who have these skills are better problem solvers and are judged to be better adjusted than those who don't (Spivack *et al.*, 1976). But one has to remember that means-end reasoning, consequential thinking, and social-perspective-taking skills are just beginning to emerge; parents may have to help the child with these skills initially.

By the time children reach adolescence, they are able to generate alternatives, specify plans to execute them, conceptualise the consequences associated with various alternatives, spontaneously link cause and effect, and see the situation from another's vantage point. In the work done by Spivack and associates, the generation of alternatives, means-end thinking, consequential thinking, and social perspective taking best predict social adjustment. In contrast to younger children, older children and adolescents are developmentally capable of learning all the problem-solving subskills and of applying them to social situations.

Social perspective taking, the ability to imagine oneself in another's position and understand how that person might think, feel, and react, is such an important skill that it requires further discussion. Robert Selman (1980), a psychologist, has studied how children develop social-perspective-taking skills. Selman found that children pass through specific stages as they acquire this skill. In the first stage, called egocentric role-taking, children aged three to four fail to see the difference between their own view of a social situation and the view that others hold of that situation, believing that others see things the same way they do. Around the age of five, children move into the subjective or differentiated perspective stage. Children in this stage do acknowledge the point of view of others, but they cannot consider their own viewpoint and the viewpoint of another at the same time. Nor can they accurately judge the other's perspective. As a result, children still appear egocentric, placing their own viewpoint above others without clearly thinking about the consequences of such actions.

At around age six, children move into Stage 2, the self-reflective or reciprocal perspective stage. At this point children understand that others may have a different perspective and realise that other people have the same level of understanding about them. Such an understanding allows the child to consider the thoughts and feelings of others. However, children of this age have a difficult time considering the perspective of a third party; for example, they have difficulty understanding how a parent can view their perspective and a sibling's perspective of the same situation at the same time.

The ability to assume a third-party perspective (mutual perspective taking), which emerges around the age of ten, characterises the mutual perspective stage. Children can now conceptualise how a third person might see their point of view and the point of view of the others involved in a situation. For example, Louisa may now be able to imagine what Mom might think about her reaction to her little sister as well as understand her little sister's perspective.

The fourth and final stage is characterised by a societal or indepth perspective. This perspective refers to the ability to conceptualise a social group's perspective; for example, the point of view of women or of Native Americans. This ability emerges during adolsecence and continues to develop during adulthood.

Perspective taking impacts on decision making because it influences how the person weighs various alternatives. For example, if the only perspective that I can imagine is my own, then all the alternatives I consider favour only my desires and goals. If, however, I can also take the other person's perspective, then I not only will come up with other alternatives but will consider the impact of those alternatives on others when I weigh the costs and benefits of a given alternative.

Perspective taking is not the only factor that influences the kinds of decisions made. Moral judgments often come into play for those decisions requiring moral choices and actions. Like perspective taking, moral reasoning has distinct features at different stages of development. Jean Piaget and Lawrence Kohlberg studied moral reasoning during childhood using situations that involved rule keeping and transgressions. While both theorists have their critics, their theories are consistent with empirical findings.

According to these theorists, younger children are generally motivated to avoid punishment and gain tangible rewards. They use moral absolutism to make judgements, meaning that everything is perceived as right or wrong, with nothing in between. The implication of this kind of reasoning for problem-solving is that younger children's choices of alternatives are restricted. As a result, they may require assistance seeing the worth of choices that are not clearly black or white.

As they mature, children become more flexible in their judgments and are able to consider such things as a person's intent. Their choices of behavioural alternatives are now influenced by the approval value of such alternatives; that is, children at this stage (eight to ten years old) are concerned about how others will view them should they engage in a particular behaviour.

The most advanced stage of moral reasoning is one marked by flexibility. Moral judgments are now based on norms that are democratically decided upon or that relete to some higher-order principle. William Damon (1977) has looked at how children think about positive justice. Positive justice has to do with the distribution of resources and fairness. During the preschool years children equate fairness with getting what they want ("I should get it because I want it"). Older preschoolers may offer external justification for their claims ("I should get it because I am bigger" or "I should get it because I am smaller"). These hedonistic notions gradually give way to positive justice determined by strict equality. Now justice means that everyone should get the same, no matter what. Around the age of six or seven, children start using the principle of reciprocity to make judgments about what is fair and what isn't: "He helped me, so I will help him" or "If I work hard, I should get the reward, too." During middle childhood (ages eight to ten) and into adolescence children become more sophisticated about their social justice reasoning. They become sensitive to the equity principle, believing that people should receive in proportion to what they give: "Mary should get four and Susie one because Mary did more of the work." And at around the age of ten, children are able to consider extenuating circumstances and balance equity, equality, and reciprocity principles: "John should get a little more than Bill, even though they did the same amount of work, because John had less to start with and needs more right now."

Social justice norms impact on decision making in several ways: For one, they influence whether or not an action will be perceived as a problem. Secondly, perceptions of social justice influence the alternatives that are considered. Finally, social justice norms affect how alternatives are weighed and which ones are ultimately chosen.

I hope that the developmental information presented here prepares readers for what they can reasonably expect of children of different ages in terms of decision making. The ages are meant only as approximate guides. The important point is to understand how children at different stages of development reason about problems and alternatives. With this information in hand, let us now consider how parents can promote good problem-solving skills in their children.

Parents as Promoters of Good Decision Making

Parents can facilitate good decision making in their children by modelling it for them. Children learn from what they see and hear. Parents who make good decisions provide good models for their children. To get the most mileage out of good decision making, parents are advised to occasionally share their decision-making steps with their children: "Hey, Alex, let me tell you how I decided to wait and buy this car instead of the first one I saw." (The explanation not only helps Alex understand the steps involved in decision making, but it also shows him the benefits of delaying immediate gratification for a better option in the future.)

Parents can facilitate good decision making in their children by pointing out the steps involved in the decision-making process used by characters in stories. Stories are a great way to introduce children to the process of decision making. Parents can use stories as an introduction to actually instructing children on the steps of problem-solving. For example, in Martha Alexander's book *More Over Twerp* young Robert decides on an excellent solution to the bully problem on the school bus. A parent can use this story with young children and literally detail the steps, including the alternatives considered, that Robert took to deal with the problem. It can then be followed up with a discussion about a problem or decision the child has to make.

Parents should give children the opportunity to make choices. The major rule to follow here is to avoid solving those problems that children can solve for themselves. Even young children need to be encouraged to problem-solve and to choose solutions whenever possible. The opportunities can be as simple as deciding between nutritious snacks and as sophisticated as being included in a discussion of some family problem. When children have the opportunity to choose, they learn to choose. As with any other skill, practice and exposure to decision making promote proficiency. Parents who decide everything for their children or who attempt to shelter them from all problems are pampering their children. Pampering is one of the major obstacles to the development of good problem-solving skills.

Is helping children problem-solve the same as pampering them? The answer to this question is, it depends. Initially, children require instruction. Young children require adult guidance. If they need help, it should be given to them. If you don't know how much help a child requires, ask him or her to talk through the problem. Sometimes in hearing a child talk through a problem, the parent can determine the child's deficiencies and help him or her make up for them. And sometimes verbalising the problem can help a child become aware of missing links in his or her understanding and can enable the child to correct these on his or her own. In any case, the child's attempt to make a good decision needs to be encouraged and fostered.

Parents can practice problem-solving strategies with their children. Role playing provides a good opportunity for children to try out problem-solving strategies. In role play children can experience the perspective of another person by pretending to be that person, and they can practice what to say or do in a given situation. (Recall Karen's use of role play to help her deal with the difficult coach.) By practicing beforehand, children become more familiar with and adept at problem-solving. As a result, they are more likely to be successful in the actual situation.

15

Cultivating Social Skills in Your Child

Our relationships with others pervade almost every aspect of our lives. People who have good social skills and strong interpersonal connections are more positive about themselves, more productive and successful on the job, better adjusted, and physically healthier than those who do not (Johnson, 1990). Why? Because feedback from others is one of the pieces of information people use to establish their self-esteem. Also, researchers have discovered that healthy interpersonal relationships protect people from the negative effects of stress. Good interpersonal skills, then, are self-esteem builders and resilience boosters.

Technically speaking, social skills are socially acceptable behaviours that are used by people when they interact with each other. Children and adults are considered socially skilled when their interactions are "personally beneficial, mutually beneficial, or beneficial primarily to others" (Combs & Slaby, 1977, p.162). Trower (1980) makes a distinction between skill components and the social skill process. Skill components are the individual behaviours that are socially appropriate and valued. Greeting someone with a "Hello" or "How do you do?" Is an example of a social skill. The skill process refers to the application of an appropriate set of skills to a situation initially and a following through with the "right" kind of responses for the social situation. Examples of children successfully engaged in a social process are those who know how and when to respond to another child who has asked them to do something they can't do and those who know how and when to make a request of a parent or teacher.

Types of Social Skills

There are a number of taxonomies or inventories of social skills. I will discuss each of the skill areas separately.

Self-Awareness Skills

While a feeling or emotion is a private affair, the manifestation of the emotion has social consequences. For example, an expression of anger needs to be appropriately vented or it is likely to result in negative social consequences.

The first step in teaching self-awareness to children is encouraging them to recognise their own feeling states and how those feelings influence behaviour. Because young children have less trouble identifying positive emotions than recognising negative and surprise feelings (Moyer, 1974), parents and teachers may need to spend more time helping them identify the latter. Moreover, because young children tend to center on one aspect of the situation only, they sometimes miss important information that could help them decide feeling states and may need help from time to time recognising the emotions and situations that influence their behaviour.

Table 12.1 Types of Social Skills

Self-awareness skills
Awareness of one's own feeling states and how they affect one's behaviour
Awareness of one's own strengths and weaknesses (and consequent tolerance for the strengths and weaknesses of others)
Awareness of how one communicates feelings and attitudes to others
Interpersonal skills
Communication skills
Ability to identify and respond appropriately to nonverbal cues of others
Ability to appropriately express positive and negative feelings and attitudes
Ability to actively listen, including making eye contact and refraining from distracting the other
Ability to accept positive and negative sentiments from others
Ability to initiate and sustain conversations with other

Role-taking skills

Ability to recognise how feeling states in others affect their behaviour

Ability to express empathy

Ability to recognise how situations affect others' behaviour

General ability to engage in prosocial, cooperative, and other-directed behaviour (e.g., sharing, taking turns, helping out)

Problem-solving skills

Ability to generate alternative solutions

Ability to evaluate alternatives and react appropriately

Ability to maintain self-control

Ability to avoid confrontation

Ability to size up situation (i.e., to view it objectively, to conceptualise the effects of various behaviours on it, and to know the required behaviours and actions).

Ability to manage conflicts amicably (conflict management skills)

Self-understanding and self-acceptance are valuable assets. People feel better about themselves when they accept their personal strengths and weaknesses. This positive attitude is reflected in their behaviour and demeanor and results in positive feedback from others. Moreover, people are more likely to accept others' strengths and weaknesses when they have accepted their own. Self-acceptance does not necessarily assure acceptance of others, but it does contribute to it. If you truly accept the fact that you are poor at a particular activity, you are less likely to negatively evaluate someone else who is equally poor at the same activity.

Acceptance of self and other starts with a descriptive evaluation of oneself and others. Very young preschool children describe themselves only in terms of their physical characteristics ("I have brown hair") or in terms of their abilities and traits ("I am good at running"; Harris & Liebert, 1984). Self-acceptance starts out with an awareness and acceptance of one's basic physical characteristics and later extends to intellectual and psychological traits as well.

To help children develop self-acceptance and tolerance toward others, parents need to evaluate children realistically, communicate to them the value of their unique talents, and help them put their weaknesses in perspective. Let your child know that everyone has weaknesses, and share with your child your own strengths and shortcomings. Being realistic about your own strengths and weaknesses and liking yourself are behaviours that set a good example for your child and encourage her or him to do the same. Communicate to your child the value of accepting other people for their strengths and weaknesses. Acceptance of others can be taught by example, as when a parent congratulates another person or shows good sportsmanship. Praising children for accepting and valuing differences found in others and praising them for being good sports are other methods that help them learn to accept others. An unhealthy attitude toward self or other people results in destructive competition, which has the potential for creating a state of chronic distress and promoting defensive social interchanges.

There are children's books that deal with the issue of acceptance of self and others. For example, in *Mr Tall and Mr Small* by B. J. Brenner (1966) a giraffe and a mouse meet in the forest. At first, each thinks the other looks peculiar. They engage in a series of arguments, each attempting to convince the other of his own superiority. Then a forest fire breaks out, and the two must combine their individual strengths to save themselves. C. S. Zolotow (1968) develops a similar theme in her book entitled *My Friend John*. In this book two boys respect each other's strengths and weaknesses, and each uses his strength to compensate for the other's weakness.

Reading stories of this kind to your child and drawing attention to the need for individual differences will help your child learn self-acceptance and tolerance for others. For example, you might read *Mr. Tall and Mr. Small* and ask the following questions:

1. What were Mr Giraffe's strengths?
2. What were Mr Mouse's strengths?
3. What was Mr. Giraffe unable to do?
4. What was Mr. Mouse unable to do?
5. How did Mr. Giraffe and Mr. Mouse think about each other before the fire?

6. What did they learn about each other when the fire broke out?

You could then follow up the discussion with questions like these:

1. What are you good at?
2. What is your (sister, brother, friend) good at?
3. How can you and your (sister, brother, friend) work together?

The final self-awareness skill to discuss involves presenting a positive image to others. How you appear to others affects how they evaluate and react to you, and how you in turn respond to them. This is the kind of social feedback that impacts on self-esteem directly. Presenting a positive image requires that children have some understanding that others might view them differently from the way they view themselves. According to Selman and Jasquatte (1978), this third-party perspective develops around the age of eight. Adults cannot assume that children are automatically concerned about how others see them; young children need to be enlightened about the impressions they leave with others. A good way for parents to teach this skill is to give children direct, concrete feedback about what they are projecting. For example, in a positive situation the comment from the parent might go something like this: "Mary, when you smile and volunteer to do the dishes, I think you are being very cooperative." To help the child identify negative nonverbal communication, the parent might say, "Mary, when you pout, I get the impression that you are angry because you did not get your own way. I prefer for you to tell me you are angry." Parents have to be careful to be specific and concrete if the child is going to benefit. Furthermore, this kind of feedback is best given when you and your child have the time to discuss the issues and when the atmosphere is positive or neutral.

It is helpful to point out to children the verbal and nonverbal behaviour in others, explaining the impressions such behaviours create. The models of these behaviours can be people seen on TV or those familiar to the child.

Communication Skills

Interpersonal communication is all of the verbal and nonverbal messages that pass between two people. When people communicate, they receive, send, interpret, and infer information from the messages they exchange with each other. These messages have meanings attached to them that influence the quality, kind, and duration of the interaction.

It is essential that children understand nonverbal language, since this is the most frequent kind of communication. Nonverbal information provides the cues for how and when to communicate with others. A child needs to know, for example, that a worried look on Mom's face means that this is not a good time to ask her for a new bike. To teach children how to accurately interpret nonverbal language, Minskoff (1980a) suggests focusing on five different kinds of nonverbal communication:

1. Body language such as posture, facial expressions, and gestures.
2. Spatial relationships between people (e.g., if two people are standing far apart, as they converse, what does this mean about their relationship?).
3. Loudness and different kinds of intonations.
4. Paralanguage (such as yawns and interruptions).
5. Artifactual cues, badges, uniforms, clothing, jewelry, and the specifics of a situation (e.g., everyone is quiet or busy).

There are several ways that parents can teach their children the skills necessary for understanding nonverbal language. For very young children, a game of nonverbal charades is a possibility. Making a game out of what people look and sound like when they're feeling different ways helps children become sensitive to important nonverbal communications. For older children and adolescents, analysing the nonverbal content in movies or magazine pictures serves a similar function. For example, sometimes it's fun to shut off the sound track of a movie and infer what is going on solely on the basis of nonverbal cues. Talking about nonverbal behaviour in yourself and others is the most direct way of educating children about nonverbal communication. This instruction needs to take place using the constructive communication techniques; it should also take place during a calm or neutral time. Discussing how your child or another person sends nonverbal messages when you and your child are engaged in a disagreement or are in an emotion-charged situation is not appropriate or useful. The child will most likely discount what you are saying and interpret your attempts to instruct defensively.

A word of caution is in order. Sometimes nonverbal messages are ambiguous. For example, joy can be expressed through laughter or tears, and a blush may be a sign of embarrassment, pleasure, or anger. Cultural differences also play a part in determining the meaning of a nonverbal message. Standing close to another while conversing is a sign of warmth in one culture but an indication of a power difference or hostile exchange in another (Johnson, 1990). The best we can do is to help our children understand that nonverbal messages may mean different things to different people.

In addition to teaching children how to interpret nonverbal communication, social skills training also teaches the art of constructive verbal communication. Teaching constructive communication begins with instructing children to be good listeners, which involves maintaining eye contact and refraining from verbal and behavioural distractions when others are communicating. Instruction then focuses on helping children identify the kinds of verbal statements they like and don't like to hear from others. Positive statements include compliments, expressions of appreciation, and positive salutations; negative statements are criticisms, expressions of blame, and demands. Next, children are taught how to give and respond to both positive and negative comments. Role play is the best vehicle for accomplishing this task. In role play parents might, for example, focus on instructing children to smile and say "Thank you" when receiving a compliment from another. Or they might help their children practice receiving negative feedback by having them role-play the following behaviours:

1. Keeping a serious face when receiving negative feedback.

2. Maintaining eye contact.
3. Keeping calm.
4. Repeating back the concern expressed by the other person ("What you are saying is that you don't like it when I. . .")
5. Thinking constructively about the negative comment or request (admitedly, this is quite difficult to do, but this ability is a valuable social skill).
6. Choosing the best alternative to deal with the situation (problem-solving strategies are discussed later in this chapter).

Here is an example of a situation where the child accepts negative feedback from a teacher in a socially skillful way: Jeremy has a difficult time keeping his desk organised. As a result, he often loses important papers and assignments. One day his teacher confronts him: "Jeremy, your desk is a mess! Look at it! How can you keep anything straight? You will need to stay in during recess and clean it out." Jeremy looks directly at his teacher and nods his head in agreement. Now, Jeremy does not like to stay in at recess. He is not happy with the teacher's form of discipline, but he keeps his compusure by telling himself to keep calm. In the past Jeremy argued with his teacher, a response that resulted in a week's restriction from recess. Now he takes the opportunity to think about the teacher's negative feedback. He realises that what she is saying is true, but he wishes that she would not yell at him in front of the whole class! He decides not to say anything to her until recess time, when he is alone with her. At recess time Jeremy approaches the teacher and says, "Ms. Smith, I know that my desk is a mess and that's why I have trouble finding papers. Maybe I can think about a way to keep my desk clean. But could you please not yell at me in front of the other kids? They make fun of me when you do this."

Jeremy discusses the problem with his mother. He proposes keeping in his desk a folder with different pockets for organising his papers. His mother commands him for his solution and for how he managed the negative feedback from the teacher. The teacher is also impressed with Jeremy's acceptance of her criticism and with his solution to the problem. She apologises to him for reprimanding him in front of the other children and promises not to do it again.

This example demonstrates all the principles of accepting negative feedback cited earlier: Jeremy maintained eye contact. He remained calm, even though he was angry with the teacher for yelling at him in front of the whole class. He generated a solution to the problem and addressed the teacher in an assertive way about his concerns. Jeremy, who is nine years old, was not always able to do this, but with some help and encouragement from his parents he now is much better at accepting negative feedback from others.

Parents can also help children learn how to give both positive and negative messages to others. Role play is an ideal technique to use in instructing children in this social skill. Through role play children can practice using the following rules when giving a positive or negative message to another:

1. Use "I" statements: "I like your. . ." or, in the case of a negative comment, "I feel bad when you. . ."
2. Use clear and specific statements: "I like the way you share your crayons with me" or "I don't like it when you interrupt me." Younger children have difficulty being specific, but with practice and good examples they can learn.
3. Use consistent verbal and nonverbal messages. If you are giving another person a compliment, smile; if you're expressing a concern, keep a serious face. When verbal and nonverbal communications are incongruent, people become suspicious of the verbal message and question your credibility.
4. Use clear descriptors for your feelings. There are three main ways that feelings are expressed verbally: with a label ("I am happy"), in terms of an action ("I could jump for joy"), or with a figure of speech ("I'm flying!").
5. Use words that describe the other person's actions. A mistake most people make is to place an evaluation or

interpretation on the behaviour of others. Instead of just saying, "I don't like it when you won't share your cars," a child might say, "You are selfish because you won't share your cars." The use of the evaluator "selfish" automatically increases the likelihood of a conflict.

Handling negative feedback from others is the ultimate challenge for social skills training. Training that focuses on behavioural control over negative emotions must take into consideration the points made in this chapter. Obtaining physical control over emotions and thinking in a constructive way about negative feedback increases the likelihood of responding in a socially appropriate way. Cartledge and Milburn (1986) cite the work of Fagan and associates, who suggest that parents and teachers convey to children the following truths:

1. The way we think and feel is our own private business. We have a right to feel or think angry or sad thoughts.
2. All actions are not okay. Some behaviours are illegal and harmful.
3. You can think and feel differently from how you behave. You can think and feel angry without having to hurt someone or get into trouble yourself. There is a right way to get your feelings out and a way that will just get you into trouble.

When children and adults are able to control their feelings and thoughts, they are in a much better position to problem-solve. Problem-solving means venting our feelings appropriately as well as finding a reasonable resolution to the negative situation.

Finally, good communication requires good conversational skills. These skills, which are indispensable to initiating and maintaining friendships, include the following:

1. Taking the initiative and getting involved in an activity.
2. Introducing oneself to the other.
3. Showing interest by paying attention and asking relevant questions.

4. Showing interest in the other person or activity.
5. Giving accurate positive feedback. (Be careful not to overdo the compliment; people who give too many compliments are sometimes perceived negatively, that is, as insincere or as ingratiating themselves in order to get something from others.)

Role-Taking Skills

Role-taking is the ability to see a situation from another's perspective. It is a vital social skill because it facilitates communication, interpersonal problem-solving, and interpersonal relations. Role-taking or perspective taking involves first recognising feeling states in others and then understanding how those feeling states affect their behaviour. There are developmental differences in children's ability to take the perspective of another person. While experts disagree as to when most children are capable of taking another's perspective, they all agree that the very young child (five and younger) has to be instructed to do so. In other words, the child has to be taught to consider another person's point of view. As the child matures, perspective taking develops naturally.

An addition to recognising and understanding how another might feel, role-taking skills also involve responding appropriately to the feelings and needs of others. Appropriate responding includes emphathetic responses, cooperative behaviour, and sharing.

Parents can promote role-taking skills in a number of different ways. They can teach children to be sensitive to the feelings of others by encouraging children to think about others. For exampie, praising the child on an outing who wants to bring something home for a sibling is reinforcing the child to think about others. Commending the child who volunteers to share and encouraging the child who responds to another person's distress in a helpful and appropriate way are other ways parents can encourage children to be "other-directed." Stories and naturally occurring events are good ways to introduce the skill of role-taking. By highlighting for a child how a particular character in a story interpreted and then responded to the needs and feelings of another, the parent is instructing the child in the subskills that go into role-taking. The parent can then identify opportunities for the child to do the same. Giving children the opportunity to learn about different people and cultures exposes them to other perspectives and viewpoints. Experiences of this sort also encourage and perfect role-taking skills. Of course, parents who show consideration for others, act in cooperative ways, and verbalise their understanding of how others feel are teaching perspective taking by example.

Sometimes children who are having difficulty seeing a situation from the other's perspective require direct instruction: "Yes, John, I understand that you were only joking when you called Susie a dork, but Susie did not think it was a joke. You will need to think about how Susie feels the next time you want to joke with her." Instruction of this nature, given in a neutral, calm, and nonevaluative way, effectively communicates the other person's perspective.

Teaching children to cooperate is one of the more important ways that parents and teachers educate children to be other-oriented. Cooperation is a mind-set as well as a set of specific skills: to be cooperative, you have to "want to" in addition to knowing how. The "knowing how" includes listening to what another has to say, coordinating one's own activities and efforts with those of other people, and engaging in behaviours that are inclusive of others (Sapon-Shevin, 1986). Cooperative games are a good way to promote this cooperative mind-set. Sapon-Shevin (1986) offers four criteria for judging a game as cooperative: (1) the game directs children to include, rather than exclude, others; (2) the game requires turn taking and sharing; (3) the game requires participants to help each other out; and (4) the game requires participants to focus on each other's strengths. Although some games promote cooperation, others do just the opposite. Games like "king of the castle" encourage name calling, and musical chairs and "steal the bacon" foster exclusion. These kinds of games need to be discouraged and replaced with games that are more cooperative in nature. Cooperation can also be taught through stories and actions. Stories like *Two Good Friends* (Dalton, 1974) and *The Blind Man and the Elephant: An Old Tale from the Land of India* (Quigley, 1959) emphasise the value and necessity of working together.

Problem-Solving Skills

Every relationship contains the potential for conflict and disagreement. Even healthy relationships have their share of conflict. Resilient personalities employ good problem-solving skills to resolve conflict in productive ways. What I will elaborate on now is conflict management skills.

Confronting a conflict and negotiating a resolution generally involve the following steps (Johnson, 1990): (1) addressing the person directly about the conflict, (2) expressing your perspective on the problem, (3) taking the perspective of the other person, (4) expressing cooperative intent, and (5) developing a plan. Conflict management is no easy task. Most children require some level of assistance. If children are exposed to these skills early in life, there is a greater probability that they will master them by the time they reach adulthood.

What do children need to know in order to be successful at conflict management? First of all, they need to know when and how to confront the problem situation or person. Self-awareness and communication and role-taking skills play a major role in conflict management and negotiations. Children need to know, for example, that if the nonverbal and verbal cues of others indicate high arousal, it is not a good time to confront them. Confronting others when you or they are upset only serves to escalate the conflict. Expressing a desire to resolve the conflict and setting up a time to talk about the problem are good conflict management responses. Children need to be instructed to express their perceptions of the problem in an objective, nonthreatening way when confronting another person. One way to ensure such a delivery is to use "I" statements and to focus the anger one has on the other person's behaviour, not his or her character: "Amy, I have a problem with the kinds of names you call me on the bus."

After expressing one's perspective on the problem, the next step is to try to understand the other's point of view. This requires active listening skills and is difficult for adults as well as children when they are emotionally charged. This is why it is better to manage the conflict when tempers and anxieties are under physical and mental control. Children need to be instructed to check out their interpretation of the other person's perspective by paraphrasing his or her statement: "Sue, let me see if I got this right. You called me a dork because you thought I took your notebook?" This is a good example of a paraphrase statement that clarifies the nature of the problem.

Finally, expressing an openness to cooperate and resolve the conflict sets the stage for negotiating a resolution. The resolution plan might involve a compromise, or it might involve some other resolution or agreement—including an agreement to disagree. Ideally, it involves (Johnson, 1990) (1) a negotiated understanding of the problem, (2) an agreement on how the parties will act differently in the future, (3) an agreement on what to do if one of the parties deviates from the agreement, and (4) a time the opposing parties will meet to review the plan.

Here is an example of a dialogue between two ten-year-old girls as they attempt to manage a conflict:

Sue: What a jerk you are, Amy! Can't you keep your hands off my stuff?

Amy: Look, Sue, you always blame me when you are careless and lose your own things.

S: Yeah, well everyone knows you are the biggest thief in the whole class!

A: And everyone knows that you are the biggest liar, too!

At this point the argument escalates, and the two girls actually become physically involved. This scenario is a good example of poor conflict management. Allow me to replay the dialogue, this time with Amy using an appropriate conflict management strategy:

Sue: What a jerk you are, Amy! Can't you keep your hands off my stuff?

Amy: Excuse me, Sue, but I don't have your notebook. Maybe you forgot it at home or something!

S: No, I didn't. You took it. Everyone knows that you are the biggest thief in the class.

A: Listen, Sue, I don't like to be called a thief, and I didn't take your notebook. If you want, I'll help you find it.

S: I know you took it. Don't try to cover it up!

A: Listen, Sue, I think we'd better talk about this later. I am too mad at you to do it now.

S: I don't want to. I want to settle it now.

A: I can't. I need to cool down.

(Amy walks away and Sue follows, harassing her all the way. Amy keeps herself under control by thinking constructive thoughts: "I am not going to let Sue get to me. She can't get me to start this fight. I will get to class, and she will have to stop." When the girls reach their classroom, Sue proceeds to tell the teacher that Amy stole her notebook. The teacher calls Amy up to her desk and asks her about the incident.)

Amy: Mrs. Smith, I told Sue that I did not take her notebook. I even offered to help her find it. She kept saying that I took the notebook and even called me a thief. I walked away from her because I was getting mad. I did not want to get into trouble like I did before, so I came right to class.

Ms. Smith: Okay, Amy. I am pleased that you decided to do what you did. Sue, you and Amy need to work this out after math class.

(Amy approaches Sue after math class.)

Amy: Look, Sue, I know you think I took your notebook. But I didn't. I would be upset too if I thought you took my notebook. I will help you find it. But I cannot help you if you keep saying that I took the notebook or if you call me names. If you think I took the notebook, ask me first; don't accuse me. I promised you the last time that I would not take anything that belongs to you—and I haven't.

(Sue finally accepts Amy's offer. They find the notebook—in Sue's desk. While the girls are not the best of friends, they have managed to reduce the conflict between them).

In this scenario Amy used all the right steps to solve the conflict. She told Sue directly and clearly what she did not like about what was happening, and she did so in a nonjudgmental way. She expressed an understanding of Sue's problem and communicated a cooperative intent. She ended the conversation by offering Sue a conflict management approach should another disagreement arise between then.

Parents can teach children conflict management skills in much the same way they teach any other social skill. Reading and discussing stories that show different conflict management strategies is a good way to introduce the relevant ideas and skills. Role-playing particularly difficult situations, while practicing constructive communication, constructive thinking, and good problem-solving strategies, is an excellent way to prepare children for problem situations. And, finally, engaging in good conflict management strategies yourself encourages your child to do the same.

